INTERNATIONAL LAW IN DOMESTIC LEGAL ORDERS

Series Editors

ANDRÉ NOLLKAEMPER

Professor of Public International Law at the University of Amsterdam

AUGUST REINISCH

Professor of International and European Law at the University of Vienna

Justice and Memory after Dictatorship

INTERNATIONAL LAW IN DOMESTIC LEGAL ORDERS

The topic of international law in domestic legal orders has risen in prominence since the end of the Cold War. Recent decades have witnessed a tremendous increase in international agreements on various subjects, impacting on domestic law and proving to be relevant to domestic litigation. These changes mean that domestic courts have the potential to make a greater contribution to the application and development of international law. This series analyses and examines these trends, looking at questions of international law in domestic legal orders from a variety of perspectives.

OTHER BOOKS PUBLISHED IN THIS SERIES

The UN Convention on the Rights of Persons with Disabilities in Practice
A Comparative Analysis of the Role of the Courts
Edited by Lisa Waddington and Anna Lawson

Legal Monism
Law, Philosophy, and Politics
Paul Gragl

The Interpretation of International Law by Domestic Courts
Uniformity, Diversity, Convergence
Edited by Helmut Philipp Aust and Georg Nolte

Domestic Application of the ECHR
Courts as Faithful Trustees
Eirik Bjorge

The Role of National Courts in Applying International Humanitarian Law
Sharon Weill

The Privileges and Immunities of International Organizations in Domestic Courts
Edited by August Reinisch

Justice and Memory after Dictatorship

Latin America, Central Eastern Europe, and the Fragmentation of International Criminal Law

RALUCA GROSESCU

OXFORD
UNIVERSITY PRESS

OXFORD
UNIVERSITY PRESS

Great Clarendon Street, Oxford, OX2 6DP,
United Kingdom

Oxford University Press is a department of the University of Oxford.
It furthers the University's objective of excellence in research, scholarship,
and education by publishing worldwide. Oxford is a registered trade mark of
Oxford University Press in the UK and in certain other countries

First Edition published in 2024

Published in the United States of America by Oxford University Press
198 Madison Avenue, New York, NY 10016, United States of America

British Library Cataloguing in Publication Data

Data available

Library of Congress Control Number: 2023948085

ISBN 978–0–19–287034–6

DOI: 10.1093/oso/9780192870346.001.0001

Printed and bound by
CPI Group (UK) Ltd, Croydon, CR0 4YY

To my mother, Georgeta, and to the memory of my father, Radu

Acknowledgements

In 2014, I embarked on an amazing research journey that led to the writing of this book. I joined the project '1989 after 1989: The Fall of State Socialism in Global Perspective', funded by Leverhulme Trust and coordinated by James Mark at Exeter University. I began to study the trials of former authoritarian officials in Latin America and Eastern Europe after the 'third wave of democratization' from a global perspective. Until that moment, I had only explored justice and memory politics in Eastern Europe, with a special focus on my native country, Romania. While fascinated by Latin American engagements with justice after dictatorship, I had never had the institutional and financial support to carry out empirical research in the region. James made this possible. Our encounter opened new research outlooks: from comparative politics to global history, and from Eastern Europe to Latin America and beyond. Within the same project, James gathered an interdisciplinary team of scholars, some of whom became my friends and long-term collaborators: Nelly Bekus, Bogdan Iacob, and Ned Richardson-Little accompanied me in developing this monograph. In our Exeter office, in coffee shops and bars in Bucharest, Berlin, and Paris, or during online meetings, we constantly discussed my questions, dilemmas, and solutions. Bogdan Iacob in particular has been a steadfast conversation partner: he carefully read every single chapter of this book and helped me improve the entire argument and structure.

In November 2014, I travelled to Buenos Aires for the first time. I returned several times over the following years and expanded my research to Brazil, Guatemala, Paraguay, and then Spain—an important link for understanding the transnational mobilizations against impunity of various Latin American groups. In parallel, I continued my research in Eastern Europe, in Romania, Bulgaria, and Lithuania. I owe many ideas in this book to the conversations I had with judges, prosecutors, and human rights activists from these countries, including Leopoldo Schiffrin, Gabriel Cavallo, and Pablo Parenti from Argentina; Paulo Fontes from Brazil; Vasil Kadrinov from Bulgaria; Dainius Žalimas and Egidijus Kūris from Lithuania; Dan Voinea from Romania; and Aitor Martínez Jiménez and José Ricardo de Prada from Spain. The hours they spent talking and corresponding with me were essential for the construction of this book, although I expect that they will not always agree with my interpretations.

I am also grateful to Laure Neumayer, Anemona Constantin, Eva-Clarita Pettai, Leigh Payne, and Ruxandra Ivan for their time, valuable exchanges, and key comments on various chapters. Their criticism has motivated, challenged, and inspired me. Of course, the ideas presented in this monograph do not necessarily reflect their views. All problematic interpretations and potential mistakes are mine alone. I also thank Julia Sittmann, my English copyeditor. She made this manuscript much better and helped me improve my often Latinized English.

My family and friends kept me grounded. They coped with my absences and my longwinded speeches about concepts far removed from their usual interests. They made me laugh and showed me that joy existed in so different parts of our life, when writing a book was becoming the centre of my universe. Their support and humour are irreplaceable. While I was writing this book, my partner, Vasile Leac, and I worked on a joint project: a small dendrologic park in the South-Central Romanian countryside made up of over 100 trees, including Eastern European pines, weeping willows and birches, Latin American araucarias, Lebanese cedars, Chinese gingko biloba and bamboo, and Japanese willows. I owe him for the idea of this project and the enormous energy and time he has invested to make it possible.

Finally, at different stages, this research was supported by three institutions: the Leverhulme Trust, through the project '1989 after 1989: The Fall of State Socialism in Global Perspective', implemented at Exeter University between 2014 and 2018; the Paris Institute for Advanced Studies, through a fellowship awarded in 2019 with the financial support from the European Union's Horizon 2020 research and innovation programme under the Marie Skłodowska-Curie Grant agreement no. 945408, and from the French State programme 'Investissements d'avenir', managed by the Agence Nationale de la Recherche (ANR-11-LABX-0027-01 Labex RFIEA+); and the Romanian Research Council (UEFISCDI), through the Exploratory Research Grant, 'The Contributions of State Socialist Countries of Eastern Europe to the Development of International Criminal and Humanitarian Law after 1945' PN-III-P4-ID-PCE-2020-1337, at the National University of Political Science and Public Administration, Bucharest, between 2021 and 2023.

I dedicate this book to my mother, Georgeta, and to the memory of my father, Radu. They taught me kindness, solidarity, and disobedience. They did everything possible to allow me to travel, see the world, and think critically about its inequalities.

Contents

List of Abbreviations

ACHR	American Convention of Human Rights
ADCT	Ato das Disposições Constitucionais Transitórias (Transitory Constitutional Disposition Act), Brazil
AJR	Asociación Justicía y Reconciliación (Association for Justice and Reconciliation), Guatemala
BCP	Bulgarian Communist Party
CALDH	Center for Human Rights Legal Action, United States
CBA	Comitê Brasileiro pela Anistia (Brazilian Committee for Amnesty), Brazil
CCIG	Comisión Internacional contra la Impunidad en Guatemala (Guatemalan International Commission against Impunity), Guatemala
CCR	Centre for Constitutional Rights, United States
CCRL	Constitutional Court of the Republic of Lithuania
CEAQUA	Coordinadora Estadal de Apoyo a la Querella Argentina contra Crímenes del Franquismo, Spain
CELS	Centro de Estudios Legales y Sociales (Centre for Social and Legal Studies, NGO) Argentina
CEE	Central Eastern Europe
CEH	Comisión para el Esclarecimiento Histórico (Commission for Historical Clarification), Guatemala
CICROC	Council for Investigation of Crimes of Communist Regimes
CNV	Comissão Nacional da Verdade (National Truth Commission) Brazil
CVJ	Comisión de Verdad y Justicia (Truth and Justice Commission), Paraguay
ECHR	European Convention on Human Rights
ECtHR	European Court of Human Rights
EP	European Parliament
FDAA	Falun Dafa Association of Argentina
FEDEFAM	Latin American Federation of Associations for Relatives of the Detained-Disappeared
FIBGAR	Fundación Internacional Baltasar Garzón (Baltasar Garzón International Foundation), Spain
GCC	Guatemalan Constitutional Court
GDR	German Democratic Republic

GERB	Citizens for European Development, political party, Bulgaria
IACtHR	Inter-American Court of Human Rights
ICC	International Criminal Court, The Hague, The Netherlands
ICCPR	International Covenant on Civil and Political Rights
ICL	international criminal law
ICTR	International Criminal Tribunal for Rwanda
ICTY	International Criminal Tribunal for the former Yugoslavia
IICCR	Institute for the Investigation of Communist Crimes in Romania
IMT	International Military Tribunal, Nuremberg, 1946
INM	Institutes of National Memory
IPN	Institute of National Remembrance, Poland
JNCCF4	Juzgado Nacional en lo Criminal y Correccional Federal 4, Argentina
LSSR	Lithuanian Soviet Socialist Republic
MEP	Member of European Parliament
MPF	Ministerio Publico Federal (Federal Prosecutor's Office), Brazil
OAB	Ordem dos Advogados (Lawyers' Organization), Brazil
OAS	Organization of American States
RSCJ	Romanian Supreme Court of Justice
SJC	Supreme Judicial Council, Bulgaria
STF	Supremo Tribunal Federal (Supreme Court of Justice), Brazil
STJ	Superior Tribunal de Justiça (Superior Court of Justice), Brazil
TPSPNDA	Tribunal Primero de Sentencia Penal, Narcoactividad y Delitos contra el Ambiente, Guatemala
TRC	Truth and Reconciliation Commission, South Africa
UDF	Union of Democratic Forces, political party, Bulgaria
UN	United Nations
USTR	Ústav pro studium totalitních režimů (Institute for the Study of Totalitarian Regimes), Czechia

Jurisprudence

European Court of Human Rights

ECtHR, *Ireland v. the United Kingdom*, Judgment of 18 January 1978
European Commission of Human Rights, *Abiloglu and 96 Others v. Bulgaria*, no. 39553/98, Decision of 20 May 1998
ECtHR, *Streletz, Kessler and Krenz v. Germany*, Judgment of 22 March 2001
ECtHR, *Papon v. France*, Decision of 15 November 2001
ECtHR, *Slivenko v. Latvia*, Judgment of 9 October 2003
ECtHR, *Kolk and Kislyiy v. Estonia*, Decision of 17 January 2006
ECtHR, *Kononov v. Latvia*, Judgment of 17 May 2010
ECtHR, *Association '21 December 1989' and Others v. Romania*, Judgment of 24 May 2011
ECtHR, *Vasiliauskas v. Lithuania*, Judgment of 20 October 2015
ECtHR, *Drėlingas v. Lithuania*, Judgment of 12 March 2019

Inter-American Court of Human Rights

IACtHR, *Velásquez Rodríguez v. Honduras*, Judgment of 29 July 1988
IACtHR, *Barrios Altos v. Peru*, Judgment of 14 March 2001
IACtHR, *Plan de Sánchez Massacre v. Guatemala*, Judgment of 29 April 2004
IACtHR, *Goiburú and Others v Paraguay*, Judgment of 22 September 2006
IACtHR, *'Las Dos Erres' Massacre v. Guatemala*, Judgment of 24 November 2009
IACtHR, *Gomes Lund* et al. *v. Brazil*, Judgment of 24 November 2010
IACtHR, *The Río Negro Massacres v. Guatemala*, Judgment of 4 September 2012
IACtHR, *Miembros de la Aldea de Chichupac y Comunidades Vecinas del Municipio de Rabinal v. Guatemala*, Judgment of 30 November 2016
IACtHR, *Herzog* et al. *v Brazil*, Judgment of 12 March 2018

Argentina

Camera Federal de La Plata, Sala III Penal, 'Schwammberger, J.F.L. s/ extradicción', Decision 41, 979 (30 August 1989)

Corte Suprema de la Nación, 'Priebke, Erich s/solicitud de extradición', CSJN Fallos 318:2148 (2 November 1995)

Juzgado Nacional en lo Criminal y Correccional Federal 4, Causa 8686/2000 'Simon, Julio, Del Cerro, Juan Antonio s/sustracción de menores de 10 años', Sentencia (6 March 2001)

Tribunal Oral en lo Criminal Federal Nro. 1 de La Plata, 'Sentencia contra Miguel Osvaldo Etchecolatz' (26 September 2006)

Juzgado Nacional en lo Criminal y Correccional Federal Nro. 9, Autos y Vistos, Causa 17.885/2005, caratulada 'LUO GAN s/ imposición de torturas (art. 144 ter inciso 1° del Código Penal) y genocidio' (12 December 2009)

Juzgado Nacional en lo Criminal y Correccional Federal Nro. 9, Decision, Causa 17.885/05 (21 December 2010)

Juzgado Nacional en lo Criminal y Correccional Federal Nro. 1, Autos y Vistos, Causa 4591/2010, caratulada 'N.N. / genocidio' (18 September 2013)

Juzgado Nacional en lo Criminal y Correccional Federal Nro. 1, Autos y Vistos, Causa 4591/2010, caratulada 'Galvan Abascal Celso; Muñecas Aguilar; Giralte Gónzález, José Ignacio. . .y otros s/ imposición de torturas. . .' (30 October 2014)

Brazil

Tribunal Supremo Federal, Arguição de Descumprimento de Preceito Fundamental-ADPF 153 (29 April 2010)

São Paulo Appellate Court, Recurso em Sentido Estrito 0004823-25.2013.4.03.6181/SP (11 December 2015)

São Paulo Appellate Court, Embargos Infringentes e de Nulidad 0004823-25.2013.4.03.6181/SP (10 December 2015)

Superior Tribunal de Justiça, Recurso Especial 1798903/RJ (25 September 2019)

Bulgaria

Bulgarian Supreme Court of Justice, Accusation Act 2 / 1994
Bulgarian Supreme Court of Justice, Decision 3 / 2002
Bulgarian Constitutional Court, Case 13/2015, Decision 12 / 13.10.2016

Guatemala

Tribunal Primero de Sentencia Penal, Narcoactividad y Delitos contra el Ambiente, Sentencia c-01076-2011-00015 Of. 2do (10 May 2013)

Italy

Procura della Republica. Presi Il Tribunale di Roma, Procedimento Penale 31079/2005

Lithuania

The Constitution Court of the Republic of Lithuania, Decision of 18 March 2014

Paraguay

Corte Suprema de Justicia, Sala Penal, Sentencia 412 (28 July 1999)
Tribunal de Apelación en lo Criminal, Primera Sala, Sentencia 1988 (11 December 2002)
Juzgado Penal de Liquidación y Sentencia No. 3, Sentencia 14 (2 November 2007)
Querella criminal por la comisión de los delitos de genocidio y / o lessa humanidad que tuvieron lugar en Paraguay en el periodo comprendido entre el 15 de augosto 1954 e el 3 de febrero 1989 (6 August 2013)

Romania

Romanian Supreme Court of Justice, Decision 2579/2009
Romanian Supreme Court of Justice, Indictment of 16 June 2014
Bucharest Appellate Court, Criminal Section No. 1, Verdict 122/F of 24 July 2015
Romanian Supreme Court of Justice, Decision 51/A of 10 February 2016

Spain

Auto de la Sala de lo Penal de la Audiencia Nacional confirmando la jurisdicción de España para conocer de los crímenes de genocidio y terrorismo cometidos durante la dictadura argentina, Madrid (4 October 1998)
Juzgado Central de Instruccion No. 5, Audiencia Nacional Madrid, Auto de Procesamiento a 98 Militares Argentinos (2 November 1999)
Audiencia Nacional Sala de lo Penal Sección Tercera, Sentencia 15 / 2006 (19 February 2005)
Tribunal Supremo, Sal Segunda, Sentencia 237 / 2005 (26 September 2005)
Tribunal Supremo: Sala de lo Penal, Judicial Appeal 10049/2006 (Ruling: 2 July 2007/ Judgment: 1 October 2007)

1
International Criminal Law from the Semi-Periphery: A Socio-Historical Approach

1. Introduction

The twentieth and twenty-first centuries have witnessed some of the most horrific human rights violations in history. In parallel, practitioners of international criminal law (ICL) have engaged in concerted efforts to bring the perpetrators of these crimes to justice. In the last thirty years, the proliferation of ICL as a means of addressing mass atrocities has been accompanied by a global fragmentation, contestation, and remaking of this body of law. Legal pluralism and heterogeneity have become key issues in the evolution of ICL, visible in the development of a diverse jurisprudence of ad hoc international and hybrid tribunals, an emerging body of case law at the International Criminal Court (ICC), and a growing number of domestic prosecutions, often followed by reinterpretations at regional human rights courts. Moreover, the recent contestations of the ICC by African nations, arguing against a perceived neocolonialism and the reluctance of major international players (such as the United States, Russia, and China) to recognize the ICC's jurisdiction, have contributed to an increasingly disputed ICL order.

This book contributes to current debates on the fragmentation of ICL by exploring how national courts in Latin America and Central Eastern Europe (CEE) challenged and transformed ICL in trials held against former authoritarian officials after the fall of the respective military and communist dictatorships at the end of the 1980s. After decades of national political and legal obstacles that constrained justice for gross human rights violations in the aftermath of these regimes, human rights activists, judges, and prosecutors turned to ICL as a potential tool to fight impunity. Faced, however, with the limits of ICL codification at both the national and international levels, they began to adjust and reinterpret this body of law to make prosecutions for past injustices possible and enforce particular historical narratives about their dictatorial

Justice and Memory after Dictatorship. Raluca Grosescu, Oxford University Press. © Raluca Grosescu 2024.
DOI: 10.1093/oso/9780192870346.003.0001

pasts. They selectively used and remade ICL to address national historical and political realities and often departed from dominant UN interpretations. They enlarged the definitions of international crimes, re-wrote or resisted established ICL principles, and created new strategies for internationalizing justice. These developments reverberated within the international system through the circulation of ideas and jurisprudence across borders and jurisdictions and through the debates they generated within the international legal community.

I argue that Latin American and CEE legal actors engaged in specific readings of ICL due both to their legal education and visions about the relationship between law and politics, and to their historical understandings of the dictatorial regime in question and the subsequent 'best' solutions for reckoning with its egregious crimes and legacies. Faced with normative critiques concerning their supposed deviation from accepted interpretations, legal actors from both regions often legitimized their approach as principled disobedience. They took bold stands against a perceived Western-centrism that has governed ICL making and global memory politics or sought—through national jurisprudence—to correct what they considered to be the faulty imprints of Cold War divisions on ICL. The volume offers an innovative perspective on the fragmentation of ICL in two respects: it highlights *why* semi-peripheries of the global system contest hegemonic readings of ICL and underlines *how* legal actors' subjective attitudes towards their national histories and political landscapes impact ICL interpretations and revisions.

2. Limits of Current Approaches to the Fragmentation of ICL

The increasing, but often multifaceted, application of ICL to address gross human rights violations has generated a growing interest in the nexus between globalization and the diversification of ICL. Scholars have, in particular, examined variations and inconsistencies in the judicial practice of UN international tribunals[1]—long the main focus of ICL historiography. While a large body of literature exists on ICL incorporation and application in national settings, the

[1] Martti Koskiennemi and Päivi Leino, 'Hague International Tribunals: Fragmentation of International Law? Postmodern Anxieties', *Leiden Journal of International Law* 15, no. 3 (2002): pp. 553–579; Larissa van den Herik and Carsten Stahn, eds., *The Diversification and Fragmentation of International Criminal Law* (Leiden: Martinus Nijhoff, 2012); Andrea Carcano, 'Of Fragmentation and Precedents in International Criminal Law: Possible Lessons from Recent Jurisprudence on Aiding and Abetting Liability', *Journal of International Criminal Justice* 14, no. 4 (2016): pp. 771–792.

impact of domestic courts on the global disparities within ICL remains understudied and, with very few exceptions, centred on Western European or North American jurisdictions.[2]

Furthermore, researchers have generally explained fragmentation through institutional or structural legal factors. Some have pointed out the competition between various courts to control the meaning of human rights and ICL as a way to enhance their legitimacy and hegemonic international status. In the absence of a singular authoritative court appointed to decide upon ICL interpretation and impose binding precedents, different institutions and jurisdictions seek to translate their own interpretations 'into a global Esperanto' in order to make their special interests appear as 'the natural interests of everybody'.[3] However, this approach has treated courts as abstract and often monolithic entities and did not engage with the diversity of judicial opinions within the same tribunals or the convergence of interpretations formulated by judges from different institutions and regions.

Other scholars have underlined a series of explanatory legal factors, from ICL's origins in both domestic and international law and in different branches of law (including criminal, humanitarian, and human rights law) to the diversity of legal systems and cultures in which ICL is applied, and the lack of dialogue between various jurisdictions across regions, UN bodies, and national states.[4] Nevertheless, the analysis of these structural factors alone does little to explain how norms evolve over time, why the fragmentation of legal ideas exists within similar legal cultures, and why equivalent ICL interpretations transcend them.

[2] Robert J. Currie and Hugh M. Kindred, 'Flux and Fragmentation in International Law of State Jurisdiction: The Synecdochal Example of Canada's Domestic Court Conflicts over Accountability for International Human Rights Violations', in *The Practice of International and National Courts and the (De-)Fragmentation of International Law*, edited by Ole Kristian Fauchald and André Nollkaemper (London: Hart Publishing, 2012): pp. 217–243; Cristina Fernández-Pacheco Estrada, 'Domestic Prosecution of Genocide: Fragmentation or Natural Diversity?' in *The Diversification and Fragmentation of International Criminal Law*, edited by Larissa van den Herik and Carsten Stahn (Leiden: Martinus Nijhoff, 2012): pp. 429–459. See also the chapter on Spain in Sharon Weill, *The Role of National Courts in Applying International Humanitarian Law* (Oxford: Oxford University Press, 2014); one notable exception that brings together case studies from outside the Western world is Edda Kristjánsdóttir, André Nollkaemper, and Cedric Ryngaert, eds., *International Law in Domestic Courts: Rule of Law Reform in Post-Conflict States* (Cambridge: Intersentia, 2012).

[3] Koskiennemi and Leino, 'Hague International Tribunals', p. 578. See also Yuval Shany, *The Competing Jurisdictions of International Courts and Tribunals* (New York: Oxford University Press, 2003).

[4] Antonio Cassese and Paula Gaeta, *Cassese's International Criminal Law*, third edition (Oxford: Oxford University Press, 2013): pp. 5–21; Flavia Lattanzi, 'Introduction', in *The Diversification and Fragmentation of International Criminal Law*, edited by Larissa van den Herik and Carsten Stahn (Leiden: Martinus Nijhoff, 2012): pp. 1–20; Ole Kristian Fauchald and André Nollkaemper, 'Conclusion', in *The Practice of International and National Courts and the (De-)Fragmentation of International Law*, edited by Ole Kristian Fauchald and André Nollkaemper (London: Hart Publishing, 2012): pp. 344–367.

Finally, researchers have identified the political and nationalist biases of domestic courts as a major cause of ICL fragmentation. However, the ensuing literature has generally been normative in nature, lamenting the threat of 'deviant' jurisprudences in comparison to a supposed 'universal' agreement over the meaning of ICL without explaining how and why these non-hegemonic readings emerge.[5] This approach has often analysed the application of ICL by national courts through a Eurocentric lens, without interrogating how Western political interests—and their epistemological legitimation—have removed numerous conflicts and affected groups, including victims of colonialism, racial segregation, and economic deprivation due to capitalist accumulation, from the purview of ICL.[6]

This book's innovative approach rests on two pillars. First, it proposes a socio-historical analysis of how national courts from Latin America and CEE developed novel readings of ICL in trials against former authoritarian officials after the 'third wave of democratization'. It places the subjective attitudes of legal actors towards the relationship between law, memory, and the historical episodes they address through ICL at the centre of the analysis. Since individual actors do not act in a political vacuum, the book also examines their options in connection to national and international institutional arrangements and opportunity structures. Based on ethnographic observation, analysis of jurisprudence, and over eighty interviews with lawyers and judicial officials, I argue that Latin American and CEE judges, prosecutors, and human rights activists interpreted and reshaped ICL through the lens of their legal education and theoretical perspectives on the law, but also according to specific historical narratives they wanted to enforce with regard to their dictatorial national past. The political and ideological inclinations of these actors, in addition to their interpretations of the history of the previous repressive regime, flowed into their approaches to dealing with gross human rights violations and were crucial factors in the evolution of ICL in these two regions.

Second, by moving the debates on ICL fragmentation from UN international tribunals to domestic courts, and from Western jurisdictions to CEE and Latin America, the volume emphasizes the role of what world-systems analysts

[5] See for instance Kai Ambos, 'The Crime of Genocide and the Principle of Legality under Article 7 of the European Court of Human Rights', *Human Rights Law Review* 17 (2017): pp. 175–186; Christian Tomuschat, 'Issue of Universal Jurisdiction in the Scilingo Case', *Journal of International Criminal Justice* 3, no. 5 (2005): pp. 1074–1081; Howard Schneider, 'Political Genocide in Latin America: The Need of Reconsidering the Current Internationally Accepted Definition of Genocide in the Light of Spanish and Latin America Jurisprudence', *American University Law Review* 25, no. 2 (2010): pp. 313–355.

[6] For an overview of critiques of Eurocentrism in ICL, see Julie Crutchley, 'How Can a Decolonial Critique Rearticulate Concepts of Peace and Victims in International Criminal Law?' Research Paper no. 2017/05 (London: The City Law School, 2017).

called semi-peripheries as essential agents in the construction and reframing of ICL. By enlarging definitions of international crimes and reinterpreting ICL principles, legal actors from these regions—directly or indirectly—questioned an international order which rendered ICL irrelevant—or at least very difficult to apply—to their historical contexts. Writing a history of ICL and its fragmentation from the vantage point of semi-peripheries enables a new account that moves beyond Western-centric visions of international law that relegated Eastern Europe and Latin America to subaltern positions.[7]

3. Latin America, CEE, and the Study of ICL

Latin America and CEE are both fertile terrains for examining how national courts contribute to the application, development, and fragmentation of ICL. Since the 'third wave of democratization', these two world regions have witnessed the highest number of prosecutions of former authoritarian officials,[8] most of which took place starting in the first decade of the twenty-first century and used ICL to enhance accountability. Given that no international tribunal was established to deal with political crimes committed during the military or the communist regimes, national judiciaries took a leading role in deciding upon the legal dilemmas surrounding justice after dictatorship. They had the freedom to employ or disregard, interpret, and adjust notions of ICL to particular domestic historical events and legal systems. Moreover, these regions not only faced similar patterns of impunity in the first two decades of democratic transition but also similar legal and political constraints that eventually led to the use of ICL as an anti-impunity tool.

Despite their different ideological foundations, the right-wing Latin American military regimes and the left-wing CEE communist regimes were both characterized by widespread human rights violations, including illegal arrest, torture, and extrajudicial killings—and, in Latin America, forced disappearances. The Gulag atrocities, the terror of the Stalinist period across CEE, Pinochet's Caravan of Death, and the Argentinian death flights are well-known

[7] For the subaltern status of Eastern Europe and Latin America in international law and its epistemology, see Tamás Hoffmann, 'Should the East Have a Voice? International Legal Life on the Semiperiphery', *OpinioJuris*, 16 December 2022, available at http://opiniojuris.org (accessed 1 October 2023); Arnulf Becker Lorca, 'International Law in Latin America or Latin American International Law? Rise, Fall, and Retrieval of a Tradition of Legal Thinking and Political Imagination', *Harvard International Law Journal* 47, no. 1 (2006): pp. 283–305.

[8] Tricia D. Olsen, Leigh A. Payne, and Andrew G. Reiter, 'Transitional Justice in the World, 1970–2007: Insights from a New Dataset', *Journal of Peace Research* 47, no. 6 (2010): pp. 803–809.

examples of mass murder and political repression perpetrated in the two regions. After the breakdown of these dictatorships in the mid- and late 1980s, activists and victims' associations formulated demands for justice, calling for criminal prosecutions against former regime officials and reparatory measures for victims and their relatives. For almost two decades, however, political and legal constraints impeded the realization of these claims, especially as far as criminal justice was concerned.

The ideological polarization in which Latin American and CEE dictatorships developed made an international agreement regarding the condemnation of gross human rights violation committed by these regimes impossible. Throughout the Cold War, the Soviet Union—as one of two superpowers—prevented any sanctions against Eastern European governments by the UN Security Council or the General Assembly. In addition, leftist intellectuals and activists across the world found inspiration in Marxist–Leninist ideology and in the Soviet revolutionary project, at least initially. In the 1960s, Western leftists denounced Stalinism but many continued to praise various aspects of CEE political systems, including their aspirations of social equality and a human rights doctrine oriented towards social and economic rights.[9] African and Asian critiques of Eastern European human rights records were also lenient, since the Soviet Union and its CEE allies backed the Afro-Asian bloc at the UN on multiple major issues, including decolonization, anti-imperialism, anti-racism, and demands for a more inclusive global economic order.[10] Similarly, the United States—with the brief exception of the administration of President Jimmy Carter—as the second Cold War superpower, alongside conservative elites and governments across Western Europe, supported the Latin American dictatorships in the name of fighting communism. Their commitment to human rights remained hostage to both anti-communist policies and the stability of right-wing authoritarian regimes, which was seen as instrumental to the containment of left-wing ideology and activism.[11] In contrast to the gradual consolidation (from the late 1970s to the beginning of the 1990s) of a Western consensus on the criminalization of the Holocaust, Cold War political divides generated ideological selectivity as far as the condemnation of gross human rights violations perpetrated in Latin America and CEE were concerned.[12]

[9] Vladimir Tismaneanu and Bogdan C. Iacob, eds., *Ideological Storms. Intellectuals, Dictators, and the Totalitarian Temperton* (Budapest: CEU Press, 2019).

[10] For these alliances, see James Mark and Paul Betts, eds., *Socialism Goes Global: The Soviet Union and Eastern Europe in the Age of Decolonization* (Oxford: Oxford University Press, 2022).

[11] Lars Schoultz, *Human Rights and United States Policy toward Latin America* (Princeton: Princeton University Press, 1981).

[12] Samuel Moyn, *The Last Utopia: Human Rights in History* (Cambridge, MA: Harvard University Press, 2012).

Furthermore, in both Latin America and CEE, most democratic transitions took place before the fall of the Soviet Union in 1991—in a context in which the competition between the two superpowers had not completely vanished and continued to impede debates on UN interventions for justice. Moreover, most countries in these two regions pursued democratization either through negotiations between authoritarian elites and oppositional groups or through coups d'état orchestrated from within reformist dictatorial circles. These transitions secured the political survival of many former officials and resulted in agreements across the political spectrum that circumvented retributive justice measures in the name of a reconciliatory project oriented towards future democratic stability.[13]

In Latin America, the reluctance to engage in retributive justice was reinforced by the unintended political consequences of Argentinian endeavours to judge military crimes in the immediate aftermath of the dictatorship's fall. As one of the first Latin American country to transition to democracy in 1983, Argentina inaugurated its political shift with criminal prosecutions against a number of military leaders. While acclaimed by victims and rights activists, these trials triggered attempted coups d'états against the democratic government and motivated President Raúl Alfonsín to put a stop to further criminal investigations through the adoption of two impunity laws: the 1986 Full Stop Law (Ley de Punto Final) and the 1987 Due Obedience Law (Ley de Obediencia Debida).[14] The Argentinian experience worried both Latin American democratic elites and international experts, who concluded by the end of the 1980s that criminal trials for gross human rights violations should be avoided in the name of democratic consolidation. Instead, milder measures for dealing with the past were recommended, from reparations for victims to history-writing through truth commissions and other investigative bodies.[15]

Similarly, in CEE in the 1990s, the idea of drawing a 'thick line' between the past and the present was embraced by both communist elites who maintained their political power (especially in countries such as Bulgaria, Romania, and

[13] For political transitions in Latin America and CEE and their subsequent approaches to transitional justice, see Vesselin Popovsky and Mónica Serrano, eds., *After Oppression: Transnational Justice in Latin America and Eastern Europe* (New York: United Nations University, 2012).

[14] Carlos H. Acuña and Catalina Smulovitz, 'Guarding the Guardians in Argentina: Some Lessons about the Risks and Benefits of Empowering the Courts', in *Transitional Justice and the Rule of Law in New Democracies*, edited by James McAdams (Notre Dame: University of Notre Dame Press, 1997): pp. 93–122.

[15] For early debates on transitional justice and its framework in terms of 'truth versus justice', see Neil Kritz, ed., *Transitional Justice: How Emerging Democracies Reckon with Former Regimes*, Volume I (Washington, DC: United States Institute of Peace Press, 1995); Naomi Roht-Arriaza and Javier Mariezcurrena, eds., *Transitional Justice in the Twenty-First Century: Beyond Truth versus Justice* (Cambridge: Cambridge University Press, 2006).

Slovenia) and centre-left groups (particularly in Poland and Hungary, but not only) who opposed the communist dictatorship but feared that the prosecution and purging of former elites would result in radicalism and acts of revenge that could potentially derail the process of democratization.[16] In both regions, this conciliatory discourse was inspired by Spain's *consenso* model, implemented after the death of the military authoritarian leader Francisco Franco in 1975. This blueprint was based on forgiving and forgetting as the ostensible best solution for dealing with the past in order to assure a peaceful transition and democratic consolidation.[17] While this lenient approach to reckoning with dictatorial violence polarized Latin American and CEE societies, the politics of consensus and historical compromise prevailed almost everywhere in both regions.

Lastly, from a legal point of view, human rights lawyers, judges, and prosecutors who attempted to open investigations into dictatorial crimes, despite political reluctance, faced two major difficulties. In Latin America, many dictatorial regimes had adopted amnesties that forbade prosecutions of acts of political violence committed by both political opponents and the military itself. Such amnesty laws were adopted, for example, in Chile (1978), Brazil (1979), and Argentina (1983). Annulling these laws after the end of the dictatorship posed a problem of infringement of non-retroactivity—a fundamental pillar of the liberal rule of law. Moreover, countries such as Argentina and Uruguay also enacted amnesty laws immediately after the transition to democracy to avoid military unrest.[18] This practice was still globally accepted at the time as an important instrument for pacifying divided societies, even if it meant pardoning international crimes. Not until 2001 would this legal constraint gradually be lifted across the region, following the milestone decision of the Inter-American Court of Human Rights in *Barrios Altos v. Peru*, which ruled that amnesties could not apply to gross human rights violations.

In CEE, the main juridical restriction to prosecuting acts of political violence were statutory limitations.[19] Most political crimes had been perpetrated

[16] James Mark, Bogdan C. Iacob, Tobias Rupprecht, and Ljubica Spaskovska, *1989: A Global History of Eastern Europe* (Cambridge: Cambridge University Press, 2019): pp. 95–101.

[17] For the circulation of the Spanish *consenso* model in Latin America and CEE, see Daniel Gunnar Kressel, '"Getting off the Tiger": The Spanish Transitional Model and Its Influence on the Democratic Transitions in Argentina and Chile 1977–1990', *Global Society* 33, no. 3 (2019): pp. 316–331; Mark et al., *1989*, pp. 95–101.

[18] For the amnesty laws and their consequences in Latin America, see Francesca Lessa and Leigh Payne, eds., *Amnesty in the Age of Human Rights Accountability: Comparative and International Perspectives* (Cambridge: Cambridge University Press, 2012).

[19] Statutory limitations, statutes of limitations, or prescriptions are the legal terms that refer to the regulation of periods within which judicial investigations and proceedings can be instituted. These terms are used interchangeably in the book.

by the communist regimes from the mid-1940s until the mid-1960s. Mass repression continued in the decades that followed, although with less intensity—for instance, Martial Law in Poland (1981–1983), the forced assimilation of ethnic Turks in Bulgaria (1984–1989), or the violent events of December 1989 in Romania. As most socialist criminal codes provided a statutory limitation of fifteen to twenty years for murder and eight to ten years for torture, it was no longer possible in the 1990s to judge such criminal offences committed during the 1950s,[20] unless they were classified as international crimes, inscribed in national legislations, and not subject to prescription. Statutory limitations also affected justice demands in Latin America, in particular for crimes committed in the 1960s and the early 1970s. Most criminal codes limited investigations into homicides to fifteen or twenty years after their commission, while acts of torture could not be punished after ten, five, and even two years, depending on the national legislation. Lifting or annulling the statute of limitations for ordinary crimes posed a problem of retroactivity in both regions and was seen as an infringement of the liberal rule of law.

As I will develop further, some categories of international crimes did exist in criminal codes across CEE and the Americas, but the lack of legal education and previous judicial practice in terms of ICL prevented the national judiciary from considering about their application in the early years of the transition to democracy. In fact, until the mid-1990s, ICL remained a 'rudimentary branch of law', with very limited application at both the international and domestic levels.[21] The majority of legal experts and judicial officials across the globe lacked training in ICL and even human rights law.[22] This phenomenon was even more persistent in countries with dualist systems of international law, as was the case in Latin America and CEE. Such systems required the official adoption of international principles and conventions within national legislations before they could be applied in legal cases: hence, education on international law was subordinated to or subsumed under education on national legal systems and legislations.[23]

[20] For an overview of these legal constraints in Eastern Europe in the 1990s, see Raluca Grosescu and Raluca Ursachi, *Justiția penală de tranziție de la Nürnberg la postcomunismul românesc* (Iași: Polirom, 2009).

[21] Cassese and Gaeta, *Cassese's International Criminal Law*, p. 4.

[22] Mark Berlin illustrates how ICL was often incorporated in national legislations during the Cold War but was the enterprise of a very restricted group of experts. Mark Berlin, *Criminalizing Atrocity: The Global Spread of Criminal Laws against International Crimes* (Oxford: Oxford University Press, 2020).

[23] See, for instance, Antonio Cassese and Mireille Delmas-Marty, *Juridictions Nationales et Crimes Internationaux* (Paris: PUF, 2002); Raluca Grosescu and Agata Fijalkowski, 'Retrospective Justice and Legal Culture', in *Justice, Memory and Redress in Romania: New Insights*, edited by Lavinia Stan and Lucian Turcescu (Cambridge: Cambridge Scholars, 2017): pp. 100–123.

The turn to ICL in both regions took place in the context of a shift in the global politics of ICL which took place in the mid-1990s and the early-2000s. Following the savage wars in Yugoslavia and Rwanda, the UN established the first ad hoc international tribunals since the Nuremberg trial ended in 1946: the International Criminal Tribunal for the former Yugoslavia (ICTY) in 1993 and the International Criminal Tribunal for Rwanda (ICTR) in 1994. They were followed by other hybrid courts for East Timor in 2000, Cambodia in 2003, and Sierra Leone in 2004. The adoption of the Rome Statute in 1998, creating the ICC, sparked a new anti-impunity ethos worldwide and affirmed the duty to prosecute international crimes. Moreover, the Rome Statute for the first time codified a generally agreed-upon definition of crimes against humanity, which condemned these crimes in times of peace (and not only in times of war, as the Nuremberg Charter had done in 1945).

These tribunals inaugurated novel legislation and jurisprudence. Nevertheless, they also operated selections and subsequent hierarchies of episodes of mass murder which were deemed by the UN sufficiently abhorrent and dangerous for the current order to enforce international justice. Together with the Nuremberg and the Tokyo tribunals in the direct aftermath of the Second World War, these new UN courts put the international crimes committed by the Axis powers during the war—including the Holocaust—and mass atrocities committed in Yugoslavia and Rwanda (and to a lesser extent in Cambodia or Sierra Leone) at the centre of global justice and memory politics.[24] For its part, the Rome Statute was applicable only to crimes committed after its ratification in 2002 and clearly prohibited retroactivity. This UN selectivity thus left demands for justice for crimes perpetrated in many other parts of the world—including Latin America and CEE—to be resolved entirely by national governments and courts, enhancing their peripheral status in global justice politics.

Nonetheless, these developments in international criminal justice provided an impetus for justice activists in Latin America and CEE to employ ICL as an anti-impunity tool at home and to affirm the centrality of their authoritarian pasts in the global memory of mass murder during the twentieth century. Yet, turning to ICL involved an engagement with the constraints inherent to the specific codifications, principles, and dominant interpretations of this body of law. Starting in the 1950s, most legislations in the two regions had criminalized war crimes, a category that was however not applicable to the military

[24] For the selectivity of UN tribunals, see Robert Cryer, *Prosecuting International Crimes: Selectivity and the International Criminal Law Regime* (New York: Cambridge University Press, 2005); Andre Vartan Armenian, 'Selectivity in International Criminal Law: An Assessment of the "Progress Narrative"', *International Criminal Law Review* 16, no. 4 (2016): pp. 642–672.

and communist repression that took place in times of peace—and not during armed conflicts as defined by international law. Some legislations (especially in CEE, and less frequently in Latin America) also criminalized genocide, a category that prohibited the extermination of racial, national, ethnic, and religious groups, but did not cover crimes against political groups—the most frequent form of violence perpetrated by military and communist dictatorships. Instead, crimes against humanity—which also encompasses persecutions on political grounds—was absent from national legislations in the two regions. Far from being a Latin American and CEE exception, the non-codification of this category in national legislations had been the rule worldwide until the ratification of the Rome Statute in 2002 and the subsequent implementation of its provisions by various states. For more than fifty years after the Nuremberg trial, the international community could not reach a consensus about a definition of crimes against humanity that would cover atrocities committed in peacetime. Furthermore, since Nuremberg, this category included persecutions of political groups—which increased the reluctance of many governments, regardless of ideological outlook, to codify it in domestic law.[25] Torture was incorporated in criminal codes in Latin America and CEE, but was classified as an ordinary and not as an international crime, making it subject to statutory limitations. Forced disappearances were also missing, a huge gap that prevented the prosecution of one of the most frequent crimes perpetrated by right-wing dictatorships in Latin America. Most of these international categories would only be codified decades later.[26]

Judging military and communist crimes based on standard categories and interpretations of ICL lacked thus a legal basis in the written national legislations enacted at the moment when these crimes were committed. This constraint was particularly important for civil law systems, such as those in Latin America and CEE—making an analysis of these regions central to ICL fragmentation in such settings. In these cases, positive written law remains the main source of law applicable in the courts; customary law, judge-written law, and judicial precedents remain secondary and, more importantly, optional. Moreover, the statutes and jurisprudence of ad hoc international tribunals were not binding on other jurisdictions and could be easily overlooked by

[25] Leila Nadya Sadat, 'Codifying the "Laws of Humanity" and the "Dictates of the Public Conscience": Towards a New Global Treaty on Crimes against Humanity', in *On the Proposed Crimes against Humanity Convention*, edited by Morten Bergsmo and Tianying Song (Brussels: Torkel Opsahl, 2014): pp. 17–46.

[26] Kai Ambos and Ezequiel Malarino, eds., *Persecución penal nacional de crímenes internacionales en América Latina y España* (Montevideo: Konrad Adenauer Stiftung, 2003); Grosescu and Ursachi, *Justiția penală*.

domestic courts in Latin America and CEE as irrelevant to their national political contexts. As the Rome Statute was not applicable to crimes committed before its ratification in 2002 and clearly banned retroactivity, justice activists from the two regions could not address the ICC, nor could they directly employ this instrument to judge crimes committed decades before its adoption. In their attempts to achieve justice in Latin America and CEE, activists were thus confronted with serious constraints of ICL codification: from the prohibition of the retroactive application of law inscribed in almost all international treaties to the exclusion of political groups from the international definition of genocide, the absence of a specific international convention to punish crimes against humanity, and the lack of an international consensus (until very recently) on the non-applicability of amnesties and statutory limitations to gross human rights violations.

In the face of these obstacles, human rights lawyers, prosecutors, and judges who sought prosecutions for dictatorial crimes in the two regions began to adapt and reinterpret ICL categories and principles to fit their specific legal and historical contexts. As the book will show, these reinterpretations were intended to fight impunity but were also designed to reinforce particular historical narratives about the past, including the condemnation of the given dictatorial regime, the questioning of the political agreements that had led to impunity, and the de-peripheralization of communist and right-wing military repression, which the UN had left without response. This deployment of ICL was however rejected by other sectors of the national judiciary (and sometimes by international experts). Opponents warned of deviations from conventional legal readings and the instrumentalization of the law for political purposes. They proposed instead more formalist interpretations in the name of legal stability and predictability and often defended the impunity status quo in the name of national reconciliation. The new ICL readings formulated in Latin America and CEE were frequently debated at the two regional human rights courts, the Inter-American Court of Human Rights (IACtHR) and the European Court of Human Rights (ECtHR), again underpinned by differing interpretations of the authoritarian past in these regions. As judicial decisions often play an epistemic function within history-writing and the consolidation of collective memory,[27] battles over the meaning of the law were intrinsically

[27] Marc Osiel, *Mass Atrocity, Collective Memory, and the Law* (New Brunswick, NJ: Transaction, 1997); Ashby Richard Wilson, *Writing History in International Criminal Trials* (Cambridge: Cambridge University Press, 2011).

connected to clashes over the historical narratives about dictatorships in Latin America and CEE.

4. Case Law Selection and the Structure of the Book

The book examines a series of paradigmatic court cases from Latin America and CEE where human rights lawyers and domestic judiciaries acted as law developers in four major ICL subjects: the principle of non-retroactivity of law, the definition of the crime of genocide, the efforts to transnationalize justice, and the duty to prosecute. The volume provides in-depth analysis of these themes, such as they emerged in trials held in eight countries—Argentina, Brazil, Bulgaria, Estonia, Guatemala, Lithuania, Paraguay, and Romania—as well as the debates they triggered at the IACtHR and the ECtHR and in the academic scholarship. The transnational mobilizations for justice are also examined, together with their impact on the development of ICL. The diversity of jurisdictions and topics analysed, which often reveal patterns of convergence towards similar reinterpretations of ICL across the two regions, provide a comprehensive empirical foundation for studying the fragmentation and transformation of ICL.

Chapter 2 examines how courts in Estonia, Romania, Argentina, and Paraguay fostered a flexible understanding of the principle of non-retroactivity. They did so by reviving a marginal and controversial UN instrument that allows for the retrospective application of ICL—namely the 1968 UN Convention on the Non-Applicability of Statutory Limitations for War Crimes and Crimes against Humanity—and by interpreting it in connection to the evolution of international customary law developed from the 1945 Nuremberg Charter to the 1998 Rome Statute. Put on the UN agenda in the 1960s by Eastern European socialist countries to prevent Nazi war criminals from escaping justice, this is the only ICL convention that permits retroactivity in the adjudication of international crimes. Owing to its retroactive effect (but also long-standing Cold War divisions and their legacies), the document was rejected by Western governments as irrelevant to the ICL order and thus has only been ratified by a small number of states. In the twenty-first century, national courts from Latin America and CEE nonetheless increasingly employed this peripheral ICL instrument to unblock prosecutions and define military and communist crimes as crimes against humanity.

Chapter 3 explores how courts in Lithuania, Argentina, and Guatemala expanded the international definition of genocide. Faced with the limits of the 1948 UN Genocide Convention in addressing the crimes of communist and military regimes, CEE and Latin American legal actors sought to correct through national jurisprudence what they saw as the biased impact of Cold War geopolitical hegemons (the Soviet Union, the United States, and Western Europe) on this ICL instrument. In particular, they rejected the conceptualization of genocide as a non-political hate crime modelled on the Holocaust and proposed a more inclusive reading that was also applicable to mass atrocities perpetrated for political, social, and cultural motives. For CEE actors, this contestation was intrinsically linked to their desire to equate the mass crimes of Nazism and communism. For Latin American actors, it was a matter of disputing a Western order that had omitted gross human rights violations committed in the Third World—including the political crimes of military regimes or the cultural genocide against Indigenous populations—from the scope of ICL.

Chapter 4 demonstrates the crucial role of Latin American activists in boosting universal jurisdiction as a key principle in ICL. Their transnational mobilization in foreign courts across Europe led to numerous international arrest warrants and triggered global debates about why and how universal jurisdiction should evolve. Moreover, the appeals they submitted to the Inter-American Commission on Human Rights resulted in breakthrough IACtHR jurisprudence that radically challenged impunity across the Americas and globally. Legal activists justified their cause in the name of a liberal humanitarian language of human rights that claimed justice for and solidarity with victims of oppressive regimes, no matter the political ideology. Furthermore, after 2010, Argentinian courts assumed a role of global pioneer of universal jurisdiction, opening a variety of extraterritorial criminal investigations into the crimes of Francoism in Spain, human rights violations in Paraguay under Alfredo Stroessner's dictatorship, and the repression of the Falun Gong in China and the Rohingya ethnic minority in Myanmar. For their part, CEE justice entrepreneurs contributed to the transnationalization of criminal and civil trials based on the passive personality principle—wherein a state claims jurisdiction over a crime committed abroad based on the nationality of the victim—although their impact on the international system was far weaker. This faint influence was due to the lack of mobilization in Western jurisdictions and to the highly ideological discourses extolled by CEE actors. They remained confined to conservative politics and sought to delegitimize any kind of leftist thinking. At the same time, while trying to achieve an equivalent treatment of Nazi and communist crimes, they often downplayed the role of their own societies in the perpetration of the Holocaust.

Lastly, Chapter 5 discusses two cases—Bulgaria and Brazil—where the national judiciary rejected the ICL principle of a duty to prosecute which acquired global relevance in the first decade of the twenty-first century. In Brazil, the 1979 amnesty law was still in force in 2023, despite various IACtHR decisions which called upon the national government and courts to void it. In Bulgaria, the application of the 1968 UN Convention on the Non-Applicability of Statutory Limitations for War Crimes and Crimes against Humanity to crimes committed under communism was declared unconstitutional in 2016, despite its frequent use in other post-communist settings. The highest courts in both countries resisted the application of ICL principles that imposed the prosecution of gross human rights violations and defended a state policy of closing the book on the past. In both cases, the highly judicialized repression during the dictatorships, the lack of radical legal reforms after the transition to democracy, and the absence of political will to engage in critical debates about the former authoritarian regimes consolidated conservative readings of international law that maintained impunity.

Through these case studies, the book identifies similar trends in the deployment of ICL within and across CEE and Latin America. On the one hand, ICL reinterpretations circulated in each region through the transnational cooperation between justice activists and judicial officials, or through indirect transjudicial communication, by way of cross-referencing and borrowing legal arguments. Regional human rights courts were often called to review these applications of ICL and acted as catalyst for the circulation of ideas within regions and globally. On the other hand, while not necessarily in dialogue with each other, CEE and Latin American legal actors converged towards similar interpretations of key aspects of ICL. They were often inspired by earlier contestations of the international order originating in postcolonial and state socialist settings. The book thus examines the battles over the meaning of ICL within and between various national judiciaries and among international experts who either endorsed or criticized these transformative discourses. By doing so, the volume emphasizes national and global fragmentations generated by different visions of law, politics, and representations of the history of military and communist regimes.

5. Methodological Approach and Sources

The book provides a new approach to the analysis of ICL fragmentation by combining global history and political sociology in order to illuminate the ways in which two semi-peripheries of the international system understood and reframed ICL. It integrates these cases into broader global trends and debates about the reinterpretation, reform, and contestation of the hegemonic ICL order since 1945. Each chapter traces the development of a particular issue within ICL since the end of the Second World War with a spotlight on Latin American and CEE interventions and their departure from UN-established principles. In doing so, the book goes beyond Western-centred narratives that have dominated the historiography of ICL and contributes to recent efforts to write a polycentric history of international law.[28] The global history approach[29] emphasizes the diverse geographies involved in the crafting of ICL and brings in previously ignored or dismissed voices. It connects developments at the international level with national phenomena and addresses how legal ideas are shaped by political and cultural interactions both between different countries and world regions, and between institutional and individual agencies. Global history also helps explain why Latin American and CEE actors contested the often Western-centric ICL categories and interpretations established at the UN. From this perspective, the book argues that Latin American and CEE challenges reflected a quest to overcome both a national impunity status quo and the region's peripheral position in the arenas of international justice and memory politics.

Furthermore, the book provides a sociological alternative to the assumption of many studies in both law and political science that the functioning of the law can exclusively be explained through institutional and structural factors. Norms and jurisprudence do not enact themselves. They require actors to construct and endorse them. Rather than a set of doctrines, rules, and procedures, law is a 'living body'[30] fashioned and refashioned at the intersection of history, politics, and the subjective attitudes towards the social world of the legal actors involved. The book thus focuses, analytically and historically, on the individual agents (lawyers, judges, experts, etc.) who implement ICL—through the lens of their legal educations, political values, and visions about the past—and on the ways in which they navigate, adapt to, or rise against structural political

[28] Surya Prakash Sinha, *Legal Polycentricity and International Law* (Durham, NC: Carolina Academic Press, 1996); Jan Eckel, *The Ambivalence of Good: Human Rights in International Politics since the 1940s* (Oxford: Oxford University Press, 2019).

[29] For the—still undeveloped—global history approaches to international law, see Ignacio de la Rasilla, *International Law and History: Modern Interfaces* (Cambridge: Cambridge University Press, 2021): pp. 152–182.

[30] This coinage is borrowed from Lawrence Friedman, who developed it in numerous works on legal culture and comparative law. See Lawrence Friedman, 'Some Thoughts on Comparative Legal Culture', in *Comparative and Private International Law: Essays in Honor of John Henry Merryman on His Seventieth Birthday*, edited by David S. Clark (Berlin: Duncker and Humblot, 1990): pp. 49–57.

and legal frameworks governing national politics and the international legal system. In line with recent works that have examined the role of human rights NGOs and lawyers in fighting impunity,[31] I argue that in order to understand changes in patterns of judicial decision-making, it is important to look beyond the structural political and legal environment, and place legal actors in the centre of the analysis.

As law is an important instrument for imposing meaning on the world and for shaping collective memory,[32] a focus on agency deconstructs the idea of an 'objective' juridical rationality. The book thus shows how ICL interpretations are formed by the interests and subjectivities of individual actors in their attempts to enforce specific historical justice agendas. It shows that despite the impartiality and universality to which ICL aspires, legal norms are the product of the specific historical and social experiences of those who create and implement them. As law is a social field whose dynamics are associated with the question of structural and symbolic domination,[33] studying the practitioners in this field is vital for understanding how they perceive the hierarchy of ICL making and if and how they chose to contest it. Legal actors from Latin America and CEE did not conceive and apply ICL as neutral jurisprudence. Instead, they sought to establish specific historical narratives about their dictatorial past and, in certain instances, to question an international order that peripheralized the political violence that had unfolded in both regions during the military and the communist regimes.

The book is the result of almost ten years of fieldwork in Latin America and CEE and the exploration of a multiplicity of sources: jurisprudence produced in national and regional courts; national legislations and parliamentary debates on various policies of dealing with the past; academic debates concerning the application of ICL in these regions; media coverage of various trials; and memoirs and academic literature published by the legal actors involved in ICL implementation. I also conducted over eighty interviews with lawyers, judges, and prosecutors in both regions. These interviews were used to understand how individual biographies, legal educations, transnational collaborations, and visions about the dictatorial past impacted the application of ICL by individual actors. Trial documents and interview material were complemented

[31] For analysis of legal changes in Latin America inspired by sociological institutionalism, see Ezequiel A. González-Ocantos, *Shifting Legal Visions: Judicial Change and Human Rights Trials in Latin America* (Cambridge: Cambridge University Press, 2016).

[32] Osiel, *Mass Atrocity*; Susanne Karstedt, ed., *Legal Institutions and Collective Memory* (Oxford: Hart, 2009).

[33] Pierre Bourdieu, 'Le force du droit. Éléments pour une sociologie du champs juridique', *Actes de la recherche en sciences sociales* 64 (1986): pp. 3–19.

by ethnographic observation in trials held in Argentina and Romania and in debates concerning possible strategies for overcoming impunity in Romania, Paraguay, and Bulgaria. The multiplicity of sources and jurisdictions analysed here offer a comprehensive account of how Latin American and CEE legal actors conceived of ICL. They also help to circumvent a linear narrative and illustrate stories of both convergence and divergence within and across the two regions.

Finally, since this book maintains that ICL application and innovation are decisively shaped by the social experience of legal actors, the same should be said about any scholar engaging with this topic. A biographical word about the author of this book is thus required. I was born in the late 1970s in communist Romania—a dictatorial and semi-peripheral country within the global system. During my youth, I witnessed decades of impunity concerning gross human rights violations committed under state socialism, both in Romania and in other countries in the region. In my early thirties, I was involved in anti-impunity campaigns in Romania, including the modification of the criminal code to allow prosecutions of political crimes committed during the 1950s. I was also sympathetic to Latin American groups who sought justice across borders and to lawyers and judges who creatively interpreted the law to increase accountability. My own views about the importance of criminal trials in addressing mass atrocities, as well as my own interest in speaking from the vantage point of semi-peripheries, will surface on many pages of this book. However, I also gave voice to those who favoured more conventional readings of ICL and tried to present their views in a balanced manner. Many of their standpoints amount to strong arguments against the political instrumentalization of law. Lastly, I critically engaged with the various political agendas motivating Latin American and CEE justice activism, and emphasized how some of these initiatives were derailed in the direction of new anti-democratic projects.

2
Towards a Flexible Reading of Non-Retroactivity

One of the major obstacles in judging communist crimes was that issue of retroactivity. We then discovered the 1968 UN Convention on the Non-Applicability of Statutory Limitations for War Crimes and Crimes against Humanity. Because of its retroactive effect, it became the instrument we were searching for. No Western European state had ratified this instrument, but the communist governments had, and in doing so, they accepted its retrospective application. The 1968 UN Convention was helpful for overcoming impunity.

Oana Soare, Romanian lawyer[1]

To reopen trials in Argentina after decades of impunity we particularly used customary international law developed since Nuremberg to prove that prosecuting the crimes of the dictatorship was not a retroactive enterprise. We also referred to jurisprudence of the Inter-American Court of Human Rights and other Western European courts and we also used the 1968 UN Convention on the Non-Applicability of Statutory Limitations. Shortly after, the government ratified the 1968 UN Convention and granted constitutional status to strengthen the legal arguments to overcome impunity.

Pablo Parenti, Argentinian prosecutor[2]

1. Introduction

This chapter discusses the efforts of justice activists and national judiciaries from Central Eastern Europe (CEE) and Latin America to overcome the issue of retroactivity and allow prosecutions when amnesties and statutory

[1] Personal interview with Oana Soare, Bucharest, Romania, 12 June 2014.
[2] Personal interview with Pablo Parenti, online, 30 March 2017.

Justice and Memory after Dictatorship. Raluca Grosescu, Oxford University Press. © Raluca Grosescu 2024.
DOI: 10.1093/oso/9780192870346.003.0002

limitations were blocking investigations into crimes of former dictatorships. Anti-impunity actors searched for precedents in the history of international criminal law (ICL), creatively used international customary law, and recovered a marginal UN instrument that allows for the retrospective application of law—the 1968 UN Convention on the Non-Applicability of Statutory Limitations for War Crimes and Crimes against Humanity (hereafter: the 1968 UN Convention). Put on the UN agenda in the mid-1960s by CEE socialist regimes to prevent Nazi war criminals from escaping justice, this is the only ICL convention that allows retroactivity and imposes a duty to prosecute international crimes 'irrespective of the date of their commission'.[3] Existing Cold War political divisions, alongside the Convention's retroactivity, doomed the document to being summarily rejected by Western governments as irrelevant to the ICL order. It has thus been ratified by only a small number of states: by 2023, 55 of 193 UN members and the State of Palestine. Case studies from Estonia, Romania, Argentina, and Paraguay reveal how national courts from Latin America and CEE revived the Convention to use it as a key anti-impunity instrument and to establish a historical narrative that acknowledged that communist and military crimes were indeed crimes against humanity. Judges and prosecutors from the two regions thus left behind a formalistic legal orthodoxy strongly influenced by positivism and proposed innovative ICL readings to render justice for dictatorial crimes.

2. The Principle of Legality and the 1968 UN Convention on the Non-Applicability of Statutory Limitations to Major International Crimes

One of the fundamental challenges of seeking justice after wars and dictatorships has been the conflict between the duty to prosecute gross human rights violations and the duty to respect the basic legal principle of non-retroactivity. This clash of principles has occurred in a variety of contexts: where the crimes committed had been legal under the previous regime; where amnesties were adopted before the regime changed to prevent prosecutions; or where the statute of limitations for the crimes committed had expired. In all these circumstances, pro-accountability efforts have been forced to reconcile the desire to render justice through criminal trials with the prohibition of *ex post facto*

[3] UN Convention on the Non-Applicability of Statutory Limitations for War Crimes and Crimes against Humanity (1968), Article I.

punishment. This dilemma has been particularly thorny in civil law systems—in historical contexts ranging from continental Western Europe after the Second World War, CEE states after the demise of communist regimes, to Latin American countries after the fall of military dictatorships—as they generally rely on a doctrine of strict legality based on written law and prohibit customary law and analogical reasoning within jurisprudence. A feature of continental legal tradition, this doctrine is in significant respects foreign to the Anglo-American legal tradition, where offences and subsequent punishments can also result from judge-made law and therefore may lack the requirements of rigidity and certainty inherent to written legislation.[4]

The principle of *nullum crimen, nulla poena sine lege*, derived from Roman law and long absorbed into modern legal systems, underlines that punishing people for an act that was not a crime at the time of commission is intolerable and reprehensible. Retroactive justice and *ex post facto* laws are considered a hallmark of tyranny because they deprive individuals of a clear definition of what is legally wrong and allow for arbitrary punishment at the whim of those in power. The non-retroactivity rule thus secures the predictability of the law and prevents random changes of legal rules for political purposes.[5] While *nullum crimen sine lege*, in its modern form, emerged during the Enlightenment, it was the perversion of the rule of law by Nazi and Stalinist regimes that led legal experts to emphasize its fundamental importance for defending liberal democracy. In the 1930s and the 1940s, various philosophers and law scholars from across the political spectrum (including Friedrich Hayek, Franz Neumann, and Leo Strauss) underlined the value of non-retroactivity in opposition to the retroactive laws enacted by the Nazis and the Soviets.[6] The predictability and security of law, the right to due process, and the independence of the judiciary emerged as fundamental pillars upon which democratic systems were to be reconstructed after the Second World War.

Nevertheless, in the immediate post-war period, the Allied Powers' desire to judge Nazi crimes gave rise to important discussions about the question of

[4] Antonio Cassese and Paula Gaeta, *Cassese's International Criminal Law*, 3rd edition (Oxford: Oxford University Press, 2013), chapter 2. Nevertheless, the rule of non-retroactivity is also part of the majority of common law systems, see Machteld Boot, *Genocide, Crimes against Humanity and War Crimes: Nullum Crimen Sine Lege and the Subject Matter Jurisdiction of the International Criminal Court* (Cambridge: Intersentia, 2002): pp. 86–124.

[5] Kenneth S. Gallant, *The Principle of Legality in International and Comparative Law* (Cambridge: Cambridge University Press, 2008): pp. 11–45; Beth van Schaack, 'Crimen Sine Lege: Judicial Lawmaking at the Intersection of Law and Morals', *Georgetown Law Journal* 97, no. 119 (2008): pp. 119–192, at pp. 122–123.

[6] Kaius Tuori, *Empire of Law: Nazi Germany, Exile Scholars and the Battle for the Future of Europe* (Cambridge: Cambridge University Press, 2020): pp. 40–86.

retroactivity. The 1945 London Agreement—also known as the Nuremberg Charter—establishing the International Military Tribunal (IMT) provided for two new categories: crimes against peace and crimes against humanity. Although the Allied powers attempted to find precedents in international law that would justify the inclusion of these crimes, scholars agree that the Tribunal relied, at least in part, on *ex post facto* law.[7] Moreover, the IMT itself held that when crimes were abhorrent, and affected society as a whole, the principle of non-retroactivity could be not evoked in order to prevent their prosecution.[8]

In December 1945, Control Council Law No. 10 allowed the Allied powers to conduct trials against German officials in the occupied zones. It also authorized occupation authorities to grant German courts the jurisdiction over 'crimes against humanity', namely the murder, deportation, enslavement, and persecution of German citizens or stateless persons. Except for the American authorities, who imposed the application of ordinary German law to Nazi offences, all other occupation powers required German courts to prosecute Nazi crimes as crimes against humanity.[9] The decision put German judges in the unusual position of applying international law to what had previously been considered domestic crimes. More importantly, crimes against humanity had not been codified in German or international law prior to 1945. This situation, combined with the reluctance of numerous German judicial officials to prosecute Nazi crimes, sparked divisive debates concerning retroactivity in both judicial and academic circles—an aspect facilitated by the fact that Control Council Law No. 1 repealed various repressive Nazi laws in 1945, but left unsaid whether the measure applied retroactively to the Nazi period. Similar disputes arose in other Western countries, such as Denmark, Holland, and France, which codified new criminal categories to purge Nazi collaborators.[10]

Two opposing reasonings emerged across Europe around these retroactive laws. Those favourable to prosecutions and to the Nuremberg jurisprudence believed that Nazi crimes could not go unpunished simply because they accorded with the positive law in force at the time of their commission. Scholars such as Gustav Radbruch, Lon Fuller, and Harry Jones[11] argued that judges

[7] Cassese and Gaeta, *Cassese's International Criminal Law*, pp. 24–26.

[8] Susan Lamb and Nullum Crimen, 'Nulla Poena Sine Lege in International Criminal Law', in *The Rome Statute of the International Criminal Court: A Commentary*, vol. 1, edited by Antonio Cassese, Paola Gaeta, and John R.W.D. Jones (Oxford: Oxford University Press, 2002): p. 737.

[9] Devin O. Pendas, 'Retroactive Law and Proactive Justice: Debating Crimes against Humanity in Germany, 1945–1950', *Central European History* 43, no. 3 (2010): pp. 428–463.

[10] Nico Wouters, ed., *Transitional Justice and Memory in Europe (1945–2013)* (Cambridge: Intersentia, 2017).

[11] Gustav Radbruch, 'Injustice légale et droit supralégal', *Archives de l'Association française de Philosophie du Droit* 1 (1994): pp. 309–320; Lon L. Fuller, 'Positivism and Fidelity to Law: A Reply to

should not only be bound by positive law but also by the standards of natural law. In circumstances where a conflict exists between written law and a higher conception of justice, and the contradiction between them assumes an 'intolerable dimension', written law must be declared 'unjust' and subordinated to the cause of morality. Proponents of this line of thought advanced the idea that non-retroactivity was not an immutable principle, if it sacrificed another fundamental value of law—namely, to seek justice. They argued that non-retroactivity should not prevent prosecutions of Nazi crimes because the contradiction between Nazi legislation and the sense of justice exceeded the bearable limit. Yet, for these proponents, the rule of law continued to demand commitment to legal security, which could be relaxed only in exceptional circumstances such as those of Nazi violence.[12] Conversely, the lawyers defending Nazi officials and collaborators, as well as advocates of legal positivism such as Herbert Hart, criticized this approach in the name of the predictability of the law.[13] In their opinion, although Nazi laws had been immoral, a fidelity to the written law must prevail, as it constitutes the only unambiguous principle that assures the foreseeability of the law. They also emphasized that certain crimes committed by the Nazis were already illegal under German law. Only those crimes could be judged based on the existing legislation. Applying new laws to old crimes was in their view a dangerous form of political arbitrariness and legal instrumentalism.

In the first five years after the war, prosecutions based on *ex post facto* laws took place all over Europe, and legal arguments closer to those expounded by Radbruch predominated. In the 1950s, however, the idea of reconstructing Western Europe based on the principles of liberal democracy—as opposed to dictatorial, communist Eastern Europe, where retroactive laws were used systematically to eliminate political opponents—led to an emphasis on strict proceduralism as a fundamental feature of the rule of law. In the 1950s, Cold War ideological divisions juxtaposed a socialist collectivist vision of rights and a liberal individual approach in which the law was regarded as an instrument

Professor Hart', *Harvard Law Review* 71, no. 4 (1958): pp. 630–672; Harry W. Jones, 'The Rule of Law and the Welfare State', *Columbia Law Review* 58, no. 2 (1958): pp. 143–156.

[12] Robert Alexy, 'A Defence of Radbruch's Formula', in *Recrafting the Rule of Law: The Limits of Legal Order*, edited by David Dyzenhaus (Oxford: Hart, 1999): pp. 15–39; Julian Rivers, 'The Interpretation and Invalidity of Unjust Laws', in *Recrafting the Rule of Law: The Limits of Legal Order*, edited by David Dyzenhaus (Oxford: Hart, 1999): pp. 40–65.

[13] Herbert L.A. Hart, 'Positivism and the Separation of Law and Morals', *Harvard Law Review* 71, no. 4 (1958): pp. 593–629.

for protecting citizens from the arbitrary powers of the state.[14] From that, the principle of legality became a fundamental pillar of liberal democracy.

In 1948, the non-retroactivity rule was introduced in the Universal Declaration of Human Rights, prohibiting *ex post facto* punishment and heavier penalties.[15] During the negotiations, however, most states referred to crimes codified by written laws and refused to include crimes created via customary law.[16] In contrast, in 1950, Article 7(1) of the European Convention on Human Rights (ECHR) forbade *ex post facto* punishment, but Article 7(2) asserted that non-retroactivity should not impede prosecutions of acts which, at the time of commission, were 'criminal according to the general principles of law recognized by civilized nations'. Article 15(2) of the 1966 International Covenant on Civil and Political Rights (ICCPR) included the same rule, which was an endorsement of the judgments concluded after the Second World War against Nazi criminals based on customary international law.[17] The drafters of the ECHR and the ICCPR understood, however, the derogation from the non-retroactivity rule as exceptional, applicable only to Nazi crimes and future crimes similar to those codified by the Nuremberg Charter. They did not envisage further retroactive law-making.[18]

Concomitant to the negotiation of these treaties, the post-Second World War purges in France, Belgium, and Holland were followed, in the 1950s, by amnesties and pardons motivated by the need for national reconciliation. West German courts immediately ceased prosecuting Nazi crimes as crimes against humanity when the occupation ended, employing instead German national laws and developing a largely exculpatory jurisprudence.[19] Western countries generally embraced the idea that legal positivism could offer a more appropriate response to the problem of wicked legal systems.[20] Starting in the 1950s, the revulsion against the Nazi rejection of legality, questions about the retroactivity of the Nuremberg prosecutions, and the Cold War-inflected Western defence of individual rights against the arbitrary power of states gradually

[14] See Ned Richardson-Little, Hella Dietz, and James Mark, eds., 'New Perspectives on Socialism and Human Rights in East Central Europe after 1945', special issue of *East Central Europe* 46, nos. 2–3 (2019): pp. 169–187.

[15] Article II(2) of the Universal Declaration of Human Rights.

[16] Gallant, *The Principle*, pp. 161–175.

[17] Ibid, 198; Eve Brems, 'Transitional Justice in the Case Law of the European Court of Human Rights', *International Journal of Transitional Justice* 5, no. 2 (2011): pp. 282–303, at pp. 299–300.

[18] Gallant, *The Principle*, p. 198.

[19] Pendas, 'Retroactive Law', p. 458.

[20] Frank Haldemann, 'Gustav Radbruch v. Hans Kelsen: A Debate on Nazi Evil', *Ratio Juris* 18, no. 2 (2005): pp. 162–178, at p. 172.

made the principle of legality an international human right in the Western world.[21]

2.1 The Adoption of the 1968 UN Convention and Its Marginal Global Impact

In the 1960s, judging Nazi crimes according to the national legislation in force at the time of commission brought new challenges. The year 1965 marked the expiration of the statute of limitations for homicides committed before 1945 in the criminal code of the Federal Republic of Germany and other states across the world, especially in Continental Europe and Latin America.[22] This imminent blocking of criminal investigations into Nazi crimes triggered a global backlash, with the CEE governments taking a leading role in pressuring West Germany (and other countries with similar legal frameworks) to modify their legislations and continue holding trials. This socialist mobilization caused progressive legal scholars to engage in pan-European cooperation across the Iron Curtain in order to find ways to overcome the imminent impunity of Nazi criminals.[23]

In 1964, the Polish Association of Jurists organized a conference in Warsaw, where experts from Eastern and Western Europe gathered to discuss whether the international crimes codified by the Nuremberg Charter could be subject to prescription (a statute of limitations, in other words). The conference shaped the following international debates on the non-applicability of statutory limitations to international crimes, including the retroactive application of this principle to past crimes.[24] The subsequent Warsaw Declaration called for the international community to endorse three principles. First, it argued that prescription was neither a general rule of law nor a universal right of the accused, because it was absent from various legal systems (in particular the Anglo-American) and had only been introduced into Continental Europe in the eighteenth century. Second, it maintained that none of the previous instruments relating to prosecution of international crimes—the Nuremberg

[21] Gallant, *The Principle*, p. 156.

[22] Jacques-Bernard Herzog, 'Étude des lois concernant la prescription des crimes contre l'humanité', *Revue de Science criminelle et de Droit pénal comparé* 1 (1965): pp. 337–371.

[23] See Raluca Grosescu, 'State Socialist Endeavours for the Non-Applicability to Statutory Limitations to International Crimes: Historical Roots and Present Implications', *Journal of the History of International Law* 21, no. 2 (2019): pp. 239–269.

[24] Pierre Martens, *L'imprescriptibilité des crimes de guerre et contre l'humanité: Étude de droit international et de droit pénal comparé* (Brussels: Éditions de l'Université de Bruxelles, 1974): p. 19.

Charter and the Charter of the International Military Tribunal for the Far East—contained reference to statutory limitations. Thus, prescription was not applicable to such offences. Third, the Declaration stated that international crimes threatened the very foundations of humanity. Therefore, domestic law could not prevent prosecutions, and *jus gentium* (the law of nations) should prevail over national legislations.[25]

In the following months, the Warsaw Declaration was circulated in different governmental and professional circles, including the Juridical Commission of the Council of Europe, the UN, and the International Association of Penal Law. Prominent legal scholars and experts (such as Jean Graven, Marc-Antoine Pierson, and Maurice Rolland) endorsed the Warsaw principles. In their view, Article 7(2) of the ECHR and Article 15(2) of the ICCPR had already asserted that non-retroactivity should not prejudice the punishment of abhorrent crimes. Other experts (such as Hans-Heinrich Jescheck, Stefan Glaser, and Daniel Wilkes) however expressed strong criticism. In their view, ignoring the terms of prescriptions inscribed in national legislations contradicted the principle of legality.[26]

Between 1964 and 1965, several countries amended their criminal codes to allow for the continued prosecution of Nazi crimes. Austria and Belgium prolonged or lifted the statutory limitations for certain categories of ordinary crimes (such as murder) without any reference to international crimes. CEE governments and Israel went a step further and declared that statutory limitations would not apply to the international crimes established by the Nuremberg Charter. Nevertheless, most of these modifications referred only to offences committed by the Axis powers during the Second World War and did not apply to future crimes.[27] Conversely, France, where the statutory limitations for war crimes and acts of treason committed before 1945 also expired in 1965, codified crimes against humanity and declared their imprescriptibility no matter when committed. The legislature adopted the Nuremberg definition but stated that the law was also applicable to future crimes.[28] In parallel, a Yugoslav law of 1965 affirmed the non-applicability of statutory limitations to genocide and war crimes—past or present.[29] Crimes against humanity remained, however,

[25] Jean Graven, 'Projet de convention sur les crimes de guerre, les crimes contre la paix et les crimes contre l'humanité Introduction et Questionnaire', *Revue Internationale de Droit Pénal* 3–4 (1966): pp. 393–449, at pp. 394–396.

[26] For these debates, see *Revue Internationale de Droit Pénal* 3–4 (1966).

[27] Grosescu, 'State Socialist Endeavours', pp. 250–252.

[28] Philippe Kalfayan, *La France et l'imprescriptibilité des crimes internationaux* (Paris: Éditions Pedone, 2015): p. 53.

[29] Grosescu, 'State Socialist Endeavours', p. 252.

uncodified. The French and Yugoslav laws were the first in the world to assert that certain categories of international crimes—whether committed during the Second World War or not—were not subject to prescription and that this principle was applicable to both past and future crimes.

In March 1965, Poland called upon the UN to ratify an international convention that upheld the non-applicability of statutory limitations to Nazi war crimes. France supported the request and asked for the inclusion of crimes against humanity. The negotiations lasted between 1965 and 1968 and stirred up numerous controversies mirroring the East–West and the South–North divides specific to the Cold War in the 1960s.[30] The most contested aspects of the drafting process were the definition of the crimes under consideration—notably the category of crimes against humanity—and the temporal scope of the convention, particularly its retroactive effect.

As far as the definition was concerned, the Polish and French proposal initially concerned only crimes committed during the Second World War. Arab and African countries argued that this approach was Eurocentric and failed to address other international crimes committed worldwide, from mass violence perpetrated under colonial rule to apartheid and war crimes in Vietnam and the Middle East.[31] In response to these objections, most states agreed that the convention should apply also to present and future crimes. Conversely, the inclusion of the categories of war crimes and genocide as defined by the 1949 Geneva Conventions and the 1948 UN Genocide Convention, respectively, was without controversy. The negotiations did, however, become an opportunity for Third World countries to expand the definition of crimes against humanity established at Nuremberg and incorporate their own histories of violence.[32]

Arab states succeeded in introducing the 'eviction by armed attack or occupation', a category they considered key for condemning the alleged crimes against humanity committed by Israel in the Arab territories. African states demanded the criminalization of 'inhuman acts resulting from the policy of apartheid', which they considered to be as grievous as Nazi crimes.[33] In contrast, most Western states opposed these amendments. They argued that introducing new crimes was unnecessary, since the Nuremberg categories already covered inhuman acts against civilian populations, while 'eviction by armed attack or

[30] Robert H. Miller, 'The Convention on the Non-Applicability of Statutory Limitations to War Crimes and Crimes against Humanity', *The American Journal of International Law* 65, no. 3 (1971): pp. 476–501.

[31] Ibid, p. 491.

[32] Ibid, pp. 485 and 493.

[33] Grosescu, 'State Socialist Endeavours', pp. 254–255.

occupation' was already part, although worded differently, of the 1949 Geneva Conventions.[34] Political motives were, however, at stake. Most of the Western states were allies of Israel and had not yet engaged critically with apartheid. Nonetheless, the voting bloc made up of Asian, African, and CEE states was large enough to guarantee the inclusion of the two new crimes. Furthermore, crimes against humanity were uncoupled from the existence of a war, as was the case in the Nuremberg Charter. The adoption of the 1968 UN Convention thus crystallized the prohibition of crimes against humanity perpetrated both in time of war and in time of peace as a principle of ICL.[35]

The temporal scope of the convention was another contentious issue. Article 1 of the convention states that war crimes and crimes against humanity are not subject to prescription, 'irrespective of the date of their commission'. The provision thus applies retroactively to past crimes. During the negotiations, CEE governments maintained that the non-applicability of statutory limitations to international crimes was an already established principle of international law and that domestic law could not prevent the prosecution of crimes that threatened the entirety of human civilization. Moreover, they contended that the convention would lose its purpose—namely the continuation of trials against Nazi criminals after 1965—without its application to past crimes.[36] In contrast, American, Western European, and Latin American governments argued that a convention applicable to the past would violate the principle of legality inscribed in their constitutions. Indeed, socialist CEE constitutions, in contrast to most Western constitutions, did not contain provisions against retroactivity.[37] The alliance between CEE, Asian, and African states would ultimately override this objection, and the convention acquired an all-embracing temporal scope in that it applied to past, present, and future crimes.

The 1968 UN Convention was thus the first ICL instrument to affirm the imprescriptibility of international crimes and impose the duty to prosecute these crimes even retroactively. It also expanded the Eurocentric definition of crimes against humanity established at Nuremberg by including new criminal political contexts such as apartheid, thereby contributing to the anti-colonial and anti-racist struggle. The document also moved beyond the Nuremberg Charter by disconnecting crimes against humanity from the existence of war.

[34] Miller, 'The Convention', pp. 491–492.

[35] Antonio Cassese, 'Balancing the Prosecution of Crimes against Humanity and Non-Retroactivity of Criminal Law: The *Kolk and Kislyiy v. Estonia Case* before the ECHR', *Journal of International Criminal Justice* 4, no. 2 (2006): pp. 410–418.

[36] Grosescu, 'State Socialist Endeavours', p. 256.

[37] Ibid.

Yet, the convention's retroactive effect and the political stakes involved in the new definition of crimes against humanity led many states to abstain from the final vote. The instrument was nonetheless adopted in November 1968 but fewer than half of UN members voted in favour. No Western country approved the document. The United States and the United Kingdom went so far as to maintain that the convention should never be considered part of *jus cogens* because it infringed the non-retroactivity rule, which had become a fundamental human right since 1945.[38] Since then, no Western state has ratified the convention, and the instrument is barely mentioned in the academic literature on ICL or the principle of legality.[39]

2.2 The 1970s and the Enforcement of the Liberal Rule of Law

By the end of the 1960s, the commitment to legal proceduralism and non-retroactivity as substantive safeguards of individual rights became an overarching principle of Western democracies. The non-retroactivity rule was also incorporated in the 1969 American Convention on Human Rights and the 1977 Additional Protocols of the 1949 Geneva Conventions, as well as in the 1981 African Charter of Human and Peoples' Rights.[40]

The 1960s also marked an important change of the CEE socialist legal doctrine and practice as these countries moved away from Stalinist practices and instituted stricter procedures, legal formalism, and due process.[41] The principle of non-retroactivity was introduced in some national legislations (such as the 1960 criminal code of the Soviet Union), but legality was not fully implemented for political crimes and did not acquire constitutional status.[42] In the 1970s, the Western powers succeeded in superseding the claims of socialist states and the Global South for socio-economic rights and greater equality in the world system, with more individualistic conceptions that focused on protecting the citizens from political repression. In this context, anti-communist dissident

[38] Miller, 'The Convention', pp. 477–478.

[39] Cassese and Gaeta, *Cassese's International Criminal Law*; M. Cherif Bassiouni, *Crimes against Humanity: Historical Evolution and Contemporary Application* (New York: Cambridge University Press, 2011); Gallant, *The Principle of Legality*.

[40] Article 9 of the American Convention on Human Rights; Article 75(4)(c) of the Additional Protocol I to the 1949 Geneva Conventions; Article 6(2)(c) of the Additional Protocol II to the 1949 Geneva Conventions; Article 7(2) of the African Charter of Human and Peoples' Rights.

[41] Maria Łoś, *Communist Ideology, Law and Crime: A Comparative View of the USSR and Poland* (New York: St. Martin's Press, 1988): p. 16.

[42] Gallant, *The Principle*, pp. 267–268. There were two exceptions: Hungary and East Germany had already banned retroactivity in their constitutions in 1949, with the exception of Nazi crimes in East Germany.

movements incorporated democratic pluralism—associated with strict legalism and respect for civil and political rights—into their claims against the state.[43] These demands were similar to those of anti-military opposition groups in Latin America, where repression had no legal basis and materialized in forced disappearances, torture, and summary executions. The consolidation of the human rights movement across the world led to demands for the establishment of liberal rule of law at a global scale.[44] By the time CEE and Latin American dictatorships were falling apart, legal proceduralism, including the non-retroactivity rule, had become a desideratum of both the opposition and the reformist elites in the two regions.[45] Non-retroactivity gradually became a matter of customary human rights law and many states incorporated this principle in their constitutions in the 1980s.[46] Former socialist countries in CEE did so in the 1990s, after the demise of their communist dictatorships.

At the international level however, the ad hoc international tribunals created after the end of the Cold War—such as the International Criminal Tribunal for the former Yugoslavia (ICTY), the International Criminal Tribunal for Rwanda (ICTR), and the Special Court for Sierra Leone—applied a more flexible version of legality. Their statutes were created after the commission of the crimes, and as far as charges of crimes against humanity were concerned, they were justified in the name of customary international law, rather than on the existence of prior written law.[47] These tribunals thus rejected an absolute positivistic version of the principle of legality.[48] In contrast, a very robust form of non-retroactivity, closer to civil law systems, was integrated in the 1998 Rome Statute of the International Criminal Court (the Rome Statute), which maintains that the Court has jurisdiction only over crimes committed after its statute entered into force in 2002. Moreover, the Rome Statute mandates strict construction in favour of the defendant and limits the Court's ability to refer to more expansive customary international law prohibitions.[49]

This heavy reliance on written law at the expense of customary law continues to characterize civil law systems, such as those in CEE and Latin American

[43] Richardson-Little, Dietz, and Mark, eds., 'New Perspectives'.

[44] Jan Eckel and Samuel Moyn, eds., *The Breakthrough: Human Rights in the 1970s* (Philadelphia: University of Pennsylvania Press, 2014).

[45] Mary Albon, '"Justice in Times of Transition": Report of the Project's Inaugural Meeting', in *Transitional Justice: How Emerging Democracies Reckon with Former Regimes*, edited by Neil J. Kritz (Washington, DC: U.S. Institute of Peace Press, 1995): pp. 42–54.

[46] Gallant, *The Principle*, p. 265.

[47] William A. Schabas, *The UN International Criminal Tribunals: The Former Yugoslavia, Rwanda and Sierra Leone* (Cambridge: Cambridge University Press, 2006): p. 63.

[48] Van Schaack, 'Crimen Sine Lege', p. 141.

[49] Ibid, p. 189.

countries. Within this context, the 1968 UN Convention played a significant role in anti-impunity strategies concerning dictatorial crimes, by providing the written international law needed to overcome the non-retroactivity rule for judging gross human rights violations.

3. Using the 1968 UN Convention against Its Original Authors in Estonia and Romania

The 1968 UN Convention provided a blueprint for various CEE countries to formulate new laws and allow for the retrospective prosecution of political crimes committed in the 1940s and 1950s. Estonia and Romania are such examples. Starting in the mid-1990s, Estonia was among the first ex-communist states to prosecute these crimes and define them as international crimes. Its legislation and jurisprudence were debated at the European Court of Human Rights (ECtHR) and were subsequently borrowed by Romanian activists to model their own strategies to combat impunity. In both countries, the 1968 UN Convention also created a legal and historical narrative that defined past acts of communist repression as international crimes and inscribed them in the list of internationally condemned atrocities of the twentieth century.

3.1 Estonia: Adapting the Notion of Crimes against Humanity to Soviet Crimes

After independence in 1991, Estonian politicians—like their Lithuanian and Latvian counterparts—engaged in persistent efforts to condemn the crimes committed during the Soviet occupation, seek justice for its victims, and delegitimize the past occupational regime as illegal and criminal.[50] Investigations into the deportation of civilian populations and the killing of anti-Soviet partisans in the 1940s and 1950s[51] were launched immediately after independence and were framed legally as international crimes, specifically crimes against

[50] For retrospective justice in the Baltic states, see Lauri Mälksoo, 'Soviet Genocide? Communist Mass Deportations in the Baltic States and International Law', *Leiden Journal of International Law* 14 (2001): pp. 757–787; Eva-Clarita Pettai and Vello Pettai, *Transitional and Retrospective Justice in the Baltic States* (Cambridge: Cambridge University Press, 2014).

[51] The two largest deportations of Baltic civilians occurred in June 1941 and March 1949. They targeted various segments of the population deemed to be 'anti-Soviet elements', including kulaks, pro-independence elites, and supporters of anti-Soviet partisans. Between 20,000 and 29,000 Estonians were deported between 1941 and 1949.

humanity. This strategy was due, on the one hand, to the fact that international crimes, in contrast to ordinary crimes, were not subject to statutory limitations. On the other hand, Baltic legislators were keen to prove that Soviet authorities had committed international crimes and to establish a parallel both between the criminality of communist and Nazi regimes and between the illegitimacy of the Soviet and Nazi occupations.[52]

In 1991, prosecuting communist crimes based on the Soviet Estonian criminal code was a difficult enterprise. Homicide had a statutory limitation of twenty years,[53] which meant that it was no longer possible to prosecute extra-judicial killings of anti-Soviet partisans in the 1940s and the 1950s. More importantly, the deportations of the civilian population did not constitute a crime under the Soviet legislation; the massive re-settling of Estonians to other Soviet regions could thus not be criminalized. Furthermore, although the Soviet Union had ratified the 1948 Genocide Convention in 1954 and the 1968 UN Convention in 1969, genocide and crimes against humanity had not been codified in Soviet Estonian legislation.[54]

Within this context, Estonian political elites designed a strategy of retrospective justice based on international law. In 1991, Estonia accessed various ICL conventions, including the 1968 UN Convention. In 1992, the Estonian Constitution underlined that the general principles of international law were part of the Estonian domestic law and that international treaties ratified by Estonia superseded national laws.[55] In 1994, the criminal code was amended to include genocide and crimes against humanity but did not provide for separate definitions of each, and instead unified them under a single article—Article 61—as:

> crimes against humanity, including genocide, as these crimes are defined in norms of international law, i.e. [x] wilful acts which aimed to completely or partially destroy a national, ethnic, racial, religious group, a group offering resistance to the occupation regime or other social group, [x] killing a member of such group or inflicting upon him serious or very serious bodily or mental damage or torturing him, [x] forced removal of children, [x] the deportation or expulsion of the Indigenous population during an armed attack,

[52] Dovile Budytre, *Taming Nationalism? Political Community Building in the Post-Soviet Baltic States* (Aldershot: Ashgate, 2013); Eva-Clarita Pettai, 'Negotiating History for Reconciliation: A Comparative Evaluation of the Baltic Presidential Commissions', *Europe-Asia Studies* 67, no. 7 (2015): pp. 1079–1101.

[53] Criminal Code of the Estonian Soviet Socialist Republic, 1961.

[54] As summarized in ECtHR, *Kolk and Kislyiy v. Estonia*, Judgment of 17 January 2006.

[55] Estonian Constitution, 1992, Articles 3 and 123.

> occupation or annexation, or the denial of their economic, political and social human rights or the stripping of such rights.[56]

The imprint of the 1968 UN Convention on this definition is striking. First, similar to Article 1(b) of the Convention, the Estonian criminal code included genocide within the category of crimes against humanity, although the UN document provided separate definitions whereas Estonian politicians combined the two categories into a single definition. According to Estonian legal scholar Lauri Mälksoo, the unification of genocide and crimes against humanity under a single definition was the result of a 'considerable lacunae in the knowledge [of Baltic legislators] of international law',[57] one that marked the legal education of many CEE legal experts during the Cold War.[58] Second, the crime against humanity of 'eviction by armed attack and occupation' under the Convention was incorporated as 'the deportation or expulsion of the indigenous population during an armed attack, occupation or annexation'. Third, like the 1968 UN Convention, Estonian law uncoupled crimes against humanity from the existence of war and criminalized them even if committed in time of peace. Finally, based on the 1968 UN Convention, these crimes were punishable 'regardless of the time of commission'.[59]

Estonian legislators also expanded the definitions of genocide and crimes against humanity provided in international law to make these categories applicable to acts of Soviet repression.[60] In the definition of 'genocide', they included crimes committed against 'groups resisting the occupation regime or other social groups', a category designed to fit the repression against anti-Soviet partisans and against kulaks. In addition, the incorporation of the 'denial or stripping of economic, political or social human rights (in the case of armed attack, occupation or annexation)' expanded the definition of crimes against humanity under international law, in order to criminalize the forced expropriations imposed by the communist state. Some Estonian scholars warned that if judges were to apply these definitions to crimes committed in the 1940s and the 1950s, they would infringe the principle of legality, since international crimes had a much narrower definition during that period.[61] Nevertheless,

[56] Estonian Criminal Code 1994, Article 61. Translated by Mälksoo in 'Soviet Genocide?', p. 772.

[57] Mälksoo, 'Soviet Genocide?', p. 761.

[58] Raluca Grosescu and Agata Fijalkowski, 'Retrospective Justice and Legal Culture', in *Justice, Memory and Redress in Romania: New Insights*, edited by Lavinia Stan and Lucian Turcescu (Cambridge: Cambridge Scholars, 2017): pp. 100–123.

[59] Estonian Criminal Code, 1994, Article 6(4).

[60] Mälksoo, 'Soviet Genocide?', p. 772.

[61] For example, professors Jüri Saar and Jaan Sootak from the University of Tartu, quoted in Mälksoo, 'Soviet Genocide?', p. 772.

Article 61 remained the legal basis for the prosecution of Stalinist crimes from 1996 to 2001.

During this period, the Estonian prosecutor's office charged several former operatives of the Soviet secret services for the deportation of civilian populations and the killing of partisans and civilian supporters under Article 61.[62] From the point of view of dominant international legal standards, these cases provoked confusion, since it was unclear whether the defendants were charged with genocide or crimes against humanity. Also, issues related to retroactivity were not debated in these early cases. Only after the adoption of a new criminal code in 2001, which incorporated the Rome Statute's definition of crimes against humanity and erased any deviations from international standards,[63] were convictions for communist crimes challenged for infringing the principle of legality.

Starting in 2001, all trials of communist crimes in Estonia began to employ the category of crimes against humanity exclusively, an approach connected to the activities of the Estonian International Commission for the Investigation of Crimes against Humanity—a historical commission created in 1998 to identify political crimes committed during the Nazi and the Soviet periods. By 1999, the Commission had largely dropped the term genocide in connection to communist crimes, while maintaining it with regard to Nazi atrocities against Jewish individuals.[64] In contrast to their Lithuanian counterparts, who insisted—as we will see in Chapter 3—on the 'double Nazi and communist genocide', the members of the Estonian Commission examined the mass violence of the two regimes through the prism of 'crimes against humanity', as defined by the Rome Statute.[65] This was due to the fact that all members of the Estonian Commission were foreigners and paid attention to how Soviet-era crimes fit the standard definitions of international crimes. The Commission's work was primarily aimed at obtaining international recognition for the suffering inflicted on the nation by the Stalinist regime.[66] Since most Stalinist crimes had been politically motivated, the category of crimes against humanity

[62] Pettai and Pettai, *Transitional and Retrospective Justice*, pp. 85 and 105–110; Mälksoo, 'Soviet Genocide?', pp. 772–778.

[63] The definition of genocide continued, however, to expand the protected groups and include those 'offering resistance to the occupation regime or other social groups'. All international crimes were punishable irrespective of the time of commission, Estonian Criminal Code, 2001, Article 5(4).

[64] Kirstyn Hevey, 'Estonian Transitional Justice: Predicated on a Collective Memory', PhD Dissertation (Budapest: Central European University, 2014): pp. 41–49.

[65] Eva-Clarita Pettai, 'Negotiating History'; Onur Baniker, 'Between Politics and History: The Baltic Truth Commissions in Global Perspective', in *Transitional Justice and the Former Soviet Union: Reviewing the Past, Looking toward the Future*, edited by Lavinia Stan and Nadya Nedelsky (Cambridge: Cambridge University Press): pp. 155–176.

[66] Eva-Clarita Pettai, 'Negotiating History'.

was deemed more suitable than that of genocide. The members of the Commission opted for the definition of crimes against humanity included in the Rome Statute because it was the most comprehensive under international law: It no longer required a nexus between these crimes and the existence of a war, and it allowed the incorporation of crimes committed during both the Nazi and Soviet regimes.[67]

Various legal scholars criticized this approach, however, because the definition of crimes against humanity included in the Rome Statute was far broader than the definition in place during the 1940s and the 1950s. They argued that by applying this expanded definition to Stalinist crimes, the Commission was endorsing a legal narrative based on retroactivity, which could be borrowed by courts and produce judicial injustice.[68] These critiques would be repeated in an emblematic case concerning deportation of civilian populations in the 1940s—a case that would be debated at the ECtHR and later used by Romanian anti-impunity activists.

In 2003, August Kolk and Petr Kislyiy, two former military officials in Soviet Estonia, were convicted of crimes against humanity for preparing and implementing the deportation of Estonian civilians to remote areas of the Soviet Union in 1949. The court argued that deportation was a crime against humanity penalized both by Article 61 of the 1994 criminal code and Article 89 of the 2001 penal code.[69] The judges also stated that according to Estonian criminal codes and the 1968 UN Convention, international crimes were punishable no matter when they were committed. The latter document also referred to deportations conducted under a regime of occupation, as it had been the case in Estonia. The defendants appealed the verdict and accused the court of a retroactive application of the law. They argued that in 1949, the Soviet criminal code applicable to Estonian territory did not codify the category of crimes against humanity. Moreover, the definition of crimes against humanity under international law applicable in 1949 was the definition in the Nuremberg Charter, which required a connection between these crimes and the existence of war. Since the deportations in question did not take place before or during the Second World War and had not been committed in connection with a crime against peace or a war crime, they did not qualify as crimes

[67] Agata Fijalkowski, 'Historical Politics and Court Redress in the Baltic States', in *Transitional Justice and the Former Soviet Union: Reviewing the Past, Looking toward the Future*, edited by Lavinia Stan and Nadya Nedelsky (Cambridge: Cambridge University Press): pp. 216–240, at p. 222.

[68] Mälksoo, 'Soviet Genocide?', p. 770.

[69] The charges were initially brought under the 2011 Estonian Criminal Code, Article 89, but because crimes against humanity had a milder penalty in the 1994 criminal code, the verdict referred to both criminal codes.

against humanity. The defendants also pointed out that deportations had been legal under Soviet law, making it impossible to foresee that their acts could be considered crimes against humanity decades later under international law.[70]

In 2004, an appeals court upheld the initial judgment. It argued that even if the category of crimes against humanity had not been codified in the Soviet legislation, Article 7(2) of the ECHR did not prevent the punishment of heinous crimes recognized by international law. In addition, the 1968 UN Convention, which had been ratified by the Soviet Union in 1969 and had been absorbed into Estonian legislation in 1991, had eliminated the nexus between crimes against humanity and the existence of a war. The instrument had also specified that 'eviction by armed attack and occupation' constituted a crime against humanity—a category that applied to the Estonian deportations. Moreover, the judges argued that the Nuremberg Charter and the ICTY Statute enshrined norms of customary international law, which were binding irrespective of whether a state had acceded to an international treaty.[71]

Subsequently, Kolk and Kislyiy lodged a complaint with the ECtHR in 2004, alleging a breach of Article 7(1) of the European Convention—which prohibits the *ex post facto* application of law—and reiterating the arguments they had made before the Estonian courts. In 2006, the Fourth Section of the ECtHR dismissed their application. Some of the sitting judges, such as Nicolas Bratza, Matti Pellonpää, and Rait Maruste, had previously indicated their favourable positions towards the condemnation of communist crimes in other ECtHR cases. The first two endorsed the German Constitutional Court's application of the Radbruch formula in *Streletz, Kessler and Krenz v. Germany*, a case that acknowledged the criminality of the murders committed at the East German border of those trying to flee to the West—despite the fact that these killings had been legal under contemporary law.[72] In *Slivenko v. Latvia*, Bratza and Maruste ruled in favour of those defending the expulsion from Latvia of family members of Russian military personnel, following the Russian troop withdrawal agreement in 1994. They argued that the presence of Russian personnel and their relatives could still represent a threat in the imaginary of the Latvian population after long years of Soviet occupation.[73]

In *Kolk and Kislyiy v. Estonia*, the majority stated that between 1941 and 1991, while Estonia was under occupation, the Soviet regime committed

[70] ECtHR, *Kolk and Kislyiy v. Estonia*, Decision of 17 January 2006, pp. 2–3.

[71] Ibid, p. 3.

[72] ECtHR, *Streletz, Kessler and Krenz v. Germany*, Judgment of 22 March 2001.

[73] ECtHR, *Slivenko v. Latvia*, Judgment of 9 October 2003, 'Joint Dissenting Opinion of Mr Wildhaber, Mr Ress, Sir Nicolas Bratza, Mr Cabral Barreto, Mrs Greve and Mr Maruste'.

large-scale attacks against the Estonian population, including the deportation of about 30,000 individuals in the 1940s, and that the accused had participated in these larger operations. Given the occupation regime, Estonia could not have redressed these injustices before its independence. Only after 1991 could the country become party to international treaties and implement its own legislation to prosecute international crimes. It was thus legitimate for Estonian judges to convict based on recent national legal developments, including the ratification of the 1968 UN Convention.[74] The ECtHR thereby enforced a legal and historical account that recognized the illegality of the Soviet occupation, acknowledged the criminality of the previous regime, and legitimized Estonia's right to criminalize Soviet repression after 1991.

The judges argued that the Nuremberg Charter recognized the deportation of civilians as a crime against humanity and that the universal validity of the Nuremberg principles (beyond crimes committed during the Second World War by the Axis powers) was confirmed, inter alia, by Resolution 95 of the UN General Assembly (11 December 1946) and by the International Law Commission. Article 7(2) of the ECHR also provided that the non-retroactivity rule could not impede prosecutions of acts which, at the time they were committed, were criminal according to the general principles of international law. The judges also quoted the ECtHR rulings in *Touvier v. France* and *Papon v. France*, which acknowledged that prosecuting crimes against humanity committed during the Second World War based on a law adopted in 1964 was legal because these crimes were already criminalized under customary international law.[75]

Furthermore, the judges emphasized that the 1968 UN Convention expressly stated that crimes against humanity were punishable irrespective of the date of commission and of the connection to war or peace time. The responsibility for such acts was not limited to the time frame of the Second World War. The Soviet Union had itself endorsed the Nuremberg principles and ratified the 1968 UN Convention, as had Estonia after independence.[76] Following this legal reasoning, the ECtHR endorsed the approach taken by the Estonian courts: the deportation of the Estonian civilian population by Soviet authorities constituted a crime against humanity and such crimes were not time limited. For the first time in its jurisprudence, the ECtHR acknowledged that crimes against humanity did not necessarily have to be committed during wartime. Moreover,

[74] ECtHR, *Kolk and Kislyiy v. Estonia*, Decision of 17 January 2006, p. 8.
[75] Ibid, p. 9.
[76] Ibid, pp. 9–10.

the Court underlined the importance of the 1968 UN Convention for legitimizing the Estonian prosecutorial strategy as the key ICL treaty on which to base accusations of crimes against humanity in times of peace and no matter the lapse of time.

According to one of the judges involved, the decision was four to three.[77] In his view, the main problem with the majority's interpretation was that there is 'no precise definition of the general principles of law recognized by civilized nations'. Consequently, it was impossible for the applicants to foresee in 1949 that their actions were illegal without a written law that prohibited the crime and imposed punishment. According to the same judge, other dissenting voices in *Kolk and Kislyiy v. Estonia* argued that in 1949 crimes against humanity were still connected to the existence of the war, so deportations during peacetime were not criminal under international law at that time.

Similar critiques were voiced by legal scholars. Estonian academics such as Jüri Saar, Jaan Sootak, and Lauri Mälksoo had warned already in the 1990s that trials for deportations posed a retroactivity problem because they concerned crimes against humanity committed in times of peace, while ICL in 1949 still required these crimes to be committed during times of war.[78] In his analysis of the ECtHR jurisprudence, ICL scholar Antonio Cassese similarly contended that in 1949, international law required a nexus between crimes against humanity and the commission of other war crimes or crimes against peace. He also argued that in 1949, 'there surely did not exist a general principle of law recognized by civilized nations prohibiting crimes against humanity', since this rule had not yet been upheld by most countries in the world. Only in the 1960s, with the adoption of the 1968 UN Convention, did the prohibition of crimes against humanity perpetrated in times of peace start to crystallize as a principle of ICL. In Cassese's view, the deportation of the Estonian civilian population qualified, however, as a crime against humanity because it had been committed in connection with a crime against peace, namely the Soviet war of aggression against Estonia. Cassese believed that the Estonian courts did not infringe upon the principle of legality when they convicted Kolk and Kislyiy, but they would have had to connect deportations to the Soviet war of aggression.[79]

Other ICL scholars such as M. Cherif Bassiouni and Sonja Grover agreed with the ECtHR decision but did not discuss whether crimes against humanity

[77] Personal interview with the ECtHR judge, online, 26 May 2020. In accordance with ECtHR procedures, when the case is not judged by the Great Chamber, only majority opinions are made public when the application is dismissed. The interviewee asked to remain anonymous.

[78] Jüri Saar and Jaan Sootak, 'Landesbericht Estland', quoted in Mälksoo, 'Soviet Genocide?', p. 770.

[79] Cassese, 'Balancing the Prosecution of Crimes against Humanity'.

in 1949 related to the state of war.[80] Grover criticized the European judges for not engaging with the lenient sentence of the Estonian court, which had sentenced Kolk and Kislyiy to a suspended eight-year prison term, due to their advanced age. In Grover's view, Article 7(2) of the ECHR also requires a lack of prejudice towards the punishment of defendants. She argued that such a light sentence was in fact a 'wrongful barrier to the rightful punishment of those who commit crimes that are an outrage to humanity'.[81] Grover's criticism overlooked, however, the fact that the ECtHR is bound by the 'margin of appreciation' rule, which gives member states of the Convention the right to interpret their own laws and impose their own penalties. For their part, transitional justice scholars have generally praised the ECtHR decision for enforcing a historical and legal narrative that acknowledged the illegality and the criminality of Soviet occupation and deportations at a European level.[82] Last but not least, the ECtHR ruling in *Kolk and Kislyiy v. Estonia* and the Estonian approach to retrospective justice inspired Romanian activists in their quest to overcome impunity for political crimes committed during the Stalinist era.

3.2 Romania: Deploying International Criminal Law to Overcome Impunity

In 2016, over twenty-five years after the fall of the communist regime, the Romanian Supreme Court of Justice convicted for the first time two former military officials for political crimes perpetrated in the 1950s, the harshest period of the communist dictatorship. The verdicts marked a radical break from previous legal approaches to investigating gross human rights violations in this country. After almost three decades of interpreting extrajudicial killings and the inhuman treatment of political prisoners as ordinary legal categories (such as murder or abuse of office) subject to statutory limitations, the Romanian judiciary employed ICL to overcome impunity. Communist crimes were classified as crimes against humanity and, as in Estonia, the 1968 UN Convention was used to justify their prosecution fifty years later and counteract accusations of retroactivity.

[80] Bassiouni, *Crimes against Humanity*, pp. 705–706; Sonja Grover, *The European Court of Human Rights as a Pathway to Impunity for International Crimes* (Berlin: Springer, 2010): pp. 232–236.
[81] Grover, *The European Court*, p. 234.
[82] Pettai and Pettai, *Transitional and Retrospective Justice*, p. 278; Fijalkowski, 'Historical Politics', p. 225.

3.2.1 The Long 1990s of Impunity: Statutory Limitations and Strong Non-Retroactivity

Like Estonia and other CEE countries, after 1989, Romania faced legal constraints in prosecuting political crimes committed in the 1950s. The socialist criminal code—in force until 2014, albeit with certain amendments—provided for a fifteen-year statute of limitations for homicide and an eight-year statute for torture,[83] meaning that by 1990 it was no longer possible to investigate murders committed before 1975 and acts of torture committed before 1981. While the Baltic states adopted laws that allowed for retrospective justice, and countries such as Germany and Poland lifted or prolonged the statute of limitations for certain categories of crimes to allow for prosecutions,[84] such efforts were blocked in Romania by the continuity of the former nomenklatura, the weak mobilization of civil society, and the lack of radical judicial reforms. Between 1990 and 1996, former communist elites continued to govern the country and promote a discourse of national reconciliation which excluded prosecutions. In 1996, the right-wing anti-communist camp acceded to power, but, once there, was more concerned with economic reforms than with changing legislation to allow for investigations.[85]

The socialist criminal code in Romania included three categories of international crimes—war crimes, genocide, and inhuman treatment (*tratamente neomenoase*)—introduced into national legislation in 1960 to fulfil Romania's commitments under the 1948 Genocide Convention and the 1949 Geneva Conventions, ratified by Romania in 1950 and 1954, respectively. Starting in 1968, the criminal code stipulated that all such crimes were not subject to statutory limitations, reflecting Romania's engagements under the 1968 UN Convention.[86]

In the 1990s, communist crimes were investigated by military prosecutors educated during the socialist period, including Dan Voinea and Mihai Popov. Born in 1950, Dan Voinea graduated in law in 1977 and became a military prosecutor in 1982. In December 1989, he drafted the indictment in the controversial trial of Nicolae and Elena Ceaușescu, which accused the dictators of genocide, based on problematic evidence. Between 1997 and 2000, he was the

[83] Romanian Criminal Code 1968, Article 122.

[84] In Germany in 1991, and in Poland in 1995 and again in 1998. Guillaume Mouralis, *Une épuration allemande: La RDA en procès 1949–2004* (Paris: Fayard, 2008); Maria Łoś and Andrzej Zybertowicz, *Privatizing the Police-State: The Case of Poland* (New York: St. Martin's Press, 2000).

[85] Lavinia Stan, 'Reckoning with the Communist Past in Romania: A Scorecard', *Europe–Asia Studies* 65, no. 1 (2013): pp. 127–146.

[86] Romanian Criminal Code 1968, Articles 356–359 defined international crimes and Article 121 mandated that they not be subject to statutory limitations.

head of the military prosecutor's office within the Romanian Supreme Court of Justice. Born in 1947, Mihai Popov graduated in law in 1974 and worked as a military prosecutor until 2016. Both were part of a generation of military prosecutors educated in a system where international human rights law mattered little, while judicial practice was under strong political control. Socialist legal culture prevented both the independence of the judiciary from the executive branch and the judges' possibility to engage in progressive interpretations of the law. Judges were supposed to apply the positive regular laws, without interconnections with constitutional or international law.[87]

From the perspective of prosecutors involved in the investigation of communist crimes in the 1990s, none of the international crimes codified in Romanian law were applicable to the acts of political repression perpetrated under communism.[88] Genocide referred only to racial, religious, ethnic, or national groups, thus excluding crimes against political groups (the most frequent target of communist regimes). War crimes were not applicable either, given that repression had taken place in times of peace. The third category, inhuman treatment, referred to acts (transposed from the 1949 Geneva Conventions) such as deportation, torture, extrajudicial killings, and the illegal deprivation of liberty perpetrated against specific groups: 'the wounded or the sick, civilian health personnel […], the shipwrecked, prisoners of war' and '*any other person who has fallen into enemy hands*' [emphasis author's own].[89] These offences carried harsher punishments if perpetrated in times of war. Victims' lawyers used this provision in order to demand the prosecutions for inhuman treatment. They argued that political opponents had 'fallen into enemy hands' and that the difference between inhuman treatment and crimes against humanity was only a matter of wording.[90]

In contrast, the prosecutors believed that the provision of 'fallen into enemy hands' was 'introduced to implement the obligations of the Geneva Conventions. It is not the same as crimes against humanity. It refers only to international or civil wars and not to political repression in times of peace'.[91] Even for certain lawyers involved in anti-impunity movements, 'inhuman treatment' was a problematic category when applied to communist crimes, since the article implied that 'such crimes are sanctioned even when committed

[87] Grosescu and Fijalkowski, 'Retrospective Justice'.
[88] Personal interview with Mihai Popov, Bucharest, Romania, 22 February 2007; personal interview with Dan Voinea, Bucharest, Romania, 18 June 2014.
[89] Romanian Criminal Code 1968, Article 358.
[90] Personal interview with Antonie Popescu, Bucharest, Romania, 16 September 2015.
[91] Personal interview with Mihai Popov, Bucharest, Romania, 22 February 2007.

in times of peace, [but] fallen into enemy hands' is difficult to interpret outside of a military conflict. It is not the same with crimes against humanity which refer to attacks on civilian populations both in times of war and in times of peace.[92] Indeed, until 2014, the criminal code did not contain a specific provision for crimes against humanity, although socialist Romania, like the Soviet Union, had ratified the 1968 UN Convention in 1969.

Given the existing legal context and the lack of political will to modify it, most investigations into communist crimes were closed. In two exceptional cases the prosecutors invoked Article 128 of the socialist criminal code, which states that the prescribed terms can be suspended if a 'legal disposition or an irremovable circumstance' had hindered a trial. Here, the indictments suspended the statutory limitations for the entire period of the communist regime, arguing that political interference in the justice system rendered impossible the investigation of such cases before 1989.[93] As we shall see in Section 4.2, this strategy would also be employed in Paraguay to allow prosecutions of crimes stemming from the dictatorship of Alfredo Stroessner. In Romania, the two defendants died before any conviction was handed down. Although these cases could have served as a precedent, the prosecution closed the investigations in all other cases, arguing that an indictment would violate the principle of non-retroactivity, since the statutory limitations had expired. Asked later about the possibility of interpreting national legislation in relation to international law on crimes against humanity, Voinea answered,

> At that time, international law did not have the importance it has today. It was national law that mattered ... We had no legal education during communism on how to use international law in court. Also, the jurisprudence of the European Court or of the international tribunals that could have helped us to adopt a different approach did not exist yet.[94]

Socialist legal education had indeed paid little attention to international human rights and ICL. Legal practitioners who graduated before 1989 recall that concepts like genocide and crimes against humanity represented 'exotic crimes mentioned only in connection with the Second World War'.[95] Although the 1992 Constitution elevated international human rights law above national norms and Romania became part of the ECHR in 1994, European

92 Personal correspondence with Valerian Stan, 27 August 2007.
93 Archives of the Bucharest Appellate Military Court, File no. 15/P/1999, 'Indictment of 8 April 1993'.
94 Personal interview with Dan Voinea, Bucharest, Romania, 18 June 2014.
95 Personal interview with Adriana Stamatescu, Bucharest, Romania, 8 April 2013.

jurisprudence and ICL only began to play a role in legal education in the 2000s. Furthermore, long after the fall of state socialism, the judiciary continued to be de facto subordinated to the executive power. In the absence of a political will to judge communist crimes, judicial officials were hesitant to engage with such cases.[96] However, these prosecutors were also cautious in admitting individual responsibility of military personnel under communism. As Popov put it in an interview from 2007, 'administrative and military officials, especially low-rank officials, were under systematic pressure from a dictatorial regime, and they could have hardly opposed the general practice of political repression'.[97] These kinds of political views, corroborated with a formalist legal education under communism, and the lack of training in international law explain the 1990s impunity status quo.

3.2.2 Towards a More Flexible Approach to Retroactivity: The Revival of the 1968 UN Convention

In 2004, a centre-right coalition won the election in Romania on the promise to reckon with the communist past, which they denounced as a source of corruption and backwardness in relation to Western Europe. In 2006, a Presidential Commission for the Analysis of the Communist Dictatorship and an Institute for the Investigation of Communist Crimes in Romania (IICCR) were created. Inspired by similar initiatives established in the 1990s throughout CEE,[98] these institutions were tasked with documenting gross human rights violations committed during the previous regime. Their activity, as well as the Romanian president's condemnation of the communist regime as 'illegitimate and criminal' in December 2006, following a report by the Commission, gave a new impetus to investigations into communist crimes[99] and generated new debates about the legal framework applied in these cases.

Between 2006 and 2010, the IICCR filed several criminal complaints, most of them referring to political crimes committed in the 1950s. As in the 1990s, the prosecutors closed all investigations, arguing that the statutory limitations had expired. Within this context, a young team of historians and legal experts

[96] Grosescu and Fijalkowski, 'Retrospective Justice'.
[97] Personal interview with Mihai Popov, Bucharest, Romania, 22 February 2007.
[98] Such as the German Zentrale Ermittlungsstelle für Regierungs- und Vereinigungskriminalität (the Central Investigative Office for Governmental and Unification Criminality) or the Polish Institute of National Remembrance.
[99] For transitional justice in Romania, see Lavinia Stan, *Transitional Justice in Post-Communist Romania: The Politics of Memory* (Cambridge: Cambridge University Press, 2013).

working at the IICCR began to construct an anti-impunity strategy.[100] As Marius Oprea, head of the IICCR between 2006 and 2010, remarked,

> The main purpose was to find a way to open trials. But it was also a matter of showing that political crimes committed in the 1950s had been part of a systematic state policy that amounted to crimes against humanity. We were not looking only for a conviction for ordinary crimes. It was also important to demonstrate that the communist regime had committed international crimes and had to be condemned by the European community.[101]

Writing the history of the communist repression in terms of international law and gaining its condemnation at a European level was as important as obtaining guilty verdicts. From this vantage point, the Institute's lawyers, Valerian Stan and Oana Soare, started to document pro-accountability strategies at a global level.

> We started to look into how other countries overcame the problem of retroactivity and statutory limitations. We were mainly interested in cases concerning communist crimes and European jurisprudence, but we also studied other cases, such as Pinochet's arrest in London and the Argentinean jurisprudence.[102]

Born in 1955, Valerian Stan held administrative positions in the Romanian army before graduating in law in 1987. In the 1990s, he was at the forefront of the movement for the democratization of the army and partnered with various human rights organizations, including the Helsinki Committee for Human Rights in Romania. Here, he became acquainted with international human rights law and with the new ICL developments after the establishment of the ICTY. For Stan, bringing former communist officials to justice was a matter of both reparation of past injustices and a form of consolidating democracy, in a context in which former members of the army and the political police retained important power after 1989.[103] Born in 1976, Oana Soare graduated with a law degree in 1999. She received little training in human rights and ICL

[100] For an analysis of this strategy, see Raluca Grosescu, 'Judging Communist Crimes in Romania: Transnational and Global Influences', *International Journal of Transitional Justice* 11, no. 3 (2017): pp. 505–524.

[101] Personal interview with Marius Oprea, Bucharest, Romania, 1 March 2008.

[102] Personal interview with Oana Soare, Bucharest, Romania, 12 June 2014.

[103] Personal correspondence with Valerian Stan, 27 August 2007.

at university, but once she joined the IICCR in 2008 it became a major preoccupation. Her grandparents had themselves been victims of the communist regime, with one grandfather imprisoned for opposing the collectivization process in the 1950s.[104]

Stan and Soare ultimately proposed a legislative solution which, similarly to the Estonian legislation, would introduce crimes against humanity into the criminal code and allow their prosecution no matter when committed. In his writings on the subject, Stan argued that Romania's commitment to the implementation of the Rome Statute—including the obligation to define crimes against humanity in the national legislation—had to be read in conjunction with the evolution of customary international law which, since the Nuremberg Charter, had systematically affirmed the duty to prosecute gross human rights violations. The 1968 UN Convention was a key document in this respect, as Romania had ratified it during the communist period and it stipulated a duty to punish international crimes no matter when committed.[105] As quoted in the introduction of this chapter, IICCR experts were aware of the rejection of this instrument by Western European states, but the Convention was useful since it had been accepted by socialist states.[106]

The IICCR experts relied in particular on the Estonian model, evoking both the 2001 criminal code and the ECtHR decision in *Kolk & Kislyiy v. Estonia*, as well as the 1964 French law on crimes against humanity and the ECtHR rulings in *Touvier v. France* and *Papon v. France*. According to Soare,

> the fact that, in *Kolk & Kislyiy v. Estonia*, the ECtHR legitimized the approach we wanted to take was a key aspect for us. In the end, our anti-impunity strategy was close to the Estonian one and to the French legislation on crimes against humanity adopted in 1964.[107]

Between 2007 and 2009, the IICCR petitioned the Ministry of Justice three times to introduce crimes against humanity into the criminal code and include the provision 'punishable no matter when committed' from the 1968 UN Convention. The Institute's experts argued that the principle of non-retroactivity would not be violated, since Romania had ratified the Convention during the communist period. They also underlined that crimes against

[104] Personal interview with Oana Soare, Bucharest, Romania, 12 June 2014.
[105] Valerian Stan, 'Crimele Comunismului: Injustiţie şi Cinism (II)', 2008, available at www.valerianstan.ro/a613-crimele-comunismului-injustitie-si-cinism-ii.html (accessed 1 October 2023).
[106] Personal interview with Oana Soare, Bucharest, Romania, 12 June 2014.
[107] Ibid.

humanity had been criminalized by the Nuremberg Charter and that the Nuremberg principles had been embraced by all UN members, including Romania. Moreover, Article 15(2) of the ICCPR and Article 7(2) of the ECHR, as well as the ECtHR jurisprudence in *Papon v. France* and *Kolk & Kislyiy v. Estonia*, did not allow for non-retroactivity to impede the prosecution of heinous crimes.[108] Still, the Ministry of Justice rejected their petitions, emphasizing that Article 15(2) of the Romanian Constitution and Article 7(1) of the ECHR forbade *ex post facto* law and punishment. The Ministry did not engage, however, in a discussion about Romania's obligations under the 1968 UN Convention or the evolution of customary international law.[109]

Parallel to the IICCR's efforts, the Supreme Court of Justice provided a new reading of the legal category of inhuman treatment in 2009. In 1995, the family of a former political prisoner, who had been tortured and left to die without medical treatment in a communist jail in 1948, lodged a criminal complaint against three military officials implicated in the incident. In 1999, the military prosecutors closed the investigation, arguing that the statutory limitations for torture and murder had expired, and that the category of inhuman treatment was not applicable outside the context of war. The plaintiffs appealed, asking for further investigations into inhuman treatment. Ten years later, after lengthy procedural delays, the case reached the Supreme Court of Justice. For the first time, Romanian judges contended that the category of inhuman treatment was applicable outside the context of international or civil wars, in cases of 'adversarial relations' between the state and its citizens. They quoted the 1978 ECtHR decision in *Ireland v. the United Kingdom*,[110] which referred to acts of ill treatment committed by the British authorities under the Special Powers Act in Northern Ireland in 1971 and drew a parallel with the situation in Romania in 1948. The Court stated that the communist state had been in an 'adversarial relation' with its political opponents and imposed a 'regime of physical and psychological extermination' upon them. The Court concluded that such acts violated Article 3 of the ECHR, which prohibits torture and inhuman punishment. Prosecutors were compelled to resume investigations under the charge

[108] The Archives of the Institute for the Investigation of Communist Crimes in Romania, 'Proposal Regarding the Modification of the Criminal Code and the Modification of Law No. 80/1995 Concerning the Status of Military Personnel, 19 September 2007'; 'Proposal Regarding the Modification of the Title XI of the Criminal Code, 22 February 2008'; and 'Proposal Regarding the Modification of the Title XI of the Criminal Code, 22 October 2009'.

[109] The Archives of the Institute for the Investigation of Communist Crimes in Romania, 'Answer of the Ministry of Justice Regarding the Proposal of IICCR with Respect to the Modification of the Title XI of the Criminal Code, 20 April 2008'.

[110] ECtHR, *Ireland v. the United Kingdom*, Judgment of 18 January 1978.

of inhuman treatment.[111] The decision thus modified the previous interpretation of this legal category, rendering it applicable to political crimes committed by communist authorities in times of peace. Nevertheless, no case was ever opened based on these charges and the prosecutors continued to reject the IICCR's criminal complaints.

In 2011, as the Parliament was adopting a new criminal code, IICCR experts lobbied several politicians to back their anti-impunity strategy. They won the support of Monica Macovei, a member of the European Parliament, former minister of justice between 2004 and 2008, and former president of the Helsinki Committee for Human Rights in Romania in the early 2000s. Macovei had also advised the associations of the victims of the 1989 Revolution in their quest for justice.[112] As 2012 marked the expiry of statutory limitations for criminal investigations into murders committed in December 1989,[113] Macovei was keen to support initiatives combatting impunity. While the IICCR's representatives proposed the introduction of crimes against humanity 'punishable no matter when committed', based on the 1968 UN Convention and the Estonian and French precedents, Macovei thought to replicate the German model of lifting the statutory limitations for homicides, which permitted the continuation of prosecutions of Nazi crimes in the 1970s.[114] While Macovei's strategy did not provide a solution for crimes committed in the 1950s, it might have made it possible to continue the prosecution of murders committed in December 1989. This was not a satisfying solution for the IICCR's experts, who wanted the recognition of communist crimes as international, and not only as ordinary crimes: 'Our goal was to legally acknowledge that these crimes were crimes against humanity. They were not random murders; they were part of a systematic plan to exterminate political opponents and thus qualify as international crimes'.[115] Finally, Macovei proposed both amendments, which were adopted by the Parliament in 2012 and incorporated in the new criminal code in 2014.[116]

111 Romanian Supreme Court of Justice (hereafter RSCJ), 'Decision No. 2579/2009', pp. 17–18.

112 For the trials of the Romanian Revolution, see Raluca Grosescu and Raluca Ursachi, *Justiția penală de tranziție de la Nürnberg la postcomunismul românesc* (Iași: Polirom, 2009): pp. 134–206.

113 Where a criminal investigation had already been initiated, the statutory limitation of fifteen years for murder was prolonged by another seven-and-a-half years. Many investigations into the violent events of December 1989 had commenced in the 1990s but were subsequently delayed. July 2012 would have marked the closure of these cases.

114 Participants observation, meeting between Monica Macovei and IICCR experts, Bucharest, 4 January 2011.

115 Personal interview with Oana Soare, Bucharest, Romania, 12 June 2014.

116 Romanian Criminal Code 2014, Articles 439 and 121.

Subsequently, the IICCR lodged a criminal complaint against Alexandru Vişinescu, former director of a political prison between 1956 and 1963. Vişinescu was accused of crimes against humanity for deploying 'a regime of physical and psychological extermination' against the inmates. The prisoners, members of the pre-1945 political elite, were held for years in solitary confinement, subjected to torture, undernourishment, and lack of medical care. At least fourteen people died due to the appalling conditions, and many others suffered permanent injuries.[117]

Owing to the demilitarization of the administration of Romanian prisons in 2004, the case was investigated by civilian prosecutors, and not by military prosecutors as it had been the case of previous complaints. The case was assigned to Denisa Cristodor, who had graduated from the National Institute of Magistrates—a postgraduate institution that trains judicial officials in Romania—in 2004. She was part of a new generation of lawyers trained in human rights law and European jurisprudence: '[Vincent] Berger's collection, *Case Law of the European Court of Human Rights*, was a sort of Bible at the Institute of Magistracy. Everyone had this book in their pocket—if I can put it like that. And we were simulating trials based on the ECtHR's jurisprudence'. A firm belief in constitutionalism and the prevalence of international human rights law over domestic legislation were also important aspects of her legal education.[118]

In 2014, Cristodor indicted Vişinescu for crimes against humanity under the new criminal code. She provided nearly 100 pages of historical contextualization, placing Vişinescu's deeds in the larger history of the communist political repression. Murder and the inhuman treatment of political prisoners emerged as a systematic phenomenon that had dominated Romania for more than four decades, and thus amounted to international crimes. From a legal point of view, she maintained that until 1989 it was politically impossible to investigate such crimes. Only after 1989 could Vişinescu be put on trial for inhuman treatment, a category replaced in 2014 by crimes against humanity. Cristodor underlined Romania's constitutional obligations to respect international law and, consequently, to prosecute international crimes no matter when committed, according to the 1968 UN Convention. She argued that in 1956, when Vişinescu started to run the political prison, crimes against humanity had already been defined in international law by the Nuremberg Charter and various UN resolutions and that this definition included persecutions of political groups.

117 RSCJ, 'Indictment of 16 June 2014'.
118 Personal interview with Denisa Cristodor, Bucharest, Romania, 15 September 2014.

Vişinescu had also infringed Article 5 of the 1948 Universal Declaration of Human Rights which prohibits torture and cruel and inhuman treatment or punishment. Moreover, Cristodor argued that the establishment of the ICTY, the ICTR, and the ICC affirmed the duty to prosecute international crimes, and Romanian courts had to interpret national legislation in light of these developments.[119]

Vişinescu's defence denounced the retroactive application of the law, arguing that crimes against humanity had not been codified in the national criminal code until 2014, while inhuman treatment was introduced only in 1960. The defence also asserted that in the 1950s and 1960s, international law had not been part of military education in Romania. Moreover, Romanian military officials were bound by laws imposing a duty to obey superior orders. Vişinescu thus could not have foreseen the illegality of his actions.[120]

In 2015, the Bucharest Appellate Court rejected the arguments of the defence. The judge, Carmen Găină, was part of the same generation of young lawyers who received training in European law and jurisprudence in the mid-2000s. She maintained that no Romanian law justified obedience to illegal orders, and that both the socialist Romanian Constitution and the 1948 Universal Declaration of Human Rights protected the right to life and to physical and psychological integrity. She then evoked the cases of *K.-H.W. v. Germany*, *Kononov v. Latvia*, and *Polednová v. the Czech Republic* to state that 'even a soldier cannot blindly obey orders that violate domestic laws or human rights recognized at an international level'.[121] As far as retroactivity was concerned, Găină argued that crimes against humanity had been part of customary international law since Nuremberg, and that Romania was bound by the 1968 UN Convention. Romanian courts were thus obligated to prosecute crimes against humanity, no matter the lapse of time.[122]

Găină did, however, change the accusation from crimes against humanity to inhuman treatment, because the 1968 criminal code provided a lighter penalty for inhuman treatment than the 2014 criminal code stipulated for crimes against humanity. The judge considered that Vişinescu's acts qualified as both crimes against humanity and inhuman treatment, but the Romanian Constitution imposed the application of the more lenient law. She sentenced Vişinescu to twenty years in prison. She used the 2009 Supreme Court decision to conclude that the communist state had been in an 'adversarial relation'

119 RSCJ, 'Indictment of 16 June 2014'.
120 Bucharest Appellate Court, Criminal Section no. 1, 'Verdict No. 122/F of 24 July 2015'.
121 Ibid, 131.
122 Ibid.

with its political opponents and had implemented a 'regime of extermination' against them.[123] Moreover, she argued that while this legal category could have been read differently prior to 1989, the ECtHR ruled in *Streletz, Kessler and Krenz v. Germany* that the laws of dictatorial regimes can be interpreted according to a democratic, rule-of-law reading.[124] In February 2016, the Supreme Court of Justice upheld the verdict,[125] which was followed by two similar trials concerned with the murder of political opponents before 1989.[126]

Romanian courts thus used the 1968 UN Convention as an instrument that allows prosecutions of international crimes retroactively. As in Estonia, the Convention was interpreted in light of the evolution of customary international law since 1945. Through this approach, the Romanian judiciary overcame impunity and created a historical account that recognized the systemic nature of communist repression and its illegality under international law.

4. Customary International Law and the 1968 UN Convention in Argentina and Paraguay

Although no country in the region adopted it until the twenty-first century, the 1968 UN Convention also became a key anti-impunity instrument in Latin America. The cases of Argentina and Paraguay illustrate how this ICL instrument was first considered to be part of customary international law and then ratified with the specific aim of creating a basis in conventional law for prosecuting crimes committed under military dictatorships. The jurisprudence of both countries is similar and reflects a departure from a strict interpretation of the principle of non-retroactivity: anti-impunity solutions relied on the direct application of ICL categories that had not been transposed into national legislation. Nevertheless, the two cases also differ. The Argentinian judiciary provided a broad legal and historical contextualization of the crimes committed by the dictatorship to prove their categorization as crimes against humanity, whereas the Paraguayan judiciary remained schematic and did not engage with the legal and political history that would have delegitimized the former regime as a perpetrator of international crimes.

123 RSCJ, 'Decision No. 2579/2009', p. 17.

124 Bucharest Appellate Court, Criminal Section no. 1, 'Verdict No. 122/F of 24 July 2015'.

125 RSCJ, 'Decision No. 51/A of 10 February 2016'.

126 Ion Ficior, former director of a political prison in the 1950s, and Vasile Pirvulescu, former Securitate officer, were indicted for crimes against humanity in 2016 and 2018, respectively.

4.1 Argentinian Struggles against Amnesties and Statutory Limitations

Between 1987 and 2001, two impunity laws (the 1986 Full Stop Law and the 1987 Due Obedience Law) blocked the prosecution of political crimes committed during the military dictatorship in Argentina.[127] Enshrined by President Raúl Alfosín, after several attempted military coups d'état against his government, these laws were motivated by the need to consolidate peace and democracy. They prohibited any investigation into dictatorial crimes, with the exception of the illegal 'appropriation' of children of left-wing militants executed by the military juntas. In 1987, the Argentinian Supreme Court of Justice declared these laws to be constitutional, establishing a *de jure* and de facto regime of impunity.[128] This decision was facilitated by the fact that there was no consensus at an international level at the time on whether political crimes of dictatorial regimes should be prosecuted, and no international institutions pressured Argentina to seek justice.[129]

While the 1853 Argentinian Constitution (in force until 1994) recognized that international treaties were part of Argentinian legislation, it did not specify whether they could be applied directly or if national laws were needed to enforce them.[130] In 1992, the Argentinian Supreme Court of Justice clarified that international treaties approved by Parliament could be applied directly by national courts. This did not apply, however, to customary international law.[131] Two years later, the newly adopted Constitution elevated international law above national norms and gave a series of human rights treaties constitutional rank.[132] Among these treaties were the 1948 UN Genocide Convention, the 1984 UN Convention against Torture, the 1966 Covenants on Human

[127] The Argentinian transition to democracy began with trials against members of the military juntas and other officers involved in human rights violations. Due to military unrest, this process was halted in 1987. For these early trials and the 1986 Full Stop Law and the 1987 Due Obedience Law, see Carlos Acuña and Catalina Smulovitz, 'Guarding the Guardians in Argentina: Some Lessons about the Risks and Benefits of Empowering the Courts', in *Transitional Justice and the Rule of Law in New Democracies*, edited by James McAdams (Notre Dame: University of Notre Dame Press, 1997): pp. 93–122.

[128] Pablo Parenti, 'Argentina', in *Jurisprudencia Latinoamericana sobre Derecho Penal International: Con Informes Adicionales de España e Italia*, edited by Kai Ambos and Ezequiel Malarino (Montevideo: Konrad Adenauer Stiftung, 2008): pp. 21–66, at pp. 51–53.

[129] Paige Arthur, 'How "Transitions" Reshaped Human Rights: A Conceptual History of Transitional Justice', *Human Rights Quarterly* 31, no. 2 (2009): pp. 321–367.

[130] Alejandro E. Alvarez, Eduardo A. Bertoni, and Mihuel Boo, 'Droit Argentin', in *Juridictions Nationales et Crimes Internationaux*, edited by Antonio Cassese and Mireille Delmas-Marty (Paris: Presses Universitaires de France, 2002): pp. 299–331, at pp. 302–303.

[131] Ezequil Malarino, 'Argentina', in *Persecución penal nacional de crímenes internacionales en América Latina y España*, edited by Kai Ambos and Ezequil Malarino (Montevideo: Konrad Adenauer Stiftung, 2003): pp. 35–81, at p. 40.

[132] Argentinian Constitution 1994, Article 75.

Rights, and the American Convention on Human Rights (ACHR). Other international instruments were assigned constitutional status later, such as the Inter-American Convention on Forced Disappearances in 1997 and the 1968 UN Convention in 2003.[133] Yet, the same Constitution prohibited *ex post facto* law, meaning that these treaties could not have constitutional status retroactively.[134] As a civil law country, Argentina required a strict interpretation of non-retroactivity, based on *lex praevia, scripta, certa, stricta.*[135]

Despite the 1994 constitutional changes, major international crimes (except for torture) were not included in the criminal code. Argentina had ratified the 1948 UN Genocide Convention and the 1949 Geneva Conventions in 1956 but did not transpose these instruments onto the national level. In 2023, genocide, war crimes, and crimes against humanity were still not criminalized in the Argentinian penal code.[136] Moreover, in 1986, when Argentina ratified the ICCPR, it made a reservation to Article 15(2), opposing the prosecution of international crimes if they had not been criminalized by national legislation.[137] The imprescriptibility of international crimes and the duty to prosecute them was acknowledged only in 2003, when the country ratified the 1968 UN Convention.[138]

The impunity regime imposed by Alfonsín's government thus remained unquestioned by the Argentinian judiciary until 2001. Nonetheless, victims' associations and human rights lawyers mobilized across borders to seek justice at the Inter-American Commission on Human Rights and in European courts, based on universal jurisdiction (see Chapter 3).[139] In 1992, the Inter-American Commission concluded that the impunity laws were incompatible with several articles of the ACHR, including the right to truth and a fair trial (Articles 1, 2, 8, and 25). The Commission did not demand that Argentina reopen trials but recommended the elucidation of forced disappearances. The Commission's ruling did not influence criminal justice but led to the creation of the so-called truth trials held in civil courts to reveal cases of forced disappearances, without, however, assigning criminal guilt.[140] More important for criminal justice, from

[133] Alvarez, Bertoni, and Boo, 'Droit Argentin', pp. 305–306.

[134] Argentinian Constitution 1994, Article 18.

[135] Parenti, 'Argentina', pp. 30–31.

[136] Malarino, 'Argentina', p. 37. In 2007, law 26.200 implemented the Rome Statute and criminalized both categories. Yet the law refers only to crimes committed after the ratification of the Rome Statute in 2002 and cannot be applied retroactively to the crimes of the 'Dirty War'.

[137] Alvarez, Bertoni, and Boo, 'Droit Argentin', p. 306.

[138] Parenti, 'Argentina', p. 23.

[139] Within the Inter-American Human Rights system, claimants must first address the Commission, which then decides whether a court case can move forward at the Inter-American Court of Human Rights (IACtHR).

[140] Kathryn Sikkink, 'From Pariah State to Global Protagonist: Argentina and the Struggle for International Human Rights', *Latin American Politics and Society* 50, no. 1 (2008): pp. 1–29.

1996 onwards, judges in Spain, France, and Belgium issued international arrest warrants against various Argentinian ex-military officials, accusing them of gross human rights violations.[141] These developments, together with powerful national anti-impunity movements, put pressure on the Argentinian judiciary, which was not only forbidden from investigating gross human rights violations, but also, by a 2000 decree signed by President Fernando de la Rúa, was prohibited from responding to any extradition request.[142]

4.1.1 Reversing Impunity Based on Customary International Law

In March 2001, Gabriel Cavallo, a judge from a court of first instance in Buenos Aires, announced a judicial decision that sent shockwaves across the Argentinian judiciary and political elite. In a case related to the illegal appropriation of children, Cavallo extended the investigations to the forced disappearances of their parents. He argued that the 1986 and 1987 impunity laws were unconstitutional and that political crimes committed under the military dictatorship could not be subject to amnesties and statutory limitations, since they constituted crimes against humanity under international law. Consequently, he opened criminal proceedings against two ex-military officials accused of illegal detention, torture, and the murder of political opponents in the 1970s.[143]

Born in 1958, Cavallo graduated in law from Buenos Aires University in 1985. The same year, he was appointed as the public defender for three military officials involved in political crimes, an experience he recalls as decisive in crystallizing his understanding of the recent Argentinian past and the sheer scale of the repression. Between 1993 and 1995, Cavallo worked as a prosecutor and subsequently was appointed investigative judge. He probed cases of transnational human and narcotics trafficking and was thus familiarized with international law and judicial cooperation across borders. As a judge specialized in transnational criminality, Cavallo had been part of various transnational networks of judicial officials and had received international extradition requests that he was unable to respond to. The inability to take action against impunity made him feel excluded from the 'serious' community of jurists. In his words, 'it became evident that unless something changed in the attitude of Argentinian judges, we couldn't be considered a serious judiciary and a serious country'.[144]

[141] See Naomi Roht-Arriaza, *The Pinochet Effect: Transitional Justice in the Age of Human Rights* (Philadelphia, PA: University of Pennsylvania Press, 2005).

[142] U.S. Department of State, Argentina—Country Report on Human Rights Practices 2002.

[143] Causa Nro. 8686/2000 'Simon, Julio, Del Cerro, Juan Antonio s/sustracción de menores de 10 años', Sentencia de 6 Marzo 2001.

[144] Personal interview with Gabriel Cavallo, Buenos Aires, Argentina, 14 June 2016.

In drafting his anti-impunity decision, Cavallo was assisted by judicial assistants Hernan Folgueiro and Pablo Parenti, who belonged to a new generation of lawyers trained in the spirit of the 1994 Constitution, which had elevated international law above national legislation. Both had received training in the Inter-American legal system and the jurisprudence of the Inter-American Court of Human Rights (IACtHR). Parenti had also participated in anti-impunity marches organized by victims' associations in Buenos Aires since 1987.[145] He would later coordinate a section of the Argentinian public prosecutor's office in charge of investigations into dictatorial crimes.

Cavallo's ruling combined constitutional principles and international law. He maintained that Article 102 of the 1853 Argentinian Constitution (transposed as Article 118 of the 1994 Constitution) stipulated the duty to investigate crimes against *jus gentium*, meaning violations of peremptory norms recognized by the international community. Invoking an inventory of international instruments and jurisprudence developed since the Nuremberg trials, he concluded that the Argentinian judiciary was bound by customary international law to investigate crimes against humanity, war crimes, and genocide. He also argued that crimes committed during the so-called Dirty War qualified as crimes against humanity. Their amnesty infringed several principles of the ACHR, such as the right to truth and the right to a fair trial. Furthermore, these crimes were not subject to statutory limitations, according to the 1968 UN Convention and Article 15(2) of the ICCPR. While Argentina had not yet ratified the 1968 UN Convention in 2001 and made a specific reservation to Article 15(2) of the ICCPR, Cavallo argued that these conventions were part of *jus cogens* and Argentina was bound by them according to its 1853 and 1994 Constitutions.[146]

In his decision, Cavallo built upon two extradition cases of former Nazi criminals, formulated by the Argentinian judiciary in 1989 and 1995. The first referred to the extradition of Josef Schwammberger, a former director of forced labour camps in Poland during the Second World War, who had immigrated to Argentina in 1948 and was tracked down by the Argentinian authorities in 1987. West Germany requested Schwammberger's extradition on homicide charges—the legal category applied by West German courts in trials of Nazi criminals. In 1989, the La Plata Appellate Court approved the extradition. Two

[145] Personal interview with Hernan Folgueiro, Buenos Aires, Argentina, 6 July 2016; personal interview with Pablo Parenti, online, 30 March 2017.

[146] JNCCF4, Causa no. 8686/2000 'Simon, Julio, Del Cerro, Juan Antonio s/sustracción de menores de 10 años', Sentencia de 6 Marzo 2001; Pablo F. Parenti, 'The Prosecution of International Crimes in Argentina', *International Criminal Law Review* 10 (2010): pp. 491–507.

of the sitting judges ruled that although homicide committed before 1945 had already been prescribed under Argentinian law, this was not the case under German law. The absence of an extradition treaty between Argentina and Germany allowed the judges to apply either German or Argentinian law. They chose the former, so that Schwammberger could be indicted for murder.[147]

The third judge, Leopoldo Schiffrin, argued that Schwammberger's deeds should be qualified as crimes against humanity, and in the absence of an extradition treaty, the extradition request should be granted based on international law and not on German law. Born in Buenos Aires in 1936 to a mixed Jewish-Christian family, Schiffrin had been interested in ICL and justice for the victims of Nazi crimes since his student days. In 1976, when the Argentinian military dictatorship took power, he was forced into exile in Germany, where he spent five years at the Institute for Public International Law at the University of Bonn. Schiffrin recalled those years as formative:

> I learned that Germans never used international criminal law categories and convicted Nazi crimes as simple murders. This seemed to me a conservative jurisprudence, and a way to avoid the magnitude of the Nazi horrors. I studied the debates around the 1968 UN Convention—it's somehow ironic that the proposal came from the communist bloc which committed its own crimes against humanity—but I believe that it was an important instrument stating that prosecutions of Nazi international crimes were more important than a strict approach to the principle of legality, which actually allowed so many Nazi criminals to go unpunished.[148]

In the Schwammberger case, Schiffrin underlined how West Germany never employed international law in judging Nazi crimes, but prolonged and then lifted the statute of limitations for homicide in 1969 and 1979 to continue prosecutions. He argued that these had been *ex post facto* modifications of statutory limitations, an approach prohibited by Article 18 of the Argentinian Constitution in cases of ordinary crimes such as homicide. In contrast, Schiffrin qualified Schwammberger's actions as crimes against humanity under international law, not subject to statutory limitations according to the 1968 UN Convention and to customary international law predating the Convention. During an interview from 2016, Schiffrin asked me if Eastern

[147] Camera Federal de La Plata, Sala III Penal, 'Schwammberger, J.F.L. s/extradicción', Decision no. 41.979, 30 August 1989.

[148] Personal interview with Leopoldo Schiffrin, La Plata, Argentina, 1 July 2016.

Europeans used the 1989 UN Convention in trials against former communists. He continued: 'it is interesting that this Convention was their enterprise, and this is why it was probably so marginal for the Western world. But this instrument is very important and helps against impunity'.[149] In the Schwammberger case, the judge also contended that the retrospective prosecution of heinous crimes was permitted by Article 15(2) of the ICCPR and Article 7(2) of the ECHR. Hence, a strict interpretation of the principle *nullum crimen sine lege* in cases of international crimes was contrary to *jus cogens*. He then argued that Article 102 of the 1853 Argentinian Constitution affirmed the duty to prosecute crimes against *jus gentium* and to extradite perpetrators when other countries opened investigations.[150]

In 1995, the Argentinian Supreme Court of Justice employed Schiffrin's approach in the extradition case of Eric Priebke to Italy.[151] A former SS officer, Priebke had taken part in the 1944 Ardeatine massacre in which more than 330 Italian civilians were executed. The extradition treaty between Argentina and Italy allowed for extraditions only when the actions were criminal in both countries. Because a murder committed in 1944 had already been prescribed in Argentina, the judges would have had to refuse extradition if they considered Priebke's acts to be ordinary crimes. The Court argued instead that Priebke had committed war crimes and crimes against humanity. Under customary international law—whose rules Argentina had to respect according to the 1853 and 1994 Constitutions—and based on the 1968 UN Convention, these crimes were not subject to statutory limitations.[152] Priebke was eventually sentenced in Italy, at the age of eighty-three, to five years in prison. The Supreme Court of Justice thus enshrined Schiffrin's approach as a precedent in Argentinian jurisprudence and established that crimes against humanity, even those committed long ago, were subject to prosecution. Both the Schwammberger and Priebke cases were, however, extradition trials. As Malarino has underlined, it was improbable that the Supreme Court would approve the same approach in a criminal trial of Argentinian military officials. The Court had endorsed the impunity laws in 1987, and international crimes remained absent from domestic legislation.[153]

[149] Ibid.

[150] Camera Federal de La Plata, Sala III Penal, 'Schwammberger, J.F.L. s/extradicción', Decision no. 41.979, 30 August 1989, 'Separate Opinion of Leopoldo Héctor Schiffrin'.

[151] Corte Suprema de la Nación, 'Priebke, Erich s/solicitud de extradición', CSJN Fallos 318:2148, 2 November 1995.

[152] Leopoldo Schiffrin, 'La primacía del derecho internacional sobre el derecho argentino', in *La aplicación de los tratados sobre derechos humanos por los tribunales locales*, edited by Martin Abregú and Christian Courtis (Buenos Aires: Del Puerto, 1997): pp. 115–125, at pp. 116–117.

[153] Malarino, 'Argentina', pp. 72–73.

Transposing Schiffrin's approach into their own ruling, Cavallo and his team still had to prove that what had been applicable to Nazi crimes could be valid for the crimes of the Argentinian dictatorship. More precisely, they had to show the international nature of military crimes, which Cavallo did by engaging at great length with the historical background of the system of political repression and forced disappearances. He concluded that the military had carried out a systematic attack against a civil population based on political motives, which qualified as crimes against humanity.

> We had to write the history of the repression at length, in order to show that the crimes of the dictatorships had not been simply murder or kidnapping, but constituted international crimes, therefore subject to international criminal law principles. The result was that legally and historically we proved that these were not ordinary crimes, but universal crimes.[154]

Cavallo and his team sought to demonstrate that the crimes committed in Argentina concerned a broad community of states and individuals. They thus listed a series of international warrants and convictions in absentia issued by foreign courts against Argentinian military officials, such as *France v. Alfredo Astiz* (1990), *Italy v. Suárez Mason and Santiago Omar Riveros* (2000), *Switzerland v. Emilio Eduardo Massera* (1998), and *Spain v. Adolfo Scilingo* (1998).[155] Discussing these cases also provided an opportunity to de-peripheralize Argentinian military repression. As Folgueiro puts it: 'We wanted to solve legal constraints, but also to write the history of the repression in such way that it would become relevant to the entire world'.[156] Dictatorial crimes were no longer a matter of domestic justice but affected the wider international community. The crimes were depicted as part of a global history of twentieth-century mass murder, insofar as the jurisprudence on Argentinian crimes represented a continuity with the jurisprudence on the Holocaust and the Yugoslav and the Rwandan civil wars.

Consequently, Cavallo argued for an international duty to investigate such crimes stemming from customary international law developed since Nuremberg and international treaties such as the 1968 UN Convention, the 1984 Convention against Torture, the 1994 Inter-American Convention against Forced Disappearances of Persons, and the 1998 Rome Statute, as well

[154] Personal interview with Gabriel Cavallo, Buenos Aires, Argentina, 14 June 2016.

[155] JNCCF4, Causa Nro. 8686/2000 'Simon, Julio, Del Cerro, Juan Antonio s/sustracción de menores de 10 años', Sentencia de 6 Marzo 2001, pp. 22–24.

[156] Personal interview with Hernan Folgueiro, Buenos Aires, Argentina, 6 July 2016.

as the 1988 IACtHR decision in *Velásquez Rodríguez v. Honduras*, which affirmed the duties of states to prevent, investigate, and prosecute human rights violations. He also referred to the Inter-American Commission's report of 1992, which concluded that the Argentinian impunity laws infringed the ACHR, including the right to truth and a fair trial. According to Cavallo, these international instruments and jurisprudence corroborated with Article 102 of the 1853 Argentinian Constitution (and Article 118 of the 1994 Constitution) rendered the impunity laws illegal at both national and international levels.[157]

After rejecting the impunity laws, Cavallo faced another dilemma: the selection of charges and the application of penalties according to the national criminal code. Not only were major international crimes not codified in the Argentinian legislation, but the statutory limitations for murders, kidnappings, or torture committed in the 1970s had already expired. Within this context, Cavallo and his collaborators proposed a *double classification* of deeds. The defendants' conduct was classified under national law as murder, illegal deprivation of liberty, or torture, but as crimes against humanity under international law, not liable to statutory limitations and punishable no matter when committed.[158] In Parenti's view, this was a 'crazy strategy', particularly for a civil law country which requires the strict codification of crimes and applicable penalties.[159] In an interview in 2016, Cavallo also assessed his decision with caution:

> It was a necessary judicial answer for the victims and for Argentinean society in general. It was the only anti-impunity solution we found. But it was problematic. When I discussed this approach with German lawyers and with the President of the Spanish Supreme Court, they told me that such approach could be interpreted as a political instrumentalization of the law and a risk for the rule of law. And I think they were not entirely wrong. I am not sure I would write this decision again.[160]

Cavallo's jurisprudence polarized the Argentinian legal experts. Some hailed the decision as a progressive and innovative anti-impunity strategy,[161] while

[157] JNCCF4, Causa Nro. 8686/2000 'Simon, Julio, Del Cerro, Juan Antonio s/sustracción de menores de 10 años', Sentencia de 6 Marzo 2001, pp. 70–78; 115–125.

[158] Parenti, 'The Prosecution', p. 498.

[159] Personal interview with Pablo Parenti, online, 30 March 2017.

[160] Personal interview with Gabriel Cavallo, Buenos Aires, Argentina, 14 June 2016.

[161] Oded Balaban and Amos Megged, eds., *Impunidad y Derechos Humanos en America Latina: Perspectivas Teóricas* (La Plata: Ediciones al Margen, 2003); Ricardo Gil Lavedra, 'The Possibility of Criminal Justice: The Argentinean Experience', in *The Role of Courts in Transitional Justice: Voices from Latin America and Spain*, edited by Jessica Almqvist and Carlos Espósito (New York: Routledge, 2012): pp. 56–80.

others considered it to be contrary to the rule of law and to the Argentinian Constitution which imposed non-retroactivity and the application of the most lenient law to the defendant.[162] At an international level, Cavallo's decision was followed several days later by the historical IACtHR judgment in *Barrios Altos v. Peru*, which ruled that amnesties and statutory limitations could not apply to major international crimes.[163] In June 2001, Amnesty International, Human Rights Watch, and the International Commission of Jurists submitted an Amicus Curiae to the Appellate Court of Buenos Aires in support of Cavallo's approach. The document dealt with international law and the jurisprudence that prohibited amnesties but did not engage with the issue of statutory limitations or the double classification of deeds.[164] Following this international endorsement and the IACtHR decision in *Barrios Altos v. Peru*, other Argentine judges opened investigations into dictatorial crimes.

4.1.2 The Adoption of the 1968 UN Convention as a Retrospective Anti-Impunity Tool

Cavallo's decision was followed by similar indictments issued by other Argentinian courts, but such an approach could have been overruled by the Supreme Court of Justice, which in 1987 had endorsed the impunity laws. In 2003, Nestor Kirchner, a former anti-dictatorship militant who had been involved in anti-impunity campaigns, won the presidential election. Immediately thereafter, the Kirchner administration adopted a two-step anti-impunity strategy, inspired by a leading Argentinian NGO, the Centre for Social and Legal Studies (CELS). In May 2003, the president ratified the 1968 UN Convention. In August 2003, Parliament assigned it constitutional status,[165] before annulling the two anti-impunity laws.[166] These measures were closely interrelated: While the latter allowed courts to resume prosecutions, the former declared that crimes against humanity were not subject to prescription and punishable no matter when committed. According to Carolina Varsky, previously a legal expert at CELS,

> the 1968 UN Convention was a key instrument for creating a favourable framework for reopening prosecutions. Other solutions would have been

[162] Malarino, 'Argentina', p. 58.

[163] IACtHR, *Barrios Altos v. Peru*, Judgment of 14 March 2001.

[164] Amnesty International, 'Argentina Memorial en Derecho Amicus Curiae sobre la incompatibilidad de las leyes de punto final y obediencia debida con el derecho internacional', AMR 13/012/2001, 31 July 2001.

[165] Argentina, Law no. 25778 / 20 August 2003.

[166] Argentina, Law no. 25779 / 21 August 2003.

> possible, based on customary international law, but in a civil law country, like Argentina, it's always better to use conventional law. This ratification was thus essential for legitimizing the annulment of the two impunity laws.[167]

Various lawyers and politicians criticized these measures as retroactive and a dangerous political instrumentalization of law.[168] Parliamentary debates were also heated, as some MPs argued that the retroactive effect of the 1968 UN Convention violated Article 18 of the Argentinian Constitution, which prohibited *ex post facto* laws and punishment. The dissenters argued that the Constitution clearly stated that any international treaty could only be incorporated if it did not infringe upon the principle of legality. They considered the use of the 1968 UN Convention for prosecutions of dictatorial crimes as an encroachment on the rule of law—and deeply reminiscent of the actions of the former military authorities themselves. Some opponents questioned the validity of the 1968 UN Convention, since it had itself been instigated by dictatorial communist regimes and had never been ratified by Western democracies.[169] Despite this, a parliamentary majority voted in favour of this anti-impunity strategy, reflecting the political resolve of the new administration to resume prosecutions.

In 2005, the Supreme Court of Justice upheld the constitutionality of this approach, stating that the application of the 1968 UN Convention was legal, since its adoption by the UN simply confirmed a consolidated principle of customary international law, namely the non-applicability of statutory limitations to international crimes.[170] Judge Eugenio Raúl Zaffaroni was among the main proponents of this approach. Judge Carmen María Argibay went even further, affirming that the instrument had been adopted by the international community in 1968 with the specific intention of producting a retroactive effect. When Argentina ratified the Convention, it approved this retroactive rule.[171] Only one judge dissented, stating that Article 18 of the Constitution prohibited retroactivity, including *ex post facto* application of international law. This counterargument was however dismissed also based on the 2001 IACtHR decision in *Barrios Altos v. Peru*. The majority did not engage in any way with the fact that Argentina had ratified the ACHR only in 1984, whereas the crimes under

[167] Personal interview with Carolina Varsky, Buenos Aires, Argentina, 3 December 2014.

[168] Pablo Luis Manili, 'Sobre la Constitucionalidad de la ley 25779, Nos guste o no nos guste', *Antecedentes Parlamentarios* 1 (2003): pp. 1749–1752.

[169] Archives of the Argentinian Parliament, 'Debates of the Argentinean Senate, 20–21 August 2003', pp. 27–122.

[170] Quoted by Parenti, 'Argentina', p. 43.

[171] Ibid, p. 45.

scrutiny had been perpetrated in the 1970s. As Pablo Parenti points out, this was due to the fact that the ACHR did not represent the major reference in this case. The foundation for the Court's decision was primarily customary international law and then the 1968 UN Convention.[172] From the Supreme Court's 2005 decision to 2015, more than 800 former military officials and civilian collaborators were convicted for crimes committed during the 'Dirty War'.[173]

4.1.3 The International Reverberations of Argentinian Jurisprudence

The reopening of trials in Argentina was widely hailed by international experts and scholars who applauded the country for moving from 'pariah' to 'global protagonist' of justice.[174] Even when acknowledging the peculiar double classification of criminal acts under national and international law, ICL analysts considered the Argentinian strategy to be an 'important historical precedent' that created new anti-impunity solutions and novel ICL constructs.[175] Argentinian judges such as Cavallo and Zaffaroni travelled to various Latin American countries, as well as Spain, Israel, and Cambodia, to promote their jurisprudence.[176] CELS became a leading Latin American NGO and exported its expertise transnationally in countries such as Paraguay, Uruguay, Peru, and Colombia.[177] Romanian activists interested in the prosecutions of communist crimes also studied the relevant Argentinian jurisprudence, although they considered it to be too problematic for civil law contexts.[178]

The Argentinian legal reasoning was also employed in 2007 by the Spanish Supreme Court of Justice in the trial of former Argentinian military officer Adolfo Scilingo, who was arrested in Spain in 1997 based on universal jurisdiction. Scilingo was first convicted in 2005 for crimes against humanity, a category introduced into the Spanish criminal code in 2004. The judge in that case, José Ricardo de Prada, employed similar arguments as in Estonia and Romania. He contended that even if crimes against humanity had not been codified in Spanish legislation until 2004, the category itself had been criminalized in customary international law since the Nuremberg trial and in the 1968 UN Convention. Hence, Scilingo's conviction did not pose a problem

[172] Ibid, p. 47.

[173] Procuraduría de Crímenes Contra la Humanidad, *El estado de las causas por delitos de lesa humanidad en Argentina. Balance y Desafíos*, available at www.fiscales.gob.ar/wp-content/uploads/2015/12/Ver-Informe.pdf (accessed 27 October 2023).

[174] Sikkink, 'From Pariah'; Roht-Arriaza, *The Pinochet Effect*, pp. 115–116.

[175] Bassiouni, *Crimes against Humanity*, p. 692.

[176] Personal interview with Gabriel Cavallo, Buenos Aires, Argentina, 14 June 2016.

[177] Personal interview with Luz Palmas, Buenos Aires, Argentina, 14 June 2016.

[178] Personal interview with Oana Soare, Bucharest, Romania, 12 June 2014.

of retroactivity.[179] In 2007, the Supreme Court of Justice overruled the verdict and considered de Prada's sentence to be retroactive. However, the Court found Scilingo guilty. Here, the judges deployed the Argentinian double classification of criminal acts. They convicted Scilingo on charges of murder and illegal arrest—crimes inscribed in the Spanish criminal code in the 1970s—and considered them to be crimes against humanity under customary international law, and thus not subject to statutory limitations.[180] It is unclear how the Supreme Court came to employ this approach, but it nonetheless underlined the legitimacy of the Argentinian jurisprudence on the issue.

As we will see below, as well as in Chapter 4, the changes that occurred in Argentina after 2001 also impacted Paraguay. Paraguayan victims addressed the Argentinian judiciary to open investigations into Stroessner-era crimes, based on universal jurisdiction. These investigations eventually accelerated prosecutions in the Paraguayan national courts.

4.2 Paraguay: A Schematic Connection between National and International Law

Paraguay is another case where the 1968 UN Convention was employed as a legal tool against impunity. However, in contrast to Argentina, Estonia, and Romania, the Paraguayan judiciary used ICL to overcome the issue of statutory limitations but refrained from a broader legal and historical contextualization that would have delegitimized Alfredo Stroessner's dictatorial regime at the national and international levels. The Paraguayan jurisprudence reflects the judiciary's uncomfortable position between societal pressures to respond to past abuses and the need to conform to structural continuities, such as the lack of independence of the judiciary and the dominance of Stroessner-era interest groups long after the end of the dictatorship.

In contrast to Argentina and other Latin American countries, Paraguay had no amnesty law that impeded investigations into dictatorial crimes. Anti-impunity efforts were confronted instead with the issue of statutory limitations and the lack of political and judicial will to prosecute former authoritarian officials. From a political point of view, Paraguay's transition to democracy was characterized by the continuity of former military and political elites and the

[179] See Alicia Gil Gil, 'The Flaws of the Scilingo Judgement', *Journal of International Criminal Justice* 3, no. 5 (2005): pp. 1082–1091.

[180] Spanish Supreme Court of Justice—Criminal Chamber, Tribunal Supremo—Sala de lo Penal, Judicial Appeal no. 10049/2006 P, Judgment of 1 October 2007 (Ruling of 2 July 2007), STS 798/2007.

lasting domination of the Colorado Party, which had endorsed Stroessner's corporatist and clientelist dictatorship for thirty-five years (1956–1989). Reforms designed to create a procedural democracy were initiated in 1989, including free elections, the restoration of civil liberties, and the adoption of a new Constitution in 1992. Yet, structural social inequalities, corruption, and the informal political and economic networks controlled by the Colorados and the army continued to dominate Paraguayan politics for more than three decades after the end of the dictatorship.[181] Furthermore, the executive branch continued to exercise strong pressure on the judiciary despite judicial reforms in 1996 that removed many corrupt judges.[182] In 2019, Paraguay was ranked the second most corrupt country in South America after Venezuela.[183]

From a legal point of view, the Paraguayan criminal code in force during Stroessner's regime provided a statute of limitations of twenty years for murder, meaning that in 1989 it was no longer possible to prosecute homicides committed before 1969. As in Romania, torture—a practice frequently inflicted upon political opponents—was codified as an ordinary crime (and not an international one) under the heading of 'serious injury' (lesión grave) to physical and mental health.[184] It had a statute of limitations of two years. Moreover, none of the core international crimes had been criminalized in the Paraguayan national legislation before the regime changed. Paraguay adopted the 1949 Geneva Conventions in 1961 but did not transpose them into domestic law. The 1948 UN Genocide Convention was only ratified in 2001, and Paraguay did not become a member of the 1968 UN Convention until 2008. Until the early years of the twenty-first century, the country was thus not bound by conventional international law in terms of genocide and crimes against humanity.

After the fall of the dictatorship, the new Paraguayan government led by an anti-Stroessner branch of the Colorado Party introduced legal changes in terms of human rights and ICL. The purpose of these modifications was to dissociate the Colorados from their previous record of political repression and to overcome the country's long-term international isolationism. In August 1989, Paraguay ratified the ACHR, and in 1993 it accepted the jurisdiction of IACtHR. In 1992, Article 5 of the new Constitution stipulated that 'genocide,

[181] For Stroessner's regime and democratization in Paraguay, see Peter Lambert and Andrew Nickson, eds., *The Transition to Democracy in Paraguay* (London: MacMillan, 1997); Dominique Fournier and Sean W. Burges, 'Form before Function: Democratization in Paraguay', *Canadian Journal of Latin American and Caribbean Studies* 25, no. 49 (2000): pp. 5–32; Diego Abente Brun, 'Estatalidad y calidad de la democracia en Paraguay', *América Latina Hoy* 60 (2012): pp. 43–66.

[182] Fournier and Burges, 'Form before Function', p. 18.

[183] According to Transparency International, quoted in Nathaniel Parish Flannery, 'What Are the Most Corrupt Countries in Latin America?', *Forbes*, 24 January 2020.

[184] Paraguayan Criminal Code 1914, Article 112.

torture, forced disappearances, and kidnapping and homicide committed on political grounds are not subject to statutory limitations'.[185] Nevertheless, this provision was thought to be future-oriented, since the same Constitution prohibited retroactivity.[186] A new criminal code adopted in 1997 criminalized genocide, war crimes, and torture, but the legislature left the category of crimes against humanity uncodified.[187] In 2023, there was still no provision on crimes against humanity (including forced disappearances) in the Paraguayan criminal code, although the country ratified the Inter-American Convention on the Forced Disappearances of Persons in 1996, the Rome Statute in 2001, and the 1968 UN Convention in 2008. The 1997 criminal code also reduced the statute of limitations for murder from twenty to fifteen years, but provided that the crimes listed in Article 5 of the Constitution were not subject to prescription.[188]

It is within this legal context that victims and human rights associations advocated for the prosecution of gross human rights violations committed under the dictatorship. During the 1990s, several former military officials—including Pastor Milciades Coronel, the head of the Investigation Department of the National Police, and General Francisco Alcibiades Britez Borges, chief of Police of Asunción—were convicted for murdering political opponents in the 1970s.[189] These cases were not constrained by the question of retroactivity, since the statutory limitations of twenty years for murder had not yet expired. In cases of murder committed before 1969, the judges found a solution to prolong the statute of limitations in a fashion similar to the Romanian prosecutors in the early trials of communist crimes. They evoked Article 13 of the Paraguayan criminal code, which—similarly to the Romanian legislation—states that the prescribed terms can be suspended if 'insurmountable circumstances' hindered investigations. The judges suspended the prescriptions for political crimes for the entire period of the Stroessner regime, arguing that political interference in the justice system rendered the investigation of such cases impossible.[190] Trials for murder could thus proceed until 2009, a solution that was facilitated by the fact that in the 1990s, judicial denunciations against

[185] Paraguayan Constitution 1992, Article 3.

[186] Paraguayan Constitution 1992, Article 14.

[187] Paraguayan Criminal Code 1997, Chapter IX.

[188] Paraguayan Criminal Code 1997, Article 102(2).

[189] Cath Collins, 'Paraguay: Accountability in the Shadow of Stroessner', in *Transitional Justice in Latin America: The Uneven Road from Impunity towards Accountability*, edited by Elin Skaar, Jemima Garcia-Godos, and Cath Collins (London: Routledge, 2016): pp. 151–177, at pp. 157–158.

[190] Rodolfo Manuel Aseretto, ed., *Fallos judiciales sobre casos de violaciones a los DD.HH* (Asunción: CIPAE, 2011): pp. 148–151.

Stroessner's close collaborators were used to resolve internal disputes with the Colorados while preserving party dominance.[191]

Trials concerning torture—the most frequent form of repression in Stroessner's Paraguay—remained problematic, given that, in 1989, it was no longer possible to prosecute 'serious injuries' perpetrated before 1987. Investigations into acts of torture were contested by the accused on the grounds of retroactivity of the law. They argued that torture had not been codified as such in the Paraguayan criminal code, and since the statute of limitations for 'serious injury' had expired, any conviction would apply *ex post facto* punishment.[192]

In 1999, a case initiated against Pastor Coronel and other police officers for the illegal detention and torture of political opponent Julian Cubas in the 1970s reached the Supreme Court.[193] The judges rejected the defence based entirely on international law, yet in a manner particular to the Paraguayan legal system. They first argued that the 1967 Paraguayan Constitution recognized the general principles of international law and that the country thus was bound by the international human rights regime. They then evoked Article 5 of the Universal Declaration of Human Rights and Article 50 of the 1949 Geneva Conventions which prohibit torture and inhuman treatment. Finally, they referred to the 1968 UN Convention, arguing that international crimes are not subject to statutory limitations no matter when committed.[194] In consequence, the Supreme Court convicted the defendants of 'serious injury'. The verdict was however schematic, without any real engagement between national and international law. First, the judges did not take into consideration the dualist Paraguayan system in terms of international law. While the 1967 Constitution recognized the general principles of international law, it also stipulated that treaties and conventions were part of the national law only after ratification and approval by the Congress.[195] Neither the 1949 Geneva Conventions nor the 1968 UN Convention had been ratified by Paraguay during Stroessner's regime. The judges did not discuss how to accommodate this contradiction. Second, the Geneva Conventions apply to international and internal conflicts, while political crimes in Paraguay had been committed in peace time. Third, the verdict did not legally and historically explain how the actions of

[191] Collins, 'Paraguay', 157.

[192] Rodolfo Manuel Aseretto, ed., *Compañero Julián Cubas* (Asunción: CIPAE, 2003): pp. 90–91.

[193] The jurisprudence of this case was published in Aseretto, *Compañero Julián Cubas*.

[194] Cesar Alfonso, 'Paraguay', in *Jurisprudencia latinoamericana sobre derecho penal internacional: Con un informe adicional sobre la jurisprudencia italiana*, edited by Kai Ambos, Ezequil Malarino, and Gisela Elsner (Montevideo: Konrad Adenauer Stiftung, 2008): pp. 261–270.

[195] Paraguayan Constitution 1967, Article 8.

the defendants constituted crimes against humanity. The sentence was devoid of historical context or legal analysis on the evolution of international crimes under international law.

The verdict was formulated by then President of the Paraguayan Supreme Court of Justice Wildo Rienzi Galeano and endorsed by Judge Luis Lezcano Claude. Both had been appointed to the Supreme Court in 1995, when the Colorado Party established a pact of governability with the opposition. This political arrangement led to a judicial reform, whereby several judges unconnected to the Colorado Party were appointed to the Supreme Court.[196] Rienzi was affiliated to a Colorado reformist wing which had been outlawed during Stroessner. Lezcano Claude was endorsed by the Liberals. His father had been a member of the Liberal Radical Party—the largest legal opposition group during Stroessner's regime—and was banned from practicing law in the 1960s due to his political opinions. According to Lezcano Claude, when the case reached the Supreme Court in 1999, both judges were inclined to support victims' claims. Resorting to ICL was the only solution, but a problematic one.

> The problem with this decision is that it emphasized the international duties to prosecute torture and crimes against humanity based on conventions which had not been incorporated by the Paraguayan Congress. This was in particular the case of the 1968 UN Convention […] Also, criminal law requires a strict definition of the crime in the criminal code. And crimes against humanity were not codified in Paraguayan legislation. We argued that Paraguay had accepted the general principles of international law in its Constitution, including the Universal Declaration of Human Rights. […] But this was indeed an unorthodox solution.[197]

Starting in 1999, the Supreme Court of Justice confirmed a series of convictions for torture and murder—considered to be crimes against humanity under international law without, however, legal and historical contextualization.[198] The judges employed the 1968 UN Convention to justify the imprescriptibility of the crimes, even though Paraguay had not yet ratified the Convention. These trials targeted a narrow group of ten to fifteen police officials, without any accusation brought against army officers involved in the repression. While victims called for prosecutions against Stroessner and his Minister of

[196] Fournier and Burges, 'Form before Function', pp. 18–19.
[197] Personal interview with Luis Lezcano Claude, Asunción, Paraguay, 18 July 2016.
[198] See Aseretto, *Fallos judiciales*.

Interior, Sabino Montanaro, those cases did not reach the courts since the two had fled to Brazil and Honduras.[199] Trials concerning the forced disappearances of prominent political opponents such as Agustín Goiburú, the Ramírez Villalba brothers, and Carlos Mancuello were also delayed for decades. It was only after the IACtHR issued a decision against Paraguay in 2006, accusing the country of inefficient justice,[200] that these three trials were accelerated, ending in guilty verdicts in 2008. Other complaints lodged by victims were however left without answer. This led analysts to label trials in Paraguay as *Opareí*, a syntagm that means 'a thing ending in nothing' or a judicial cause that expires without investigation.[201]

In 2004, President Nicanor Duarte established a Truth and Justice Commission (Comisión de Verdad y Justicia, CVJ) as a way to mark a break with previous administrations. Duarte pursued the most left-wing policies ever adopted by the Colorado Party over its sixty-year rule and promised new investigations into dictatorial crimes. The 2008 CVJ report was one of the most comprehensive accounts produced by such an institution in Latin America.[202] It historicized the systematic silencing of political opponents and oppression of Indigenous groups in detail and concluded that Stroessner-era crimes amounted to crimes against humanity as defined by the Rome Statute. CVJ legal experts also lodged several criminal complaints for political crimes committed before 1989.[203] Together with anti-impunity movements such as the Churches' Committee for Emergency Assistance, they pushed Duarte to initiate the ratification of the 1968 UN Convention, inspired by the Argentinian anti-impunity strategy.[204] Ratification was achieved in September 2008, one month after socialist Fernando Lugo became the new president—the only one since 1989 not affiliated with the Colorados.

Investigations were however delayed due to the belief among judges that these cases were potentially career-ending. In an interview in 2015, Arnaldo Fleitas Ortiz, a judge who had reopened the Goiburú case after the IACtHR decision against Paraguay, pointed out that

199 Collins, 'Paraguay', p. 158.

200 IACtHR, *Goiburú and Others v Paraguay*, Judgment of 22 September 2006. Claudio Nash Rojas, *El Sistema Interamericano de Derechos Humanos en Acción: Aciertos y Desafíos* (México: Porrua, 2010): pp. 211–226.

201 Maria Rosaria Stabili, 'OPAREI. La Justicia de Transición en Paraguay', *America Latina Hoy: Revista de Ciencias Sociales* 61 (2012): pp. 137–162.

202 Collins, 'Paraguay'; Kai Ambos, Cesar Alfonso, and Roberto Ubeda, 'Paraguay', in *Encyclopaedia of Transitional Justice*, edited by Lavinia Stan and Nadya Nedelsky (Cambridge: Cambridge University Press, 2013): pp. 364–370.

203 Comisión de Verdad y Justicia, *Memoria de Gestion 2004–2008* (Asunción: Vangraf, 2008): pp. 37–39.

204 Personal interview with Carlos Portillo, Asunción, Paraguay, 13 February 2015.

> There were investigations in Paraguay, I myself conducted trials which ended in guilty verdicts. But there was a lot of caution about these cases because they were politically sensitive. Look what happened to Baltasar Garzón in Spain. When he disturbed the political arrangements of the transition, he was excluded from the judiciary.[205]

Beyond protecting their judicial careers, some judges also argued for the discontinuation of cases because statutory limitations for murder committed under the previous regime had expired in 2009. As Carlos Portillo, a CVJ commissioner, explained in an interview from 2015:

> The Supreme Court's decision of 1999 was contested by many jurists. There was no consensus about whether courts can use customary international law in a country of civil law tradition to suspend statutory limitations. Paraguay ratified the 1968 UN Convention in 2008, but crimes against humanity are not codified in national legislation. The judiciary had to use codified crimes, such as murder, that were in fact prescribed. In short, certain jurists accept the Supreme Court's approach, while others consider it against the rule of law.[206]

According to Santiago Bibolini, one of the prosecutors in charge of criminal complaints lodged by the CVJ, the prosecutor's office was still analysing the validity of this approach in 2015:

> We are working on a report on whether we can use customary law to justify prosecutions no matter the lapse of time. We must conform the national legislation in force when the crimes were committed to international law, including the 1968 UN Convention. But we must conduct a study because there is no jurisprudential consensus on this matter. [. . .] This problem arises in cases of torture and extrajudicial killings. For forced disappearances, we argue that this is a continued crime, so there is no statute of limitation.[207]

These legal dilemmas were heightened by the political impunity conferred by the Colorados to certain Stroessner-era officials. For instance, in 2014, President Horacio Cartes bestowed the national medal of honour to ex-police officer Eusebio Torres Romero, under investigation since 2007 for murder and

205 Personal interview with Arnaldo Fleitas Ortiz, Asunción, Paraguay, 18 February 2015.
206 Personal interview with Carlos Portillo, Asunción, Paraguay, 13 February 2015.
207 Personal interview with Santiago Bibolini, Asunción, Paraguay, 11 February 2015.

torture—a gesture that sent a clear message about the lack of political will to push for effective prosecutions.[208]

Within this context, in 2013, victims' associations—such as the National Movement of the Victims of the Dictatorship and the Foundation Celestina Pérez de Almada—requested the Argentinian judiciary to investigate gross human rights violations committed in Paraguay, based on universal jurisdiction and on the fact that some victims had been Argentinian citizens, persecuted under Operation Condor.[209] The complaint was formulated by Aitor Martínez Jiménez, a young Spanish lawyer trained in international law who worked for the Baltasar Garzón Foundation. Based on the CVJ's research, the complaint underlined the systematic repression in Stroessner's Paraguay and labelled the crimes as crimes against humanity. Martínez quoted extensively from Argentinian jurisprudence, underlining the imprescriptibility of international crimes and pointing to Schwammberger's and Priebke's extraditions and the guilty verdicts against military officials. He also emphasized the duty to prosecute imposed by the 1968 UN Convention, which was now part of Paraguayan legislation.[210] Martínez Jiménez's intervention also gave impetus to Paraguayan justice activists to use this kind of legal reasoning in their long-standing efforts to open prosecutions and write a critical historical account about the former dictatorship.[211]

Following this request, Argentinian judges pressured the Paraguayan judiciary, requesting information on current investigations. After six years of national and transnational pressure, Paraguayan courts opened trials in 2019 and convicted three former officials (all of whom had already been convicted in other trials in the 1990s) for torture and the murder of political opponents in the 1970s.[212] The judges who led the case employed the Supreme Court's 1999 approach, without discussing the relationship between international and national law during Stroessner's regime. They also evoked the 1968 UN

[208] Daniel Carísimo, 'Paraguay—Gobierno de Cartes condecora al torturador Eusebio Torres', *Alternatifos America Latina*, 16 December 2014, available at www.alterinfos.org/spip.php?article6750 (accessed 29 October 2023).

[209] Operation Condor was a transnational repressive system instituted by South American dictatorships in the 1970s to track down and silence left-wing activists. Francesca Lessa, 'Operation Condor on Trial: Justice for Transnational Human Rights Crimes in South America', *Journal of Latin American Studies* 51 (2019): pp. 409–439.

[210] 'Querella criminal por la comisión de los delitos de genocidio y / o lessa humanidad que tuvieron lugar en Paraguay en el periodo comprendido entre el 15 de augosto 1954 e el 3 de febrero 1989' (6 August 2013). Document shared with the author by Aitor Martínez Jiménez.

[211] Personal Interview with Yudith Rolón, Asunción, Paraguay, 4 February 2015.

[212] 'Tres torturadores stronistas son condenados por crimen de Celestina', *UltimaHora*, 21 December 2023, available at www.ultimahora.com/tres-torturadores-stronistas-son-condenados-crimen-celestina-n2861078.html (accessed 29 October 2023).

Convention as an instrument ratified by democratic Paraguay, which allowed prosecutions of crimes against humanity without any statute of limitations. Nevertheless, in 2019 during a similar trial against Eusebio Torres, the Paraguayan Appellate Court acquitted the accused. The judges argued this time that crimes against humanity were indeed not subject to statutory limitations, but the indictment drafted in 2017 was based on criminal investigations that had continued for two decades and such a long enquiry infringed on the defendant's right to a fair trial.[213] The judges did not engage with the issue of non-retroactivity or the duty to prosecute international crimes, but dismissed the case based on the defendant's right to a fair trial.

The Paraguayan jurisprudence reflects a convergence towards the idea that the prohibition of torture and crimes against humanity was a *jus cogens* rule in the 1970s irrespective of whether domestic law explicitly prohibited them. Furthermore, as in Argentina, the 1968 UN Convention was first envisaged as an instrument contributing to the development of *jus cogens* in terms of egregious crimes and then ratified with the specific purpose of providing a conventional legal basis for prosecutions of Stroessner-era crimes, no matter the lapse of time. Nevertheless, the strong politicization of the judiciary and the informal impunity granted to many former officials by current leaders of the Colorado Party resulted in delayed investigations and contradictory results.

In the four cases analysed in this chapter, courts gradually abandoned a strict interpretation of the principle of legality as far as dictatorial crimes were concerned. Anti-impunity strategies were built upon a combination of customary international law and the 1968 UN Convention. The Estonian jurisprudence, and its endorsement by the ECtHR, created a legal precedent which affirmed—for the first time in global jurisprudence—that deportation of civilian populations in time of peace constituted a crime against humanity even in the 1940s. Romanian courts found inspiration in the Estonian cases, and after almost thirty years of impunity, judged political crimes perpetrated in the 1950s as crimes against humanity based on a new criminal code adopted in 2014 and interpreted according to the 1968 UN Convention. Argentinian and Paraguayan courts used the peculiar double classification of criminal acts under national and international law, which was later also employed by the Spanish judiciary. These approaches endorsed a historical narrative in which dictatorial crimes were acknowledged as international crimes with the same gravity as crimes

[213] 'Dos emblemas de la dictadura, acusados por tortura y otros delitos contra DDHH, absueltos', *Hoy*, 23 May 2019, available at www.hoy.com.py/nacionales/dos-emblemas-de-la-dictadura-acusados-por-tortura-y-otros-delitos-contra-dd-hh-absueltos (accessed 29 October 2023).

judged by international tribunals since Nuremberg. The communist and military regimes were thus inscribed in the global history of twentieth-century bureaucratically organized atrocities, including the Holocaust and the crimes committed in Rwanda and the former Yugoslavia.

In all cases, the 1968 UN Convention played an important role in counter-attacking accusations of retroactivity. It offered a written international law that allowed retrospective prosecutions of crimes against humanity. In Estonia and Romania, the Convention had already been ratified in the 1960s by the communist states. The Convention was also deployed in other former socialist countries, such as Hungary,[214] but its application to communist crimes was rejected in Bulgaria, which is discussed in Chapter 5. In Argentina and Paraguay, the instrument was initially interpreted as part of the evolution of *jus cogens* since 1945, despite the marginality of the Convention internationally. The instrument was then ratified in both countries specifically to allow prosecutions. Similar paths have been taken by other Latin American countries, such as Chile and Uruguay.[215] The Convention's utility in prosecuting past dictatorial crimes is also visible in the significant rise in the number of ratifications in the last two decades, including countries such as Uruguay, Ecuador, Honduras, Ghana, and Palestine.

[214] Tamás Hoffmann, 'Trying Communism through International Criminal Law? The Experiences of the Hungarian Historical Justice Trials', in *Hidden Histories of War Crimes Trials*, edited by Kevin Jon Heller and Gerry Simpson (Oxford: Oxford University Press, 2013): pp. 229–247.

[215] Jean Pierre Matus Acuña, 'Informe sobre la ejecución de la sentencia en el caso Almonacid presentado a la Cámara de Diputados', *Revista Ius et Praxis* 12, no. 2 (2006): pp. 385–396.

3
Broadening the Definition of Genocide

> The European experts on the Holocaust have a hegemonic position that limits the possibility of genocide to two or three phenomena in the world: The Holocaust, Rwanda and maybe the Armenian genocide. […] I understand the desire not to devalue genocides like the Holocaust. But this doesn't mean we don't have to recognize other genocides, other plans of extermination committed on political and economic grounds, as for example in the Southern Cone. What I tried to do in my jurisprudence, and here I followed Judge Baltasar Garzón, was to provide a more inclusive reading of the 1948 UN Convention, one that would also be applicable to political victims such as those of the Latin American military dictatorships.
>
> Carlos Rozanski, Argentinian judge[1]

> The consequences of this ECHR decision, unprecedented in international practice, are fundamental. This is the first time that ethno-political genocide has been recognized by an international Court. Such genocide is now claimed by a multitude of states and populations. Once the ECHR accepts the "ethno-political" label, other countries will be tempted to follow in Lithuania's footsteps. By delivering this judgment the majority are expanding the scope of genocide far beyond the approach taken so far in international criminal law.
>
> Iulia Motoc, judge at the ECtHR[2]

1. Introduction

This chapter examines how national courts in Lithuania, Argentina, and Guatemala challenged and transformed the international definition of genocide in order to include crimes committed against political opponents and

[1] Personal interview with Carlos Rozanski, La Plata, Argentina, 16 June 2016.
[2] ECtHR, *Drėlingas v. Lithuania*, Judgment of 12 March 2019, 'Dissenting Opinion of Judge Motoc'.

Justice and Memory after Dictatorship. Raluca Grosescu, Oxford University Press. © Raluca Grosescu 2024.
DOI: 10.1093/oso/9780192870346.003.0003

national resistance movements, and cultural genocide against Indigenous populations—two categories explicitly excluded from the 1948 UN Genocide Convention. Critiques concerning the limits of the Convention to address crimes committed on political, social, and cultural motives have been voiced since 1948 by legal experts and social scientists.[3] Nonetheless, this was the first time that courts of law reformulated the UN definition of genocide, rejected the conceptualization of this category as a non-political hate crime modelled on the Holocaust and shaped by Cold War politics, and expanded its scope to reflect the national histories of mass violence in these three countries.

In Lithuania, the category of *ethno-national-political genocide* was developed to frame the repression of anti-Soviet partisans in the 1940s and 1950s. This new concept was an attempt to enforce an equal condemnation of the mass atrocities committed by the Nazi and Soviet regimes during their occupations of the Baltic states. In parallel, Argentinian judges employed the notion of *ideological auto-genocide*—a term coined in the 1980s by American legal experts to condemn the crimes of the Khmer Rouge in Cambodia—to label the military repression of left-wing opponents in the 1970s. Its purpose was to centre the Argentinian dictatorship in the global history of twentieth-century bureaucratically organized atrocities such as the Holocaust. In Guatemala, the genocide charges against former dictator Efraín Ríos Montt incorporated not only the massacres of Indigenous groups but also acts of *cultural genocide*, including the destruction of Mayan culture and social cohesion. This jurisprudence reflected the efforts by a pan-Mayan cultural rights movement to interpret both the civil war and the whole of Guatemalan history through the prism of racism, cultural destruction, and neocolonial oppression against Indigenous populations.

This jurisprudence triggered international debates and controversies, including at regional human rights courts (the European Court of Human Rights, ECtHR, and the Inter-American Court of Human Rights, IACtHR) and between legal scholars. When criticized for departing from the dominant understanding of genocide, legal actors from these countries argued against the ostensibly biased sway of Cold War political hegemons (the United States, the Soviet Union, and Western Europe) on this ICL instrument and on the

[3] Benjamin Whitaker, 'Revised and Updated Report on the Question of the Prevention and Punishment of the Crime of Genocide', UN Doc. E/CN.4/Sub/1985/6; Beth van Schaack, 'The Crime of Political Genocide: Repairing the Genocide Convention's Blind Sport', *Yale Law Journal* 106 (1997): pp. 2259–2291; Hurst Hannum, 'International Law and Cambodian Genocide: The Sounds of Silence', *Human Rights Quarterly* 11, no. 1 (1989): pp. 82–138; Kristina Hon, 'Bringing Cultural Genocide in by the Backdoor: Victim Participation at the ICC', *Seton Hall Law Review* 43, no. 1 (2013): pp. 359–407.

mnemonic hierarchy of violent pasts. They criticized the exoneration and the downplaying of communist crimes and of violence in the Third World, including the cultural genocide against Indigenous populations, in favour of the Western-driven centrality of the Holocaust.

Although still marginal in the international arena, this jurisprudence could circulate to other jurisdictions and alter the dominant interpretation of genocide. Currently endorsed by the ECtHR, the Lithuanian application of genocide in cases concerning the killing of anti-Soviet partisans might also be applied to crimes committed by former colonial powers against national liberation movements (such as those in Algeria, Kenya, and Indonesia). Conversely, the Argentinian judiciary's revival of the concept of *ideological auto-genocide* is unlikely to find application in other settings, since the category of crimes against humanity is now clearly defined in international law and is more suitable to address crimes committed for political reasons. For its part, the Guatemalan creation of a means of framing colonial and postcolonial cultural and economic oppression against Indigenous populations as genocidal could find wider import as other Indigenous communities use it to seek redress for past violence.

2. Critiques of the Genocide Convention since 1948

The jurisprudence analysed here builds and expands upon a set of legal and political ideas that have delineated, since 1948, the limits of the UN Genocide Convention in addressing a wide range of episodes of political violence in the twentieth century. This criticism concerned two main aspects: the restrictive list of victim groups protected by the Convention and the restrictive list of genocidal acts, most of which refer to the physical and biological destruction of specific communities at the expense of their cultural destruction.[4]

The elimination of political groups from the scope of this international instrument—an essential consideration in the three countries under scrutiny—has likely provoked more criticism than any other aspect of the Convention.[5] As formulated in 1948 and replicated in the statutes of all ad hoc international tribunals and the 1998 Rome Statute of the International Criminal Court,

[4] Whitaker, 'Revised and Updated Report'; van Schaack, 'The Crime'; Hannum, 'International Law'; Hon, 'Bringing Cultural Genocide'.

[5] William A. Schabas, *Genocide in International Law: The Crimes of Crimes* (Cambridge: Cambridge University Press, 2009): p. 117. For the drafting process of the Convention, see also Matthew Lippman, 'The 1948 UN Convention on the Prevention and Punishment of the Crime of Genocide: Forty Years Later', *Temple International & Comparative Law Journal* 8, no. 1 (1994): pp. 1–84.

genocide refers exclusively to the destruction of national, ethnic, racial, or religious groups. However, UN General Assembly Resolution 96(1), which called for a UN convention on genocide in 1946, as well as the initial draft of the convention (formulated by the UN Secretariat in 1947), covered a much wider range of protected groups, including linguistic, social, and political groups. Due to the systematic repression of kulaks and political opponents, the Soviet Union (and its CEE allies) resisted the inclusion of social and political categories. Great Britain also endorsed this approach, since it feared that its repression of insurgencies in the colonies might be denounced as genocide. Latin American countries similarly opposed the inclusion of political groups, given their history of political violence and coups d'état since independence in the nineteenth century.[6] While the legal argument for this omission centred around the idea that political and social groups lacked permanence and stability, scholars agree that the decision was made for 'political reasons, rather than reasons of principle'.[7] Since 1948, this restrictive selection of protected groups has provoked widespread dissatisfaction. Critics have argued that most episodes of mass murder over the course of the twentieth century were committed not on grounds of identity but for political and economic motives (such as the crimes of communist regimes, the enforced disappearances engaged in by the military regimes in Latin America, and the destruction of Indigenous populations across the globe).[8]

These critiques were intensified by the fact that for several decades, the Genocide Convention was the only ICL instrument that was widely ratified and imposed concrete obligations upon states in cases of atrocities committed within their borders and, as a general rule, by their officials.[9] The category of crimes against humanity—which also covers persecutions on political and cultural grounds—did not enjoy the same success: as discussed in Chapter 2, the 1968 Convention on the Non-Applicability of Statutory Limitations to War

[6] Schabas, *Genocide in International Law*, pp. 117–171; Lippman, 'The 1948 UN Convention'; Anton Weiss-Wendt, *The Soviet Union and the Gutting of the UN Genocide Convention* (Madison, WI: University of Wisconsin Press, 2017): pp. 97–113.

[7] Schabas, *Genocide in International Law*, p. 39. Linguistic and cultural groups were also excluded from the final text of the Convention. The forced assimilation of Native American, First Nations, and Inuit communities in the United States and Canada, and certain cultural policies instituted by Great Britain in its colonies, made these countries particularly reluctant to include linguistic and cultural categories. See Lippman, 'The 1948 UN Convention', pp. 36–39.

[8] Whitaker, 'Revised and Updated Report'; van Schaack, 'The Crime'; A. Dirk Moses, 'Empire, Colony, Genocide: Keywords and the Philosophy of History', in *Empire, Colony, Genocide: Conquest, Occupation, and Subaltern Resistance in World History*, edited by Dirk Moses (New York: Berghahn, 2010): pp. 3–54.

[9] Matthew Lippman, 'The Drafting of the 1948 Convention on the Prevention and Punishment of the Crime of Genocide', *Boston University International Law Journal* 3, no.1 (1985): pp. 1–65, p. 62.

Crimes and Crimes against Humanity was ratified by only a handful of states and was unanimously ignored by Western governments. Until the ratification of the Rome Statute in 2002, there was no agreed definition of crimes against humanity under international law and, in contrast to genocide, the category was absent from most national legislations. Even today, no specific convention on crimes against humanity exists, and the Rome Statute is compulsory only for state parties.[10] Due to this absence of other comparable legal tools, demands were increasingly voiced to subsume a variety of state-perpetrated acts of political violence within the scope of the Genocide Convention, even though, from a legal point of view, the Convention was inapplicable to many conflicts and gross human rights violations.[11]

Consequently, various international law scholars and social scientists have called for the enlargement of the number of protected groups.[12] UN Special Rapporteurs on genocide, Nicodème Ruhashyankiko and Benjamin Whitaker, acknowledged in 1978 and 1985, respectively, that the limited scope of the protected groups rendered the Convention inefficient and might have even encouraged atrocities committed on political, social, and cultural grounds. Whitaker listed a long series of mass atrocities perpetrated against groups which did not fall under the Convention's scope and proposed the broadening of the protected categories to at least include political groups and possibly women, homosexuals, and economic and professional classes.[13] Other international lawyers have argued that jurisprudence on genocide should take into consideration elements of customary international law (such as General Assembly Resolution 96(1) and earlier drafts of the Convention) that would make genocide applicable to crimes committed on political and social grounds.[14]

[10] M. Cherif Bassiouni, *Crimes against Humanity: Historical Evolution and Contemporary Application* (Cambridge: Cambridge University Press, 2011). The 1984 Convention against Torture and Other Cruel, Inhuman or Degrading Treatment or Punishment and the 2006 International Convention for the Protection of All Persons from Enforced Disappearance only entered into force in 1987 and 2010, respectively.

[11] Lippman, 'The Drafting of the 1948 Convention', p. 62.

[12] Stefan Glaser, *Droit International Pénal Conventionnel* (Brussels: Bruylant, 1970); Frank Chalk and Kurt Jonassohn, 'The Conceptual Framework', in *The History and Sociology of Genocide*, edited by Frank Chalk and Kurt Jonassohn (New Haven: Yale University Press, 1991): pp. 17–26; Israel W. Charney, 'Toward a Generic Definition of Genocide', in *Genocide, Conceptual and Historical Dimensions*, edited by George J. Andreopoulos (Philadelphia: University of Pennsylvania Press: 1994): pp. 64–94; Helen Fein, 'Scenarios of Genocide: Models of Genocide and Critical Responses', in *Towards the Understanding and Prevention of Genocide*, edited by Israel W. Charny (Boulder, CO: Westview Press, 1984): pp. 3–31.

[13] Whitaker, 'Revised and Updated Report'.

[14] Lory Lyman Bruun, 'Beyond the 1948 Convention: Emerging Principles of Genocide in Customary International Law', *Maryland Journal of International Law and Trade* 17, no. 2 (1993): pp. 193–226, at pp. 210–218.

Furthermore, some states extended the list of protected groups as part of national legislation (for example, Bolivia, Costa Rica, Ethiopia, France, Portugal, and Spain). Most of these countries involved social and political groups, although some states opted for open-ended categories such as France's formulation of 'groups determined by another arbitrary criteria'.[15] Nevertheless, the practice of broadening the definition of the protected groups did not prevail everywhere, and it is not yet a rule of international customary law.[16] Despite still-ongoing criticism, the 1948 definition of genocide remains confined in international law to the protection of national, ethnic, racial, and religious categories. Jurisprudence in national and international courts also applied and reinforced this definition.[17]

A second major critique of the Genocide Convention—of particular relevance to the Guatemalan debates on genocide—was the restriction of the definition to acts of biological and physical destruction and the exclusion of 'cultural genocide'. This latter category, present in the initial drafts of the Convention, referred to acts intended to destroy the language, religion, or culture of a group. It encompassed the forcible transfer of children from one group to another, the forced exile of individuals representing the culture of a group; the prohibition of the use of a national language; and the systematic destruction of books and religious, historical, and artistic monuments and objects.[18] These acts were however excluded from the final text of the Convention—with the exception of the forcible transfer of children—due to pressure exerted in particular by the existing colonial powers (Great Britain, France, and Belgium) and by states with Indigenous populations (the United States, Canada, and Brazil) that feared that their assimilationist policies would be labelled as genocide.[19] Those seeking to narrow the definition argued that 'culture' was not a fixed characteristic of a group, but an evolving notion that could not be easily defined in legal terms. Moreover, since the destruction of culture ostensibly did not directly threaten human life, it was better to leave this matter to 'the sphere of

[15] See for example N. Ward Ferdinandusse, *Direct Application of International Criminal Law in National Courts* (Hague: T.M.C. Asser, 2006).

[16] Schabas, *Genocide in International Law*, p. 23.

[17] One notable exception was the trial in absentia of Cambodian Khmer Rouge leader Pol Pot organized by the Vietnamese authorities. The conviction on charges of genocide referred to mass atrocities committed by the Khmer Rouge, including the extermination of political and economic groups that did not reflect their ideology. Howard J. De Nike, John Quigley, and Kenneth J. Robinson, *Genocide in Cambodia: Documents of the Trial of Pol Pot and Ieng Sary* (Pennsylvania, PA: University of Pennsylvania Press, 2000).

[18] Schabas, *Genocide in International Law*, p. 207.

[19] On the negotiations surrounding the issue of cultural genocide and the 1948 UN Convention, see Schabas, *Genocide in International Law*, pp. 207–213; Elisa Novic, *The Concept of Cultural Genocide: An International Law Perspective* (Oxford: Oxford University Press, 2016): pp. 22–30.

protection of minorities'—and thus outside of ICL.[20] In contrast, critics of this approach contended that the exclusion of cultural destruction was designed to prevent the international community from criminalizing as genocide the acts perpetrated by Western liberal democracies against minorities in their countries and colonies.[21]

Since 1948, scholars and practitioners have argued for a more flexible interpretation that includes the non-physical destruction of a group as a social unit.[22] Scholars working on violence against Indigenous populations have been particularly vocal in stressing the limits of the Convention to address the destruction of Indigenous cultures and traditional ways of life as a consequence of Western economic modernization projects developed on Indigenous lands.[23] According to them, this cultural destruction—which ultimately threatens the survival of groups—had not only an economic basis but also a racist foundation that emphasized the superiority of the Western, white, and capitalist culture over the Indigenous one.[24] It was thus necessary to include cultural genocide in a Protocol to the Genocide Convention or in a new treaty.[25] Yet, as both William Schabas and Elisa Novic stress, cultural genocide seems to be a dead letter among international lawmakers. Proposals to criminalize this category in the Rome Statute were dismissed, and the adoption of a new treaty seems improbable.[26]

Within the jurisprudence, in the aftermath of the Second World War, the Polish trials against Nazi criminals Arthur Greiser (1948) and Amon Göth (1946) included accusations of cultural genocide. The defendants were convicted not only for the extermination of Poles and Jews but also for 'the destruction of Polish culture and political thought'. Cultural genocide became a

[20] Hon, 'Bringing Cultural Genocide', p. 10.

[21] Leora Bilsky and Rachel Klagsbrun, 'The Return of Cultural Genocide?', *European Journal of International Law* 29, no. 2 (2018): pp. 373–396, at pp. 387–388; Moses, 'Empire, Colony, Genocide', pp. 3–54.

[22] Lippman, 'The Drafting of the 1948 Convention', pp. 62–63; Larry May, *Genocide: A Normative Account* (Cambridge: Cambridge University Press, 2010); David Nersessian, 'Rethinking Cultural Genocide under International Law. *Human Rights Dialogue* 2, no. 12 (Spring 2005) available at www.carnegiecouncil.org (accessed 5 October 2023).

[23] Chalk and Jonassohn, 'The Conceptual Framework'; Elazar Barkan, 'Genocide of Indigenous People', in *The Spectre of Genocide: Mass Murder in Historical Perspective*, edited by Robert Gellately and Ben Kiernan (Cambridge: Cambridge University Press, 2003): pp. 117–140; Lindsey Kingston, 'The Destruction of Identity: Cultural Genocide and Indigenous People', *Journal of Human Rights* 14 (2015): pp. 63–83.

[24] Robert Jaulin, *La Paix Blanche: Introduction à l'Éthnocide* (Paris: Seuil, 1970).

[25] Whitaker, 'Revised and Updated Report'; Daphne Anayiotos, 'The Cultural Genocide Debate: Should the UN Genocide Convention Include a Provision on Cultural Genocide, or Should the Phenomenon Be Encompassed in a Separate International Treaty?', *New York International Law Review* 99, no. 2 (2009): pp. 99–129.

[26] Schabas, *Genocide in International Law*, p. 220; Novic, *The Concept of Cultural Genocide*, p. 12.

central issue in these trials because it allowed the tribunals to criminalize 'the destruction of the Polish people', whereas a narrow focus on physical genocide would have emphasized the centrality of the Jewish victimhood.[27] These cases were however largely ignored by international law scholars because they were adjudicated before the adoption of the Genocide Convention and by the communist authorities based on retroactive special laws.[28]

More recently, the concept of cultural genocide re-emerged in the legal sphere in two contexts. In Australia and Canada, national courts took up cases in the 2000s that involved the forcible transfer of aboriginal, First Nations and Inuit children to residential schools and white families in the 1960s and 1970s. Although the forcible transfer of children from one group to another is criminalized under the Genocide Convention, the judges in question dismissed the accusations, arguing that the purpose of residential schools was not to physically destroy Indigenous peoples. Although such policies may have endangered the survival of aboriginal, First Nations and Inuit culture, this was not germane to the charges, since the Genocide Convention did not include cultural genocide.[29] The issue of cultural destruction also emerged at the ICTY, although the tribunal's jurisprudence on the matter is limited to a few cases, in particular *The Prosecutor v. Radislav Krstić* and *The Prosecutor v. Blagojević et al.* In both cases, the judges ruled that the cultural component was relevant as evidence of the intent to destroy a group but acts of cultural genocide were not punishable as such if they remained unrelated to physical or biological genocide.[30] Thus, both in international law and in jurisprudence, the tendency remains to pit cultural genocide against physical and biological genocide and leave the former out of criminalization processes.

As shall be seen, Lithuanian, Argentinian, and Guatemalan jurisprudence departs from these dominant international standards in terms of both the protected groups and the question of cultural destruction.

[27] Bilsky and Klagsbrun, 'The Return of Cultural Genocide?', pp. 384–385.

[28] Alexander Prusin, 'Poland's Nuremberg: The Seven Court Cases at the Supreme National Tribunal 1946–1948', *Holocaust and Genocide Studies* 24, no. 1 (2010): pp. 1–25.

[29] For cases related to the forced transfer of children in Australia and Canada, see Novic, *The Concept of Cultural Genocide*, pp. 38–45.

[30] ICTY, *The Prosecutor v. Radislav Krstić*, Judgment of 19 April 2004; 'Separate and partly dissenting opinion by Judge Shahabuddeen', IT-98- 33-A, paras. 48–49; ICTY, *The Prosecutor v. Blagojević et al.*, Judgment of 17 January 2005, IT-02-60-T, para. 666.

3. Lithuania and the Ethno-National-Political Genocide

Since Lithuania's independence in 1991, its courts have handed down around twenty genocide convictions against former operatives of the Soviet secret services, most of them accused of having killed Lithuanian anti-Soviet partisans in the 1940s and the 1950s.[31] Rooted in a long-standing historical narrative which had denounced both the Nazi and the Soviet occupations as genocidal, this jurisprudence affirmed the overlapping nature of national and political groups of the Lithuanian anti-Soviet armed resistance and broadened, under the concept of *ethno-national-political genocide*, the application of the notion of genocide to national liberation movements.

3.1 Legal and Historical Aspects of the 'Double Genocide' in the 1990s

In 1992, the Lithuanian parliament adopted a law on the Responsibility for the Genocide of Lithuanian Inhabitants, which codified for the first time the category of genocide in Lithuanian legislation. Although the Soviet Union ratified the 1948 UN Convention in 1954, genocide was never criminalized into the national law of the Lithuanian Soviet Socialist Republic (LSSR) (inter alia, the 1961 Criminal Code). Except for certain war crimes, no liability for international crimes was established in LSSR legislation.[32] Lithuania accessed the 1948 UN Convention in 1992 and ratified it in 1996. The 1992 Law on the Responsibility for Genocide added to the conventional definition of genocide that:

> the killing and torture and deportation of Lithuanian inhabitants committed during the occupation and annexation of Lithuania by Nazi Germany and the USSR corresponded to the crime of genocide as understood by international law.[33]

The law was valid retroactively, and acts of genocide were not subject to a statute of limitations.[34]

[31] For details, see Eva-Clarita Pettai and Vello Pettai, *Transitional and Retrospective Justice in the Baltic States* (Cambridge: Cambridge University Press, 2014): pp. 85–97.
[32] For the crime of genocide in Lithuanian legislation, see The Constitutional Court of the Republic of Lithuania (hereafter CCRL), 'Decision of 18 March 2014', pp. 25–28.
[33] Ibid, pp. 25–26.
[34] Ibid, p. 27.

The law endorsed a historical narrative of the 'double Nazi and Soviet genocide' that had emerged during the 1940s in the anti-communist campaigns of Baltic émigrés in North America and Western Europe. Immediately after the Second World War, various organizations of Baltic citizens had mobilized from the United States against the Soviet occupation, accusing the USSR (including at the UN) of a premeditated plan to destroy the nations under its occupation through mass deportations, forced labour, and the physical elimination of national elites and anti-Soviet partisans.[35] These Baltic campaigns associated prison camps in Siberia, China, and North Korea with Auschwitz and Dachau, and equated Stalinism and Nazism. Raphael Lemkin himself provided these organizations with legal advice and took the lead in campaigns that equated the communist repression with the Holocaust.[36] This narrative became the official mnemonic account of the Lithuanian state after 1991. The country adopted various laws that denounced the illegality of both the Nazi and the Soviet occupations, affirmed the continuity of the Lithuanian state under international law, and elevated anti-Soviet partisans to the status of national heroes. Moreover, the legislature held that institutions organized by the partisans had been the sole legitimate authority during the Soviet occupation—the direct prolongation in fact of the Lithuanian Republic.[37]

This national legislative package was accompanied by Lithuania's efforts to achieve international recognition of the illegitimacy of the Soviet occupation. The annexation of the Baltic states by the Soviet Union was a rather peculiar case under international law. In 1940, none of the Baltic states actively resisted the USSR's occupation, and the Lithuanian government ordered the regular army not to oppose. In 1941, the Nazi troops attacked the Soviet Union and occupied the Baltic territories. Subsequently, the recapturing of the Baltic states by the USSR in 1944 was presented by Moscow as a 'liberation' and a 'voluntary accession' to the Soviet Union.[38] In 1991, Moscow engaged through a bilateral treaty with Lithuania to eliminate the consequences of the 1940 annexation. Despite this agreement and the recognition by most Western powers of the illegal annexation of the Baltic states, the Russian Federation continued to question the idea of an illegal occupation and of a legitimate anti-Soviet armed

[35] Dovilė Budrytė, 'We Call It Genocide: Soviet Deportations in the Memory of the Lithuanians', in *The Genocidal Temptation: Auschwitz, Hiroshima, Rwanda, and Beyond*, edited by Robert S. Frey (Lanham, MD: University Press of America, 2004): pp. 79–95.

[36] Weiss-Wendt, *The Soviet Union*, pp. 159–174.

[37] CCRL, 'Decision of 18 March 2014', pp. 42–43.

[38] Justinas Žilinskas, 'Status of Members of Anti-Soviet Armed Resistance (Partisans' War) of 1944–1953 in Lithuania under International Law', *Baltic Yearbook of International Law* 11 (2011): pp. 31–65, at p. 42.

resistance. In Moscow's view, Baltic partisans had been nothing more than Nazi collaborators or—at best—unlawful groups that opposed the rightful government of the Soviet Union.[39] Consequently, the Baltic–Russian 'memory war' over the Second World War and its aftermath fundamentally shaped Lithuanian mnemopolitics.[40]

The 1992 Law on the Responsibility for Genocide was thus part of a broader Lithuanian effort to condemn the illegal Nazi and the Soviet occupations, and to qualify the crimes committed by the Soviet regime in terms of international, and not just domestic, law. In 1998, two years after Lithuania ratified the 1948 UN Convention, the crime of genocide was introduced into the criminal code.[41] In addition to the four groups protected by the 1948 UN Convention, the Lithuanian legislature included social and political groups—a provision designed to criminalize the Soviet repression of kulaks and political opponents.[42] Yet crimes against humanity, a category better suited to the political crimes engaged in by the communist regimes, was not codified. This would be achieved only in 2003, following Lithuania's ratification of the Rome Statute that same year. A new criminal code adopted in 2003 included crimes against humanity while maintaining the broader definition of genocide.[43]

Within this context, a Special Investigative Division for Nazi and Communist Crimes drafted various indictments, from 1991 to 2003, against former officials of both regimes, although Soviet crimes predominated. The indictments involved executions of Jewish individuals by Lithuanian Nazi collaborators, and of civilians and armed resistance fighters by Soviet secret service operatives (most of them of Lithuanian origin). The courts used mainly the charges of genocide, provoking confusion when compared to international legal standards.[44] Under the umbrella of genocide, courts mixed crimes committed against both civilians and armed fighters. Also, in some instances, the courts referred solely to the extermination of political groups—explicitly departing from the 1948 UN Convention—while in others, they overlapped national, political, and social groups. Moreover, they punished acts perpetrated prior

[39] Dainius Žalimas, 'Legal Issues on the Continuity of the Republic of Lithuania', *Baltic Yearbook of International Law* 1 (2001): pp. 1–22, at pp. 10–11.

[40] Maria Mälksoo, 'The Memory Politics of Becoming European: The East European Subalterns and the Collective Memory of Europe', *European Journal of International Relations* 15, no. 4 (2009): pp. 653–680; see also Maria Mälksoo, 'A Baltic Struggle for a "European Memory": The Militant Mnemopolitics of *The Soviet Story*', *Journal of Genocide Research* 20, no. 8 (2018): pp. 530–544.

[41] Lithuanian Criminal Code 1998, Article 71.

[42] Justinas Žilinskas, 'Broadening the Concept of Genocide in Lithuania's Criminal Law and the Principle of Nullum Crimen Sine Lege', *Jurisprudencija/Jurisprudence* 4, 118 (2009): pp. 333–348, at p. 337.

[43] Lithuanian Criminal Code 2003, Articles 99–113.

[44] Žilinskas, 'Broadening the Concept of Genocide'.

to the drafting of the 1948 UN Convention, thus setting a precedent for the *ex post facto* application of international law.[45] As various Baltic commentators observed, prior to Lithuania's accession to the European Union in 2004, courts were rarely interested in elucidating the differences between national and international law.[46] According to Dainius Žalimas, president of the Lithuanian Constitutional Court in 2018:

> The 1992 Law was a strong political statement about the criminality of the Soviet regime and its similarity to the Nazi regime. Genocide has a much stronger impact on public opinion, especially when dealing with historical injustices, unlike crimes against humanity, whose nature is much less understood by the public. Framing the Soviet repression as genocide brought us a lot of criticism, but it was rooted in Lithuania's history, where the Soviet repression was conducted against the most eminent representatives of the nation.[47]

Prosecutors in charge of Nazi and communist crimes also viewed the broad Lithuanian definition of genocide as a correct political act designed to reshape the 1948 UN Convention and render it applicable to the Lithuanian context. Rimvydas Valentukevičius—head of the Special Investigative Division for Nazi and Communist Crimes for more than fifteen years—saw the expansion of the notion of genocide 'totally valid and necessary' to include the destruction of the Lithuanian national elite and correct the narrow international definition which had ignored the annihilation of social and political groups:

> Such an expansion of the concept of genocide is totally valid and necessary, because the classical concept of genocide established in international law is confined to four characteristics of the destroyed group and thus excludes the victims of so many twentieth-century massacres, including the mass destruction of the Lithuanian population. In our country, we corrected this error in the 1948 UN Convention by including two other protected groups: political and social.[48]

Through this approach, the Lithuanian judiciary took on both the role of international law reformers and the didactic mission to rewrite the national history.

[45] Pettai and Pettai, *Transitional and Retrospective Justice*, p. 93.
[46] Žilinskas, 'Broadening the Concept of Genocide'.
[47] Personal interview with Dainius Žalimas, Vilnius, Lithuania, 17 October 2018.
[48] Personal interview with Rimvydas Valentukevičius, Vilnius, Lithuania, 16 October 2018.

Yet, this legal approach was very soon the target of international criticism. According to Valentukevičius, the first critiques came in 1996, when the Lithuanian courts issued two extradition warrants for former Soviet officials, now residing in Russia and Israel, accused of killing anti-Soviet partisans in the 1940s. Both states refused extradition and protested an alleged historical revisionism and misinterpretation of international law. They argued that Lithuania was departing from the international definition of genocide because the cases referred to the repression of armed political groups and not to extermination committed on ethnic, racial, and religious grounds. The Russian and Israeli authorities also engaged in historical debates, arguing that the accused had been anti-fascist partisans who had fought the Nazi occupation and thus ought to be considered heroes of the Second World War.[49] Western European left-wing movements and Jewish associations also accused Lithuanian courts of trivializing Nazism, denying the uniqueness of the Holocaust, and downplaying the participation of Eastern European societies in the extermination of the Jews during the Second World War.[50]

This criticism, together with a growing internationalization of Lithuanian judiciary following Lithuania's accession to the European Union, generated debates at a national level about the appropriate use of the umbrella term genocide in all cases of Soviet repression. After the adoption of the 2003 criminal code (which incorporated crimes against humanity), cases of deportations of civilian populations began to be classified as war crimes and crimes against humanity, but procedures concerning the killing of anti-Soviet partisans continued with charges of genocide. According to Lithuanian legal scholar Justinas Žilinskas, this approach was due not only to the will to enforce the narrative of the genocidal Soviet repression but also to find a legal solution for prosecutions:

> It was difficult to frame crimes committed against partisans as war crimes, first because during war soldiers can kill each other, and second because it is not clear if the partisans' war against Soviet occupation can be labelled as war under international law. The Soviet Union never recognized the existence of an internal conflict, and the Russian government maintains this argument. And framing them as simple murder would lead to impunity, given that the statutory limitations for this crime had passed a long time ago.[51]

[49] Ibid.

[50] Michael Shafir, *Between Denial and 'Comparative Trivialization': Holocaust Negationism in Post-Communist East Central Europe*. Jerusalem: Vidal Sassoon International Center for the Study of Antisemitism, ACTA, no. 19, 2002.

[51] Personal interview with Justinas Žilinskas, Vilnius, Lithuania, 17 October, 2018.

Courts thus argued that the killing of 20,000 partisans was part of a campaign aimed 'to destroy the former Lithuanian way of life and to replace it by a new Soviet order comprised of persons without nationality or ethnicity'.[52] In this vein, special NKVD units (such as the 'Fighter Battalions', Istrebitelnye bataliony) had been established by the Soviet authorities to crush any Lithuanian national resistance.[53] However, starting in 2004, Lithuanian courts began to pay closer attention to the accommodation of the national within international law. In *Vasiliauskas and Zukaitine*—a case that eventually reached the ECtHR (see *infra*)—the Lithuanian Court of Appeal elaborated on the overlapping nature of political and national groups as it related to the partisans:

> Lithuanian partisans, that is to say, participants in armed resistance to occupational power, [. . .] had at the same time been representatives of the Lithuanian nation, that is, the national group. The Soviet genocide was carried out precisely on the criteria of the inhabitants' nationality-ethnicity. [. . .] Lithuanian partisans could be attributed not only to political, but also to national and ethnic groups, [. . .] groups listed in the Genocide Convention.[54]

The Court thus argued for the impossibility of establishing a clear-cut division between political and national groups in the context of the Lithuanian anti-Soviet struggle. It then concluded that an *ethno-national-political genocide* had been committed.

In response, Vasiliauskas lodged a complaint at the ECtHR, accusing the infringement of Article 7(1) of the European Convention on Human Rights through the retroactive application of the broad 1998 Lithuanian definition of genocide to acts perpetrated in 1953. In 2009, the ECtHR's decision to hear the case led social-democratic politicians and several judges to request the official position of the Constitutional Court on whether the concept of genocide could be applied to the killings of anti-Soviet partisans.

[52] As summarized in ECtHR, *Vasiliauskas v. Lithuania*, Judgment of 20 October 2015, p. 27.
[53] Rytis Satkauskas, 'Soviet Genocide Trials in the Baltic States: The Relevance of International Law', *Yearbook of International Humanitarian Law* 7 (2004): pp. 388–409, at pp. 392–393.
[54] Quoted in ECtHR, *Vasiliauskas v. Lithuania*, Judgment of 20 October 2015, p. 9.

3.2 The Constitutional Endorsement of the Notion of Ethno-National-Political Genocide

The decision of the Constitutional Court, handed down in 2014, was drafted in large part by Dainius Žalimas, a professor of international law at Vilnius University and a firm advocate for the equal treatment of crimes committed by the Nazi or Soviet regimes.[55] The judgment concluded that it was legal for domestic legislation to broaden the category of protected groups included in the international definition of genocide, as various other countries, such as France, Spain, and Bolivia, had already done.[56] According to Žalimas, such an extension was not only legal under international law but also legitimate in post-communist countries, given Soviet efforts to design the 1948 UN Convention in such a way as to decriminalize its own mass crimes:

> One cannot look at an international convention as an immutable rule. We must be aware of the political context and interests which framed the Convention. We should not forget that the Soviet Union insisted on eliminating political and social groups, in an attempt to decriminalize its own acts of repression against these categories.[57]

While the Constitutional Court acknowledged the legality of reframing the 1948 UN Convention according to specific national contexts, it ruled, however, against the retroactive application of an expanded definition of genocide adopted in the 1990s to acts committed in the 1950s. The judges argued that given the lack of codification of genocide in LSSR legislation, Lithuanian courts could have resorted to the definition of genocide under international law in force when the crimes were perpetrated. Conventional law at the time had however restricted the list of protected groups to ethnic, racial, religious, and national categories. As far as customary international law was concerned, they noted that Resolution 96(1) of UN General Assembly and earlier drafts of the 1948 UN Convention reflected certain tendencies in the development of international law but did not amount to a prevailing rule.[58] The Court thus maintained that applying the categories of social and political genocide *ex post*

[55] See Dainius Žalimas, 'Crimes Committed by the Communist Regimes from the Standpoint of International Legislation: Lithuanian Case Study', in *Crimes of the Communist Regimes: An Assessment by Historian and Legal Experts. Proceedings of an International Conference* (Prague: Institute of the Study of Totalitarian Regimes, 2011): pp. 43–81.

[56] CCRL, 'Decision of 18 March 2014', pp. 12–13.

[57] Personal interview with Dainius Žalimas, Vilnius, Lithuania, 17 October 2018.

[58] CCRL, 'Decision of 18 March 2014', p. 10.

facto would represent a breach of the Lithuanian Constitution, which prohibited retroactivity.[59]

Nonetheless, argued the judges, if one could prove that a political or social group was also representative of the survival of a national group, then convictions of genocide did not pose any problems.[60] In Žalimas's view, it was difficult to draw a clear line between political and national groups in Lithuania, as in other cases of armed resistance to foreign occupation:

> The partisans constituted a liberation movement, fighting for the independent Lithuanian nation. One can label them as a political group, because they took up arms and fought against the occupant [. . .]. But this group was representative of the Lithuanian nation and of its independent survival. Consequently, it was also a national group. I believe that every judiciary should evaluate the definition of national, social, political groups in their respective historical contexts and not blindly apply supposed universal categorizations.[61]

Žalimas thus proposed a historically contextualized application of international law to local settings. In this vein, the Constitutional Court quoted the ICTR cases *The Prosecutor v. Semanza* and *The Prosecutor v. Kamuhanda* which state that 'a group enjoys no generally or internationally accepted definition, rather each group must be assessed in the light of a particular political, social, historical, and cultural context'.[62] The Constitutional Court also asserted that 'the groups indicated in the Convention cannot be easily distinguished among themselves', particularly in the context of the Baltic states, where 'historical sources had provided evidence that, in certain cases, the Soviet system had conducted repression against national groups (nations) while at the same time acting against social and political groups'.[63]

A number of Baltic and Western historians have also endorsed this line of thought, arguing that the extrajudicial killing of anti-Soviet partisans and the deportation of civilian populations had the purpose to destroy not only political groups but all nationalist representatives, and thus Baltic national values.[64] As Estonian legal scholar Lauri Mälksoo put it, 'in the context of the occupied

[59] Ibid, p. 64.
[60] Ibid, p. 38.
[61] Personal interview with Dainius Žalimas, Vilnius, Lithuania, 17 October 2018.
[62] CCRL, 'Decision of 18 March 2014', pp. 16–17.
[63] Ibid, p. 6.
[64] See Rudolf Joseph Rummel, *Lethal Politics: Soviet Genocide and Mass Murder since 1917* (New Brunswick, NJ: Transaction, 1990); Birutė Burauskaite, ed., *Genocide of Lithuanian People*, Volume II (1944–1947) (Vilnius: Institute of Philosophy, Sociology and Law, Research Center of Repressions in Lithuania, 1998).

Baltic states, the "anti-Soviet element" [against whom the repression had been conducted] had a different meaning from the rest of the USSR, [namely] the meaning of destroying three young nation states'.[65] Supporting the notion of two, Nazi and Soviet, totalitarianisms and genocides, some authors also claim to accommodate events occurring under both Nazism and communism into a common European memory framework through the equal recognition of the suffering of their victims.[66] The Baltic states have, in fact, emerged (together with Poland and Czechia) as the vanguard of a so-called new European commemorative politics, demanding the inclusion of their experiences under communist regimes within the pan-European master narrative centred on the condemnation of the Nazi regime. These claims have however been met with opposition from 'the old Western Europe' for whom the Holocaust has been, since the 1970s, a 'founding myth' and a canonical representation of totalitarian (Nazi) evil.[67]

Žalimas himself criticized the ostensible double standard in the mnemonic treatment of Nazism and communism at a European level and called for a pan-European moral, political, and legal condemnation of the communist crimes. He decried the alleged lack of will of Western Europe to condemn the communist crimes and ideology with the same vigour applied to Nazi crimes or to mass atrocities committed in former Yugoslavia, although the scale of all these crimes was comparable.[68] The decision of the Constitutional Court also reflected the narrative of two, Nazi and Soviet, occupations and genocides, and tried to accommodate the respect for the non-retroactivity rule with the application of the category of genocide within the historical context of the Baltic states. The Constitutional Court acknowledged that a retroactive application of the categories of social and political genocide would amount to an infringement of the principle of legality. Yet, if courts were able to prove that a targeted political or social group represented a significant component of a national group, they could convict the perpetrators of genocide without contravening the Lithuanian Constitution or the 1948 UN Convention. This approach endorsed the application of the category of *ethno-national-political genocide* in

[65] Lauri Mälksoo, 'Soviet Genocide? Communist Mass Deportations in the Baltic States and International Law', *Leiden Journal of International Law* 14 (2001): pp. 757–787, at p. 783.

[66] Mälksoo, 'The Memory Politics'; Siobhan Kattago, 'Agreeing to Disagree on the Legacies of Recent History: Memory, Pluralism and Europe after 1989', *European Journal of Social Theory* 12, no. 3 (2009): pp. 1–21.

[67] For these debates, see Laure Neumayer, *Criminalising Communism in the European Political Space after the Cold War* (London: Routledge, 2018).

[68] Žalimas, 'Crimes'.

cases of repression of national resistance movements, represented here by anti-Soviet partisans.

4 Argentina and Ideological Auto-Genocide

In the first fifteen years after trials of military officers resumed in Argentina, 32 per cent of the verdicts for political crimes committed during the so-called Dirty War framed these crimes as genocide under international law.[69] While most of the sentences continue to refer to 'a context of crimes against humanity', the military repression has increasingly been defined as genocide, both in the courts and public history in the past ten years.[70] Drawing on Spanish proceedings initiated in the 1990s against former Latin American officials (including Augusto Pinochet), Argentinian judges resuscitated the concept of *ideological auto-genocide*. The term was coined in the 1980s by American scholars to criminalize the atrocities of the Khmer Rouge in Cambodia and treat political and social groups as a subcategory of the national group in order to define crimes perpetrated on political/social grounds as genocide. In Argentina, this approach reflected the desire of certain legal actors to depoliticize the 'Dirty War' and create a national consensus concerning the evil of the dictatorship. It also mirrored the will to de-peripheralize the memory of the Argentinian military repression and affirm its centrality to the global history of twentieth-century mass atrocities.

4.1 From Cambodia to Argentina via Spain: The Travelling Category of Ideological Auto-Genocide

In contrast to Lithuanian jurisprudence, which was based on national legislation, the Argentinian courts relied exclusively on the direct application of international law. Argentina ratified the 1948 UN Convention in 1956, but up until the present there is no provision in the national criminal code that defines genocide or crimes against humanity. As discussed in Chapter 2, Argentinian judges used a 'double classification of deeds' under national and international law to combat impunity. This approach, endorsed by the Supreme Court of

[69] Alejandra Dandán, 'Deben ser juzgados por genocidio', *Página/12*, 11 April 2016. Available at www.pagina12.com.ar/diario/elpais/1-296670-2016-04-11.html (accessed 12 October 2023).
[70] Emilio Crenzel, 'The Crimes of the Last Dictatorship in Argentina and Its Qualification as Genocide: A Historicization', *Global Society* 33, no. 3 (2019): pp. 365–381.

Justice in 2005, argued that dictatorial crimes had been committed in 'a context of crimes against humanity' and could thus be prosecuted no matter the lapse of time. Yet, starting in 2006, judges across Argentina started to hand down verdicts referring to 'a context of genocide'.[71]

Carlos Rozanski, the first judge who formulated such a sentence, was known for his left-wing political views, victim-centred jurisprudence, and judicial activism. Born in 1951 to a family of Jewish origin, Rozanski came to the attention of the Argentinian media in 2003, when he authored a law on child sexual abuse which prohibited the cross-examination of minors in court and lifted the statute of limitations for sexual violence. Rozanski endorsed the social reforms of the Kirchner administrations and presented himself as an activist judge, 'attentive towards the needs of the victim [and] concerned not only with the application of the law, but also with its modification'.[72] Rozanski affirmed that his decision to employ the category of genocide was motivated by a didactic mission to foster solidarity with the victims.[73] Genocide, as the 'crime of crimes', was the best legal means to achieve a social consensus about the criminality of the dictatorship and legitimize a historical narrative that victims themselves have tried to impose since the 1970s. In a 2016 interview, he added that his jurisprudence was also part of a transnational flow of ideas and judicial activism that sought to provide a more inclusive reading of the 1948 Genocide Convention, one that would render the instrument applicable to the multiplicity of twentieth-century instances of mass murder, most of them motivated by political and economic interests.[74]

Rozanski was close to the circle of lawyers who searched for justice in Spain in the 1990s based on claims of universal jurisdiction (see Chapter 4). He practically replicated the legal reasoning employed by the Spanish judge, Baltasar Garzón, and confirmed by the special court Audiencia Nacional in various international arrest warrants issued against Argentinian military officers (and against Augusto Pinochet).[75] In the 1990s, Spanish law allowed prosecutions based on universal jurisdiction only for the crimes of genocide, terrorism, and

[71] Tribunal Oral en lo Criminal Federal N 1 de La Plata, 'Sentencia contra Miguel Osvaldo Etchecolatz, 19 Septiembre 2006'.

[72] Personal interview with Carlos Rozanski, La Plata, Argentina, 16 June 2016.

[73] Carlos Rozanski, 'Delitos de lesa humanidad y genocidio, origen y sentido de las prohibiciones', in *Juicios por crímenes de lesa humanidad en Argentina*, edited by Gabriele Andreozzi (Buenos Aires: Editorial Atuel, 2011): pp. 177–198, at pp. 185 and 196.

[74] Personal interview with Carlos Rozanski, La Plata, Argentina, 16 June 2016.

[75] For an analysis of Garzón's jurisprudence, see Naomi Roht-Arriaza, *The Pinochet Effect: Transitional Justice in the Age of Human Rights* (Philadelphia, PA: University of Pennsylvania Press, 2005): pp. 44–50; Richard J. Wilson, 'Prosecuting Pinochet: International Crimes in Spanish Domestic Law', *Human Rights Quarterly* 21, no. 4 (1999): pp. 927–979.

torture, as crimes against humanity was only introduced into the Spanish criminal code in 2003.[76] Since military crimes in Argentina were political in nature, using the category of genocide required an expansion of the dominant understanding of the term under international law. Garzón—a well-known but controversial judge, who had already provided contentious interpretations of law in cases concerning Basque terrorism—justified his jurisprudence as a strategy against impunity, with historical intellectual arguments:

> In the 1990s, it was a question of either providing a more comprehensive interpretation of the definition of genocide or of doing nothing. Crimes against humanity were not yet codified in Spanish legislation and there was no international convention on crimes against humanity. I couldn't work with that category. [...] I thus searched for a solution to reinterpret the definition of genocide in a more inclusive way. And I found a key framework that had been used in connection with the Cambodian genocide, including in a report formulated in 1985 by Special Rapporteur Benjamin Whitaker regarding the need to revise the Genocide Convention.[77]

Starting in the 1980s, various American legal scholars (including Hurst Hannum, Gregory H. Stanton, and UN Special Rapporteur Benjamin Whitaker) argued that in Cambodia, an 'ideological auto-genocide' had been committed by the Khmer Rouge against those parts of the Cambodian national group that did not fit their vision of the nation.[78] They contended that in an attempt to impose a new socio-political order, the Khmer Rouge planned to wipe out both ethnic and religious minorities (the Vietnamese, Chinese, Cham Muslim, and Buddhist communities) and any members of the Khmer national group considered incompatible with Khmer Rouge social engineering. The destruction of these different groups had been part of one and the same violent process of remaking Cambodian society according to a particular ideology. In 1979, a report of the UN Commission on Human Rights stated that this extermination amounted to 'nothing less than an auto-genocide'.[79] According to

[76] Roht-Arriaza, *The Pinochet Effect*, pp. 44–50.

[77] Personal interview with Baltasar Garzón, Madrid, Spain, 18 November 2015.

[78] Hannum, 'International Law'; Gregory H. Stanton, 'The Cambodian Genocide and International Law', in *Genocide and Democracy in Cambodia: The Khmer Rouge, the United Nations and the International Community*, edited by Ben Kiernan (New Haven: Yale University Southeast Asia Studies, 1993).

[79] Quoted by Bertrand Ramcharan, *The Advent of Universal Protection of Human Rights: Theo van Boven and the Transformation of the UN Role* (Cham, Switzerland: Springer, 2018): p. 47. The same approach was employed in 1979 by the People's Revolutionary Tribunal during Pol Pot's trial. See Tara H. Gutman, 'Cambodia, 1979: Trying Khmer Rouge Leaders for Genocide', in *Trials for International Crimes in Asia*, edited by Kirsten Sellars (Cambridge: Cambridge University Press, 2016): pp. 167–190.

legal scholar Hurst Hannum, while the term 'auto-genocide' had no legal status per se, the reality it described was what the Genocide Convention defined as the destruction 'in part' of a 'national group'.[80] Although the destruction in part of a national group by another segment of the same national group may not have been contemplated in 1948, Hannum contended, an innovative interpretation of the Convention could not automatically be excluded. In fact, both the drafters of the Convention and the 1971 decision of the International Court of Justice on the Mandatory Agreement concerning Namibia had agreed that the concepts embodied in the Genocide Convention 'were not static, but were by definition evolutionary [. . .] as law must never be oblivious to the changes in life, circumstance and community standards in which it functions'.[81] Consequently, just as the 1985 UN Study on Genocide drafted by Special Rapporteur Benjamin Whitaker had also emphasized, the definition of genocide did not exclude cases where victims were part of the perpetrator's own group, and could hence be applied to the crimes committed by the Khmer Rouge.[82]

This approach was however criticized by other lawyers (including the International Commission of Jurists) for fostering confusion between national and political groups and thus departing from the conventional definition of genocide under international law.[83] Human rights activists involved in the Cambodian Genocide Project at Yale University and the Cambodia Documentation Commission nonetheless continued to put forward this argument in various political and legal arenas. Their mobilization culminated in the adoption by the US Congress of the 1994 *Cambodian Genocide Justice Act*, which called for prosecutions of, and reparations for, 'the Khmer Rouge genocide'. In the 1990s, debates around the legal classification of Khmer Rouge crimes also generated an influential current that contested the dominant interpretation of genocide under international law and called for repairing 'the Genocide Convention's blind spots', particularly by including the crime of 'political genocide'.[84]

Inspired by this narrative, Garzón argued that as in Cambodia, a kind of 'auto-genocide' had been committed in Argentina (and in the Southern Cone

[80] Hannum, 'International Law', p. 112.
[81] Ibid, p. 113.
[82] Whitaker, 'Revised and Updated Report'.
[83] Stanton, 'The Cambodian Genocide'.
[84] van Schaack, 'The Crime'. Yet, as did other international tribunals, the Courts in Cambodia continued to apply the notion of genocide only to crimes committed against ethnic and religious groups (such as the Vietnamese or Buddhist communities); the extermination of members of the Khmer Rouge group continued to be classified as a crime against humanity.

in general) against a national subgroup formed by individuals who were not deemed suitable to the new political and economic order, whether they actively opposed the regime or simply had a passive attitude towards it.[85] This approach was facilitated by a slight difference between the definition established by the 1948 UN Convention and the definition of genocide introduced in Spanish legislation in 1973, wherein the term 'social' was used instead of 'racial' until 1983, when the definition was amended.[86] Based on this departure, Garzón and other judges from the Spanish Audiencia Nacional, willing to open investigations into Latin American crimes, claimed that genocide could actually apply to any social category that was under threat of extermination. They argued that a national group could not mean 'a group formed by people who belong to the same nation' but a human group (belonging to a nation or ethnicity) with specific social characteristics (be they political, economic, or based on gender or age). A more restrictive understanding of the term would prevent genocide from being applied to such 'odious' practices as killing all HIV positive individuals, all older people, all political elites, or specific economic classes.[87] Garzón also resorted to international customary law that predated the 1948 UN Convention, such as Resolution 96(1) of 1946 and the first drafts of the Convention which included the extermination of social, political, and 'other groups'. The Spanish legislation had thus to be interpreted not only considering the 1948 UN Convention but also in light of its precedents, which the judges deemed to be accepted components of customary international law. The Audiencia Nacional also deployed this approach in 2006 in cases concerning crimes committed by the Guatemalan army during the civil war (see *infra*).

This view was however repudiated by other judicial officials and academics, who emphasized that the repression carried out in Argentina had political motivations and exceeded the scope of the 1948 UN Convention. In their view, Garzón and the Audiencia Nacional had provided 'a controversial, expansive interpretation of genocide' that amounted to a political act to change the definition of genocide crafted by the governments.[88] In response, Garzón underlined

[85] Roht-Arriaza, *The Pinochet Effect*, p. 47.

[86] Wilson, 'Prosecuting Pinochet', p. 959.

[87] 'Auto de la Sala de lo Penal de la Audiencia Nacional confirmando la jurisdicción de España para conocer de los crímenes de genocidio y terrorismo cometidos durante la dictadura argentina', Madrid, 4 October 1998, www.derechos.org/nizkor/arg/espana/audi.html (accessed 25 April 2022).

[88] Christian Tomuschat, 'Issue of Universal Jurisdiction in the Scilingo Case', *Journal of International Criminal Justice* 3, no. 5 (2005): pp. 1074–1081, at p. 1080; see also Alicia Gil Gil, 'La sentencia de la Audiencia Nacional en el caso Scilingo', *Revista Electrónica de Ciencia Penal y Criminología* 7 (2005): pp. 1–18; Howard Schneider, 'Political Genocide in Latin America: The Need of Reconsidering the Current Internationally Accepted Definition of Genocide in the Light of Spanish and Latin America Jurisprudence', *American University Law Review* 25, no. 2 (2010): pp. 313–355.

the shortcomings of the 1948 UN Convention which 'left political groups unprotected and made genocide an almost unemployable category from a legal point of view'. Paralleling his Lithuanian colleagues, he argued that

> in the end, the legal definition of genocide under international law was a political product of the Cold War. The interests of the Soviets and others imposed the eliminations of political groups. Mass murder after the Second World War was committed mainly on political grounds. The conservative reading of genocide allows impunity for all these crimes. [. . .] Why allow this limited interpretation introduced fifty years ago for political reasons to govern the present interpretation of the Convention? If we, judges, are to do justice, we must use our creative power and come up with more progressive readings. My vision is that legal texts must be seen as living documents that can be interpreted in order to prevent and punish current injustices.[89]

This frustration with the Genocide Convention's narrow definition reflects the criticism of those legal scholars and historians for whom the Convention remains a conservative document, inapplicable to most twentieth-century massacres and in need of reform to include political groups.[90] In contrast to legal scholars who call for a reformulation by legislative means, Garzón stands for a judicial commitment to recast international law through jurisprudence and emphasizes the need to use the creative power of the judiciary to repair the ostensible shortcomings of this UN ICL instrument.

4.2 Depoliticizing and De-Peripheralizing the Memory of the 'Dirty War'

In the late 1990s, various lawyers—many of whom represented the victims' associations in the cases opened in Spain—promoted the paradigm of *ideological auto-genocide* in Argentina as a possible strategy to combat impunity. The most prominent advocate was Carlos Slepoy, a lawyer jailed for political reasons from 1976 to 1977 and then exiled to Spain. Framing military repression as

[89] Personal interview with Baltasar Garzón, Madrid, Spain, 18 November 2015.

[90] Lippman, 'The 1948 UN Convention'; van Schaack, 'The Crime'; Israel W. Charney, 'Toward a Generic Definition of Genocide', in *Genocide: Conceptual and Historical Dimensions*, edited by George J. Andreopoulos (Philadelphia, PA: University of Pennsylvania Press, 1994): pp. 64 and 74; Eduardo Rezses, 'La Figura de Genocidio y el Caso Argentino: La Posibilidad de Adecuar Jurídicamente una Figura Penal a Una Realidad Política', in *Aportes Jurídicos para el análisis y juzgamiento del genocidio en Argentina*, edited by Eduardo Rezses (Buenos Aires: Secretaria de Derechos Humanos, 2007): pp. 61–63.

genocide was embraced by the Argentinian anti-impunity movement, because it corresponded to an existing historical narrative dating back to the 1970s and developed further by a multitude of actors—from victim associations to human rights lawyers to academics.[91]

In this narrative, the victims of the military dictatorship were disconnected from politics and the guerrilla movements and were presented as apolitical individuals, often classified by gender, age, profession, or religion. This account underscored an indiscriminate violence perpetrated against diverse social categories and aimed to counter the justification presented by the dictatorship of violence as a necessity in the fight against left-wing 'subversion'. This discourse did not reflect on genocide in legal terms but used the category as a rhetorical tool designed to fit a global humanitarian vocabulary emerging in the 1970s based on the defence of individual rights and the moral obligation to empathize with all victims of oppressive regimes, irrespective of political conviction.[92] In addition, comparisons with Nazism were made, particularly by left-wing Jewish activists targeted by the military, who had suffered harsher treatment than non-Jewish victims. This discrepancy suggested that the regime was by nature antisemitic and facilitated the association between military repression and the Holocaust, helping to consolidate the rhetoric of an ongoing genocide.[93]

After the fall of the dictatorship, the report of the National Commission on the Disappearance of Persons lent further credence to the narrative of arbitrary and widespread violence against victims from a variety of social and professional groups. Although the report mentioned only briefly the notion of genocide, it did imply an association between the dictatorship and Nazism. In the 1990s, during a period of total impunity in Argentina and the rise of the Holocaust as the global symbol of victimhood,[94] memory entrepreneurs adopted the language of the memory of Nazi genocide to equate the

[91] Other proponents were Horacio Ravenna of the Permanent Association of Human Rights and Ana Chávez of Servicio Paz y Justicia (SERPAJ). Crenzel, 'The Crimes of the Last Dictatorship', p. 374.

[92] For the depoliticization of pro-victim campaigns in the 1970s, see Barbara Keys, 'Anti-Torture Politics: Amnesty International, the Greek Junta, and the Origins of the Human Rights "Boom" in the United States', in *The Human Rights Revolution: An International History*, edited by Akira Iriye, Petra Goedde, and William I. Hitchcock (New York: Oxford University Press, 2012): pp. 201–222.

[93] For the use of the Holocaust in memory politics in Argentina, see Emmanuel Kahan and Daniel Lvovich, 'Los usos del Holocausto en Argentina: Apuntes sobre las apropiaciones y resignificaciones de la memoria del genocidio nazi', *Revista Mexicana de Ciencias Políticas y Sociales* LXI, no. 228 (2016): pp. 1–26; Estelle Tarica, 'The Holocaust Again? Dispatches from the Jewish "Internal Front" in Dictatorship Argentina', *Journal of Jewish Identities*, 5, no. 1 (2012): pp. 89–110.

[94] For the rise of the global memory of the Holocaust, see Daniel Levy and Natan Sznaider, *Human Rights and Memory* (University Park, PA: Pennsylvania State University Press, 2010).

Argentinian military repression with the Holocaust.[95] Their efforts were endorsed by sociologists like Daniel Feierstein and Marcelo Raffin, whose works sought to inscribe the Argentinian dictatorship into the dreadful twentieth-century history of bureaucratically organized atrocities and to promote an understanding of genocide that included mass murder committed on political grounds.[96] After 2003, as memory and justice projects promoted by the Kirchner administrations proliferated, this discourse became dominant: from victims' associations and their lawyers to historians and museum curators, a wide range of experts involved in criminalizing the past combined forces to promote a discourse that framed the dictatorship as a genocidal regime.[97]

Rozanski himself was a proponent of this historical narrative and was in contact with Garzón, Slepoy, and other anti-impunity activists involved in the Spanish proceedings, and promoting the legal framework of the military repression in terms of genocide. Like Garzón and Lithuanian actors, Rozanski believed that justice demanded a more comprehensive interpretation of the 1948 UN Convention, to produce a new social cohesion around the victims both in Latin America and in other regions where massive political crimes had been committed:

> We must go beyond a conservative reading of the Convention. Political groups were excluded in 1948, but we don't have to consider only the Convention, but also customary international law. […] Genocides were committed in most cases on political grounds. We must take into consideration the systematic plan to exterminate a sector of the population, even if we were to call it a national group or a group of intellectuals. In the case of Argentina, not only left-wing activists, but also apolitical people were exterminated because they did not fit the neo-liberal, conservative, military project.[98]

Rozanski also argued against the Eurocentric bias in the treatment of genocide, whereby the centrality of memory of the Holocaust encouraged the peripheralization of other episodes of mass murder, as can be seen in the quote introducing this chapter.[99] Along with other Argentinian judges employing

[95] Liliana Feierstein, '"A Quilt of Memory": The Shoah as a Prism in the Testimonies of Survivors of the Dictatorship in Argentina', *European Review* 22 (2014): pp. 585–593.

[96] Daniel Feierstein, *Cinco Estudios Sobre Genocidio* (Buenos Aires: Acervo Cultural, 1997) and El genocidio como práctica social: *Entre el nazismo y la experiencia argentina* (Buenos Aires: Fondo de Cultura, 2007); Marcelo Raffin, *La experiencia del horror* (Buenos Aires: Ed. Del Puerto, 2006).

[97] Crenzel, 'The Crimes of the Last Dictatorship'.

[98] Personal interview with Carlos Rozanski, La Plata, Argentina, 16 June 2016.

[99] Ibid.

the genocide paradigm, this critique has also been voiced by scholars working on the history of violence in the Third World. They consider that the conception of genocide as an apolitical mass hate was modelled on the Holocaust of European Jewry. This approach removed ICL from Third World priorities and forced many societies to frame their memory of mass repression in reference to the Holocaust.[100] In Argentina, leading scholar Eugenio Zaffaroni, a member of the Supreme Court of Justice from 2003 to 2015 and a judge at the IACtHR from 2016 to 2022, has argued that

> the Genocide Convention is in certain aspects parochial. It has been shaped to specifically fit the Holocaust and has left aside, among other massacres, those committed by colonial Europe and those of Hiroshima and Nagasaki [. . .] the forced displacements of Soviet Stalinism, the murder by Pol Pot of a quarter of Cambodia's population, only because it was said they didn't intend to annihilate the population entirely.[101]

His stance reflected the broader preoccupation of the Latin American school of critical criminology—one of its main representatives being Zaffaroni himself—with the asymmetry and dependency between the Global North and the Global South in the production of legal knowledge and practice.[102] Rozanski, Zaffaroni, and other Argentinian judicial officials (such as Norberto Lorenzo and Horacio Insaurralde) thus sought to enforce a more inclusive reading of the 1948 UN Convention that would de-peripheralize the memory of various dictatorial repressions (the Argentinian one included) and would inscribe them in the history of widely recognized cases of genocide, such as the Holocaust, or the Rwandan and the Yugoslav genocides.

Hailed by victims' associations, this approach has however been faulted by other Argentinian jurists, such as Daniel Rafecas, Gabriel Cavallo, and Pablo Parenti, who argue that the victims of the dictatorship were persecuted on political grounds (not because they were Argentinian nationals). Hence, there is no legal basis for the invocation of genocide since such crimes constitute

[100] For these critiques, see Dirk Moses, *The Problems of Genocide: Permanent Security and the Language of Transgression* (Cambridge: Cambridge University Press, 2021).

[101] 'Zaffaroni: "La Convención Internacional Contra el Genocidio es en algunos aspectos mezquina"', *Télam Digital*, 21 March, 2014, available at www.telam.com.ar/notas/201403/56282-zaffaroni-la-convencion-internacional-contra-el-genocidio-es-en-algunos-aspectos-mezquina.html (accessed 12 October 2023).

[102] Nicolás Garcia and Máximo Sozzo, 'For a "Marginal Criminological Realism": Zaffaroni and the Birth of a Critical Perspective on the Criminal Question from the Global South', *Justice, Power and Resistance* XX, no. XX (2023): pp. 1–19.

crimes against humanity.[103] Similarly, certain historians and sociologists argue that framing the victims of the regime as a national (and not a political) group results in forgetting the political dimension of the leftist insurgency, and possibly frustrating former militants who could see in it a negation of their political project.[104]

Since 2006, the concept of *ideological auto-genocide* has gained traction within the Argentinian judiciary, reflecting the intensification of the rhetoric of genocide at a societal level. As Pablo Parenti, head (from 2007 to 2023) of the prosecutors' unit in charge of human rights violations, put it,

> many judicial officials think that genocide is more serious than crimes against humanity, at least at a symbolic level. Also, the genocide idea is so deeply rooted in the fight against the dictatorship and against impunity. We keep talking about 'genocidaires' at every corner. This narrative proposed by victims has now been transposed into jurisprudence, even if the current legal definition of genocide does not fit in the Argentinean case.[105]

The expansion of the international definition of genocide was thus the result of a desire to endorse a historical narrative that has been developing in Argentina since the 1970s and became dominant under the Kirchner administration. It was viewed as a duty of the courts to affirm a historical account that would respond to victims' claims and would reach all of society. But this interpretation also resulted from the frustration of certain judges with the current definition of genocide and their desire to change the prevailing international standards through national jurisprudence, which could then travel abroad to blossom into customary international law.

5. The Criminalization of Cultural Genocide in Guatemala

In May 2013, a Guatemalan court sentenced former President José Efraín Ríos Montt to eighty years in prison for genocide and war crimes committed against the Indigenous population during his mandate (from March 1982 to August

[103] Daniel Rafecas, 'La reapertura de los procesos judiciales por crímenes contra la humanidad en la Argentina', in *Juicios por crímenes de Lesa Humanidad en Argentina*, edited by Gabriele Andreozzi (Buenos Aires: Cara o ceca, 2011): pp. 155–176. Personal interview with Gabriel Cavallo, Buenos Aires, Argentina, 4 December 2014.

[104] Crenzel, 'The Crimes of the Last Dictatorship'; Hugo Vezetti, *Pasado y Presente: Guerra, Dictadura y Sociedad en Argentina* (Buenos Aires: Siglo Veintiuno, 2002).

[105] Personal interview with Pablo Parenti, online, 14 February 2018.

1983). Although the Constitutional Court annulled the verdict soon thereafter on procedural grounds, the sentence nonetheless represents a significant recast by a national court of the dominant definition of genocide under international law. The trial generated wide-ranging debates on whether the violence against Mayan groups was based on identity or political motivations and whether it could be classified as genocide, especially since the charges related not only to large-scale massacres but also to the destruction of Indigenous culture and social cohesion. Ultimately, Ríos Montt's conviction reflected the anti-impunity efforts of a pan-Mayan cultural rights movement, which had consolidated in the 1990s and pushed for the criminalization of acts of cultural genocide, thus expanding the framework of the 1948 UN Convention.

5.1 'Acts of Genocide' versus 'Policy of Genocide' in the Historical Clarification Commission

The initial engagement with the concept of genocide and its pertinence to the Guatemalan civil war arose during the drafting of the 1999 Report of the UN-sponsored Commission for Historical Clarification—La Comisión para el Esclarecimiento Histórico (CEH). The report found that over the course of the 36-year civil war (1961–1996), 200,000 people were killed, 45,000 forcibly disappeared, and 1 million displaced. The document attributed 93 per cent of the violence to the army and its paramilitary allies and acknowledged that the Mayan Indigenous population was the victim of 83 per cent of the crimes committed. The CEH compiled a long list of inhuman acts, including torture, massacres, burning people alive, the killing of children, and the systematic rape of women. The CEH drew on theories of skewed modernization to explain authoritarianism and the causes of the civil war, tracing the roots of a political culture based on racism and economic subordination of Mayans back to the Spanish period.[106]

The CEH—presided over by German international law scholar Christian Tomuschat, Guatemalan legal scholar Alfredo Balsells, and Mayan activist Otilia Lux de Cotí—also reflected upon historical events in legal terms. The Report argued that 'acts of genocide' had been committed in four regions of Guatemala during Ríos Montt's presidential tenure. According to the CEH, while the military had engaged in the repression of the Mayan population with the declared purpose of putting an end to the guerrilla movement (which was

[106] CEH, *Guatemala: Memoria del Silencio*, vol. 1 (Guatemala: UNOPS, 1999): pp. 79–81.

supported by segments of Mayan groups), the Mayan 'enemy' had been conceived of in ethnic terms. Racism fostered the belief that Indigenous communities were distinct, inferior, a little less than human and thus removed them from the moral universe of the perpetrators. The massacres, but also the destruction of entire Mayan villages and religious and cultural symbols, had been carried out with the intent to destroy a 'substantial part' of the Mayan population present in the military areas at the time of the attacks. In the Commission's view, the motive for these genocidal acts (to win the war) was distinguishable from the intent with which they had been carried out (the destruction of the Mayan groups as such).[107]

The CEH did however draw a distinction between a 'genocide policy' and 'acts of genocide', arguing that

> a genocide policy exists when the final objective of the actions is the total or partial extermination of a group. Genocidal acts occur when the final objective is not necessarily the extermination of the group, but specific political, economic, military or other goals, yet the means to achieve this final objective include the total or partial extermination of the group.[108]

This line of reasoning departed from the UN Genocide Convention, which implies a specific intent to exterminate on ethnic, national, racial, or religious grounds. In the Guatemalan context, the concept was broadened, as the intent could be economic, political, or military, while still affecting the survival of an ethnic group. According to Tomuschat, the CEH did not necessarily depart from the substance of the 1948 UN Convention, as it was clear that the mass killings had a racial premise. Yet, as in many cases of twentieth-century genocides, proving the intent to exterminate the 'group as such' was difficult, since political and identity motives overlapped in many conflicts, including the one in Guatemalan.[109] Given this context, the CEH experts took a more cautious approach when referring to genocide. They did not overgeneralize the entire policy of repression against Mayans as genocidal but selected specific regions and specific time periods in which abhorrent crimes had been perpetrated. The same logic led them to make the distinction between genocidal 'policy' and 'acts' of genocide. While it is not certain where this distinction originated, it

[107] Ibid, pp. 315–316.
[108] Ibid, p. 316.
[109] Personal interview with Christian Tomuschat, Berlin, Germany, 3 July 2019.

reflects an attempt at reconciling the historical Guatemalan context with the dominant interpretation of genocide under international law.

However, the 'acts of genocide' cited by the CEH referred not only to acts of physical destruction but also included acts traditionally categorized as *cultural genocide*, which were omitted from the 1948 UN Convention. Such acts included the bombing of sacred Mayan temples, the scorching of Mayan crops and lands, the burning of *huipiles*—traditional dress reflecting ethnicity—and the prohibition of burial rituals. The CEH also condemned the creation of 'model villages', where Mayans who recognized the military authority were compelled to 'Latinize' and 're-educate' themselves in the spirit of Guatemalan nationalism, renounce their social and cultural practices, and participate in Civil Self-Defence Patrols which assisted the army in pursuing the Ixil group who continued to oppose the regime. The purpose of such practices, the CEH argued, was to destroy the Mayan culture and social cohesion, which were seen by the military as subversive and inferior in comparison to Ladino culture.[110]

The labelling of the repression as genocidal and the introduction of elements of cultural genocide were largely the result of an emerging pan-Mayan cultural rights movement that interpreted not only the war but the whole of Guatemalan national history through the prism of racism and the internal colonialism of the Ladinos, and demanded that the CEH do the same.[111] This Guatemalan Indigenous mobilization was part of a transnational current across Latin America to change the hegemonic perception of Indigenous worlds and propose a new vision of the nation-state which acknowledged the Indigenous as a differentiated political and cultural identity.[112] Mayan activists linked racism and economic dispossession of Indigenous populations to Western capitalism and colonialism, the consequences of which continued to grant Ladinos hegemony over the Indigenous community.[113] The influence of this movement led to Otilia Lux de Cotí's appointment to the Commission. Along Mayan rights groups, she pushed for an acknowledgement of the genocidal intent of the military actions against Mayans.[114] Although the CEH's

[110] Summarized by Jan Perlin, 'The Guatemalan Historical Clarification Commissions Finds Genocide', *ILSA Journal of International & Comparative Law* 6, no. 2 (2000): pp. 289–413.

[111] Greg Grandin, 'The Instruction of Great Catastrophe: Truth Commissions, National History, and State Formation in Argentina, Chile, and Guatemala', *The American Historical Review* 110, no. 1 (2005): pp. 46–67, at p. 59.

[112] For the Mayan cultural movement, see Emilio del Valle Escalante, *Maya Nationalisms and Postcolonial Challenges in Guatemala: Coloniality, Modernity, and Identity Politics* (Santa Fe, NM: School for Advanced Research, 2009); Arturo Arias, 'The Maya Movement, Postcolonialism and Cultural Agency', *Journal of Latin American Cultural Studies* 15, no. 2 (2006): pp. 251–262.

[113] María Iñigo Clavo, 'Conversation with Aura Cumes on Mayan Epistemology, Postcolonial Theory and the Struggle for Identity', *Re-visiones* 7 (2017).

[114] Grandin, 'The Instruction', p. 59.

conclusions were hailed by victims, human rights NGOs, and historians, the report was disavowed by government officials and economic elites, who refused to accept this narrative, arguing instead that the military had acted in defence of national security.[115]

5.2 The Guatemalan 'Auto-Genocide' in Spanish Courts

The crimes committed during the civil war stood without judicial response for more than two decades. The 1996 Peace Accords were accompanied by a Law of National Reconciliation which granted amnesty for political crimes committed during the conflict but excluded international crimes. Nevertheless, the weak Guatemalan judicial system and the continuity of military influence in politics impeded prosecutions.[116]

Inspired by the transnational Argentinean anti-impunity movement, Guatemalan victims mobilized across borders, seeking justice in Spain. In 1999, Nobel Peace Prize winner Rigoberta Menchú—together with Guatemalan NGOs and Spanish solidarity groups—filed a complaint before the Audiencia Nacional, accusing eight people (Ríos Montt included) of genocide, terrorism, and torture. Argentinian lawyer Carlos Slepoy and Spanish lawyers José Luis Galán and Manuel Ollé Sesé, who had also represented Argentinean claimants in Spain, assisted the victims.[117] In 2006, Judge Santiago Pedraz of the Audiencia Nacional issued international warrants for the eight suspects on charges of genocide. The accusation included both the targeting of ethnic Mayans and the elimination of a part of the 'national group due to its ideology'—a departure from the 1948 UN Convention that Audiencia Nacional had already accepted in the Argentinian case. Pedraz used the concept of *ideological auto-genocide* to argue that the Guatemalan army conducted a planned campaign of physical extermination of entire segments of the Guatemalan population (Mayans and non-Mayans) that were perceived by the military as insurrectional, anti-national, and supportive of the guerrillas. In the case of Mayans, mass atrocities had been committed both on political and ethnic grounds. As far as

[115] Héctor Centeno Martin, 'Comisión del Esclarecimiento Histórico: Guatemala, entre la memoria del silencio y el silencio de la memoria', *Informe de CMI* 13 (2018): pp. 1–74.

[116] Guatemala has one of the weakest judicial systems in the world. In 2009, the impunity rate was 99.75 per cent. For obstacles to prosecutions and anti-impunity mobilizations, see Naomi Roht-Arriaza, 'Making the State Do Justice: Transnational Prosecutions and International Support for Criminal Investigations in Post-Armed Conflict Guatemala', *Chicago Journal of International Law* 9, no. 1 (2008): pp. 79–104.

[117] Roht-Arriaza, *The Pinochet Effect*, p. 173.

non-Mayan victims were concerned, Pedraz employed Garzón's logic in the Argentinian cases, maintaining that the anti-military opponents constituted a part of the Guatemalan national group which was targeted by the military on ideological grounds.[118]

In 2007, the Guatemalan Constitutional Court (GCC) ruled that the Spanish warrants had no legal basis within the Guatemalan–Spanish extradition treaty and declined the extradition. Since Spain prohibits trials in absentia, this decision put an end to the Guatemalan genocide case in Madrid, but the anti-impunity struggle continued at the IACtHR and at the national level. Already by the end of the 1990s, in parallel to the complaint lodged in Spain, Mayan groups assisted by NGOs such as the Association for Justice and Reconciliation (AJR) and the Center for Human Rights Legal Action (CALDH) filed charges against Ríos Montt and other members of the Guatemalan High Command for the crime of genocide. The lack of domestic investigations led these groups to address the IACtHR on the right to truth, the right to information, and the right to effective justice. Starting in 2004, the IACtHR handed down various decisions in which it compelled the Guatemalan authorities to investigate large-scale massacres.[119] These decisions and the Audiencia Nacional's warrants exerted significant pressure on the Guatemalan judicial system.

Between 2000 and 2006, the European Parliament also issued several resolutions, urging the Guatemalan government to investigate the crimes identified by the CEH.[120] During the same period, the UN called on Guatemala to initiate a radical judicial reform, which led to the creation of the Guatemalan International Commission against Impunity (CCIG). Established in 2009 through an agreement between the UN and the Guatemalan government, the CCIG investigated corruption, organized crime, and criminality in the ranks of clandestine networks with roots in Guatemala's military structures.[121] Although the CCIG was not authorized to investigate crimes committed during the civil war, it helped consolidate the independence of the judiciary and the establishment of high-risk tribunals which incorporated judges trained in international law who later prosecuted crimes committed during the internal

[118] Naomi Roht-Arriaza, 'Guatemala Genocide Case', *The American Journal of International Law* 100 (2008): pp. 207–231.

[119] For the Inter-American system and anti-impunity in Guatemala until 2007, see Marcie Mersky and Naomi Roht-Arriaza, 'Guatemala', in *Victims Unsilenced: The Inter-American System and Transitional Justice in Latin America* (Washington, DC: Due Process of Law Foundation, 2007): pp. 7–32.

[120] 'European Parliament resolution on the proceedings against Rios Montt', 26 October 2006; 'European Parliament resolution on the human rights situation in Guatemala', 11 April 2002.

[121] Andrew Hudson and Alexandra W. Taylor, 'The International Commission against Impunity in Guatemala: A New Model for International Criminal Justice Mechanisms', *Journal of International Criminal Justice* 8, no.1 (2010): pp. 53–74.

conflict. This gradual reform of the judicial system imposed by the UN, the transnational pressures for justice, and the local anti-impunity mobilizations led to investigations into gross human rights violations. Starting in 2008, several (mostly low-ranking) military officers and soldiers were convicted for their participation in massacres such as Plan de Sánchez, Dos Erres, and Río Negro. While those cases used charges of homicide or forced disappearances, Ríos Montt's trial was the first to employ the category of genocide.[122]

5.3 Expanding the Notion of Genocide to Cultural Destruction in Ríos Montt's Trial

In May 2013, Efraín Ríos Montt was convicted of genocide committed against the Mayan Ixil population during his presidential mandate in the early 1980s.[123] In contrast to the Spanish proceedings, which had also referred to massacres against non-Mayans, the Guatemalan case focused exclusively on the Ixil Indigenous group which had been among the most affected Mayan communities during the conflict. The charges included the killing of 1771 civilians, the displacement of around 29,000 people (or around 75 per cent of the Ixil population), the transfer of Mayan children to other groups (namely Ladinos), and the destruction of Mayan culture and social cohesion through the creation of 'model villages' and attacks on Indigenous religion.[124]

From a legal point of view, the accusation of genocide relied on the national criminal code, which had criminalized genocide in 1973, twenty-three years after Guatemala ratified the 1948 UN Convention.[125] The verdict represented an innovation regarding the dominant understanding of genocide. First, building upon the narrative crafted by the CEH, the judges advanced a distinction between purpose (what the perpetrator sought to achieve) and motive (why he wanted to achieve it) in order to dismiss the defence argument that

[122] Jo-Marie Burt, 'From Heaven to Hell in Ten Days: The Genocide Trial in Guatemala', *Journal of Genocide Research* 18, no. 2–3 (2016): pp. 143–169, at p. 146.

[123] For detailed analysis of the trial, see Susan Kemp, 'Guatemala Prosecutes Former President Rios Montt', *Journal of International Criminal Justice* 12 (2014): pp. 133–156; Hanna Bosdriesz and Sander Wirken, 'An Imperfect Success: The Guatemalan Genocide Trial and the Struggle against Impunity for International Crimes', *International Criminal Law Review* 14, no. 6 (2014): pp. 1067–1094; Burt, 'From Heaven to Hell'.

[124] Tribunal Primero de Sentencia Penal, Narcoactividad y Delitos contra el Ambiente (hereafter: TPSPNDA), Sentencia c-01076-2011-00015 Of. 2do (10 May 2013), available at www.derechos.org/nizkor/guatemala/doc/montt41.html (accessed 25 October 2023).

[125] Since 1973, the criminal code contained provisions on genocide (Article 376) and 'crimes against obligations to humanity' (crimenes contra los deberes de la humanidad) (Article 378), which were incorporated as part of Guatemala's obligations under the 1949 Geneva Conventions.

the repression had been political in nature and not directed against the Mayan ethnic group as such. From the very beginning, Ríos Montt's lawyers maintained that the military had intended to curb the insurgency of the guerrillas—not to eradicate the Ixiles on ethnic criteria. They argued that the military operations had been a legitimate defence of the state; any harm done to civilians was the consequence of abuses committed by individual officers or soldiers. Consequently, accusations of genocide were precluded, as there was no proof of a systematic plan of destruction perpetrated against Mayan communities. In contrast, the judges stated that while the military might have intended to 'only' end the insurgency, they thought to do it by destroying substantial segments of the Ixil group, which, in the regime's view, were synonymous with the guerrilla fighters. According to the Court, the identification of the Ixil as an internal enemy was not only political but embedded in the pervasive racism of the Guatemalan ruling class.[126]

The Court drew on the expert testimony of social scientists Marta Casáus Arzú and Angel Valdez, whose works emphasized that racism had characterized the Guatemalan society since the Spanish Conquista. During the conflict, it became part of state ideology together with the national security doctrine. According to the Court, counter-insurgency considerations, combined with endemic racism, led the military command to seek the destruction of the Ixil population, including its culture and way of life.[127] The judges also underlined the blurry line between various motives and refused to hierarchize them. As in the Lithuanian case, the Guatemalan judges argued that the existence of political motives did not exclude the ethnic (or national, in Lithuania) criteria that had been central to attacks carried out against the Ixil population.[128]

Second, the accusation included acts of cultural genocide. This approach was strongly supported by human rights organizations such as CALDH and AJR, which argued that physical violence against Indigenous people could not be dissociated from the military's view that Mayan culture was inferior and undermined their project of militarizing and Westernizing Guatemalan society. The attacks on Mayan culture were thus also part of a plan to destroy the Ixil group.[129] The use of this approach in Ríos Montt's indictment was facilitated by the fact that Claudia Paz y Paz, Guatemala's general prosecutor overseeing

[126] TPSPNDA, Sentencia c-01076-2011-00015 Of. 2do (10 May 2013), available at www.derechos.org/nizkor/guatemala/doc/montt41.html (accessed 25 October 2023). See also Marta Casáus Arzú, *Genocidio: ¿la máxima expresión del racismo en Guatemala?* (Guatemala: F&G Editores, 2008).

[127] TPSPNDA, Sentencia c-01076-2011-00015 Of. 2do (10 May 2013), available at www.derechos.org/nizkor/guatemala/doc/montt41.html (accessed 25 October 2023).

[128] Ibid.

[129] Burt, 'From Heaven to Hell', pp. 148–149.

the case, had previously been a CEH member and an Indigenous rights activist. Moreover, in her doctoral dissertation, she argued for a more inclusive reading of genocide, one that would enhance the protection of Indigenous people, including their culture.[130]

Against this backdrop, the prosecutors proposed a novel interpretation of the categories of 'mental harm' and 'conditions of life' included in the 1948 UN Convention in order to encompass not only acts of physical violence but also the destruction of Mayan social cohesion and culture.[131] Previously, these categories—as constituent elements of genocide under international law—had generally been limited to physical or biological destruction, a view confirmed by much of the international case law.[132]

In Ríos Montt's trial, the accusations included, on the one hand, the acts of genocide incorporated in the 1948 UN Convention, such as massacres, the forced transfer of Mayan children to other groups, preventing birth (through rape and the forcible removal of foetuses), or deliberately inflicting conditions of life that would bring about the physical destruction of a group (such as the scorched-earth campaigns that led to forced displacement and starvation). On the other hand, the indictment referred to the 'life conditions' and 'mental harm' caused by the establishment of so-called model villages, where the Ixil group under military rule were 'Latinized', 're-educated' in the spirit of the regime, and were compelled to participate in Civil Self-Defence Patrols. According to Edwin Canil, a Mayan lawyer who supported the victims on behalf of CALDH, the charges included acts of cultural destruction in order to contextualize the physical violence and present evidence of intent to destroy a group.

> Nobody sought to punish cultural genocide as such, disconnected from physical violence. Yet the destruction of the Mayan culture, the attempt to erase our way of life, our cosmovision, our beliefs, cannot be dissociated and should not be dissociated from the massacres. This cultural destruction, including the re-education system of the so-called model villages, was a fundamental purpose of the military and it has to be classified and punished as genocide.[133]

130 Claudia Paz y Paz Bailey, La protección penal de los pueblos: Especial consideración del delito de genocidio, PhD Thesis, University of Salamanca, 2006; for Paz y Paz's biography, https://womenslinkworldwide.org/premios/jurado/20 (1 June 2019).

131 Kemp, 'Guatemala', pp. 139–140.

132 Schabas, *Genocide in International Law*, pp. 271–272. Novic, *The Concept of Cultural Genocide*, pp. 52–56. The 2016 ICC decision in *Prosecutor v. Al Mahdi* confirmed this exclusion. The ICC returned its first verdict that dealt entirely with cultural destruction, but did not invoke the crime of genocide, and indicted the accused for the more limited war crime of destruction of cultural property. Bilsky and Klagsbrun, 'The Return of Cultural Genocide?'.

133 Personal interview with Edwin Canil, Guatemala City, Guatemala, 21 August 2019.

Angel Valdez also emphasizes that conversations about cultural genocide were necessary not only to prove the exterminatory intent of the military but also to render justice to the victims for whom their culture and way of life was intrinsically linked with their physical existence.[134] In contrast, the defence opposed this accusation, claiming that the Ixil groups in 'model villages' had received care, education, and decent living conditions, making any charges of ill-treatment false.[135]

In response, the Court considered that altering Indigenous ways of life was an explicit goal of the military that constituted mental harm. It argued that the 're-education' process imposed new social relations and new forms of cultural and religious practice entirely at odds with the Ixil 'cosmovision'.[136] By depriving them of their lands, burning their crops, and forcibly displacing them, the military sought to undermine the Mayan view of the universe and creation, which is intrinsically linked to the relationship between 'motherland' and the essence of existence. The Court thus incorporated a Mayan vision of rights, which goes beyond the Western construct of human rights. As Indigenous activist Aura Cumes points out, 'for Indigenous peoples, everything has life, and therefore it should have rights just like people do; for many Indigenous communities, this is very clear, but this is not true for the capitalist West, which sees every living thing as something to be exploited'.[137] Moreover, according to the Court, the Ixil group underwent a political re-education to instil loyalty to the military and hatred of their own group members. These measures aimed to extinguish the social fabric of the Ixil group, whose social unit included physical, linguistic, customary, territorial, and spiritual links.[138] The military sought to transform Mayans into compliant individuals defined by their new Guatemalan national identity and stripped of their own ethnic identity and culture, which was understood by the military as a subversive means of resistance since the Spanish conquest.[139]

Although acclaimed by victims' associations and anti-impunity organizations, Ríos Montt's conviction was annulled by the GCC ten days later on procedural grounds, in a split three-two ruling. None of the substantive points of the trial played any role whatsoever, with the decision focusing on

[134] Personal interview with Angel Valdez, Guatemala City, Guatemala, 21 August 2019.

[135] TPSPNDA, Sentencia c-01076-2011-00015 Of. 2do (10 May 2013), available at www.derechos.org/nizkor/guatemala/doc/montt41.html (accessed 25 October 2023).

[136] Ibid.

[137] Personal interview with Aura Cumes, Guatemala City, Guatemala, 19 August 2019.

[138] TPSPNDA, Sentencia c-01076-2011-00015 Of. 2do (10 May 2013), available at www.derechos.org/nizkor/guatemala/doc/montt41.html (accessed 25 October 2023).

[139] Kemp, 'Guatemala', p. 144.

a controversial irregularity concerning the composition of the Court.[140] The GCC ordered a retrial, which was subsequently delayed, ending with Ríos Montt's death in 2018. In 2019, another general, Luis Mendoza García, was accused of genocide against the Ixil group.[141] In April 2023, the trial was ongoing.

6. Reverberations at Regional Human Rights Courts and within the Global Legal Community

The expanded notions of genocide proposed by Lithuanian, Argentinian, and Guatemalan courts did not remain purely domestic affairs. On the one hand, they sparked debates at the ECtHR and the IACtHR, which were called upon—either by the defendants (Lithuania) or by the victims (Guatemala)—to adjudicate on the correct application of the category of genocide. On the other hand, they became the subject of academic disputes, as scholars criticized the departure from dominant international standards or demanded the national contextualization of international law. These legal debates also reveal the regional and global mnemopolitics at stake. The Lithuanian case at the ECtHR reflected both the Baltic-Russian memory struggles about the Second World War and its aftermath and the European divisions concerning the putative moral equivalence of Soviet communism and Nazism. The Argentinian case sparked discussions about the international hierarchies of mass murder, where the Holocaust and other crimes committed on the grounds of identity (such as the Yugoslav and Rwandan genocides) are placed at the centre of international memory politics, while politically motivated crimes (as in the Southern Cone or in CEE) have ostensibly been peripheralized. The Guatemalan case reinforced the mnemonic agenda of Indigenous populations in their quest for recognition as victims of colonial and postcolonial genocides.

Moreover, as will be shown below, judges and scholars became concerned with the potential circulation of these legal lines of thought across jurisdictions and their application in other political contexts. At the ECtHR, certain judges warned that other former Soviet Republics could borrow the Lithuanian concept of *ethno-national-political genocide* or that it could be used to categorize the imperial repression of anti-colonial liberation movements in Africa and Asia. The Argentinian and Spanish concept of *ideological auto-genocide* was

[140] Burt, 'From Heaven to Hell', pp. 156–157; Bosdriesz and Wirken, 'An Imperfect Success', pp. 1087–1089.

[141] 'Exjefe militar guatemalteco enfrentará juicio por genocidio de indígenas', swissinfo.ch, 16 February 2022, available at www.swissinfo.ch (accessed 25 October 2023).

highly criticized and its transposal into other historical contexts met with scepticism. In contrast, the Guatemalan reflections on cultural genocide were considered by many as progressive legal reasoning that might travel and be applied in other instances of destruction of Indigenous populations.

6.1 Controversies Surrounding the Concept of Ethno-National-Political Genocide at the ECtHR

The ECtHR was confronted with the Lithuanian jurisprudence on genocide in two cases: *Vasiliauskas v. Lithuania*, heard by the Great Chamber in 2015, and *Drėlingas v. Lithuania*, judged by the Fourth Section in 2019.[142] The hearings revealed deep divisions among European judges on the application of the category of genocide to crimes committed by the repressive Soviet system in the 1950s against Lithuanian partisans. The cases involved legal arguments about the infringement of the principle of legality but also became a matter of European mnemopolitics and history-writing. Furthermore, as Judge Iulia Motoc opined, at stake was the very concept of *ethno-national-political genocide*, which, once endorsed by the ECtHR, would establish a precedent and 'tempt other countries to follow in Lithuania's footsteps' and broaden the scope of genocide beyond the approach taken so far in international law.[143]

In 2004, Vytautas Vasiliauskas, an MGB operative (the KGB's predecessor), was convicted by a court of first instance of genocide based on the 1998 criminal code for having killed two anti-Soviet partisans in 1953. The verdict emphasized that the killings were part of a systematic Soviet plan to eliminate the anti-Soviet resistance, but it did not engage in debates about international law, nor had it elaborated whether the groups targeted by the Soviet authorities had been political, social, or national in nature. In 2005, the Appellate and the Supreme Court upheld the verdict and described the partisan movement as a 'political group' that had however been 'an essential part of [the Lithuanian] national group'. The courts referred to an *ethno-national-political genocide*, arguing that in the Lithuanian context political and national groups could not be clearly separated.[144]

In 2005, Vasiliauskas challenged the verdict at the ECtHR, arguing that it contravened Article 7(1) of the European Convention on Human Rights,

[142] ECtHR, *Vasiliauskas v. Lithuania*, Judgment of 20 October 2015; ECtHR, *Drėlingas v. Lithuania*, Judgment of 12 March 2019.

[143] ECtHR, *Drėlingas v. Lithuania*, 'Dissenting Opinion of Judge Motoc', p. 35.

[144] ECtHR, *Vasiliauskas v. Lithuania*, Judgment of 20 October 2015.

through the retroactive application of a broad definition of genocide (including social and political groups) that did not have any basis in national or international law in 1953.[145] Moscow intervened as a third party in the case. It contended that Soviet policies and legislation were not aimed at destroying the Lithuanian nation but unlawful armed groups fighting against the legitimate Soviet government of Lithuania. The repression of partisans could not be framed in terms of crimes against humanity either (since it had not targeted civilians), but only against illegal armed 'bandits'.[146]

The Lithuanian defence was constructed on two arguments which, although interconnected, seemed to contradict each other. On the one hand, it argued that 'this case is not about a wider definition of the crime of genocide' but about a specific interpretation of this category in the context of the Soviet occupation. The anti-Soviet partisans, the government stressed, were both a political and a national group, because the restoration of Lithuanian independence had both a political and a national purpose.[147] The Soviet authorities regarded the Baltic states as 'untrustworthy nations'—'the politically motivated killings had been merely a screen for national and ethnic genocidal aspirations'.[148] Through this argument, the defence tried to avoid a discussion about the expansion of the international definition of genocide and shifted the debate into the sphere of national history. Lithuanian lawyers insisted in fact that the ECtHR could not blindly impose European standards of human rights without taking into consideration national histories.[149] On the other hand, however, the defence pointed to the inclusion of political groups in customary international law prior to the adoption of the 1948 UN Convention. Renowned international law scholar William Schabas acted on behalf of Lithuania. Whereas in his previous writings Schabas had argued that there was not enough evidence that customary international law protected social and political groups under the definition of genocide,[150] he now changed his approach. He stressed that Resolution 96(1) and initial drafts of the Convention should be taken into consideration as customary law. Based on these documents, a more inclusive definition of genocide applicable to crimes with political and social motivations did not infringe on the principle of legality.[151]

145 Ibid.

146 Ibid, pp. 51–52.

147 Grand Chamber Hearing in *Vasiliauskas v. Lithuania*, 04 June 2014, available at www.echr.coe.int/Pages/home.aspx?p=hearings&w=3534305_04062014&language=lang (accessed 13 October 2019) (hereafter: Grand Chamber Hearing).

148 ECtHR, *Vasiliauskas v. Lithuania*, Judgment of 20 October 2015, pp. 47–49.

149 Grand Chamber Hearing.

150 Schabas, *Genocide in International Law*, p. 7.

151 Grand Chamber Hearing.

In 2015, the Grand Chamber ruled, with a slim majority of nine to eight votes, that Vasiliauskas's conviction had violated Article 7 of the European Convention. The judges in the majority were mainly from Western countries (France, Italy, Luxembourg, and Denmark), where genocide was deeply embedded in the Holocaust paradigm, and the equation of Nazi and communist crimes criticized. Two further judges were from Turkey and Serbia, countries that as a rule take a narrow approach to the notion of genocide to avoid the international recognition of the Armenian genocide and to downplay Serbia's role in the Yugoslav genocide. In contrast, most of the judges backing the Lithuanian approach came from former communist countries (Lithuania, Latvia, and Hungary) and former Yugoslav republics (Montenegro and Croatia). Two further judges siding with the minority were from Portugal—a country whose mass repression under Salazar is rarely addressed as part of the common European traumatic past—and Ireland, which has a strong anti-colonial tradition and whose struggle against the British Empire is also overlooked at the European level. While one cannot assess the ECtHR decisions based exclusively on the nationality of the judges, this case seemed to reflect divisions between a status quo Western European mnemopolitics centred on the Holocaust and a counter-hegemonic vision coming from European semi-peripheries.

First, the majority dismissed Schabas's position, arguing that there was no agreement among scholars on whether Resolution 96(1) reflected a *jus cogens* prohibition of genocide or not. Consequently, in 1953, customary law had not provided a definition of genocide wider than the one established in the 1948 UN Convention.[152] Second, the Court considered that, in 1953, the interpretation of the '[destruction] in part' of a group—such as that presented by the Lithuanian national courts in the case of anti-Soviet partisans—referred to a quantitative measure of the respective group. The broadening of this understanding towards a more qualitative approach (a 'distinct' or 'prominent' part) developed only later, in the jurisprudence of the ICTY and the ICTR, and had not been foreseeable by the defendant in 1953.[153] Third, according to the majority, the Lithuanian courts had not provided sufficient evidence that partisans constituted a significant share of the national group—in other words, a group protected under Article II of the Genocide Convention.[154] Taken together, the latter arguments provoked confusion among scholars and practitioners, as it

[152] ECtHR, *Vasiliauskas v. Lithuania*, Judgment of 20 October 2015, p. 60.
[153] Ibid, p. 61.
[154] Ibid, pp. 62–63.

was unclear whether or not a more articulated historical account concerning the significance of the partisans for the national group would have altered the majority's decision.[155]

Out of eight judges voting in favour of the Lithuanian government, three considered that the ECtHR had no motive to engage with the case because the Lithuanian Constitutional Court had already provided a remedy to the applicant through its 2014 decision. They thus bypassed the question of genocide entirely.[156] The other five judges dissented sharply from the majority. While accepting that social and political groups were not covered by the crime of genocide as recognized internationally in 1953, they could not accept that

> a protected group (a nation) which defends itself against the destruction of its very fabric though the mobilization of a resistance movement suddenly, by that act of resistance, transforms itself solely into a 'political group', thus placing itself outside the terms of the Genocide Convention. This would be to interpret the Convention [. . .] in an overly formalistic manner and in a spirit inconsistent with [its] purpose.[157]

Through this argument, the dissenting judges enforced the idea that national liberation movements could be protected under the Genocide Convention. Although this aspect did not come to the fore in the debates, the transfer of the concept of *ethno-national-political genocide* to other world regions was nonetheless relevant to the decision according to dissenting Lithuanian judge Egidijus Kūris:

> The Lithuanian jurisprudence reflected the limits of the 1948 UN Convention and its political underpinnings and could have future implications for crimes committed by the Khmer Rouge, or by the French government during the Algerian anti-colonial war. [. . .] It doesn't mean it could be applied to colonialism in its entirety, but only to some instances, such as the mass destruction of anti-colonial resistance.[158]

[155] Justinas Žilinskas, 'Vasiliauskas vs. Lithuania: Battle Lost in the War to Come?', International Comparative Jurisprudence 2 (2016): pp. 67–71, at p. 69.

[156] ECtHR, *Vasiliauskas v. Lithuania*, 'Dissenting Opinion of Judges Sajó, Vučinić, and Turković', p. 93.

[157] ECtHR, *Vasiliauskas v. Lithuania*, 'Dissenting Opinion of Judges Villiger, Power-Forde, Pinto de Albuquerque, and Kūris', p. 73.

[158] Personal interview with Egidijus Kūris, Strasbourg, France, 27 February 2019.

Judge Iulia Motoc would also later state, in *Drėlingas v. Lithuania*, that by endorsing Lithuania's approach, the ECtHR would establish a precedent and thereby encourage the circulation of the construct of *ethno-national-political genocide* to other former Soviet Republics, communist regimes, and contexts of anti-colonial struggle.[159]

The Baltic–Russian memory war and the condemnation of communist crimes at a European level were also at stake for the dissenting judges. They emphasized that Russia continued to deny, as third party in the case, the Stalinist atrocities committed in the Baltic states. Irish judge Ann Power-Forde even criticized the majority for missing the chance to give the Soviet era its proper name—that is: genocide. Quoting from historian Norman Davies—an advocate for the equal treatment of Nazi and Stalinist crimes—she stated that Stalin's programme 'outdid any other disaster in European history, even the Second World War'.[160] According to Judge Kūris, the majority acted as if Lithuanian courts should have explained the historical context anticipating a Strasbourg audience: 'These facts are known to every schoolchild in that society. True, they are not necessarily known in Strasbourg, but in that event, this is Strasbourg's problem'.[161] To support their argument, the dissenting judges quoted the ICTR in *Prosecutor v. Rutaganda*, arguing that 'the protected groups must be assessed in the light of a particular political, social and cultural context'.[162]

The dissenting judges also took a stance against the majority's view that a qualitative interpretation of the term 'in part' would involve retroactivity in the present case. They admitted that in 1953 there had been no jurisprudence on the meaning of the term 'in part' because trials concerning genocide occurred only in the ICTR and ICTY jurisprudence. Yet this interpretation was found to be formalistic, to ignore history and to render the Holocaust the only genuine genocide up until the mid-1990s.

> We acknowledge that in 1953 [. . .] there was no jurisprudence on the meaning of the phrase 'in part' [. . .] given that the first case in which a conviction for the crime of genocide was pronounced did not occur until 1998. [. . .] A supposition that genocides did not occur before 1998 (save the Holocaust) because no court, prior to that date, had stated that they occurred, would be not only legally inconsistent, but also offensive to numerous national, ethnic, racial or religious groups which, in various parts of the globe, fell victim to

159 ECtHR, *Drėlingas v. Lithuania*, 'Dissenting Opinion of Judge Motoc', p. 35.
160 ECtHR, *Vasiliauskas v. Lithuania*, 'Dissenting Opinion of Judge Power-Forde', p. 94.
161 Ibid, 'Dissenting Opinion of Judge Kūris', p. 96.
162 Ibid, 'Dissenting Opinion of Judges Villiger, Power-Forde, Pinto de Albuquerque, and Kūris', p. 72.

government-planned destruction, without, however, ever being able to bring their cases to international courts.[163]

According to Judge Kūris, the majority's reasoning created a vicious circle that limited the capacity of any national court to advance international law.

> The Grand Chamber rejected Lithuania's approach on the grounds that an international clarifying jurisprudence on the qualitative interpretation of the notion 'in part' did not exist when the crimes had been committed. But once a national court tries to develop such a jurisprudence, the ECtHR blocks this development.[164]

The opinions in *Vasiliauskas v. Lithuania* reflected divisions on both the framing of Soviet crimes as genocide and the endorsement of the new legal construct of *ethno-national-political genocide.* Although the Grand Chamber rejected an expansion of the 1948 UN Convention, the debates continued at the ECtHR with an unexpected twist in 2019 in *Drėlingas v. Lithuania.*

In response to the Grand Chamber's decision, the Lithuanian Supreme Court of Justice chose to conform to the ECtHR ruling while still endorsing the concept of *ethno-national-political-genocide.* In May 2016, it argued that Vasiliauskas's conviction had indeed been retroactive since the courts had not clearly proved that the partisans were representative of the Lithuanian nation. The sentence had to be quashed.[165] However, a few months later, in October 2016, in a case similar to *Vasiliauskas*, the Supreme Court convicted a former KGB officer, Stanislovas Drėlingas, of genocide for taking part in the capture, in 1956, of one of the most prominent leaders of the Lithuanian partisans, Adolfas Ramanauskas.[166]

The Supreme Court's verdict was carefully formulated to counter the ECtHR's critiques and maintain the Lithuanian jurisprudence on genocide—particularly because Drėlingas also lodged a complaint with the ECtHR in May 2016. According to a legal adviser to the Supreme Court, interviewed in 2018:

> This was an opportunity for us to persuade the European Court of the validity of our approach, namely that crimes against Lithuanian partisans constituted a genocide. Given the small margin of the decision in *Vasiliauskas*, we

163 Ibid, p. 74.
164 Interview with Egidijus Kūris, Strasbourg, France, 27 February 2019.
165 ECtHR, *Drėlingas v. Lithuania*, Judgment of 12 March 2019, pp. 19–20.
166 Ibid, pp. 2–5.

hope that providing as much historical context as possible would convince Strasbourg in this new case.[167]

The Supreme Court engaged in detail with the history of the Lithuanian partisans, Ramanauskas's role in the anti-Soviet struggle, and the defendant's activities against partisans. However, the Court did not elaborate on the interpretation of the term 'in part' in qualitative or quantitative terms. Hence, various analysts concluded that Lithuanian judges ignored Strasbourg's judgment.[168] Indeed, referring to the ECtHR decision in *Vasiliauskas*, the Court stated only that it had now provided enough evidence that Lithuanian jurisprudence did not imply retroactive enlargement of the 1948 UN Convention, because in the Lithuanian historical context political and national groups overlapped during the anti-Soviet struggle.

In March 2019, in a decision adopted by a seven to two margin, the Fourth Section of the ECtHR endorsed Lithuania's approach in *Drėlingas v. Lithuania* and provided a contrasting opinion to that adopted by the majority of the Grand Chamber in the *Vasiliauskas* case. Two judges who had dissented in the previous case were on the current panel (Judge Kūris and Portuguese judge Paulo Pinto de Albuquerque). Also, this time, most of the judges were from Eastern Europe (Hungary, Romania, Bosnia, and Herzegovina), including two former Soviet Republics (Lithuania and Ukraine). The majority argued that the Lithuanian Supreme Court had now brought enough evidence to prove that the Soviet repression had targeted the most active and prominent members of the Lithuanian nation.[169] Nevertheless, the majority ignored the Grand Chamber's argument in *Vasiliauskas v. Lithuania* about the retroactive application of the qualitative interpretation of the term 'in part' and limited their analysis to whether or not Lithuanian courts had sufficiently substantiated their judgment historically.

In response, Italian judge Ranzoni argued in his dissent that the majority had deliberately misinterpreted the Grand Chamber's decision.[170] The second dissenter was Romanian judge Motoc. While disagreeing with the Grand

[167] Interview, anonymous, Lithuanian legal advisor, Vilnius, Lithuania, 17 October 2018.

[168] Donatas Glodenis, 'Lithuanian Supreme Court of Justice Ignores Strasbourg Genocide Judgement', *Liberties*, 23 May 2016, available at www.liberties.eu/en/news/lithuania-genocide-unlawful-conviction/8624 (accessed 25 October 2023).

[169] ECtHR, *Drėlingas v. Lithuania*, Judgment of 12 March 2019, pp. 30–32.

[170] He also considered that the *Drėlingas* and *Vasiliauskas* cases were different in nature, given that the first applicant had not been directly involved in the execution of partisans. In his view, Drėlingas's conviction reflected such a dilution of the concept of genocide that it could be equated with any act of repression. ECtHR, *Drėlingas v. Lithuania*, Judgment of 12 March 2019, 'Dissenting Opinion of Judge Ranzoni', pp. 41–48.

Chamber's majority view in the *Vasiliauskas* case as far as the narrow (quantitative) interpretation of the term 'in part' was concerned, she believed that the *Drėlingas* case should be heard by the Grand Chamber, because this was the first time that 'the ethno-political genocide has been recognized by an international Court'. In her view, this precedent could now be used in contexts of mass killings that have not yet been acknowledged as genocide, where victims perished due to their belonging to a subversive class (such as victims of Stalin, Mao Tse-tung, and Pol Pot). Since the definition of protected groups in the 1948 UN Convention remained a contentious issue in international law, its enlargement had to be discussed by the Grand Chamber.[171] In 2019, however, the Grand Chamber dismissed a request by Drėlingas's lawyer to hear the case, as Drėlingas had died several months before. The ECtHR position thus remains split between the Grand Chamber's rejection of an expanded definition of genocide and the Fourth Section's endorsement of the application of the category of genocide to national liberation movements.

6.2 The IACtHR's Hesitant Jurisprudence on Genocide

The IACtHR only engaged with the concept of genocide in the Guatemalan case, as no complaint was brought to the Court from Argentina. In the 2000s, persistent impunity in Guatemala led human rights NGOs to accuse the Guatemalan judiciary at the Inter-American Commission on Human Rights of having infringed Articles 25 (right to judicial protection) and 8 (right to a fair trial) of the American Convention on Human Rights. The purpose was to instigate trials and recognize the genocide against the Mayan population at a regional level. The Commission endorsed the efforts of the victims' groups and addressed the IACtHR, asking the Court to compel Guatemala to investigate what the Commission considered to be massacres 'committed within the framework of a genocide' against Mayans.[172]

Starting in 2004, various IACtHR decisions affirmed Guatemala's duty to prosecute large-scale massacres.[173] Yet, in contrast to the Commission, the Court refused to engage in debates about the application of the category of

[171] Ibid, 'Dissenting Opinion of Judge Motoc', pp. 35, 38.

[172] See IACtHR, *Case of Plan de Sánchez Massacre v. Guatemala*, Judgment of 29 April 2004, p. 2.

[173] IACtHR, *Plan de Sánchez Massacre v. Guatemala*, Judgment of 29 April 2004; IACtHR, *The 'Las Dos Erres' Massacre v. Guatemala*, Judgment of 24 November 2009; IACtHR, *the Río Negro Massacres v. Guatemala*, Judgment of 4 September 2012; IACtHR, *Miembros de la Aldea de Chichupac y Comunidades Vecinas del Municipio de Rabinal v. Guatemala*, Judgment of 30 November 2016.

genocide. The judges argued that the Court was entitled to decide upon the infringement of the American Convention's provisions but lacked the jurisdiction and the historical fundamentals to determine whether specific acts of violence could be labelled genocide.[174] Indeed, in contrast to the ECtHR, which had to decide upon the infringement of Article 7 of the European Convention (the retroactive application of laws)—and was obliged to debate the definition of genocide and its applicability to the Lithuanian context of the 1950s—the IACtHR was asked to rule over articles of the American Convention, which did not necessarily require a discussion about the classification of crimes. According to the judges, by ruling on whether genocide had been committed or not, the IACtHR would have overstepped its jurisdiction.

Nevertheless, the Court's refusal to scrutinize the nature of the crimes was criticized by IACtHR judges known for their progressive anti-impunity jurisprudence. In 2004, in *Plan de Sánchez v. Guatemala*, Brazilian judge A.A. Cançado Trinidade formulated a separate opinion, arguing that the majority had been excessively formalistic and had failed to acknowledge the 'aggravated international responsibility of the state'.[175] Quoting from the CEH's Report and the Inter-American Commission's complaint at the IACtHR, Trinidade maintained that in order to grant victims full reparations and real access to the truth, the Court should have recognized, or at least engaged with, the nature of the crimes under international law. Moreover, the Court could have used the 1948 UN Convention and other norms of customary law to emphasize the aggravating circumstances surrounding violations of rights protected by the American Convention on Human Rights.[176] This argument was also endorsed by Guatemalan ad hoc judge Ramón Cadena Rámila in 2009 in the *Los Dos Erres* case. Following Trinidade, Rámila contended that the IACtHR should have acknowledged that Guatemala had infringed ICL conventions, such as the 1994 Inter-American Convention on Forced Disappearance of Persons or 1994 Convention of Belém do Pará on the eradication of violence against women.[177] Neither judge, however, explicitly ruled that genocide had been committed in Guatemala, their separate opinions emphasizing only the limits of the IACtHR's engagement with ICL and its inability to provide a coherent legal and historical narrative of the events in question.

[174] IACtHR, *Plan de Sánchez Massacre v. Guatemala*, Judgment of 29 April 2004, 7, 21; IACtHR, *the Río Negro Massacres v. Guatemala*, Judgment of 4 September 2012, p. 83.

[175] IACtHR, *Plan de Sánchez Massacre v. Guatemala*, Judgment of 29 April 2004, 'Separate Opinion of Judge A.A. Cançado Trinidade'.

[176] Ibid.

[177] IACtHR, *The 'Las Dos Erres' Massacre v. Guatemala*, Judgment of 24 November 2009, 'Concurring Opinion of Judge Ramón Cadena Rámila'.

7. Scholarly Divisions

Legal scholars analysing the jurisprudence on genocide in the three countries were also divided between those who found the departures from dominant international standards inacceptable and those with a more permissive attitude towards locally contextualized applications of ICL, particularly when fighting against entrenched impunity.

In 2017, German law scholar Kai Ambos criticized what he called 'the bad habits' of Eastern European, Spanish, and Latin American courts to expand established concepts of ICL, to create 'nonsensical' legal constructs, and to apply the law not according to the principles of the rule of law, but in a manner oriented towards 'policy, anti-impunity and *effet utile*'.[178] He also decried the position of the dissenting judges in *Vasiliauskas v. Lithuania* for endorsing such 'distortions'. He contended that such an approach deliberately ignored the political character of communist and military crimes, leading to absurd legal and historical claims:

> This view ignores that the driving force behind [the Soviet] repression is not nationality but political conviction, that is, the partisans are targeted as a political, not a national group. [. . .] [In Latin America,] this had led to the somewhat absurd claim that the Argentinean, Chilean and Uruguayan right-wing military perpetrators killed their fellow Argentinean, Chilean and Uruguayan left-wing victims because of their nationality, that is, Argentineans etc. killed Argentineans because of the common bond of nationality. This is, of course, nonsensical and conceals the fact that the nature of such criminality is political, that is, the political adversary is killed since the perpetrators want to exterminate the political ideology he/she stands for.[179]

Ambos stressed that such reasoning expanded the application of genocide to political groups and national liberation movements and consciously deviated from the intentions of the drafters of the 1948 UN Convention. Similar critiques were formulated by German international expert Christian Tomuschat and Spanish legal scholar Alicia Gil Gil who contended that Garzón and the Audiencia Nacional's 'controversial, expansive interpretation of genocide' amounted to a political act to change the interpretation the UN had given to

[178] Kai Ambos, 'The Crime of Genocide and the Principle of Legality under Article 7 of the European Court of Human Rights', *Human Rights Law Review* 17 (2017): pp. 175–186.

[179] Ibid, p. 183.

genocide in international law.[180] William Schabas also argued that Spanish courts went too far in considering any social group as protected by the Convention, because 'such reasoning leads to an absurdity that trivializes the very nature of genocide: the human race itself constitutes a protected group, and therefore genocide covers any mass killing'.[181] Looking at Argentina, Howard Schneider labelled Rozanski's verdict as 'tormented' reasoning which ignored all international legal standards.[182] In the Lithuanian case, scholars underlined that national judges sought to delegitimize the Soviet occupation at any price, including deviant interpretations of international law. Russian scholars were particularly vocal proponents of this point of view. They praised the majority decision in *Vasiliauskas v. Lithuania* for establishing the limits of the notion of genocide and curbing the instrumentalization of ICL to boost the Lithuanian 'national myth' and to equate the USSR with the Third Reich.[183]

In many cases, this criticism was rooted in the liberal tradition of the rule of law, which defends strict proceduralism and privileges the right of the defendant as important norms that would prevent the instrumentalization of law for political purposes. Some proponents, like Kai Ambos, had themselves been defence counsels for various individuals judged by international tribunals.[184] Others, like Christian Tomuschat, had taken bold positions against judicial activism and the role of domestic judges in changing international law. In his words: 'Domestic judges are not called upon to amend and change international law. Their true mandate is to apply the law conscientiously and objectively. Private, subjective preferences and wishes should not determine the substance of a decision which the judge is entrusted with giving'.[185] Such approaches have however proven impermeable to Global South critiques regarding the Eurocentric nature of ICL's origins and the construction of a supposed universalism that served Western political and epistemological domination. In the Lithuania case, battles over historical narratives regarding the Second World War and the legitimacy of the Soviet Union were also at stake.

[180] Christian Tomuschat, 'Issue of Universal Jurisdiction in the Scilingo Case', *Journal of International Criminal Justice* 3, no. 5 (2005): pp. 1074–1081, at p. 1080; Alicia Gil Gil, 'La sentencia de la Audiencia Nacional en el caso Scilingo', *Revista Electrónica de Ciencia Penal y Criminología* 7 (2005): pp. 1–18.

[181] Schabas, *Genocide in International Law*, p. 171.

[182] Schneider, 'Political Genocide', pp. 351, 353.

[183] Alexander Shamshiev, 'The European Court Is against the Lithuanian National Myth', available at www.rubaltic.ru/articles/lithuanian-national-myth-27102015/ (accessed 20 October 2023).

[184] Ambos defended Mladen Markač at the ICTY and Jean-Pierre Bemba Gombo at the ICC. Both were acquitted.

[185] Prof. Christian Tomuschat, Oral Submission before the Inter-national Court of Justice for Germany in Case Concerning Jurisdictional Immunities of the State (Germany v. Italy), 12 September 2011, quoted in Sharon Weill, *The Role of National Courts in Applying International Humanitarian Law* (Oxford: Oxford University Press, 2014): p. 157.

Critiques of the Guatemalan interpretation of genocide have been less frequent but mirrored existing complaints about overlapping groups—in this case ethnic and political. Anthropologist David Stoll, a controversial scholar who questioned the genocidal narrative of the Guatemalan conflict, argued that the massacres were committed against unarmed peasants who supported the guerrillas, and, while most of them were Mayan, others were Ladino. In Stoll's view,

> this would amount to genocide only if we stretch the international convention's protected classes of victims from racial, ethnic, national and religious to political groups. [. . .] But then the same reasoning makes the Guerrilla Army of the Poor guilty of genocide—for targeting the part of the Ixil population who objected to its political agenda, considerable number of whom was accused of serving as spies for the army and executed without judicial procedure.[186]

Jan Perlin has also emphasized that the CEH report did not clarify whether the violence had been committed in order to destroy an ethnicity or to politically and economically subjugate the Mayan population.[187] For these scholars, expanding the international definition of genocide implied retroactive readings of the law, a dilution of the concept of genocide itself, and the legitimization of dangerous behaviours on the part of judicial officials who assume legislative powers and amend international law.[188]

Other scholars celebrated, however, these developments in national jurisprudence as milestones against impunity. Ríos Montt's conviction was considered by most commenters as a landmark. While acknowledging the departures from the 1948 UN Convention through the inclusion of acts of cultural destruction and even the overlapping of political and ethnic groups, most academics saw these aspects as necessary innovations for rendering justice and exposing historical truth.[189] One possible driver of this consensus might be that most of these analysts—such as Naomi Roht-Arriaza, Jo-Marie Burt, Susan Kemp, and Marta Casáus Arzú—had themselves been involved in transnational movements against impunity in Guatemala or in mobilizations

[186] David Stoll, 'Guatemala: Was It Genocide?', available at http://sites.middlebury.edu/dstoll/files/2013/10/Guatemala-Was-It-Genocide.pdf (accessed 20 October 2023).

[187] Perlin, "The Guatemalan Historical Clarification Commission", p. 411.

[188] Schabas, *Genocide in International Law*, p. 171; Schneider, 'Political Genocide', p. 352; Ambos, 'The Crime of Genocide', p. 183; Rafecas, 'La reapertura', p. 171.

[189] See Naomi Roht-Arriaza, 'Genocide and War Crimes in National Courts: The Conviction of Rios Montt in Guatemala and Its Aftermath', *ASIL Insights* 17, no. 14 (2013); Jo-Marie Burt, 'From Heaven to Hell'; Susan Kemp, 'Guatemala', Marta Casáus Arzú, 'Sobre la presunción de intencionalidad o propósito de destruir a un grupo étnico como tal', *La Hora*, 19 April 2013.

for Indigenous rights.[190] The annulment of Ríos Montt's conviction also led scholars to sympathize with the victims, rather than engage in critiques of the verdict. Certain scholars prized Garzón's jurisprudence for offering a legitimate and valuable strategy for combatting impunity in Latin America, even if he had departed from the international standards on genocide.[191] In terms of Lithuania, William Schabas endorsed the concept of *ethno-national-political genocide* and its applicability to repression of national liberation movements—a position taken by most Baltic academics.[192] These scholars contended that international customary law provided at least some basis for including crimes against political groups and acts of cultural genocide. Moreover, they preferred novel (albeit problematic) interpretations of ICL that fought against impunity to more conventional readings of ICL that maintained the status quo.

Beyond their echoes at regional human rights courts and in the academic literature, it is hard to anticipate the consequences of these novel interpretations on coming jurisprudence. Rejected by the Grand Chamber yet endorsed by the Fourth Section of the ECtHR, the Lithuanian concept of *ethno-national-political genocide* could be borrowed to classify mass crimes against national liberation movements in former Soviet Republics and former Western colonies (such as French crimes in Algeria, Portuguese crimes in Angola, Dutch crimes in Indonesia, and British crimes in Kenya). Argentinian judges promoted their interpretation of genocide at conferences and professional workshops across Latin America and in Cambodia, Bangladesh, and Sri Lanka.[193] Yet, with the global proliferation of the classification of crimes against political opponents as crimes against humanity, the concept of *ideological auto-genocide* is unlikely to take hold in other jurisdictions. Conversely, the Guatemalan verdict could be a valuable resource for building cases that include acts of *cultural genocide* against Indigenous groups alongside their physical and biological destruction and thereby connect 'mental harm' and 'conditions of life' to the destruction of their culture and social cohesion.

[190] Naomi Roht-Arriaza was a member of the Center for Justice and Accountability, an organization that helped Guatemalan victims construct cases before the Spanish Court and the IACtHR. Susan Kemp was Legal Director of CALDH, and Jo-Marie Burt was a militant academic.

[191] Roht-Arriaza, *The Pinochet Effect*, pp. 47–49.

[192] Satkauskas, 'Soviet Genocide Trials'; Žilinskas, 'Vasiliauskas'.

[193] Personal interview with Carlos Rozanski, La Plata, Argentina, 16 June 2016.

4

Strategies for Internationalizing Justice

> We had various transnational meetings to discuss the creation of a European tribunal for communist crimes. However, there was no real debate about how it could be established, where it should be based, what legislation should be used, and who would fund it. In the end, these meetings were about political discourses. It soon became clear that a real strategy for criminal justice would remain in the national sphere.
>
> Luciana Jinga, Romanian historian and activist[1]

> Many people saw the Argentinian investigations into Francoist crimes as rocambolesque and without sense. But this was far from being true. The case put pressure on Spanish authorities to reflect on the new international doctrines about the duty to prosecute major international crimes and even to interrogate potential accused. It also generated new debates about universal jurisdiction and its future in the Global South.
>
> Aitor Martínez Jiménez, Spanish human rights lawyer[2]

1. Introduction

In their quest for justice and the international legal recognition of their countries' violent past, Central Eastern European (CEE) and Latin American activists also mobilized beyond their national borders, building upon and reformulating Cold War strategies of transnationalizing justice. While Chapters 2 and 3 emphasized the stories of convergence between the two regions, the analysis of transnational mobilizations in this chapter highlights how distinct regional historical contexts, political aims, and ideological underpinnings generated dissimilar approaches to internationalizing justice—with

[1] Personal interview with Luciana Jinga, online, 8 February 2022.
[2] Personal interview with Aitor Martínez Jiménez, Asunción, Paraguay, 4 February 2015.

Justice and Memory after Dictatorship. Raluca Grosescu, Oxford University Press.
DOI: 10.1093/oso/9780192870346.003.0004

different impacts on international criminal law (ICL). CEE actors focused their mobilizations on the European level, particularly after their accession to the European Union from 2004 onwards. They lobbied for the establishment of an international tribunal for communist crimes, a legal instrument to parallel the Nuremberg trials. Through this initiative, they sought to contest a Western historical narrative based on the uniqueness of the Holocaust and to impose an equal legal and political treatment of Nazi and communist crimes. CEE mobilizations at a European level assumed a bold anti-communist stance, often connected to radical conservative politics. They particularly targeted political institutions such as the European Parliament and the European Commission, whereas mobilizations at the European Court of Human Rights were rare, as were their attempts to transnationalize criminal and civil litigations. CEE memory entrepreneurs ultimately managed to enforce a totalitarian interpretation of communism in European assemblies and to reshape the EU's remembrance policy, but failed to create an international tribunal for communist crimes. Their impact on the international justice system remained marginal.

In contrast, since the 1970s, and especially after the mid-1990s, Latin American activists deployed a variety of anti-impunity tactics and legitimized their cause through a liberal humanitarian discourse on human rights. They renounced the 1960s and early 1970s narrative of radical leftist resistance against structural socio-economic oppression and inequality and instead emphasized a moral and legal duty to punish gross human rights violations, no matter the ideology behind those crimes. They addressed the Inter-American System of Human Rights to fight impunity at home and sought prosecutions in foreign courts based on universal jurisdiction. Through their efforts in various Western European courts and the alliances they forged with progressive (and often left-wing oriented) Western lawyers and judicial officials, Latin American activists reinforced and promoted universal jurisdiction as a principle of ICL. Moreover, in response to the restriction of universal jurisdiction statutes in Western European countries such as Belgium and Spain, Argentina assumed a leading role in transnational justice efforts at the global level. Since 2009, Argentinian courts have initiated criminal investigations based on universal jurisdiction in a variety of cases, including Franco-era crimes in Spain, human rights violations under Alfredo Stroessner's dictatorship in Paraguay, crimes committed by Chinese authorities against the Falun Gong religious sect, and mass repression against the Rohingya ethnic group in Myanmar. These cases renewed hopes for victims of political repression around the world that their voices would still be heard, even if only in Argentina, a semi-peripheral country of the Global South. However, they also reflected a political use of universal jurisdiction, as right-wing and left-wing lawyers selected different cases to advance their political goals and their historical understandings of the past.

2. Limits of Internationalizing Justice during the Cold War

After the Nuremberg and the Tokyo trials, the internationalization of justice for major international crimes continued steadily, although with a limited impact on the formation of a global anti-impunity ethos. Tactics such as transnational and civil litigation, efforts to impose a prosecutorial regime based on universal jurisdiction, and demands for the establishment of international tribunals were important Cold War precedents that inspired Latin American and CEE justice activists in the 1990s and the 2000s, who then tried to expand them further.

Starting in 1945, the criminal trials of Nazi officials held in occupation courts or in the domestic courts of victim nations were the most frequent form of transnational justice. Under the 1945 Control Council Law No. 10, the Allies established occupation tribunals in Germany and judged some 8,812 Germans and Austrians accused of war crimes and crimes against humanity.[3] While not without flaws, Law No. 10 and the subsequent trials[4] wrote new jurisprudence based on the Nuremberg principles and categories of international crimes. In addition, between 1945 and 1949, domestic courts in victim nations across Europe prosecuted more than 60,000 Nazi officials.[5] These cases often entailed the extradition of the accused on ICL charges (particularly war crimes) and consolidated the legitimacy of transnational criminal prosecutions based on the territoriality principle—the right of a state to judge foreign nationals who committed crimes on its territory.

In 1961, the Adolf Eichmann trial marked a turning point in the transnationalization of criminal justice. Kidnapped from Argentina by the Israeli national intelligence service, Adolf Eichmann was accused of crimes

[3] Devin O. Pendas, 'Retroactive Law and Proactive Justice: Debating Crimes against Humanity in Germany, 1945–1950', *Central European History* 43, no. 3 (2010): pp. 428–463, at p. 429. Pendas acknowledges that the numbers might be underestimated.

[4] Trials conducted by Soviet occupation tribunals were decried for violating basic principles of the rule of law. Trials held under American jurisdiction were criticized for imposing the application of ordinary German law to Nazi offenses and abandoning jurisprudence based on ICL. See Pendas, 'Retroactive Law', p. 431.

[5] Pendas, 'Retroactive Law', p. 429. The Soviet Union also put a number of Japanese army officers on trial. Similar trials took place in the Dutch Indies and China. See Kirsten Sellars, ed., *Trials for International Crimes in Asia* (Cambridge: Cambridge University Press, 2016).

against humanity and crimes against the Jewish People, based on the 1950 Israeli Nazis and Nazi Collaborators (Punishment) Law. Given that the crimes had been committed outside Israel by a non-Israeli national, the court justified its jurisdiction through the doctrine of passive personality—namely the right of a state to bring to trial a foreign national for offences committed abroad against its own citizens. Aware, however, of critiques that Israel did not yet exist at the time when the crimes were committed, the court also made use of the principle of universal jurisdiction. It ruled that crimes against humanity were so abhorrent that any state had the standing to judge the perpetrators of such crimes, irrespective of the existence of a territorial or personal link between the respective state and the offenders or their victims. Such a ruling contradicted the dominant UN doctrine at the time, since the principle of universal jurisdiction had not yet been included in any ICL conventions, and most states clearly opposed it. From this perspective, the Eichmann trial was an important precedent which moved the law forward on the question of universal jurisdiction, setting aside the narrow jurisdictional frames of existing ICL instruments.[6] Nevertheless, as some scholars have underlined, the 1950 Law on Nazis and Nazi Collaborators, under which Eichmann was charged, covered only crimes committed by the Axis powers during the Second World War. In this sense, the trial reflected a limited understanding of the universality principle.[7]

During the Cold War, universal civil jurisdiction also gained a foothold in the United States through the landmark case *Filártiga v. Peña-Irala*, a 1980 civil case that litigated the gross human rights violations committed in Paraguay under Stroessner's regime. In 1976, Américo Peña-Irala, a police officer, tortured to death Joelito Filártiga, a Paraguayan national, in retaliation for his father's anti-Stroessner political activities. In 1978, both Peña-Irala and Joelito's sister, Dolly Filártiga, emigrated to the United States. In 1979, Dolly brought a civil lawsuit against Peña-Irala. She was assisted by the Center for Constitutional Rights (CCR), a progressive legal advocacy organization established in 1966 that specialized in strategic litigations to fight human rights

[6] Leora Bilsky, 'The Eichmann Trial and the Legacy of Jurisdiction', in *Politics in Dark Times: Encounters with Hannah Arendt*, edited by Seyla Benhabib (Cambridge: Cambridge University Press, 2010): pp. 198–218; William Schabas, 'The Contribution of the Eichmann Trial to International Criminal Law', *Leiden Journal of International Law* 26 (2013): pp. 667–699; Matthew Lippman, 'The Trial of Adolf Eichmann and the Protection of Universal Human Rights under International Law', *Huston Journal of International Law* 5, no. 1 (1982): pp. 1–34.

[7] Theodor Meron, 'Public International Law Problems and the Jurisdiction of the State of Israel', *Journal du Droit International* 88, no. 2 (1961): pp. 1054–1056; Gary J. Bass, 'The Adolf Eichmann Case: Universal and National Jurisdiction', in *Universal Jurisdiction: National Courts and the Prosecution of Serious Crimes under International Law*, edited by Stephen Macedo (Philadelphia: Pennsylvania University Press, 2004), pp. 75–90.

violations and economic injustices. The CCR reactivated a US federal law from 1789, the Alien Tort Statute, that gives federal courts jurisdiction to hear lawsuits filed by a foreign national for torts committed in violation of international law. It argued that based on universal jurisdiction, US civil courts had the right to hold perpetrators responsible for major international crimes committed abroad. In 1980, the United States Court of Appeals of the Second Circuit upheld the argument and ordered Peña to pay Dolly Filártiga over 10 million USD in damages. Peña ultimately left the United States without paying a penny, but the case set the precedent for applying the Alien Tort Statute in transnational civil litigations, thus advancing the principle of universal civil jurisdiction.[8]

Debates on the establishment of a prosecutorial regime based on universal jurisdiction also took place at the UN. After failed attempts to include such a principle in the 1948 Genocide Convention and the 1949 Geneva Conventions, some progress was made in the 1970s and the 1980s. In 1973, an alliance at the UN between CEE socialist countries and the Afro-Asian bloc led to the adoption of the International Convention on the Suppression and Punishment of the Crime of Apartheid (the Apartheid Convention). For the first time, an international ICL instrument included the principle of universal jurisdiction—meaning that any citizen participating in the crime of apartheid could be prosecuted for this offence in any state party to the Convention. This was a radical change compared to previous ICL instruments, which restricted jurisdiction to the states where the crime was committed or to an international tribunal established by the UN. However, the Apartheid Convention remained a marginal and controversial document, as Western countries never ratified it. This resistance was due both to political reasons (Western powers, such as Great Britain and the United States, continued to support the racist South African state) and legal arguments (the categories of offences were deemed overly broad, sanctioning almost any form of cooperation with South Africa, including economic exchange).[9] The Apartheid Convention moved forward the international discussion surrounding universal jurisdiction but did not bring forth a global consensus. Furthermore, no participant in the apartheid regime was ever prosecuted in South Africa or abroad.

The 1984 UN Convention against Torture also included the principle of universal jurisdiction but in a more restrictive way than the Apartheid

[8] William J. Aveces, *The Anatomy of Torture: A Documentary History of Filártiga v. Peña-Irala* (Leiden: Martinus Nijhoff, 2007); Anna Su, 'The Rise and Fall of Universal Jurisdiction', *Human Rights Quarterly* 41, no. 4 (2019): pp. 849–872.

[9] Ariel Bultz, 'Redefining Apartheid in International Criminal Law', *Criminal Law Forum* 24 (2013): pp. 205–233.

Convention. According to Bassiouni, this document is more a reflection of the duty to 'extradite or prosecute' than of universal jurisdiction: only in the event that an individual is not extradited is a state compelled to prosecute by relying on universal jurisdiction.[10] The Torture Convention did not include a 'pure' form of universal jurisdiction, but achieved the greatest consensus among the Cold War-era ICL instruments that imposed a duty to extradite or prosecute. Due to this broad-based acceptance, the Torture Convention became the key international document upon which the British courts relied in their decision to extradite Augusto Pinochet to Spain in 1999 (see *infra*).

The Cold War period also witnessed demands for the establishment of a permanent international court or ad hoc international tribunals for specific political contexts. At the UN, the attempts to create a permanent international criminal court post-Nuremberg were halted in 1954 due to Cold War tensions. Debates about the creation of such an institution re-emerged in the 1970s and 1980s, but again conflicts between East and West and now between North and South impeded any concrete results. In 1979, based on the provisions of the Apartheid Convention, the UN Commission on Human Rights appointed ICL expert M. Cherif Bassiouni to draft the statute of an international criminal tribunal for the crime of apartheid. The Commission accepted the draft in 1980, but debates about its enforcement were discontinued as Western powers critiqued the initiative as a political weapon against South Africa.[11]

During the Cold War, numerous other violent political regimes—the communist regimes in CEE and the military dictatorships in Latin America among them—generated claims for international justice. As early as the 1940s and 1950s, Eastern European exile communities in the United States and Western Europe, alongside anti-communist organizations sponsored by the National Committee for a Free Europe, denounced political repression in state socialist regimes and called for the establishment of an international tribunal to prosecute the alleged Soviet genocide against Eastern European nations. Such demands were formulated by organizations driven by nationalism, pro-Americanism, and an ideological opposition to Marxism, and were often echoed at the UN by US and British representatives.[12] Given Moscow's veto power in the Security Council, such initiatives remained nothing more than a

[10] M. Cherif Bassiouni, 'The History of Universal Jurisdiction and Its Place in International Law', in *Universal Jurisdiction: National Courts and the Prosecution of Serious Crimes under International Law*, edited by Stephen Macedo (Philadelphia: Pennsylvania University Press, 2004): pp. 39–63, at p. 55.

[11] M. Cherif Bassiouni, 'Chronology of Efforts to Establish an International Criminal Court', *Revue Internationale de Droit Penal* 86, nos. 3–4 (2015): pp. 1163–1194.

[12] Ieva Zake, ed., *Anti-Communist Minorities in the US: Political Activism of Ethnic Refugees* (New York: Palgrave Macmillan, 2009).

'trial by word'.[13] These claims lost their intensity during late socialism, but they were revived by CEE justice and memory entrepreneurs after the end of the Cold War, as this chapter will illustrate.

Starting in the early 1970s, transnational solidarity movements centred on the victims of Latin American military dictatorships formulated their own demands for international justice and the international criminalization of enforced disappearances. At the beginning of their mobilization, many of these networks were anti-American and ideologically inclined to Third Worldism and Marxism,[14]—in contrast to the pro-American, anti-communist activism. Their calls for justice were often supported at the UN by the CEE socialist states, as well as lawyers and intellectuals with socialist orientations. Still, the establishment of an international tribunal for political crimes committed in the Southern Cone was never a significant topic on the UN agenda. The 1970s marked the deradicalization of the left across the world and the rise of a liberal human rights discourse based on the defence of civil and political rights, a movement that was increasingly supported by global NGOs and liberal as well as conservative politicians. This international current, as well as the growing interaction between Latin American human rights defenders and liberal NGOs, such as Amnesty International and Human Rights Watch, caused Latin American activists to ideologically reframe their cause. They abandoned their 1960s and early 1970s radical resistance to structural socio-economic oppression and inequality, and instead focused on the struggle for civil–political rights against dictatorship. This new approach thereby aligned these activists with the emergent liberal humanitarian vocabulary of human rights which focused on the defence of individual rights and the moral obligation to empathize with all victims of oppressive regimes, irrespective of their political conviction.[15]

Starting in 1976, the weekly protests of the Madres de la Plaza del Mayo in Buenos Aires to demand information about the fate of their disappeared children gained wide international support, including from the American government and the Vatican. In 1977, Amnesty International—in collaboration with lawyers from Argentina and Chile—initiated an international campaign against enforced disappearances in Latin America. Other global NGOs, such as the

[13] Anton Weiss-Wendt, *A Rhetorical Crime: Genocide in the Geopolitical Discourse of the Cold War* (New Brunswick, NJ: Rutgers University Press, 2018): pp. 30–49.

[14] Alison Brysk, *The Politics of Human Rights in Argentina: Protest, Change and Democratization* (Stanford: Stanford University Press, 1994): p. 46.

[15] Vania Markarian, *Left in Transformation: Uruguayan Exiles and the Latin American Human Rights Networks, 1967–1984* (New York: Routledge, 2005).

International Federation of Human Rights and the International Commission of Jurists, as well as Western European governments—including France and the Nordic states—joined the initiative. This mobilization generated the establishment of a UN Working Group against Enforced Disappearances in 1980,[16] with the mission to assist families in determining the whereabouts of disappeared relatives. One year later, the Latin American Federation of Associations for Relatives of the Detained-Disappeared (FEDEFAM) was established in San José, Costa Rica, to advocate for the adoption of an international convention that would criminalize enforced disappearances as a crime against humanity.

During its second congress held in Caracas in November 1981, FEDEFAM gathered a group of international lawyers to prepare a first draft of such a convention.[17] European–Latin American solidarity networks also organized various colloquiums across Europe to push for the adoption of a UN instrument against enforced disappearances. In 1988, these efforts resulted in a first draft of the declaration for the UN Convention against Enforced Disappearances submitted by UN legal expert Luis Joinet to the UN Commission on Human Rights. Further mobilizations led to the adoption by the UN General Assembly of the Declaration on the Protection of all Persons from Enforced Disappearance (1992) and the Inter-American and the UN conventions against enforced disappearances in 1994 and 2006, respectively.

After the fall of the various dictatorships in Latin America and CEE, pro-accountability actors from both regions renewed their calls for justice, transnationalizing their mobilizations and demands, as domestic political and legal constraints hindered prosecutions at home. As we shall see below, they used and further developed Cold War precedents and, in the case of Latin American activists, pushed forward the theoretical debates and legal practice of universal jurisdiction.

3. Central Eastern Europe: The Nuremberg Obsession and Conservative Politics

After the end of communist regimes in CEE, justice and memory entrepreneurs across the region adopted two strategies of internationalizing justice, which were intensified after 2004 as former socialist countries acceded to the

[16] For these efforts, see Anne Marie Clark, *Diplomacy of Conscience: Amnesty International and Changing Human Rights Norms* (Princeton: Princeton University Press, 2011): pp. 70–100.

[17] Sophie Baby, *Juger Franco? Une approche transnationale, 1936–2010,* Habilitation à diriger des recherches (Paris: Université Sorbonne Nouvelle, 2022): pp. 269 and 271.

European Union. The first was deployed from the early 1990s onwards and targeted the establishment of a European tribunal that would replicate Nuremberg and ensure a similar treatment of Nazi and communist crimes. It aimed to enforce a historical narrative that equated the two 'totalitarianisms'—Stalinism and Nazism—and challenged the prevailing Western European narrative constructed around the uniqueness of the Holocaust as the absolute evil.[18]

The second strategy was deployed since the 2010s and envisaged transnational criminal trials based on the passive personality principle. It comprised complaints lodged in Germany and Poland against former Czechoslovak communist officials accused of the murder of East German and Polish citizens attempting to illegally cross the Czechoslovak border into the West. In these later cases, CEE justice entrepreneurs mobilized the paradigm of refugee victimhood that had gained momentum across Europe during the Syrian refugee crisis in 2015. They presented all those who had tried to cross the Iron Curtain into the West as refugees and victims of murderous communist regimes. CEE justice strategies were often accompanied by discourses that downplayed the participation of CEE states in the extermination of their Jewish communities and presented Middle Eastern refugees as a threat to a 'white and Christian' Europe. In addition, anti-communist memory entrepreneurs sought not only to achieve justice for the political crimes committed under communism but also to delegitimize any kind of neo-Marxist political thought.

3.1 Failed Attempts to Establish an International Tribunal for Communist Crimes

During the 1990s, demands for a 'Nuremberg Trial for communist crimes' were formulated in almost all CEE countries by regime victims and militants for decommunization, who aspired to the establishment of an international tribunal that would adjudicate communist crimes and condemn communist ideology. This communality of claims was rooted in several factors: many former communist elites retained their political and economic power in the post-communist period and opposed measures of radical decommunization. This elite continuity delayed investigations into communist crimes, and

[18] Laure Neumayer, 'Integrating the Central European Past into a Common Narrative: The Mobilizations around the "Crimes of Communism" in the European Parliament', *Journal of Contemporary European Studies* 23, no. 3 (2015): pp. 344–363; Maria Mälksoo, *The Politics of Becoming European: A Study of Polish and Baltic Post-Cold War Security Imaginaries* (London: Routledge, 2010).

subsequently to the very small number of trials.[19] Even in the Baltic states, which adopted broad legislative packages to condemn the double Nazi and Soviet occupation, the number of convictions for Stalinist crimes remained low.[20] Within this context, narratives about an 'unfinished revolution', which allowed former communists to maintain power and evade justice, were prominent and sometimes used by right-wing politicians to delegitimize their leftist opponents.[21] Moreover, hopes for a 'Nuremberg Trial for communist crimes' emerged from the quest to gain support from the EU to pressure Russia into acknowledging its responsibility for the imposition of communist regimes in the region and for the Soviet occupation of the Baltic states. This narrative was often accompanied by a condemnation of 'the Western betrayal of Eastern Europe' in the aftermath of the Second World War, since it had allowed the expansion of the Soviet domination in CEE.[22]

During the 1990s, liberal and conservative intellectuals, former dissidents, and members of the former exile communities transnationalized these claims through international conferences, commemorations, summer schools, and joint publications.[23] Once the recognition of the Holocaust became a precondition for accession to the European Union, anti-communist activists built their demands on a Cold War historical narrative that equated Stalinism and Nazism. They denounced the putative double standard in the political, moral, and legal judgment of Nazism and Stalinism at a European level.[24] While some Western European and American intellectuals were also involved in these transnational networks, the equation of Nazism and communism remained problematic in the West.[25] From its initial phase, the CEE anti-communist mobilization was thus at odds with various Western political and intellectual groups who were either leftist or supported the narrative of the uniqueness of the Holocaust.

[19] Lavinia Stan, ed., *Transitional Justice in Eastern Europe and Former Soviet Union: Reckoning with the Communist Past* (New York: Routledge, 2009).

[20] Seven in Latvia, eleven in Estonia, and around thirty in Lithuania until the mid-2000s. Eva Clarita Pettai and Vello Pettai, *Transitional and Retrospective Justice in the Baltic States* (Cambridge: Cambridge University Press, 2014): pp. 85–86.

[21] James Mark, *The Unfinished Revolution: Making Sense of the Communist Past in Central-Eastern* (New Haven: Yale University Press, 2014).

[22] Maria Mälksoo, 'The Memory Politics of Becoming European: The East European Subalterns and the Collective Memory of Europe', *European Journal of International Relations* 15, no. 4 (2009): pp. 653–680.

[23] Valentin Behr, Muriel Blaive, Anenoma Constantin, Laure Neumayer, and Máté Zombory, 'Anti-Communist Consensus: The Black Book of Communism in Pan-European Perspective', *Revue d'Études Comparative Est-Ouest* 2–3, nos. 2–3 (2020): pp. 55–88.

[24] Neumayer, 'Integrating the Central European Past'.

[25] Małgorzata Pakier and Bo Straåth, eds., *A European Memory? Contested Histories and Politics of Remembrance* (New York: Berghahn, 2010).

The EU accession of CEE countries accelerated the transnationalization and visibility of anti-communist discourses. Various institutes of national memory (INMs) created across the region to investigate and raise awareness about communist crimes began to elaborate collective strategies for dealing with the past on a European level. The Czech Institute for the Study of Totalitarian Regimes (USTR) was particularly active in this transnationalization process. In 2008, the USTR organized, with the support of the Czech Ministry of European Affairs, an international conference, during which participants—many of them coming from INMs—adopted the Prague Declaration on European Conscience and Totalitarianism. The document called for a pan-European condemnation of the crimes of communism, in line with the Nuremberg trials's condemnation of Nazi crimes. It asked for the establishment of an Institute of European Memory and Conscience that would study both 'totalitarianisms'. It also proposed the establishment of 23 August (the day the Molotov–Ribbentrop Pact was signed in 1939) as a day of remembrance for the victims of both Nazi and communist regimes. The Declaration was later signed by more than 7,500 individuals, including former anti-communist dissents, and liberal and conservative intellectuals and politicians from both Eastern and Western Europe.[26]

At a European level, a small group of conservative CEE members of the European Parliament (MEPs) pushed for the adoption of the Prague Declaration's principles by European institutions. Former anti-communist dissidents, such as Sandra Kalniete (Latvia), Vytautas Landsbergis (Lithuania), Tune Kelam (Estonia), and László Tőkés (Romania), lobbied MEPs across political and national lines to endorse a resolution that condemned the two European 'totalitarianisms'. These former dissidents had already called for the international judgment of communist crimes in the mid-2000s, but their campaign lacked a legal strategy. For instance, in 2008, they asked for the creation of a European investigative committee for communist crimes that would lodge complaints with the International Criminal Court (ICC)—a jurisdiction that could not investigate crimes committed before 2002. Additionally, they pointed to other potential judicial venues, such as the European Court of Human Rights and even the International Court of Justice,[27] neither of which had any competency in matters of criminal justice. Lastly, their calls for the creation of a European tribunal did not find any consensus beyond the post-communist right-wing politicians.

[26] *Declaration on European Conscience and Communism* (Prague, 2008).

[27] Laure Neumayer, *Criminalising Communism in the European Political Space after the Cold War* (London: Routledge, 2018): pp. 197 and 216.

In 2009, heated debates over the EP's endorsement of the Prague Declaration continued to reflect the East–West divisions surrounding the history of the Second World War and the uniqueness of the Holocaust. At the same time, tensions between right and left on the political spectrum emerged with regard to the equation of Nazism and communism and the application of the totalitarian paradigm to the wide spectrum of communisms that existed during the twentieth century.[28] Nevertheless, a compromise was reached when the EP adopted the Resolution of European Conscience and Totalitarianism by a large majority. The resolution acknowledged the uniqueness of the Holocaust, but condemned all totalitarian regimes in Europe (including former fascist regimes in Spain, Portugal, and Greece), and highlighted the magnitude of the crimes of communism. In addition, it established 23 August as a day of remembrance for the victims of all 'totalitarian' and 'authoritarian' regimes and called for the creation of a European-funded institution in charge of the memory of these regimes.[29]

The Resolution did not, however, mention the creation of a European tribunal for communist crimes. Such an initiative was considered by MEPs across the political spectrum to be too expensive and unnecessary, given that communist regimes were no longer a threat to contemporary Europe. Other MEPs argued that a tribunal was unsuitable as CEE countries had taken a range of different approaches to reckoning with their dictatorial past, from trials to amnesties and pardons. In their view, this diversity of approaches presented a political and legal obstacle to pan-European criminal justice initiatives for dealing with the memory of repressive regimes.[30] In short, the Resolution of European Conscience and Totalitarianism had a symbolic value, as it acknowledged the criminality of communist regimes at a European level, but no practical effect in terms of internationalizing justice. Furthermore, the Resolution's call for a European-funded institution centred around the legacy of 'totalitarianisms' was never realized.

In response, in 2010, the USTR decided to establish a transnational NGO that would gather together different institutions from Eastern and Western Europe to enforce a pan-European memory of 'communist criminality' and eventually achieve international justice. The NGO was named the Platform of European Memory and Conscience (the Platform). Its charter was signed in 2011 by almost all INMs in CEE, as well as Western NGOs engaged in the

[28] Neumayer, 'Integrating the Central European Past'.

[29] European Parliament 2009, 'Resolution of 29 April 2009 on European Conscience and Totalitarianism'.

[30] Neumayer, *Criminalising Communism*, pp. 181–182.

anti-communist memory cause.[31] Swedish conservative MEP Goran Lindblad was elected president, and Czech activist and politician Neela Winkelmann-Heyrovská was elected managing director. Winkelmann-Heyrovská had worked for the USTR and had played an important role in the preparation of both the Prague Declaration in 2008 and the EP Resolution of European Conscience and Totalitarianism in 2009. She was the main driver of the Platform's activity,[32] alongside an executive board of current and former conservative MEPs—Sandra Kalniete, Vytautas Landsbergis, Tune Kelam, and László Tőkés among them.

The Platform's representatives were united by a radical anti-communism that went beyond the condemnation of CEE dictatorial regimes. It aimed instead to denounce socialist regimes as 'totalitarian' regardless of national contexts and historical period. The Platform's representatives frequently called for the prohibition of Marx's works and equated Marxist and Nazi ideologies. For instance, Martin Mejstřík, a former Czech anti-communist dissident who played an important role in the establishment of both the USTR and the Platform, declared in 2010:

> Oh, yes, our academic and intellectual Marxists today are getting a free ride. They get a certain respect by mouthing rhetoric about improving the lot of the worker and the poor, their utopian pretensions. But whenever empowered, Marxism has failed utterly, as has fascism. Marxists deserve no respect, no tolerance. They should be treated as though they hope for the return of the Red Plague, which they do.[33]

On various occasions, other members of the Platform gave similar declarations,[34] which antagonized not only leftist politicians and intellectuals but also more liberal activists engaged in dealing with the communist past.

The Platform implemented transnational educational programmes that drew parallels between Nazi and communist crimes, and lobbied European and national political elites to create an international tribunal and acknowledge the

[31] In 2011, the Platform encompassed eighteen institutes of national remembrance from CEE, as well as one from Sweden and one Dutch NGO. In 2015, it had fifty-one members, including institutes and NGOs from Moldova, Russia, Ukraine, the United States, and Canada.

[32] Zoltan Dujisin, 'A History of Post-communist Remembrance: From Memory Politics to the Emergence of a Field of Anticommunism', *Theory and Society* 50, no. 1 (2021): pp. 65–96.

[33] Martin Mejstřík, 'Untitled Speech', in *International Conference: Crimes of the Communist Regimes. An Assessment by Historian and Legal Experts. Proceedings* (Prague: Institute of the Study of Totalitarian Regimes, 2011): p. 36.

[34] See for instance Zsolt Szilágyi's (member of the Executive Board of the Platform) statement in the 2019 Annual Report, available at www.memoryandconscience.eu, p. 8.

structural proximity of Nazism and communism. It also appointed a team of legal advisers—all scholars of international criminal law or European human rights law—to develop strategies for internationalizing justice. However, in contrast to the Latin American lawyers who—as we will see below—defended and publicly promoted their strategies, the Platform's lawyers were far more prudent and were often in disagreement about the best solutions for bringing perpetrators to justice. In many cases, it was in fact Neela Winkelmann-Heyrovská who led the Platform's strategies and not the lawyers themselves.

Legal advisers of the Platform of European Memory and Conscience:

Prof. Albin Eser, Director Emeritus of the Max Planck Institute of Foreign and International Criminal Law in Freiburg, Germany. A former judge at the ICTY and a member of the German delegation at the negotiations of the ICC's Statute in 1998, he was an expert in international criminal law, and the co-author of leading commentaries of the German criminal code.
Prof. Frank Meyer, Department of Criminal Law and Criminal Procedure Law at the University of Zurich, was an expert in jurisdictional conflicts in criminal matters in the European Union.
Dr. Nina Bruskina, Institute of International and European Union Law at the University of Vilnius, was an expert in the ECtHR's jurisprudence and has written critically about the ECtHR's alleged double standard in treating Nazi and communist crimes.
Dr. Jernej Letnar Černič was a lecturer in human rights law at Graduate School of Government and European Studies in Slovenia and a specialist in transitional justice in CEE, particularly the former Yugoslavia. In 2018, Černič left the Platform, arguing that it was too close to Viktor Orbán's government.
Dr. Roberta Arnold, University of Zurich, was a specialist in international criminal law. While she was not formally tied to the Platform, she assisted on several occasions in the drafting of the legal strategy.
The law firm Derra, Meyer & Partner, Berlin, was hired to draft criminal complaints in Germany.

As early as 2011, during their respective presidencies of the Council of the EU, the Hungarian and Polish governments put dealing with communist crimes on the agenda; the government of Lithuania did the same in 2013, asking for a European tribunal for communist crimes. Nevertheless, such actions had no effect as the European institutions emphasized the lack of consensus among the member states over 'best practices' for dealing with violent pasts. At a conference organized by the Platform at the EP in 2012, legal adviser Jernej Letnar Černič warned that creating a European tribunal was unlikely due to limited political support and funding from most Western and Eastern governments.[35] As emphasized in the quote introducing this chapter, Luciana Jinga, who represented the Romanian Institute for the Investigation of Communist Crimes at several Platform meetings, argued that the debates around a Nuremberg trial for communist crimes were primarily political and lacked legal focus.[36] Vasil Kadrinov, who represented the only Bulgarian institutional member of the Platform, the Hannah Arendt Centre in Sofia, also became disenchanted with this strategy:

> A Nuremberg trial for communist crimes was omnipresent in the Platform's discussions, but it was a dead end. The Czech and Estonian governments put the issue on the European agenda when they held the presidencies of the EU, but in the end, this remained a Visegrád discourse without real consequences.[37]

In 2015, two years before Estonia assumed presidency of the Council of the EU, the Estonian minister of justice announced his support for the creation of an international tribunal. He organized a meeting with representatives from the ministries of justice of Latvia, Lithuania, Poland, Czechia, Slovakia, Hungary, and Georgia in Tallinn. The group adopted the Tallin Declaration which called for the creation of an international 'Council for Investigation of Crimes of Communist Regimes' (CICROC). Debates about the CICROC continued at governmental level, particularly within the Visegrád group, and during the Estonian presidency of the Council of the EU in 2017, with several meetings organized to draft a statute and discuss funding. According to Illimar Lepik von Wirén, an Estonian government consultant in charge of preparing these meetings, the initiative was both rooted in lobbying for a pan-European

[35] Jernej Letnar Černič, 'Mass Killings, Torture, Mass Graves in the EU', Paper Presented at the International Conference Legal Settlements of Communist Crimes, European Parliament, Brussels, 5 June 2012.

[36] Personal interview with Luciana Jinga, online, 8 February 2022.

[37] Personal interview with Vasil Kadrinov, Sofia, Bulgaria, 30 March 2017.

condemnation of communism and a reaction to Vladimir Putin's memory politics after the invasion of Crimea in 2014:

> Until the Russian invasion of Ukraine, the West did not understand the danger that Putin represented to our region and to Europe in general. Our aim was to condemn communist crimes, but also to warn that rehabilitating Stalin, wearing t-shirts with Lenin and Stalin, and negating the Soviet Union's role in communist repression was in fact a danger to us all.[38]

No Western European country backed, however, the Estonian initiative. Even former communist countries such as Bulgaria and Romania, which held the presidency of Council of the EU in 2018 and 2019, abandoned the project. Their representatives prioritized instead economic convergence of EU state members and the security of Europe in the context of the Syrian civil war and the subsequent refugee crisis. Establishing the CICROC would have required a large financial investment that CEE states could hardly have afforded without the support of wealthier Western European nations. Against the backdrop of the East–West divide on the uniqueness of the Holocaust and the equation of Nazism and communism, such support was improbable. As Illimar Lepik von Wirén recalls,

> The West did not see an urgent need to fund such a tribunal and, indeed, most perpetrators were dead. Also, there was both a sort of Western consensus that dealing with communist crimes would have downplayed the Holocaust and a common leftist perception that communism had brought socio-economic rights.[39]

The 2008 economic crisis accentuated leftist critiques of neoliberal politics at the European level; issues related to socio–economic inequalities, intra-European imbalances, and democratic deficits further marginalized the criminalization of communism. Moreover, during the 2010s, conservative politics radicalized in CEE. Parties such as FIDESz in Hungary and PiS in Poland sought to legitimize their illiberalism through the narrative of two 'criminal totalitarianisms' and the downplaying of the role of CEE governments and sectors of civilian population in the extermination of European Jews during the

[38] Personal interview with Illimar Lepik von Wirén, online, 2 March 2022.
[39] Ibid.

Second World War.[40] Conservative politicians and activists concerned with the establishment of a Nuremberg trial for communist crimes also lambasted gender equality and extolled the 'battle to keep Muslims out of Europe'.[41] They promoted Eurosceptic and nationalist discourses, as well as policies that diminished freedom of speech and the independence of the judiciary. The conflation of these topics and practices in CEE conservative circles led to an increased reluctance within European institutions to endorse the condemnation of the crimes of communism.

3.2 Transnational Justice: Failed Criminal Prosecutions, Successful Civil Litigations

In 2015, the Platform also launched the project *Justice 2.0* to lodge criminal complaints concerning communist crimes that had a transnational component and where at least two different jurisdictions could be used as legal venues. According to Neela Winkelmann-Heyrovská, this strategy was adopted to overcome national political and legal constraints in countries such as Czechia, Slovakia, and Bulgaria, and to build a transnational memory of communist crimes. After the failed attempts to establish a European tribunal for communist crimes, the Platform's legal advisers agreed that using the passive personality principle would be a more realistic strategy to open investigations and prosecutions.[42]

The first case chosen by the Platform concerned crimes committed in Bulgaria during the so-called 'Revival Process' (1984–1985), during which communist authorities forced ethnic Turks to change their names to Bulgarian names and violently repressed those who refused to do so. This campaign of murder, imprisonment, and internal displacement led to a massive refugee crisis at the Bulgarian–Turkish border in 1989, when the communist authorities opened the frontier and forced Turks to leave the country. The Platform considered these repressive methods to be crimes against humanity committed on ethnic and political grounds. Bulgarian investigations into these cases at the beginning of the 1990s had resulted in the indictment of certain high-ranking

[40] Uladzislau Belavusau and Anna Wójcik, 'La criminalisation de l'expression historique en Pologne: la loi mémorielle de 2018', *Archives de Politique Criminelle* 40 (2018): pp. 175–188; Andrea Peto, 'The Illiberal Memory Politics in Hungary', *Journal of Genocide Research* 24, no. 2 (2022): pp. 241–249.

[41] James Mark, Bogdan C. Iacob, Tobias Rupprecht, and Ljubica Spaskovska. *1989: A Global History of Eastern Europe* (Cambridge: Cambridge University Press, 2019): pp. 275–298.

[42] Personal interview with Neela Winkelmann-Heyrovská, online, 27 January 2022.

communist officials (including Todor Zhivkov), accused of incitement to racial hatred, but the trial was halted in 1998 due to an alleged lack of evidence, as were most trials in Bulgaria (see Chapter 5). Representatives of the Platform intended to identify ethnic Turks who had been repressed and were now residing in Germany or Turkey and were willing to lodge criminal complaints in these countries. The Platform also identified alleged perpetrators who were still alive, among them two former members of the Politburo of the Bulgarian Communist Party and a former high rank officer of the political police.[43]

This case rapidly fell apart. The Sofia Hannah Arendt Centre—the only Bulgarian member of the Platform—stopped collaborating with the Platform in May 2016. Against the backdrop of the Syrian refugee crisis, Vasil Kadrinov, the president of the Centre, accused the Platform of receiving funding from Victor Orbán's administration and endorsing a 'government which builds fences similar to those built by the communist regimes'.[44] Consequently, the Platform no longer had a partner institution to gather documents and witness statements in Bulgaria. The Platform's legal advisers themselves were not convinced that the strategy would work. One legal adviser who preferred to remain anonymous acknowledged the difficulty of this enterprise in an interview from 2015: it entailed identifying ethnic Turks who were now German citizens, and engaging in a systematic legal and documentation effort in both countries. In addition, only cases of murder could be brought to trial in Germany as the statutory limitations for other crimes had expired. Jernej Letnar Černič also expressed his scepticism in a 2022 interview: although the forced assimilation of Turks had infringed international human rights law, it was unclear to what extent it amounted to crimes against humanity.[45] Moreover, Bulgaria, Germany, and Turkey had not incorporated this criminal category into their legislations in the 1980s. Given the withdrawal of the Hannah Arendt Centre and the procedural difficulties acknowledged by legal advisers, the Platform abandoned the case.

The second case concerned the murder of Czech, Polish, and German citizens trying to flee socialist regimes across the Western Czechoslovak border. It was inspired by the trials of communist officials and border guards convicted by German courts in the 1990s for the shooting of East German citizens who attempted to cross into the West during the Cold War. In 2015 and

[43] Platform of European Memory and Conscience, *Annual Report 2016*, available at www.sgtrs.nl/wp-content/uploads/2019/10/annual_report_2016_web.pdf (accessed 1 May 2023).
[44] 'Hannah Arendt Center: Sofia has frozen its activities with PEMC', Public Letter, 18 May 2016, document shared with the author by Vasil Kadrinov.
[45] Personal interview with Jernej Letnar Černič, online, 3 February 2022.

2016, the Platform lodged criminal complaints in Poland and Germany based on the passive personality principle. According to Winkelmann-Heyrovská, the Platform never envisaged prosecutions based on universal jurisdiction, nor was it inspired by the Latin American endeavours in Europe. It opted instead for cases based on the passive personality principle which avoided accusations of an infringement of national sovereignty, but still demonstrated the transnational character of communist crimes. As Winkelmann-Heyrovská remarked, 'The issue of cross-border crimes was systematic in the Eastern Bloc. It had happened everywhere and the transnational complaints concerning the Czechoslovak case could be replicated in other countries, for instance the killings at the Romanian-Yugoslav border'.[46] These transnational law cases could connect Eastern and Western Europe through stories of cross-border crossings of refugees in search of freedom and liberal democracy. As I discuss later in the chapter, it was a sad irony that prominent members of the same advocacy group opposed the immigration to Europe of African and Asian people fleeing from war, dictatorship, and destitution.

The complaint in Poland was lodged with the Institute of National Remembrance (IPN), an institution in charge of memorializing and investigating Nazi and communist crimes. The Platform accused the leadership of the Czechoslovak Communist Party of erecting high-voltage electric fences that killed at least ninety-one people trying to cross the border between 1951 and 1965. The Platform classified these deaths as crimes against humanity.[47] In 2017, the IPN promised to begin investigations into the cases of Poles killed by high-voltage electricity on the Czechoslovak border during communism. Nevertheless, until April 2023, there had been no major developments in the case. The statutory limitations for murder committed during the communist period had expired in Poland, and, as Czech prosecutors would later argue, the responsibility of communist leaders could amount to an abuse of power but not to crimes against humanity.[48]

The complaint in Germany concerned sixty-seven Czechoslovak communist officials—including the last three surviving members of the Politburo of the Communist Party of Czechoslovakia—who were accused of the killing of five German citizens at the Western Czechoslovak border between 1967 and 1986.[49] Again, the Platform intended to classify these deaths as crimes

[46] Personal interview with Neela Winkelmann-Heyrovská, online, 27 January 2022.

[47] Platform of European Memory and Conscience, *Annual Report 2017*, available at www.memoryandconscience.eu/ (accessed 25 April 2023).

[48] Roman Cuprik, 'Communist-era Interior Minister May Face Trial for Electric Fence Deaths', *The Slovak Spectator*, 10 March 2015.

[49] Platform of European Memory and Conscience, *Annual Report 2017*. The three main accused were Milouš Jakeš, Lubomír Štrougal, and Peter Colotka.

against humanity, but the law firm leading the case considered an accusation of murder more realistic. Murder is not subject to statutory limitations in the German criminal code; and there had been guilty verdicts in the 1990s for killings at the border between the two Germanies that could be used as precedents. Moreover, the category of crimes against humanity did not exist in the German law when the crimes were committed.[50]

Among the five victims identified, the Platform chose a highly emotional case to promote its cause: Hartmut Tautz, an eighteen-year-old East German, had attempted to cross from Czechoslovakia to Austria in 1986. He was attacked and critically wounded by the specially trained killing dogs of the Czechoslovak border guards. He was taken to the hospital too late, and died. The Platform organized various events around Tautz's death, including the unveiling of a commemorative sculpture in front of the European Parliament in Brussels in 2015 and the construction of a memorial in Bratislava in 2016. These commemorations were not couched in a universalist and apolitical human rights language, but were steeped in ideology and current political implications. The sculpture in Brussels denounced the dangers of communist ideology: the dogs and guards who killed Tautz were given the faces of Karl Marx, Slavoj Žižek, and Vladimir Putin, while the ground on which the victim lay was designed to resemble Noam Chomsky.[51] As shown before, the narrative linking communist crimes not only to state socialist regimes but also to Karl Marx and other neo-Marxist thinkers was frequent in the Platform's discourses. Massacres and political repression were presented as the direct result of an alleged criminal logic within Marxist ideology that had to be banned. The Platform's efforts to punish the killings perpetrated at the Czechoslovak border therefore aimed to both provide justice for the victims and delegitimize all forms of past, present, or future leftist thinking.

In 2017, the German prosecutor's office launched investigations into the killing at the Czech–German border, and in 2018, a joint Czech–German investigation team was established upon German request. Meanwhile, the Platform lodged a criminal complaint in Czechia requesting similar inquiries into the killing of twenty-eight victims of various nationalities. The German prosecutors contended that the murders were not subject to statutory limitations under German law, and that the killings at the border also violated the international human right to leave one's own country. However, the Czech prosecutors only brought charges of abuse of power and negligence in office,

[50] Personal interview with Neela Winkelmann-Heyrovská, online, 27 January 2022.
[51] Neumayer, *Criminalising Communism*, p. 220.

arguing that the accused did not incite to murder in any way. The case was ultimately closed in 2020 because one main defendant had died and two others were diagnosed with Alzheimer's disease and deemed unfit to stand trial. The Platform contested this decision at the Czech Supreme Court, accusing that the medical certificates had been issued by biased military doctors who had served during the communist period. In December 2021, the Supreme Court ruled in favour of the Platform and asked for a new medical assessment.[52] In May 2023, the case was still pending.

While no guilty verdict was issued with respect to the border killings, this strategy of transnationalizing justice led German prosecutors to pressure the Czech judiciary to initiate investigations. The Platform also attempted to connect all those who tried to flee communist regimes in a transnational narrative of repression and victimhood. In 2020, the Platform contacted the Romanian Institute for the Investigation of Communist Crimes to identify cases of individuals of various CEE nationalities who had attempted to cross the Romanian–Yugoslav border. Historian Luciana Jinga coordinated this project, which documented dozens of cases, and interviewed several survivors and witnesses. No legal complaint was however lodged until May 2023: Romania had a twenty-year statutory limitation for murder during the socialist period, and it was difficult to prove that such crimes constituted crimes against humanity. Also, according to Jinga, the project failed to create a common European memory about the repression conducted at socialist borders.

> The idea of creating a culture of transnational solidarity of those who were trying to flee the Eastern Bloc is more a retrospective enterprise than a historical reality. In Yugoslav refugee camps, Romanians felt frustrated because German citizens or rich individuals were immediately allowed to go to the West, while the others had to wait for months and were often forced to return to Romania. I do not think we can talk about transnational memory and solidarity in terms of border crossings during communism.[53]

From a political perspective, the transnational memory the Platform has sought to highlight no longer paralleled the memory of Nazi crimes. Instead, it deployed a different narrative of victimhood that gained momentum during the 2015 Syrian refugee crisis, casting all those who tried to cross the communist

[52] 'The Platform thanks the Constitutional Court of the Czech Republic for its precedent-setting decision and for reopening the road to justice for the victims Lubomír Štrougal and Vratislav Vajnar', available at www.memoryandconscience.eu/ (accessed 25 April 2023).

[53] Personal interview with Luciana Jinga, online, 8 February 2022.

borders into the West as refugees. This approach continued previous Cold War narratives that had denounced the communist regimes for the refugee crises provoked by the 1956 Hungarian uprising, the 1968 Prague Spring, and the 1984–1989 Revival Process in Bulgaria. It was also a strategy designed to gain support and sympathy through a parallel with the Syrian refugees trying to gain asylum in the European Union. Nevertheless, the use of the 'refugee' paradigm for the victims of communism occurred simultaneously to proclamations by some of the Platform's representatives who denounced non-European and non-Christian migrants and refugees as a threat to European identity.

László Tőkés, a member of the Platform's Executive Board, declared on several occasions that the European Union must stop receiving 'migrants' from the Middle East in order to defend the Christian origins and values of its citizens. He continued, 'In this sense, we are close to Viktor Orbán's auto-defensive and pro-European politics and not to the anti-national and anti-European politics of the liberal left'.[54] Ana Blandiana, founder of the Sighet Memorial in Romania (a museum-memorial member of the Platform), also declared that Europe was threatened by millions of immigrants whose 'cultural baggage' and 'medieval convictions' were incompatible with democracy and European values. From her perspective, the EU's 'bureaucratic and vegetative' politics, marked by political correctness and the unfiltered acceptance of Muslim migrants, would eventually lead to the dissolution of European identity.[55] These racist declarations criticized the putative Western embrace of refugees from the Middle East in comparison to its ostensible refusal to acknowledge Eastern Europeans' suffering under communism.[56]

As of 2022, the Platform was unsuccessful in its attempts to transnationalize criminal prosecutions although Czech courts opened investigations due to the German prosecutors' pressure, but closed them due to statutory limitations. However, it did succeed in transnationalizing civil litigations, which resulted in financial compensation from the Czech and Slovak states to Germans wounded at the Czechoslovak border or to the families of those killed. In 2016, the Platform contacted Lubomír Müller, a Slovak lawyer who had been convicted to six months in prison in 1976 for being a member of the Jehovah's Witnesses and practicing spiritual work without a state permit. After 1991,

[54] Radu Chis, 'Tokes Laszlo despre imigranți: "Trebuie să apărăm Europa, valorile, națiunile și țările noastre"', *Buzznews*, 8 September 2015.

[55] Andrei Pricopie, 'Blandiana: 'Milioanele de emigranți ferm hotărâți să nu se integreze vor dizolva din interior cultura și mentalitățile Europei', *TheEpochTimes*, 23 June 2016.

[56] Slavenka Drakulić, 'Competing for Victimhood: Why Eastern Europe Says No to Refugees', *Eurozine*, 4 November 2015.

he represented various victims in the Slovak courts in their attempts to obtain compensation for illegal arrest, torture, or property confiscated during the communist period, based on a law passed in Czechoslovakia in 1990. As the text was not specific about the nationality of the victim, it allowed the Platform to interpret it as applicable to foreign citizens. Müller agreed to take the case, and, in 2017, a court from Bratislava ruled that Hartmut Tautz had been killed by the Czechoslovak authorities and his family was entitled to compensation and an official apology from the Slovak state. Following this decision, the Platform initiated a communications campaign in Germany calling upon other individuals to claim compensation in Slovakia or Czechia. By December 2019, thirty-eight former East German citizens had received reparations from the Czech and Slovak courts; another twelve cases were pending.[57] These cases received significant media coverage in Slovakia, Czechia, and Germany. They consolidated a historical narrative that portrayed those who had attempted to flee to the West as refugees persecuted and murdered by a communist regime. However, transnational civil litigations remained confined to Czech and Slovak courts.

3.3 Weak Mobilizations at the European Court of Human Rights

Anti-impunity efforts of CEE activists at the European Court of Human Rights (ECtHR) were rare—a sharp contrast from Latin American pro-accountability actors who systematically appealed to the Inter-American Court of Human Rights (IACtHR) to unblock prosecutions at home (see *infra*). While victims of communist regimes often appealed to the ECtHR on matters of compensations and the restitution of property confiscated by communist authorities,[58] only two applications touched on aspects of criminal justice.

In 1996, a group of ninety-seven Bulgarian citizens of Turkish origin called upon the European Commission of Human Rights to address the ECtHR and sanction Bulgaria for postponing the investigations into the killings, unlawful detention, and forced name changes perpetrated during the Revival Process and failing to pay proper compensation for these crimes. In 1998, the Commission rejected the application, arguing that it was unclear if the

[57] Platform of European Memory and Conscience, *Annual Report 2020*, available at www.memoryandconscience.eu/ (accessed 25 April 2023).

[58] James A. Sweeney, *The European Court of Human Rights in the Post-Cold War Era: Universality in Transition* (London: Routledge, 2013).

applicants had exhausted all domestic remedies available under Bulgarian law. It also stated that the European Convention on Human Rights (ECHR) did not guarantee a right to criminal proceedings against third persons. Instead, it was the responsibility of the Bulgarian judiciary to decide whether a criminal investigation would lead to a prosecution. Moreover, the Commission argued that the ECHR only covered events after Bulgaria's ratification of the Convention in 1992.[59]

Indeed, the complaint was silent on what judicial venues the applicants had addressed at the national level and did not specify on which articles of the ECHR the Bulgarian state had allegedly infringed. Nevertheless, the Commission's response did not address the delays of the Bulgarian justice system in investigating the crimes of the Revival Process, which could have been interpreted as violations of both Article 6 (the right to a fair trial) and Article 2 (the right to life), which also calls for independent and effective investigations into suspicious deaths (particularly when perpetrated by state agents). The Commission's response reflected a conservative approach that contradicted the more progressive visions of the UN Human Rights Committee and the IACtHR, which had both ruled that a lack of investigations into gross human rights violations represented a continuation of those violations under the new regime.[60]

A second case was brought before the ECtHR by Romanian victims of the bloody events of December 1989, in which at least 1,200 individuals were killed. In 2007, after long delays in prosecuting these crimes, the Romanian judiciary closed the investigations, arguing that the statutory limitation for murders committed in 1989 had expired. That same year, the Association 21 December lodged a complaint with the ECtHR, accusing the Romanian government of failing to investigate the killing of a nineteen-year-old boy on 22 December 1989. It argued that the Romanian justice system had infringed Article 6 and Article 2 of the ECHR. In 2011, in *Association '21 Decembrie' v. Romania*, the ECtHR ruled against Romania: the delay and closure of criminal proceedings without providing truth and remedy to the victims had violated both the right to life and the right to a fair trial. Moreover, the Court stated that an investigation could not be terminated on the basis of statutory limitations when the authorities themselves were responsible for the delay due to their inactivity; this was especially inadmissible in the case of widespread use of lethal force against

[59] European Commission of Human Rights, *Abiloglu and 96 Others v. Bulgaria*, no. 39553/98, Decision of 20 May 1998.

[60] Eva Brems, 'Transitional Justice in the Case Law of the European Court of Human Rights', *The International Journal of Transitional Justice* 5, no. 2 (2011): pp. 282–303, at p. 286.

a civilian population that was trying to topple a dictatorial regime (as in the case of the events of December 1989). Similar ECtHR decisions were issued in the following years in various cases concerning the 1989 December violence.[61] After these ECtHR decisions, the Romanian judiciary reopened investigations and admitted that the crimes committed during the 1989 events could be considered crimes against humanity, not subject to statutory limitations. However, the complexity of the cases alongside the national political constellation, in which former communist elites still retained political influence, led to other delays in the investigations.[62] While the ECtHR decisions were considered a victory by the victims' associations, they had little effect on the development of criminal justice concerning the violence perpetrated in December 1989.

Attempts to transnationalize justice beyond demands for a Nuremberg for communist crimes were thus rare in CEE. Most communist crimes had been committed between the mid-1940s and the beginning of the 1960s; by the 1990s, many victims were already old, and, in many cases, marginalized individuals without financial resources and legal knowledge to seek redress at the ECtHR or through transnational prosecutions. Furthermore, legal education in European human rights law and international criminal law was slow to be introduced to CEE law curricula, in most cases only after the 2004 European enlargement.[63] Moreover, memory and justice entrepreneurs were more often interested in obtaining a symbolic condemnation of communist regimes from European institutions, rather than constructing legal actions across borders—an enterprise that entailed systematic legal and financial efforts. The anti-communist rhetoric became an important resource for creating political legitimacies at both national and European levels, with media campaigns and formal condemnations selected as privileged strategies that involved less effort than building transnational legal cases.

[61] ECtHR, *Association '21 December 1989' and Others v. Romania*, Judgment of 24 May 2011.

[62] Raluca Grosescu, 'The Trials of the Romanian Revolution', *Cultures of History Forum*, 17 January 2019, available at https://cultures-of-history.uni-jena.de/ (accessed 25 April 2023).

[63] Raluca Grosescu and Agata Fijalkowski, 'Retrospective Justice and Legal Culture', in Lavinia Stan and Lucian Turcescu, eds., *Justice, Memory and Redress in Romania: New Insights* (Cambridge: Cambridge Scholars, 2017): pp. 100–123.

4 Latin America: Liberal Humanitarianism and the Globalization of Transnational Justice

In contrast to CEE activism, which remained intertwined with conservative politics and fixated on the condemnation of communist crimes and communist ideology at a Nuremberg-style tribunal, Latin American justice entrepreneurs opted for a variety of legal strategies and jurisdictions, a tactic which increased their opportunities to achieve justice. Given that the story of Latin American transnational mobilizations against impunity during the 1980s and the 1990s has been examined at length,[64] this section only summarizes the most important trends that fuelled the success of this advocacy and emphasizes their impact on the development of ICL. It then turns to the more recent and unexplored contributions of Argentinian courts and legal experts to the development of universal jurisdiction.

Three important aspects made the tenor of Latin American activism radically different from that in CEE. First, victims, exile communities, and human rights lawyers from Latin America systematically addressed both the Inter-American System of Human Rights and Western European courts to claim justice for crimes that were left without judicial response at home. They opened legal fronts in a multiplicity of jurisdictions and thus maximized their chances of success. Second, they renounced their leftist radical vocabulary, embraced a liberal language of human rights, and deliberately selected plaintiffs who could be presented as apolitical individuals who had fallen victim to the indiscriminate violence of military regimes. While condemning right-wing dictatorships and their ideology remained important, punishing perpetrators through the instruments of criminal justice became their primary purpose. This legalist rhetoric made it easier for European judges to initiate investigations based on a liberal humanitarian vocabulary, which had gained wider acceptance in the late 1970s. After all, these mobilizations were not about delegitimizing contemporary conservative and liberal politics or resuscitating a radical left; they were about using the law to render justice for abhorrent crimes condemned by international treaties. Third, Latin American activists, many of whom were lawyers, forged alliances with progressive Western European judicial officials

[64] Naomi Roht-Arriaza, *The Pinochet Effect: Transitional Justice in the Age of Human Rights* (Philadelphia, PA: University of Pennsylvania Press, 2005); Cath Collins, *Post-Transitional Justice: Human Rights Trials in Chile and El Salvador* (Philadelphia, PA: University of Pennsylvania Press, 2010); Due Process of Law Foundation, *Victims Unsilenced: The Inter-American System and Transitional Justice in Latin America* (Washington DC: Due Process of Law Foundation, 2007); Francesca Lessa, *The Condor Trials: Transnational Repression and Human Rights in South America* (Yale: Yale University Press, 2022).

and counterparts who were disposed to applying creative interpretations of national and international law in order to move the criminalization of gross human rights violations forward. Some of these judicial officials had been part of networks specializing in transnational criminality or had been judges at the international criminal tribunals established in the 1990s. Due to this previous experience, they were familiar with the intricacies of international law and were open to its direct application in national courts.

4.1 The IACtHR and the Consolidation of the Duty to Prosecute

As early as the late 1970s, Latin American human rights activists and victims of military regimes appealed to international organizations and NGOs to stop and sanction political repression at home. One key institution they addressed was the Inter-American Commission on Human Rights, which has the mandate to investigate and report on the situation of human rights in member countries of the Organization of American States (OAS). Families of imprisoned or disappeared individuals across Latin America addressed the Commission by formulating petitions and demanding investigations in their countries. The historic visit of the Inter-American Commission to Argentina in 1979, and its subsequent report (published in 1980), was a ground-breaking moment in acknowledging the systematic repression unleashed by the military junta. As revolutionaries across the world began to reject their former violent revolutionary aims, the global debate over rights began to shift—away from its previous focus on economic and social rights towards a new emphasis on civil–political freedoms, which stood in opposition to the power of 'totalitarian states'.[65] Against this global backdrop of a re-hierarchization of rights, the Commission framed its report in a liberal language of human rights. While it did mention the revolutionary goals of leftist activists as historical background, the report depicted the military violence in terms of an infringement of civil and political rights, and particularly of the right to life and to physical integrity of large subsets of the Argentine population, no matter their political convictions. The Commission described a repressive system that targeted civil society indiscriminately and classified the victims in terms of specific ethnic, religious, and socio-occupational groups.[66] This narrative echoed previous reports by

[65] Mark et al., *1989*, pp. 75–76.
[66] Inter-American Commission on Human Rights (IACHR), *Informe sobre la situación de los derechos humanos en Argentina* (Washington: OAS, 1980).

international NGOs, such as Amnesty International, which focused on the inventory and description of crimes, rather than on an analysis of the ideological and socio-economic structural conditions that fuelled leftist mobilizations and insurgencies in Latin America.[67] The Commission recommended the clarification of enforced disappearances, the urgent responses to habeas corpus, and the prosecution of state actors involved in extrajudicial killings and acts of torture.[68] The Commission thus exhorted Argentina to judge international crimes, which were deliberately presented in the depoliticized language of human rights.

In the following years, the Commission responded to several individual petitions by issuing similar decisions in a variety of cases across Latin America. Since 1986, it has referred a series of cases to the IACtHR, which gradually developed new ICL doctrines on forced disappearance, the duty to prosecute, and the non-applicability of amnesties and statutory limitations to major international crimes.[69] In *Velásquez-Rodríguez v. Honduras*[70]—a 1988 case concerning enforced disappearances—the IACtHR ruled that the American Convention on Human Rights (ACHR) entailed a duty to investigate and punish gross human rights violations. In the 1990s, the Court began to include, as a compulsory remedy, the state's obligation to carry out criminal judicial proceedings and punish not only direct perpetrators but also the intellectual authors of the crimes committed, thereby directly targeting the high command of military regimes. Concomitantly, the Court elaborated the doctrine of enforced disappearances as 'continuous' crimes: until the fate and whereabouts of a victim are established with certainty, enforced disappearances are ongoing criminal acts and statutory limitations cannot impede their investigation.[71]

In 2001, the IACtHR ruled in *Barrios Altos v. Peru*[72] that amnesties and statutory limitations could not apply to major international crimes, including genocide, war crimes, and crimes against humanity. This decision marked a turning point in judicial discourses and memory politics in Latin America: the political consensus of the 1980s and 1990s, built upon negotiated transitions based on amnesties and pardons, was no longer acceptable. Trading justice for peace and democratic consolidation in the context of major international crimes

[67] Markarian, *Left in Transformation*, pp. 89–91.
[68] IACHR, *Informe*.
[69] Alexandra Huneeus, 'International Criminal Law by Other Means: The Quasi-Criminal Jurisdiction of Human Rights Courts', *American Journal of International Law* 107, no. 1 (2013): pp. 1–44.
[70] IACtHR, *Velasquez-Rodriguez v. Honduras*, Judgment of 29 July 1988.
[71] Ibid.
[72] IACtHR, *Barrios Altos v. Peru*, Judgment of 14 March 2001.

infringed upon the ACHR: impunity thus had to end. After 2001, the Court reaffirmed this principle in a variety of cases from countries such as Brazil, Chile, Colombia, El Salvador, Guatemala, Paraguay, Suriname, and Uruguay.[73] The Court adopted a radically monist approach to the relationship between international and national law and ruled that national laws that imposed amnesties and statutory limitations for major international crimes lacked legal validity. It gave direct effect to its judgments and obliged domestic courts to engage in a form of a decentralized control to prohibit the application of national laws that violated the ACHR.[74]

With the exception of Brazil (see Chapter 5), national courts in OAS member states complied with IACtHR rulings. High-ranking officials, including former Peruvian President Alberto Fujimori and former Guatemalan President Efraín Ríos Montt, were convicted of crimes against humanity and genocide following the implementation of the IACtHR decisions and interpretations. In Argentina, the pardons of military officials, including former head of state Rafael Videla, were declared unconstitutional and in breach of the IACtHR's jurisprudence. In line with the Commission's approach, the IACtHR deployed a liberal language of human rights, evoking the infringement of the right to life and physical integrity, the right to personal liberty, and the right to a fair trial. Nonetheless, the IACtHR remained cautious in providing political interpretations of the events in question, fearing that this would overstep its jurisdiction (see Chapters 3 and 5).

Some observers criticized the Court for too visibly engaging in judicial activism, assuming a quasi-criminal jurisdiction, and prioritizing the rights of the victims over those of the defendants.[75] Nonetheless, the IACtHR developed an innovative and far-reaching approach to the duty to prosecute. Its consistent body of law on the subject was incorporated in the jurisprudence of national courts across Latin America, contributing to the progressive advance of ICL in the region. This outcome was the result of a long struggle by individuals and groups dedicated to ensuring accountability for the atrocities committed

[73] Brian D. Tittemore, 'Ending Impunity in the Americas: The Role of the Inter-American Human Rights System in Advancing Accountability for Serious Crimes under International Law', *Southwestern Journal of Law and Trade in the Americas* 12, no. 2 (2006): pp. 429–476.

[74] Christina Binder, 'The Prohibition of Amnesties by the Inter-American Court of Human Rights', *German Law Journal* 12, no. 5 (2011): pp. 1203–1230.

[75] Gerald Neumann, 'Import, Export and Regional Consent in the Inter-American Court of Human Rights', *The European Journal of International Law* 19, no. 1 (2008): pp. 101–123; Fernando Felipe Basch, 'The Doctrine of the Inter-American Court of Human Rights Regarding States' Duty to Punish Human Rights Violations and Its Dangers', *American University International Law Review* 23, no. 1 (2007): pp. 195–229.

throughout the Americas. The struggle for justice by victims and activists at the IACtHR constituted an essential catalyst for ending impunity.[76]

4.2 Mobilizations in Europe and the Development of Principle of Universal Jurisdiction

Parallel to the mobilizations at the Inter-American System of Human Rights, Latin American activists also formulated demands for justice in European courts, based on the principles of passive personality and universal jurisdiction. In the 1970s, many political opponents of the military regimes had taken refuge in Europe and acquired European citizenships. Most of those who remained in Latin America, especially in Argentina, already held European passports, given the large European emigration to the Southern Cone during the twentieth century. Moreover, the violent repression across Latin America had also targeted European citizens who were living in the Southern Cone and were leftist militants or supporters of local anti-dictatorial movements. This transnational victimhood allowed anti-impunity activists to address European courts and demand criminal investigations. Here again, exiles set aside the heroic language that made their oppression part of their leftist political experience in favour of denouncing the specific methods of the Latin American governments that had repressed them. By way of collaborations with European NGOs that promoted a liberal language of human rights, Latin American exiles became aware of the benefits of renouncing a radical vocabulary and instead employing an anti-impunity, 'humanitarian rhetoric almost empty of calls for radical social change'.[77] In order to gain access to justice, they framed their claims in legalist terms that were compatible with the legislations of European countries.

Anti-impunity activism in France is a relevant example for the propagation of this legalist and apolitical vocabulary. In the 1980s, the Association of the Relatives and Friends of French Citizens Disappeared in Argentina, together with the French–Latin American Association, brought an initial complaint to French courts. The French legal system allows for investigations into crimes against French citizens no matter where they are committed but does not

[76] Collins, *Post-Transitional Justice*; Roht-Arriaza, *The Pinochet Effect*; Naomi Roht-Arriaza, 'Making the State Do Justice: Transnational Prosecutions and International Support for Criminal Investigations in Post-Armed Conflict Guatemala', *Chicago Journal of International Law* 9, no. 1 (2008): pp. 79–104.

[77] Markarian, *Left in Transformation*.

contain provisions on universal jurisdiction. The case was carefully chosen to include victims with French citizenship and avoid stories of leftist activism and involvement in armed insurgencies. It was centred on the enforced disappearance in Argentina of two French nuns who had supported the Madres de Plaza de Mayo. Sophie Thonon, the lawyer who led the case on behalf of the two associations, emphasized that it was important to select an emblematic, 'apolitical', and 'sacred' case in order to avoid political controversy and construct a clear case 'of Good versus Evil'.[78] In 1990, Alfredo Astiz, an Argentinian military officer, was tried in absentia and sentenced to life in prison for the kidnapping and torture of the two nuns. The Argentinian authorities refused to extradite him, but Astiz was finally convicted of crimes against humanity in 2005, after the impunity laws were revoked in Argentina. In 2010, the Paris Cour d'Assises convicted another Argentinian officer and twelve Chilean military officers, including Manuel Contreras, the former chief of Pinochet's secret police, for the kidnapping and torture of four French citizens. While the victims had been leftist militants, they were portrayed in terms of their profession (doctor, student, and chemist) and their humanitarianism (helping poor communities and political prisoners) rather than in terms of their political activism.[79]

Investigations based on the passive personality principle were also opened in other European countries and resulted in international arrest warrants in Germany and Switzerland and in guilty verdicts after trials in absentia in Italy. They were the outcome of collaborations between exile communities, victims' families and associations, and progressive human rights lawyers, such as Wolfgang Kaleck in Germany, Giancarlo Maniga and Marcello Gentili in Italy, and Sophie Thonon in France. Both the lawyers representing the victims and the investigative judges provided a neutral historical reading of leftist activism in Latin America and focused instead on the abhorrent stories of torture, rape, extrajudicial killings, and enforced disappearance. Such a focus was essential both to counterattack the argument made by the military regimes that their actions were necessary to combat leftist terrorism and to construct a consensus across the political spectrum concerning the duty to punish heinous crimes perpetrated against innocent victims.[80] While none of the accused was ultimately extradited to Europe, these trials and investigations were instrumental in

[78] Roht-Arriaza, *The Pinochet Effect*, p. 123.

[79] 'La dictature chilienne a été condamnée à Paris', *France 24*, 17 December 2010.

[80] For the construction of this apolitical victimhood, see Emilio Crenzel, 'The Crimes of the Last Dictatorship in Argentina and Its Qualification as Genocide: A Historicization', *Global Society* 33, no. 3 (2019): pp. 365–381.

putting pressure on the Argentinian and Chilean judiciary, contributing to the fight against impunity in Latin America.

The Spanish and Belgian judiciaries went a step further to include criminal investigations based on universal jurisdiction. In the 1990s, both countries allowed for such criminal proceedings for certain categories of crimes: war crimes in Belgium and genocide, terrorism, and torture in Spain. Only the Spanish investigations are discussed here[81] because they were by far the most comprehensive, resulted in numerous international arrest warrants, and led to Augusto Pinochet's arrest in London in 1999. They were also emblematic of an anti-impunity alliance between Latin American exiles and progressive Western European lawyers, prosecutors, and investigative judges, who promoted universal jurisdiction as a key principle in ICL.

The first criminal complaint brought before Spanish courts concerned political repression in Argentina,[82] and was drafted by Carlos Castresana, a Spanish anti-corruption prosecutor who had also chaired the Union of Progressive Prosecutors—a professional association with leftist political views established in the 1980s to defend constitutional rights, including the socio-economic rights of marginalized segments of Spanish society. In March 1996, Castresana lodged a complaint with the Audiencia Nacional, the court charged with judging specific crimes committed across Spanish territory, such as treason, drug and human trafficking, money laundering, and international crimes including terrorism, hijacking, and genocide. Castresana listed both Argentinian and Spanish victims, located their murders and enforced disappearances within the wider repression enforced by the military junta, and accused General Rafael Videla, General Antonio Bussi, Admiral Emilio Massera, and other lower-ranking officers of genocide, terrorism, illegal detention, disappearances, and child abduction. He invoked Article 23.4 of the Organic Law of State Power adopted in 1985 which allowed Spanish courts to prosecute certain crimes committed by non-Spaniards outside Spain, including genocide, terrorism, and other crimes recognized in international treaties ratified by Spain. While the complaint was grounded in Spanish legislation, it used categories of international crimes and affirmed the Spanish judiciary's right to investigate such crimes based on both the principles of passive personality and universal jurisdiction. The complaint was assigned by lottery to judge Baltasar Garzón, a well-known and controversial official, who had investigated transnational drug trafficking and money laundering, as well as acts of terrorism

[81] For mobilizations in Belgium, see Roht-Arriaza, *The Pinochet Effect*, pp. 118–121.
[82] For a detailed account, see Roht-Arriaza, *The Pinochet Effect*, pp. 5–8.

committed by both the Basque separatist organization, ETA, and the anti-ETA death squads run by the Socialist Party government.

In April 1996, Argentinian exiles, united under the umbrella of the Argentine Human Rights Association in Madrid, together with victims' associations and human rights NGOs in Buenos Aires—such as Madres de Plaza de Mayo and the Service, Peace and Justice group, headed by Nobel Prize winner Adolfo Pérez Esquivel—joined Castresana's complaint. They contributed information and worked to convince other Spanish associations and political parties to support their claims, bringing on board the Association of Free Lawyers (a progressive alternative to the Madrid Bar Association), the legal team of the United Left Party, and Amnesty International. Various Spanish lawyers as well as leftist political elites supported the complaint with legal assistance and public declarations.[83]

The solidarity underlying this mobilization was rooted in the long history of Argentinian and Spanish relations: Argentina had been a 'haven' for many leftist Spaniards seeking refuge from Franco's dictatorship. Cold War alliances between socialist and communist Spanish political parties and trade unions, on the one hand, and leftist Latin American exiles, on the other, were also instrumental. After the return to democracy in 1977, Spain became a preferred destination for South American émigrés fleeing dictatorial rule. Spain consolidated itself as a space for anti-dictatorial militantism driven by a mutual Spanish and Latin American denunciation of right-wing military authoritarianism.[84] At the same time, Spain and Argentina were connected through the Spanish language and the similarity of their legal systems, an aspect that facilitated investigations. By October 1996, the case included more than 300 victims, many of whom were of Spanish descent. A coalition of Argentinian and Spanish lawyers, including exiled Argentinian lawyer Carlos Slepoy and Spanish human rights lawyers José Luis Galán and Manuel Ollé Sesé, took the lead in prosecuting the case. In parallel, Chilean exiles, backed by the Association of Progressive Prosecutors in Valencia, lodged their own complaint related to crimes committed under Augusto Pinochet's rule, which was assigned to investigative judge Manuel García-Castellón.

In 1997, Judge Baltasar Garzón issued international arrest warrants against several Argentine military officials, including Leopoldo Fortunato Galtieri and Eduardo Massera. They were accused of genocide, terrorism, and torture committed during the Dirty War. He also expanded his investigations to crimes

[83] For a detailed account, see Roht-Arriaza, *The Pinochet Effect*, pp. 2–11.
[84] Baby, *Juger Franco?*

connected to Operation Condor, the transnational repressive system of South American dictatorships, introduced in the 1970s at Chile's behest, to track down and murder left-wing activists. Consequently, Garzón's investigations began to overlap with the Chilean inquiry. In 1998, when Pinochet was in London for medical treatment, Garzón also issued an arrest warrant against the former Chilean head of state, accusing him of the same crimes. As discussed in Chapter 3, these charges were problematic from the perspective of the dominant interpretation of international law. Garzón expanded the notion of genocide arguing that an 'auto-genocide' had been committed in Argentina (and in the Southern Cone in general) against a national subgroup formed by individuals who were deemed unsuitable to the new political and economic order—whether they actively opposed the regime or simply had a passive attitude towards it. Such interpretation provided an apolitical narrative regarding the military repression. The judge also used the classification of terrorism to include 'state terrorism', even though international law did not encompass such category.[85] The only category used according to standard definitions of international law was torture, but the arrest warrant also included acts of torture committed before the adoption of the 1984 UN Convention against Torture (which entered into effect in 1987), based on the argument that torture had been an international crime under customary law, long before 1984. In Garzón's view, such an interpretation was necessary to fight impunity. Crimes against humanity had not been yet integrated into the Spanish criminal code, and it was the duty of progressive judges to interpret international law in a manner that bypassed formalistic readings that allowed for impunity to continue unpunished.[86]

British judges, however, only partially endorsed Garzón's interpretation in their decision on Pinochet's extradition to Spain.[87] They did not engage in any debate about the definitions of genocide and terrorism: extradition for such crimes was illegal under British law because these crimes had not yet been incorporated into British criminal law. The majority of the judges agreed to grant the extradition, but only for acts of torture committed after the ratification of the 1984 Convention against Torture by the United Kingdom and for

[85] Juzgado Central de Instrucción no. 5 Audiencia Nacional Madrid, 'Auto de Procesamiento a 98 Militares Argentinos', available at www.derechos.org/nizkor/arg/espana/gar.html (accessed 24 April 2023). For Garzón's jurisprudence in the Pinochet case, see Richard J. Wilson, 'Prosecuting Pinochet: International Crimes in Spanish Domestic Law', *Human Rights Quarterly* 21, no. 4 (1999): pp. 927–979.

[86] Personal interview with Baltasar Garzón, Madrid, Spain, 18 November 2015.

[87] For three different British proceedings regarding Pinochet's extradition to Spain, see Roht-Arriaza, *The Pinochet Effect*, pp. 32–66; Michael Ratner and Reed Broody, eds., *The Pinochet Papers: The Case of Augusto Pinochet in Spain and Britain* (The Hague: Kluwer International Law, 2000).

conspiracy to torture prior to December 1988 (since conspiracy was considered to be a continuing offence). In taking a positivist approach, they evaded debates about the status of torture under customary international law before this date.[88] Nevertheless, the Pinochet cases in the United Kingdom were important for acknowledging several crucial issues pertaining to the UN Convention against Torture: namely, that it covered torture carried out by heads of state; it provided universal jurisdiction in national courts for the crime of torture; and it was inconsistent with the immunity of a former head of state.[89] Although Pinochet was ultimately not extradited to Spain for health reasons, the rulings of the British courts backed Spanish judicial efforts to prosecute international crimes—especially torture—based on the principle of universal jurisdiction. As various observers have underlined, the Pinochet case was one of the most important cases in the history of the prosecution of human rights,[90] one which activated other Latin American mobilizations in Spanish courts.

In 1999, Guatemalan human rights NGOs formulated their own complaint before the Audiencia Nacional. They accused eight military officials (including former President Efraín Ríos Montt) of genocide, terrorism, and torture committed in the 1980s, at the height of the Guatemalan civil war (1960–1996). Guatemalan activists were supported by Spanish solidarity groups and were also represented by the Argentinian-Spanish team of Carlos Slepoy, José Luis Galán, and Manuel Ollé Sesé that had coordinated the Argentinian complaint several years earlier.[91] In 2006, Judge Santiago Pedraz of the Audiencia Nacional issued international warrants for all eight individuals on charges of genocide. In 2007, the Guatemalan Constitutional Court ruled that the Spanish warrants had no legal basis in the Guatemalan–Spanish extradition treaty and declined the extradition. Since Spain prohibits trials in absentia, this decision put an end to the Guatemalan genocide trial in Madrid.[92] Victims from El Salvador also lodged complaints with the Audiencia Nacional but investigations were delayed, first due to questions about extraditions and later due to the amendment of the Spanish law on universal jurisdiction in 2009 and 2014 (see *infra*). In fact, the only trial and guilty verdict issued by Spanish courts based on the principle of

[88] Michael Ratner, 'The Lords Decision in Pinochet III', in *The Pinochet Papers: The Case of Augusto Pinochet in Spain and Britain*, edited by Michael Ratner and Reed Broody (The Hague: Kluwer International Law, 2000): pp. 32–52.

[89] Ibid, p. 34.

[90] Madeleine Davis, *The Pinochet Case: Origins, Progress, and Implications* (London: ILAS, University of London, 2003); *Manuel Ollé Sesé*, 'Tribuna Abierta: Contribución de la Justicia Universal a Latinoamérica', *Revista Electrónica Iberoamericana* 4, no. 2 (2010): pp. 5–7.

[91] Roht-Arriaza, *The Pinochet Effect*, p. 173.

[92] Naomi Roht-Arriaza, 'Guatemala Genocide Case', *The American Journal of International Law* 100 (2008): pp. 207–231. For more details on this case, see also Chapter 2.

universal jurisdiction concerned Adolfo Scilingo, a former Argentine naval officer involved in the 'death flights' during the 1970s. Scilingo had travelled to Spain in 1997 to testify against the leaders of the military junta during Baltasar Garzón's early investigations. Following his testimony, he was indicted and arrested in 1999. He was convicted by the Audiencia Nacional in 2005, and his conviction was confirmed in 2007 by the Supreme Court of Justice.[93]

Despite these limited results in terms of trials and convictions, the Latin American anti-impunity mobilizations in Spain and other Western European countries had important consequences in at least two respects. First, combined with the efforts at the IACtHR, they had a 'boomerang effect'[94]: due to transnational pressure, judges from Argentina, Chile, and Guatemala initiated their own investigations into dictatorial crimes and finally reversed the impunity status quo in their own countries. Second, Latin American mobilizations led to the creation of a transnational network of lawyers and NGOs committed to the promotion of universal jurisdiction as a key principle of international law. After Pinochet's arrest in London, a variety of Western European, North American, and Latin American legal experts and scholars, as well as global human rights organizations such as Amnesty International, Human Rights Watch, and the International Federation of Human Rights, organized joint campaigns to affirm the role of extraterritorial prosecutions as a means of combatting impunity at a global level.[95] This activism nurtured the hopes for victims of international crimes across the world that Spain (and Belgium) could become important venues of transnational justice. At the same time, however, it also led to a multiplication of criminal complaints based on universal jurisdiction, which accumulated in Spanish and Belgian courts and raised concerns about the effectiveness and financial cost of investigating extraterritorial crimes.[96]

[93] Alicia Gil Gil, 'The Flows of the Scilingo Judgement', *Journal of International Criminal Justice* 3, no. 5 (2005): pp. 1082–1091; Richard J. Wilson, 'Spanish Supreme Court Affirms Conviction of Argentine Former Naval Officer for Crimes against Humanity. *ASIL Insights* 12, 2008, American University, WCL Research Paper no. 2008-30, available at: https://ssrn.com/abstract=1090245 (accessed 23 April 2023).

[94] Margaret E. Keck and Kathryn Sikkink, *Activist beyond Borders: Advocacy Networks in International Politics* (Ithaca: Cornell University Press, 2014).

[95] The most active promoters of universal jurisdiction across borders include radical lawyers such as Wolfgang Kaleck in Germany, William Boudron in France, *Manuel Ollé Sesé* in Spain, and Michael Ratner in the United States; judges familiar with international law, such as Roger Le Loire in France, Damien Vandermeersch in Belgium, and Baltasar Garzón in Spain; and law professors open to universal jurisdiction, such as Eric David in Belgium and M. Cherif Bassiouni in the United States.

[96] Julian Seroussi, 'The Cause of Universal Jurisdiction: The Rise and Fall of an International Mobilisation', in *Lawyers and the Construction of Transnational Justice*, edited by Yves Dezalay and Bryant G. Garth (New York: Routledge, 2012): pp. 48–59.

In the first decade of the 2000s, Spanish and Belgian courts acknowledged jurisdiction over numerous cases, including the alleged genocide committed by Chinese authorities in Tibet and by Rwandan political and military leaders during the civil war; alleged acts of torture committed by US authorities at Guantanamo; and alleged war crimes committed by the Israeli government in Gaza.[97] While praised by human rights NGOs and victims' associations across the globe, the multiplication of these cases generated a backlash from a number of governments who accused the courts of infringing upon their national sovereignty. This sovereigntist discourse also denounced a 'tyranny of judges' who arbitrarily interfered in global affairs and transgressed the traditional jurisdiction of national judiciaries.[98] Political pressure by powerful states, such as China or the United States, but also critiques of 'neo-colonial justice' formulated by the African Union, finally led to the reformulation and narrowing of universal jurisdiction laws in Belgium (2003) and Spain (first in 2009 and then 2014) to include only prosecution based on the active or passive personality principle.[99]

Despite the gradual collapse of universal jurisdiction in Europe, the Latin American mobilizations for extraterritorial prosecutions made a significant impact on ICL. Combined with the efforts at the IACtHR, they represent the largest and most effective contemporary transnational mobilizations to end impunity for dictatorial crimes, through both the 'boomerang effect' and the global debates they sparked about the significance of transnational justice. As we shall see later in the chapter, starting in the first decade of the twenty-first century, Argentina took the lead in developing universal jurisdiction both in judicial practice and theory, although in highly politicized ways.

[97] For an inventory of these cases, see José Elías Esteve Moltó, 'Requiem for Universal Jurisdiction in Spain', *Quebec Journal of International Law* 33, no. 1 (2020): pp. 55–84; Seroussi, 'The Cause of Universal Jurisdiction'.

[98] See for instance Henry Kissinger, 'The Pitfalls of Universal Jurisdiction: Risking Judiciary Tyranny', *Foreign Affairs*, July–August 2011.

[99] Most analysts explain the 'fall' of universal jurisdiction in Europe through the lens of power politics and the political and economic pressure exercised by the great powers over small states. See Moltó, 'Requiem for Universal Jurisdiction'; Steven R. Ratner, 'Belgium's War Crimes Statute: A Postmortem', *American Journal of International Law* 97, no. 4 (2003): pp. 888–897; Ignacio Rasilla del Moral, 'The Swan Song of Universal Jurisdiction in Spain', *International Criminal Law Review* 9 (2009): pp. 777–808. Several scholars also point to the implosion of the cause from within. An increasing number of NGOs became involved in lodging complaints, without sharing a common and long-term legal strategy, using universal jurisdiction as a battlefield for their own legitimacy. See Seroussi, 'The Cause of Universal Jurisdiction'; Luc Raydams, 'The Rise and Fall of Universal Jurisdiction', Leuven Centre for Global Governance Studies, Working Paper no. 37, January 2010, available at https://ghum.kuleuven.be/ggs/publications/working_papers/2010/37Reydams (accessed 25 April 2023).

5 Argentina: The New Pioneer of Universal Jurisdiction?

After the amendment of the universal jurisdiction statutes in Belgium and Spain, transnational prosecutions of international crimes continued in various Western European courts, targeting low-ranking defendants who had become residents of the prosecuting states. These proceedings marked a shift in the role of national courts from 'global enforcers of justice' through international warrants to a more limited function of preventing 'safe heavens' for perpetrators seeking refuge in Western countries.[100] In contrast, since 2009, Argentina began to use universal jurisdiction in its broad meaning, including arrest warrants against high-profile defendants without Argentinian residence. Most of these cases were still pending as of April 2023, although some have generated investigations in the defendant's home country or created transnational solidarity movements that pressured international organizations toward supporting accountability. These trials illustrate the aspirations of a Global South semi-peripheric country, Argentina, to reverse relations of coloniality and asymmetries of power politics in global affairs by engaging with crimes committed by more powerful states, such as China or Spain. However, the cases themselves were highly politicized: ideological conflicts that originated in the Cold War continued to frame discourses on universal jurisdiction in twenty-first century Argentina. Right-wing and left-wing lawyers selected different cases to advance their politics and historical understanding of the past.

5.1 Defending the Argentinian Dictatorship, Accusing Communism: The Falun Gong Case

In 2005, the Falun Dafa Association of Argentina (FDAA) lodged a criminal complaint in Buenos Aires against Jiang Zemin (China's president from 1993 to 2003) and Luo Gan (a prominent member of the Politburo of the Chinese Communist Party), accusing them of acts of genocide and torture committed in China against members of the Falun Gong religious sect, starting in 1999.[101]

[100] Máximo Langer, 'Universal Jurisdiction Is Not Disappearing: The Shift from 'Global Enforcer' to 'No Safe Haven' Universal Jurisdiction', *Journal of International Criminal Justice* 13 (2015): pp. 245–256.

[101] Falun Dafa Association of Argentina, 'Informes sobre Causas Radicadas en la República Argentina Relacionadas con la Persecución contra Practicantes de la Falun Dafa en Territorio de China Continental, Buenos Aires, 2.02.2016', available at www.asociacionfalundafa.org.ar/wp-content/uploads/2016/09/2016-02-02-Resumen-Causas-de-Falun-Gong-en-Argentina.pdf (accessed 29 April 2023).

The FDAA filed the lawsuit while Luo Gan was visiting Argentina. A similar complaint had been lodged by Falun Gong members in Spain in 2004.[102] The Argentinian complaint was formulated in the context of a national political and judicial activist movement that had forced the reopening of trials against former military leaders accused of international crimes committed during the so-called Dirty War. As discussed in Chapter 2, in 2003, the leftist government led by Nestor Kirchner revoked the amnesty laws that had blocked prosecutions since the mid-1980s and engaged in an active memory politics that condemned the former dictatorship. On their side, judges across the country used the IACtHR's jurisprudence to dismiss amnesties and statutory limitations as justifications for curtailing justice for major international crimes. The first decade of the twenty-first century thus marked both the return to power of leftist Peronism and the multiplication of criminal trials related to gross human rights violations perpetrated during the dictatorship. The memory activism of first Nestor Kirchner and later Cristina Kirchner was acclaimed by victims' associations and human rights NGOs. Nevertheless, their activities were criticized by other sectors of the Argentinian elite as an instrumentalization of the past for the sake of reconsolidating leftist politics and enforcing a historical narrative that demonized military crimes, while hiding the leftist violent insurgencies of the 1970s under the rug.[103]

Two Argentinian lawyers constructed the Falun Gong case in Buenos Aires: during his youth, Alejandro Cowes had sympathized with the military dictatorship, but became disenchanted with right-wing military doctrines in the 1980s once he learned about the massive political repression. He nonetheless remained sceptical of leftist politics, which he associated with the communist regimes of Eastern Europe and the Latin American terrorism of the 1970s.[104] Adolfo Casabal Elía had also supported the military regime and maintained radical right-wing, anti-communist views after the fall of the dictatorship. In the mid-2000s, he defended various former Argentinian military officials accused of crimes against humanity, including Rafael Videla. He was part of an Argentinian right-wing elite that legitimized the military violence of the 1970s as a means of combatting communism.[105] While Casabal Elía helped build the legal argument, it was Cowes who represented the victims in courts. In an interview from 2022, he explained that he took the case due to this

[102] Moltó, 'Requiem for Universal Jurisdiction'.

[103] Francesca Lessa, *Memory and Transitional Justice in Argentina and Uruguay: Against Impunity* (New York: Palgrave Macmillan, 2013): pp. 120–126.

[104] Personal interview with Alejandro Cowes, online, 13 April 2022.

[105] Personal interview with Adolfo Casabal Elía, Buenos Aires, Argentina, 27 May 2022.

sympathy for Falun Gong victims, but also due to an alleged double standard in treating left- and right-wing political repression in Argentina:

> It was legitimate and necessary to judge the crimes committed by the military junta. However, Cristina Kirchner was engaging in aggressive memory politics concerning the right-wing dictatorship, but was strengthening economic relations with China and was thus validating a contemporary repressive communist regime.[106]

In January 2006, Federal Judge Octavio Aráoz de Lamadrid admitted the complaint; in December 2009, he issued arrest warrants against the two accused. The investigations were based on various reports published by the UN Commission of Human Rights, Human Rights Watch, and Amnesty International, as well as testimonies (taken in Buenos Aires and New York) of individuals who had been subjected to torture.[107] Lamadrid had studied international law in Spain between 2001 and 2002, including doctrines of universal jurisdiction. He was not, however, connected to the networks involved in constructing the Pinochet or Gualtieri cases, nor had he presided over the trials of military officials in Argentina after the reopening of prosecutions in 2001–2005. On the contrary, he considered the Argentinian human rights movement to be one-sided, focusing only on justice for right-wing military crimes, overlooking the left-wing terrorism of the 1970s and defending current socialist authoritarian regimes in Cuba and Venezuela. The Falun Gong case emerged as an opportunity to expand human rights jurisprudence to communist governments that were committing genocide in the present.[108]

From a legal point of view, Lamadrid argued that the violations perpetrated in China against Falun Gong members qualified as crimes against humanity and genocide as defined by the ICC statute. However, given that China did not recognize the jurisdiction of the ICC and had veto power at the UN Security Council, it was impossible to open investigations at the ICC. In contrast, the Argentinian law adopted in 2006 to implement the ICC statute stipulated that Argentine courts could exercise jurisdiction over foreigners who commit international crimes abroad as provided by treaties and international

[106] Personal interview with Alejandro Cowes, online, 13 April 2022.

[107] Juzgado Nacional en lo Criminal y Correccional Federal no. 9, 'Autos y Vistos de 12 de enero de 2006', and 'Autos y Vistos de 12 de diciembre 2009 / Causa no. 17.885/2005, caratulada "LUO GAN s/ imposición de torturas (art. 144 ter inciso 1° del Código Penal) y genocidio"'. Documents shared with the author by Octavio Araoz de Lamadrid.

[108] Personal interview with Octavio Araoz de Lamadrid, online, 12 April 2022.

conventions adopted by Argentina.[109] Moreover, the Argentinian Constitution of 1853, as amended in 1994 (Article 118), allowed for the exercise of jurisdiction over violations of *jus cogens* international norms outside national borders.[110] Lamadrid contextualized the oppression of the Falun Gong within the longer history of Chinese communist repression against religious groups. He argued that the Chinese authorities elevated the 'socialist ideology of Marx and Lenin' to the 'religion' of the state and denounced other religions as 'heresies'.[111]

Lamadrid's decision set an important precedent, in so far as he underlined the potential of Argentinian legislation to open prosecutions based on universal jurisdiction. His legal reasoning would later be used in other cases of extraterritorial prosecutions. However, the arrest warrants were sensitive for Cristina Kirchner's government, as it was negotiating for greater Chinese investment in Argentina. Furthermore, the case did not reverberate within the Argentinian human rights movement. According to Lamadrid,

> Nobody supported this cause. Cristina was trying to attract China's dirty money, so the government was reluctant. There was no solidarity from the Madres and Abuelas de la Plaza de Mayo, nor from the CELS [Center for Legal and Social Studies]. These organizations are too ideological and have no universal ethics that include crimes committed by the left.[112]

In 2010, Lamadrid left the bench after a conflict with the Kirchner government; another judge, Julian Ercolini, immediately revoked the arrest warrants. He argued that Argentina had no jurisdiction over crimes committed outside its territory, nor the possibility to investigate deeds perpetuated in distant places like China. In addition, the judiciary had exceeded its purview by interfering in matters of foreign affairs and put Argentina's foreign policy towards China in danger.[113] Indeed, after Lamadrid's decision, the Chinese embassy in Buenos Aires called for the closure of any criminal cases related to the Falun Gong, and Cristina Kirchner was forced to postpone a visit to Beijing.[114]

109 Argentina, Law no. 26.200/2006, Articles 3(d) and 5.

110 Juzgado Nacional en lo Criminal y Correccional Federal no. 9, 'Autos y Vistos de 12 de diciembre 2009 / Causa No. 17.885/2005, caratulada "LUO GAN s/ imposición de torturas (art. 144 ter inciso 1° del Código Penal) y genocidio"'.

111 Ibid.

112 Personal interview with Octavio Araoz de Lamadrid, online, 12 April 2022.

113 Juzgado Nacional en lo Criminal y Correccional Federal no. 9, Buenos Aires, 'Decisión de 21 Diciembre 2010, Causa Ni 17.885/05'.

114 'China Criticizes Argentina for Arrest Request of Jiang Zemin, Falun Gong Support', *VoaNews*, 23 September 2009.

Several months later, in December 2010, an appellate court confirmed the closure of the case, but based on different arguments. The judges argued that Argentina was entitled to investigate major international crimes based on universal jurisdiction, but—as the case was already under investigation in Spain—a similar Argentinian enterprise amounted to double jeopardy.[115] In a concurring opinion, Judge Eduardo G. Farah echoed the global criticism of universal jurisdiction, arguing that an arrest warrant only made sense if the accused was present in Argentina. Otherwise, such an enterprise entailed laborious extradition trials and battles over jurisdiction. Opening the Argentinian courts to practices of universal jurisdiction was likely to be costly and unproductive. Argentinian judges would be forced to consider applications from all over the world, hear witnesses outside Argentina, and have no means to access evidence and recover the 'historical truth'.[116]

The FDAA appealed the decision a second time, arguing that the judges had never requested information regarding developments in the Spanish courts. In 2012, two judges from the Federal Criminal Court of Cassation, Liliana Catucci and Eduardo Riggi, upheld the FDAA's arguments and ordered the reopening of the case.[117] Both were associated with right-wing politics, as they had found former Argentinian president Carlos Menem not guilty in various power of abuse trials, but convicted close collaborators of Cristina Kirchner for corruption. Until 2012, the case moved between jurisdictions for procedural reasons. Three years later, in Spain, the Supreme Court of Justice dismissed the Falun Gong case. The decision reflected the 2014 amendments to the law on universal jurisdiction, which allowed investigations into crimes committed outside Spain only if the victim or the perpetrator was a Spanish citizen or resident and if the perpetrator was on Spanish territory at the time of the investigations.[118] The case in Buenos Aires was still pending as of April 2023.

In the Falun Gong case, lawyers and judges with right-wing political views sought to overcome an alleged asymmetry in Argentinian memory politics, with its emphasis on right-wing military violence. Left-wing NGOs and human rights movements did not support the case. Despite this divide, judge Lamadrid's decision and its confirmation by the Federal Criminal Court of Cassation established Argentina's right to investigate major international

[115] Ibid.

[116] Ibid.

[117] 'Argentina: Cámara de Casación reabre causa por genocidio contra practicantes de Falun Gong Fuente: The Epoch Times en español', *TheEpochTimes*, 24 March 2015.

[118] Moltó, 'Requiem for Universal Jurisdiction'.

crimes committed outside its borders. The case also echoed internationally, with Lamadrid travelling to Geneva and New York to present his jurisprudence at the UN. The case did not, however, have any repercussions in China. Moreover, Chinese loans and investments in Argentina made right-wing politicians, such as President Mauricio Macri, step back from their previous criticism of human rights violations committed by Beijing. Argentina's economic dependence on China[119] kept the country in a subaltern global position, despite attempts by members of its legal elite to transform the country into a protagonist of the universal jurisprudence front.

5.2 'Moral Debts', Reversing Coloniality: The Case of Francoist Crimes

The second universal jurisdiction case in Argentina concerned crimes committed during the Spanish Civil War and the Francoist regime. In 2010, over 250 Spaniards lodged a complaint in Buenos Aires (the *Querella Argentina*), requesting investigations into genocide and crimes against humanity perpetrated by the Francoist army and administration between 1936 and 1977. The complaint was filed in reaction to the Spanish Supreme Court of Justice's 2010 decision to veto investigations into these crimes. While the Spanish Supreme Court had acknowledged that amnesties and statutory limitations did not apply to major international crimes in the Scilingo case, it rejected this reasoning as far as Francoist crimes were concerned. The majority decision contended that the Spanish Amnesty Law of 1977 was legally valid and politically legitimate, and dismissed Baltasar Garzón's attempts to open investigations.[120]

The *Querella Argentina* was constructed by a group of lawyers based in Madrid and Buenos Aires, and backed by high-profile Argentinian judges, such as Eugenio Zaffaroni.

[119] Luke Patey, 'China Made Mauricio Macri a Deal He Couldn't Refuse', *Foreign Policy*, 24 January 2017.

[120] Ulrike Capdepón, 'The Selectivity of Universal Jurisdiction: The History of Transnational Human Rights Prosecutions in Latin America and Spain', in *The Routledge History of Human Rights*, edited by Jean H. Quataert and Lora Wildenthal (London: Routledge, 2019): pp. 507–522.

Legal Advisers of the Victims of Francoism

Matias Bailone: Argentinian lawyer trained in ICL across Europe and Latin America. He was a senior adviser to the Ministries of Justice of Ecuador, Bolivia, and Peru and head of the Investigation Institute of the Argentinian Supreme Court of Justice between 2009 and 2015.
Carlos Slepoy: Argentinian lawyer jailed for political reasons from 1976 to 1977. Upon his release, he emigrated to Spain. He was a leading lawyer for the Argentinian and Guatemalan victims who mobilized in the Spanish courts in the 1990s.
Prof. Ana Messuti: Argentinian lawyer and scholar who went into exile in Madrid during the Argentinian dictatorship. She has published extensively on the duty to prosecute gross human rights violations.
David Baigún: professor of criminal law at Buenos Aires University. He had been connected to leftist human rights movements since the 1950s and suffered political persecution during both Juan Carlos Onganía's dictatorship (1966–1970) and the last military regime (1976–1983). After Argentina's democratic transition, he represented various victims in cases concerning the illegal appropriation of babies.
Beinusz Szmukler: Argentinian lawyer and leftist political militant who defended political prisoners during the Argentinian military dictatorship.
Máximo Castex: specialist in criminal law and close collaborator of David Baigún. He represented victims of the Argentinian military dictatorship in various trials during the 2000s.
Ricardo Huñis: specialist in criminal law and close collaborator of David Baigún. He represented victims of the Argentinian military dictatorship in various trials during the 2000s.
Jacinto Lara: Spanish lawyer and president of the Spanish Association Pro Derechos Humanos.
Carlos Zamorano: Leftist activist and member of the Argentinian League of Human Rights since the 1960s. He defended political prisoners during Onganía's dictatorship and was himself a political prisoner between 1974 and 1980.
Héctor Trajtemberg: member of the Argentinian League of Human Rights, who represented victims of the Argentinian military dictatorship in various trials in the 2000s.

The lawyers involved in the case all had left-wing political views; some of them had themselves been persecuted during the Argentinian military dictatorship, and some immigrated to Spain in the 1970s. Almost all had been involved in the Argentinian anti-impunity movements in Madrid or Buenos Aires and had close ties to the Madres and Abuelas de la Plaza de Mayo and the Argentinian League of Human Rights, and had collaborated with the CELS. The complaint thus maintained the alliance of Spanish and Latin American anti-impunity networks that led to Pinochet's arrest in London and the reopening of trials in Argentina and Chile in the early 2000s. Carlos Speloy's statement is relevant for most of the lawyers involved in this case:

> I have the honour of being one of the lawyers for this cause, as I was one of the lawyers involved in the cases opened in Spain in connection with the crimes committed by the Argentinean dictatorship. […] The effective application of the principle of universal jurisdiction (in Spain) was an extraordinary instrument to fight against impunity on a global level. Now is the time to apply this principle to those responsible for the crimes committed during and in the name of Francoism.[121]

According to Ana Messuti, these lawyers were connected by visions of ICL rooted in natural law philosophy and the social theory of law; but the complaint was also an opportunity to nourish their 'pride as global enforcers of justice'.[122] Since the reopening of trials in Argentina in 2001–2005, Argentinian lawyers and judges have gained international prestige as 'justice pioneers'.[123] The case concerning Franco-era crimes was an occasion to consolidate this status.

Starting in 2010, NGOs and victims' associations mobilized in Spain and Argentina to support the complaint.[124] On the Spanish side, various NGOs (including the Association for the Recovery of Historical Memory) banded together to establish the CEAQUA (Coordinadora Estadal de Apoyo a la

[121] Declaration by Carlos Slepoy in 2013, quoted by Baltasar Garzón, 'Justicia de Otro Lado del Charco: Los 10 Años de la Querella Argentina contra el Franquismo', *La Jurisdicción Universal en el Juicio al Franquismo: La Querella Argentina contra el Genocidio en España*, edited by Eugenio Raul Zaffaroni (Buenos Aires: Ediciones Olejnik, 2021): pp. 35–36.

[122] Personal interview with Ana Messuti, online, 28 April 2022.

[123] Kathryn Sikkink, 'From Pariah State to Global Protagonist: Argentina and the International Struggle for Human Rights', *Latin American Politics and Society* 50, no. 1 (2008): pp. 1–29.

[124] Maria Montoto Ugarte, 'Las víctimas del franquismo en "la Querella Argentina": luchas por el reconocimiento y nuevas desigualdades', *Papeles del CEIC*, 2017, no. 1, 28 February 2017, available at www.ehu.eus/ (accessed 30 April 2023).

Querella Argentina contra Crímenes del Franquismo) in 2012. This organization was active in consolidating Spanish–Argentinian networks and promoting the case in the Spanish Congress, at the European Parliament, and the UN.[125] Former judge Baltasar Garzón also supported the complaint through his NGO, the Baltasar Garzón International Foundation (FIBGAR). The NGO was founded in 2011 with the goal of combatting impunity and promoting the principle of universal jurisdiction across the world.[126] Global NGOs, such as Amnesty International, as well as UN rapporteurs on transitional justice, such as Pablo de Greif, also joined this transnational support network.

On the Argentinian side, organizations such as the Madres and Abuelas de la Plaza de Mayo, CELS, and the Argentinian League for Human Rights backed the complaint, describing their campaign as paying a 'historical debt' towards Spaniards who had supported their anti-impunity efforts in the 1990s.[127] The *Querella Argentina* was assigned to María Servini de Cubria, one of the first judges to investigate cases of illegal appropriation of babies during the military dictatorship and to return children to the families as early as the 1970s. Between September 2013 and October 2014, Servini issued international arrest warrants against twenty-four former Francoist officials, including two former ministers, accused of torture and the murder of political opponents in the 1970s.[128] Employing Lamadrid's legal precedent in the Falun Gong case, Servini argued that investigations had been halted in Spain due to the 1977 Amnesty Law, and that the Argentinian legislation allowed investigations based on universal jurisdiction. She used documents gathered by Baltasar Garzón as part of his 2008 inquiry, as well as new victim statements taken in Buenos Aires and Madrid. She argued that Francoist crimes amounted to crimes against humanity, and that amnesties and statutory limitations did not apply to these crimes. The arrest warrants were thus legal under Argentinian and international law.[129]

[125] For the CEAQUA mobilization, see www.ceaqua.org/dossier-de-actividad/ (accessed 30 April 2023). By 2022, CEAQUA had filed around 600 lawsuits and constructed a widespread transnational movement of more than 150 social and political organizations. Capdepón, 'The Selectivity of Universal Jurisdiction', p. 516.

[126] For FIBGAR's activities, see https://baltasargarzon.org/en/baltasar-garzon-2/in-other-countries/ (accessed 25 April 2023).

[127] Gabriel Gatti, '"Lo nuestro, como en Argentina": Humanitarian Reason and the Latin Americanization of Victimhood in Spain', *Journal of Latin American Cultural Studies* 25, no. 1 (2022): pp. 147–165, at p. 147.

[128] Juzgado Nacional en lo Criminal y Correccional Federal no. 1, 'Autos y Vistos de 18 de septiembre 2013 / Causa No. 4591/2010, caratulada 'N.N. / genocidio'; Juzgado Nacional en lo Criminal y Correccional Federal no. 1, 'Autos y Vistos de 30 octubre 2014 / Causa No. 4591/2010, caratulada '*Galvan Abascal Celso; Muñecas Aguilar; Giralte Gónzález, José Ignacio … y otros s/ imposición de torturas …*'

[129] Ibid.

In response to Servini's warrants, Spanish judge Pablo Ruz[130] summoned two former Francoist police officers accused of torture in December 2013. This was the first time that Franco's alleged torturers had to testify before a Spanish court. In 2014, the case was however closed. The Spanish Audiencia Nacional refused the extradition of the suspects to Argentina on three grounds: the 1977 Amnesty Law was valid in Spain and no prosecutions could be initiated; the statutory limitations for the crimes of torture and murder had expired; and Argentina had no legitimacy to intervene in the Spanish judicial process.[131]

The Spanish judiciary's refusal to cooperate with Servini reflected a double standard, if not a colonial attitude towards Argentina's attempts to prosecute Francoist crimes. The same Audiencia Nacional, which had condemned former Argentinian officer Adolfo Scilingo in 2005 for crimes against humanity based on universal jurisdiction, was now rejecting Argentina's judicial intervention based on the sovereignty principle. In a 2016 interview, Joaquín Giménez García, a judge at the Spanish Supreme Court of Justice who had confirmed Scilingo's conviction, declared:

> I have a very positive attitude towards universal jurisdiction. Especially if we talk about the European Union, as a common space of justice, freedom, and security. In the European Union, it is normal to have cooperation between a court in Cádiz and a court in Sofia, for instance. There are also crimes that concern the entirety of humanity. Therefore, the International Criminal Court was created. [. . .] But the case opened in Argentina refers to crimes that have been amnestied or for which the statute of limitation had expired [in Spain]. One must take national legal and historical contexts into consideration.[132]

Giménez García's statement demonstrates how universal jurisdiction remained a selective, mostly Eurocentric, mechanism in Spain. Its conceptualization was dependent on asymmetrical international political power relations and the way judges understood the legitimacy of national political and legal arrangements in their own countries. The legal reasoning used in the Scilingo case by the Spanish courts became invalid once Argentinian courts employed it to overcome impunity in Spain.

[130] Pablo Ruz had already used universal jurisdiction in Spain to open investigations into crimes committed by the Moroccan military in West Sahara between 1975 and 1991 and torture committed in Guantanamo by the George Bush II administration in the 2000s.

[131] María Manuel Márquez Velásquez, 'The Argentinian Exercise of Universal Jurisdiction 12 Years after Its Opening', *OpinioJuris*, 04 February 2022, available at http://opiniojuris.org/ (accessed 27 April 2023).

[132] Personal interview with Joaquín Giménez García, Madrid, Spain, 28 May 2016.

As of April 2023, the *Querella Argentina* had not yet resulted in any guilty verdicts in Buenos Aires or Madrid. On the contrary, in 2022, when one of the accused, Rodolfo Martín Villa, contested his international arrest warrant, the Argentinian Federal Appellate Court ruled that Servini's investigations lacked sufficient evidence. The court did not close the case but referred it to the lower courts for further inquiries.[133] Despite the lack of effective prosecutions, these initiatives revitalized the debates about justice for Francoist crimes. A growing number of Spanish city governments—including Barcelona, Pamplona, Zaragoza, and Cádiz—have joined the *Querella Argentina* and filed their own applications to the Spanish courts.[134]

Argentinian–Spanish judicial activism has instead had a significant impact beyond criminal justice. Several mass graves were exhumated by Spanish authorities in response to Argentinian pressure. Repertoires of contentious actions used by Argentinian victims in the 1970s, such as the weekly protests of the Madres of Plaza del Mayo, were reproduced in Spain, in the so-called 'Thursday round' (or Ronda de la Dignidad), organized every Thursday since 2010 at the Puerta del Sol Square in Madrid demanding justice for Francoist crimes.[135] The transitional justice tryptic, 'truth, memory, and justice', coined by Latin American anti-impunity movements, also became a demand made by Spanish NGOs and victims' associations.[136] Iconic paradigms of victimhood originating in the Southern Cone and especially in Argentina, such as 'the detained-disappeared' or 'illegally appropriated babies' were adapted to Spanish circumstances.[137] Although criticized by some analysts as artificial,[138] these paradigm transfers consolidated transnational mnemonic solidarities concerning repressive right-wing military regimes in Latin America and Europe.

The *Querella Argentina* reveals the ambivalence of Argentinian attempts to upend the peripheral, subaltern status of the Global South in relation to the Global North. On the one hand, categories of international law and repertoires of contentious action originating in Argentina were borrowed by Spanish activists. Argentina thus operated as a 'leading supplier' of mnemonic categories—a supplier that added new 'Latin', Global South, referents to a Eurocentric

[133] Ana Maria Pascual, 'Las falsedades del discurso de Martín Villa, que sigue imputado en Argentina', *Publico*, 17 January 2022.

[134] Capdepón, 'The Selectivity of Universal Jurisdiction', p. 518.

[135] Ugarte, 'Las víctimas del franquismo', p. 11.

[136] Capdepón, 'The Selectivity of Universal Jurisdiction'.

[137] Gatti, '"Lo nuestro, como en Argentina"'.

[138] See for example Vincent Druliolle, 'The Struggle for Recognition of the Stolen Children and the Politics of Victimhood in Spain', in *The Politics of Victimhood in Post-conflict Societies*, edited by Vincent Druliolle and Roddy Brett (Cham: Springer International, 2018): pp. 77–99.

memory constructed around the uniqueness of the Holocaust.[139] On the other hand, the investigations in Buenos Aires caused an 'extraterritorial backfire effect' highlighting Spain's attempts to hold universal jurisdiction proceedings for crimes committed in Latin America, while refusing to reckon with its own dictatorial past.[140] The lack of effective results can be seen as a confirmation of the recurring critiques of selectivity, neocolonialism, and paternalism raised against the principle of universal jurisdiction. As in the Falun Gong case, these pending lawsuits demonstrate that Global South semi-peripheral countries still have limited power to bring perpetrators from the Western centre—or from other global powers—to justice. However, the *Querella Argentina* became an inspiration for victims of mass repression in Myanmar and Paraguay.

Leftist human rights NGOs involved in the *Querella Argentina*, such as the Abuelas of the Plaza de Mayo and the Foundation for Peace and Justice (Fundación Servicio Paz y Justicia), also supported a criminal complaint against Myanmar's top military and political leaders—including Commander-in-Chief Senior General Min Aung Hlaing and Aung San Suu Kyi—accused of committing genocide against the Rohingya Muslim minority in 2015 and 2016.[141] The complaint was lodged in November 2019 by Argentinian lawyer Tomás Ojea Quintana—former UN Human Rights Council's Special Rapporteur on human rights in Myanmar from 2008 to 2014—on behalf of the Burmese Rohingya Organization UK. Since the 1990s, Quintana has led important trials on behalf of victims of the Argentinian military dictatorship. He had represented the Abuelas of the Plaza del Mayo in cases of illegal appropriation of babies and led a successful case against representatives of Ford Motors Argentina involved in political repression in the 1970s.[142] The support of Argentinian NGOs for the Rohingya was a direct result of their trust in Quintana as a human rights lawyer of national and international repute and reflected the solidarity of leftist Argentinian militants with victims of former (and current) military dictatorships.

The complaint was lodged with the same judge who investigated Francoist crimes. However, Judge Servini dismissed the case in December 2019, arguing that the ICC prosecutor had already launched investigations into the repression

[139] Gatti, '"Lo nuestro, como en Argentina"'.

[140] Máximo Langer and Mackenzie Eason, 'The Quiet Expansion of Universal Jurisdiction', *The European Journal of International Law* 30, no. 3 (2019): pp. 779–817, at p. 808.

[141] Kriangsak Kittichaisaree, *The Rohingya, Justice and International Law* (New York: Routledge, 2022): pp. 215–223.

[142] For Tomás Ojea Quintana's biography, see www.ohchr.org/en/special-procedures/sr-dprk (accessed 28 April 2023).

of the Rohingya, and any Argentinian initiative would duplicate the ICC endeavours. She also contended that the lack of cultural connections between Myanmar and Argentina rendered any understanding of the Burmese political context very difficult, possibly leading to biased conclusions.[143] Quintana appealed the decision and obtained an official letter from the ICC that confirmed that Argentina could investigate the crimes based on the ICC complementarity principle. In 2021, an Argentinian federal criminal court overturned Servini's decision and ordered criminal investigations. The court also allowed six Rohingya women to testify remotely about alleged acts of murder and rape committed by the Myanmar military.[144]

The investigations have however remained sluggish. In contrast to the Spanish case, the Rohingya complaint was more complicated: investigations could not be carried out in Myanmar given the return of the military to power in 2021. Documents and witness statements had to be translated into Spanish, and travel to Buenos Aires was expensive.[145] However, Quintana continued to seek support from international organizations. As the UN Special Rapporteur on human rights in the Democratic People's Republic of Korea (North Korea) starting in 2016, he had the leverage to influence international organizations to exert pressure for further investigations. His efforts resulted in a meeting, in April 2022, between experts of the UN Independent Investigative Mechanism for Myanmar and judge Servini in Buenos Aires. As of April 2023, the case had stalled however, as Servini had to deal with both the evergrowing number of complaints related to Franco-era crimes and investigations into alleged electoral fraud in Argentina—another complex and time-consuming issue.[146]

5.3 Universal Jurisdiction and Its 'Boomerang Effect' in Paraguay

The only case with an effective impact on prosecutions and guilty verdicts concerned gross human rights violations committed in Paraguay between 1954 and 1989 during Alfredo Stroessner's dictatorship. As seen in Chapter 2, certain trials had already taken place in Paraguay in the 1990s, but most investigations

[143] Ministerio Público Federal, 'La Cámara Federal porteña ordenó investigar la denuncia sobre crímenes de lesa humanidad en Myanmar', 29 January 2022, available at www.fiscales.gob.ar/fiscalias/la-camara-federal-portena-ordeno-investigar-la-denuncia-sobre-crimenes-de-lesa-humanidad-en-myanmar/ (accessed 28 April 2022).
[144] Ibid.
[145] Personal interview with Tomás Quintana, online, 12 May 2022.
[146] Ibid.

had been delayed, and only a few police officers were ever convicted. Victims' associations and the Paraguayan Truth Commission lodged various criminal complaints in Paraguay at the beginning of the 2000s, but without result. Within this context, in 2013, Paraguayan victims' associations requested the Argentinian judiciary to open investigations into the torture and the enforced disappearances of political opponents. Most of these victims had been middle-class educated individuals. The complaint pointed to around 480 alleged perpetrators identified by the Paraguay Truth Commission. It evoked both universal jurisdiction and the passive personality principle, as certain victims had been Argentinian citizens, persecuted under Operation Condor.[147] In 2014, representatives of the Indigenous Aché community signed on to the request, demanding an investigation into the destruction of their people during the 1970s—through killings, torture, rape, and internment in special colonies, where they were subject to forced labour and inhumane treatment.[148] The Aché case was thoroughly documented, revealing that more than 70 per cent of the community was exterminated in the 1970s. However, most alleged perpetrators mentioned in the complaint were already dead, while others remained unidentified.

The complaint was formulated by Aitor Martínez Jiménez, a thirty-two-year-old Spanish lawyer trained in international law. He had worked for the Spanish Ministry of Foreign Affairs in Paraguay in the early 2000s and had been involved as a consultant for justice and memory programmes surrounding the Stroessner dictatorship. In 2011, he joined the FIBGAR. The criminal complaint lodged in Argentina reflected the Foundation's aspiration to become a global justice entrepreneur. As Martínez explained in a 2015 interview, the Foundation initially searched for dual-national, Spanish and Paraguayan, victims to address the Spanish courts based on the passive personality principle. It also considered Argentina as a potential venue, due to its expansive approach to universal jurisdiction, and the arrest warrants in the Falun Gong and Francoist regime cases. Ultimately, the Foundation opted for Argentina, given that several Argentinian citizens had been victims of the Stroessner regime, and Argentina had already initiated a trial in relation to Operation Condor. Moreover, Argentina was a neighbouring country with a similar legal

[147] 'Querella criminal por la comisión de los delitos de genocidio y / o lessa humanidad que tuvieron lugar en Paraguay en el periodo comprendido entre el 15 de augosto 1954 e el 3 de febrero 1989' (6 August 2013). Document shared with the author by Aitor Martínez Jiménez.

[148] Iván Herrera, 'Indígenas Aché de Paraguay piden a juez argentino investigar crímenes de dictadura', *Servindi*, 12 April 2014, available at www.servindi.org/actualidad/104145 (accessed 25 April 2023).

system—an aspect that facilitated investigations. According to Martínez, the primary goal of the complaint was to pressure Paraguayan authorities to unblock the cases rather than initiate a trial in Argentina:

> Universal jurisdiction is not a very efficient mechanism if we expect trials and guilty verdicts in the foreign jurisdiction. Generally, there is no trial, because the defendants reside in the country where they committed the crime. However universal jurisdiction helps to unblock the situation in those respective countries.[149]

The Paraguayan complaint partially accomplished its purpose. After six years in which Argentinian judges systematically requested information about the status of investigations, Paraguayan courts launched prosecutions in 2019 and convicted three former officials for torture and the murder of political opponents during the 1970s.[150] In contrast to the limited impact of the *Querella Argentina* on Spanish courts, the Paraguayan judiciary responded to transnational pressure in order to avoid potential international warrants and international opprobrium for being a haven for impunity. The epistemic coloniality that Argentina exerted over Paraguayan legal experts might also help explain this judicial response. Paraguayan legal textbooks relied extensively on Argentinian scholarship and jurisprudence, and many Paraguayan scholars and legal practitioners saw Argentina as a source of both doctrinal inspiration and judicial practice.[151]

Conversely, no investigation into the Aché case was ever initiated. The case was inherently more problematic because the main accused had already passed away. The outcome also reflected an asymmetry between justice for middle-class political opponents and justice for Indigenous populations. According to an anthropologist who worked for decades with the Aché groups, the case lodged in Argentina presented an ambivalent picture. On the one hand, members of the Aché community had the opportunity to testify and present their own version of events. On the other hand, they were instrumentalized by Western NGOs, such as the FIBGAR, to boost their own legitimacy as global enforcers of justice.[152] In the end, the Aché remained second-class

[149] Personal interview with Aitor Martínez Jiménez, Asunción, Paraguay, 4 February 2015.
[150] 'Tres torturadores stronistas son condenados por crimen de Celestina', *Ultima Hora*, 21 December 2019.
[151] Personal interview with Luis Lezcano Claude, Asunción, Paraguay 18 July 2016.
[152] Personal interview with Philippe Edeb Piragi, Asunción, Paraguay, 8 February 2015.

victims, a reality that maintained the citizenship status they were given during Stroessner's dictatorship.[153]

5.4 The Madrid–Buenos Aires Principles: A Radical Project of Universal Jurisdiction

In addition to cases brought before the Argentinian courts, Latin American (and especially Argentinian) lawyers, judges, and activists, engaged—alongside the FIBGAR—in a process of reinterpretation and advancement of doctrinal aspects of universal jurisdiction. In 2015, these efforts materialized in the Madrid–Buenos Aires Principles of Universal Jurisdiction, formulated to improve doctrines previously articulated by Western and African experts.

In the 1990s, following the growing number of arrest warrants based on universal jurisdiction in Europe, various legal scholars sought to clarify the principles and practices of this emergent area of ICL. The first collective attempt was initiated by the International Commission of Jurists, supported by the Program in Law and Public Affairs at Princeton University. It resulted in the Princeton Principles of Universal Jurisdiction, adopted in November 2000 by a group of legal experts, mostly from North America and Western Europe. The very few non-Western scholars who participated in the debates were based at Western universities.[154] The Princeton Principles affirmed the legitimacy of extraterritorial prosecutions for major international crimes—including piracy, slavery, war crimes, crimes against peace, genocide, crimes against humanity, and torture—and underlined that national courts could use universal jurisdiction even if their national legislation did not specifically provide for it. They excluded amnesties, statutory limitations, as well as diplomatic immunity as exculpatory elements. The Principles were also well crafted in respect to the liberal rule of law, including due process, the prohibition of double jeopardy and trials in absentia, and the prohibition of the death penalty. The document called for the inclusion of universal jurisdiction

[153] Two other criminal complaints were filed in Argentina based on universal jurisdiction but none has reached the courts. The first, formulated in 2022, concerns Saudi Arabia's crown prince and minister of defence, Mohammed bin Salman al Saud, who is accused of the torture of political opponents and war crimes resulting from the Saudi-led coalition's military campaign in Yemen, which began in 2015. The second one concerns alleged war crimes and crimes against humanity perpetrated in Gaza since 2009 by five high-ranking Israeli officials, including Prime Minister Benjamin Netanyahu.

[154] See Stephen Macedo, ed., *The Princeton Principles of Universal Jurisdiction* (Princeton, NJ: Program in Law and Public Affairs, Princeton University): pp. 63–65, available at https://lapa.princeton.edu/hosteddocs/unive_jur.pdf (accessed 25 April 2023).

in all future ICL treaties and encouraged states to incorporate the principle in national legislations.[155]

However, the composition of the Princeton group embedded these principles in a Western liberal vision of human rights that was criticized by both African and Latin American legal experts and activists.[156] First, apartheid was excluded from the list of crimes—an ironic exclusion, given that the 1973 Apartheid Convention was the first and only ICL instrument to clearly include the principle of universal jurisdiction. This omission reflected a Western-centric view on major international crimes, wherein no Western government ever ratified the 1973 Apartheid Convention. Second, the Princeton Principles focused only on sanctions for violations of civil and political rights. There was no reference to violations of social, economic, and cultural rights, even though Global South activists and scholars had systematically underlined the importance of these rights for Asia, Africa, and Latin America. Third, the Princeton Principles remained confined to an ICL paradigm that envisioned responsibility only for individuals, while legal entities, such as multinational corporations that had participated in or profited from mass crimes, continued to be immune from justice. Fourth, they referred only to criminal law, leaving aside civil law complaints.

Given these critiques and the absence of participants from sub-Saharan Africa at Princeton, the Africa Legal Aid convened two meetings in Cairo (2001) and Arusha (2002) to devise principles of universal jurisdiction from an African perspective. The meetings resulted in the Cairo–Arusha Principles of Universal Jurisdiction, which departed from the Princeton Principles in several respects. The preamble mentioned apartheid as a major international crime with particular resonance in Africa. The list of crimes was enlarged to include 'serious environmental crimes', gender-based crimes, such as rape and other forms of sexual violence, and crimes with 'major adverse economic, social, or cultural consequences, such as acts of plunder and gross misappropriation of public resources'. The document stated that universal jurisdiction would apply not only to natural persons but also other legal entities, including multinational corporations that participated in or benefited from dictatorships and armed conflicts. It also called for the protection of victims and witnesses. The Cairo–Arusha Principles went further than the Princeton Principles but remained regionally confined to Africa. According to Aitor Martínez Jiménez,

[155] Ibid, pp. 28–36.

[156] See Evelyn A. Ankumah, 'The Cairo-Arusha Principles on Universal Jurisdiction in Respect of Gross Human Rights Offenses: An African Perspective', *Proceedings of the ASIL (American Society of International Law) Annual Meeting*, 98 (2004): pp. 238–240.

they were also limited as far as the protection of social, economic, and cultural rights was concerned and did not sufficiently reflect the rights of Indigenous populations connected to environmental crimes.[157]

In response to these critiques (corroborated by the absence of Latin American participants at Princeton, Cairo, and Arusha), the FIBGAR, in collaboration with Latin American lawyers, took on a reformulation of previous approaches to universal jurisdiction, leading to the adoption of the Madrid–Buenos Aires Principles in 2015. Legal experts and human rights activists who had collaborated on extraterritorial prosecutions in Spain and Argentina—including Baltasar Garzón, Carlos Slepoy, Raúl Zaffaroni, Daniel Rafecas, Rigoberta Menchú, and Dolores Delgado García—were at the forefront of the initiative. African and Asian participants also took part in the discussions, which unfolded between 2014 and 2015 during six seminars in Madrid, Puerto Rico, Asunción, The Hague, Johannesburg, and Buenos Aires. North American and Western European experts were also invited, but they were far outnumbered by Global South participants.[158]

The Madrid–Buenos Aires Principles added a set of new recommendations to previous guidelines. They enlarged the list of crimes to include economic and environmental crimes—such as acts of corruption fuelling conflicts and the destruction of ecosystems. They proposed the criminalization of forced population transfers with the purpose of exploiting the natural resources of 'ancestral lands'—a mechanism designed to protect Indigenous populations. The document also promoted universal jurisdiction for civil law cases and reinforced the Cairo–Arusha innovations regarding the criminal liability of legal persons (including multinational corporations) and the special protection of victims and witnesses.[159] Through the global scope of the participants involved in the debates, the references to violations of socio-economic rights, and the protection of Indigenous populations, the Madrid–Buenos Aires Principles represented the most comprehensive universal jurisdiction project adopted thus far. However, the reverberations of these principles were limited. Western and African scholars have not written about them, as has been the case with the Princeton Principles and to a lesser extent the Cairo–Arusha Principles. The Madrid–Buenos Aires initiative has remained a semi-peripheral proposal with little impact in Western Europe and North America.

[157] Personal interview with Aitor Martínez Jiménez, Asunción, Paraguay, 4 February 2015.

[158] For the list of participants, see https://fibgar.org/upload/proyectos/35/en/principles-of-universal-jurisdiction.pdf (accessed 25 April 2023).

[159] Ibid.

The CEE and Latin American mobilizations for transnational justice reflect different legal tactics, informed by different historical narratives, and with differing impacts on the development of ICL. The CEE attempts to establish a European tribunal for communist crimes was a dead letter due to both divisions between East and West concerning the uniqueness of the Holocaust and right- and left-wing political conflicts over the significance of communist ideology. The financial implications of creating such a tribunal also rendered this strategy problematic. In parallel, CEE justice entrepreneurs did not engage with the concept of universal jurisdiction, believing that such an endeavour would only generate accusations of an infringement of national sovereignty. In addition, employing universal jurisdiction would have entailed not only a knowledge of different legal systems but also coalitions with Western human rights lawyers to help with criminal complaints in countries such as Spain or Belgium, and financial resources for translating large numbers of documents and many hours of witness testimony. This strategy was too expensive and time consuming for CEE justice and memory entrepreneurs, who systematically sought to capitalize on an anti-communist discourse to gain political and symbolic power nationally and at a European level. At the same time, complaints at the ECtHR remained the purview of the victims. CEE justice entrepreneurs restrained from addressing the ECtHR, a time-consuming strategy that would have, again, demanded major legal and financial resources. Nonetheless, the complaints based on the passive personality principle showed that transnational pressure could be instrumental in opening investigations. German prosecutors compelled their Czech counterparts to draft an indictment although the trial was halted due to the poor health of the accused. Transnational civil trials in Czechia and Slovakia were also successful in as much as they acknowledged the crimes committed by the communist regime at their borders. However, the conflation of anti-communism, the denunciation of all forms of neo-Marxist thinking, and radical conservative politics—including an opposition to gender equality and racism against Asian and African refugees—rendered CEE justice mobilizations deeply problematic for both socialist and liberal elites and NGOs across Europe.

In contrast, Latin American activists in the 1990s renounced the radical left discourse of the 1960s and early 1970s and embraced a liberal, humanitarian rhetoric of human rights. They mobilized in various jurisdictions and found common ground with European lawyers and judges in a shared quest for justice and a progressive interpretation of international law no matter the ideology behind these crimes. The international arrest warrants issued in France, Germany, and especially in Spain, together with the IACtHR's jurisprudence, were instrumental in creating an anti-impunity ethos among judges from the Southern Cone, who gradually opened prosecutions across the region. They also contributed to the consolidation of the idea that amnesties, pardons, and statutory limitations could not apply to major international crimes. Moreover, Latin American activism was the catalyst for transnational networks that promoted universal jurisdiction as a principle of ICL, including the formulation of the Madrid–Buenos Aires Principles.

However, the engagement of Argentinian courts and legal experts with universal jurisdiction since 2009 has had mixed results, revealing both a fragmented field of activism and the limited ability of a semi-periphery to overcome global impunity. On the one hand, Argentina emerged as a promising Global South venue for extraterritorial prosecutions of major international crimes, and fed hopes that universal justice could be exerted after the limits imposed in Spain and Belgium. Mobilizations in Argentina boosted global anti-impunity movements, and encouraged transnational solidarity between victims of oppressive regimes. The Madrid–Buenos Aires Principles renewed the doctrinarian debates on this area of ICL and proposed a progressive and Global South-oriented project of universal justice. On the other hand, as of April 2023, only the Paraguayan complaint has engendered any concrete legal consequences through a 'boomerang effect' at home. In contrast, the Falun Gong and Spanish complaints reflected the semi-peripheral status of Argentinian courts, whereby attempts to hold the political and military elite of more influential states accountable were unsuccessful. The Spanish courts assumed their right to judge former Latin American military officials based on universal jurisdiction, but rejected the same principles and legal reasoning once Argentinian courts claimed the same right to investigate Franco-era crimes. Argentina's dependency on Chinese investments revealed the reluctance of Buenos Aires politicians—both from the left and the right—to criticize Beijing's human rights record. For its part, the 'boomerang effect' of the Paraguayan complaint reflected a specific Argentinian influence on Paraguayan judiciary and legal education, doctrine and practice. It also had no consequence on the opening of investigations into crimes against the Aché, who remain second-class citizens in terms of their access to justice. Similarly, the Madrid–Buenos Aires Principles were ignored by Western governments and Western academia, reflecting the impact of relations of coloniality and asymmetries of power on practices of universal justice. Moreover, the cases opened in Buenos Aires based on universal jurisdiction revealed a fracture within the community of Argentinian activists, who selectively used this principle to advance their right- or left-wing political interpretations and visions of the past.

5

Resisting the Duty to Prosecute

Bulgarian judges did everything possible to close any investigation into communist crimes. They dismissed international criminal law instruments that acknowledge the duty to prosecute gross human rights violations, arguing that they had not been part of Bulgarian legislation during the communist period. For Bulgarian judges, customary international law and even international conventions ratified during communism had no relevance despite their use in other Eastern European countries and across the globe.

Vasil Kadrinov, Bulgarian human rights activist[1]

The Amnesty Law is a political position endorsed by most Brazilian judges, even those with left-wing political views. Given the power of the military brass in contemporary Brazil and the pressures they exerted to close any debate about the past, the fear of democratic reversal remains strong. But it is also a matter of a legal culture reluctant to embrace international law.

Paulo Fontes, Brazilian judge[2]

1. Introduction

The fragmentation of international criminal law (ICL) in both Latin America and Central Eastern Europe (CEE) was further cemented by the reluctance to investigate crimes committed under dictatorships and during violent conflicts. Cultures of impunity continue to exist in the two regions and across the globe, as governments and national judiciaries continue to evade an international regime that, in recent decades, has begun to impose the duty to prosecute gross human rights violations. While a significant body of international law and jurisprudence now acknowledges that amnesties, statutory limitations, and other

[1] Personal interview with Vasil Kadrinov, Sofia, Bulgaria, 30 March 2017.
[2] Personal interview with Paulo Fontes, online, 14 December 2021.

Justice and Memory after Dictatorship. Raluca Grosescu, Oxford University Press. © Raluca Grosescu 2024.
DOI: 10.1093/oso/9780192870346.003.0005

legal provisions should not impede indictments for major international crimes, national state practice does not always follow these international trends. Given the long history of not only amnesties as a means of promoting political reconciliation, but also statutes of limitation as a means of assuring due process, domestic courts persist in invoking them as political and legal arguments against the duty to prosecute.

This chapter illustrates this tendency through two case studies—Bulgaria and Brazil—where national judiciaries endorsed legal narratives that maintained impunity for dictatorial crimes and historical accounts that circumvented a critical interrogation of the dictatorial past. Most courts applied a very restrictive notion of non-retroactivity and continued to frame the crimes of previous regimes as acts of ordinary—versus international—criminality. They resisted ICL principles that impose a duty to prosecute, arguing that such principles had not been in force in their jurisdictions when the crimes were committed. In Bulgaria, the application of the 1968 UN Convention on the Non-Applicability of Statutory Limitations to War Crimes and Crimes against Humanity to communist crimes was declared unconstitutional in 2016—even though Bulgaria had ratified this convention in 1969. In Brazil, the 1979 Amnesty Law is still in force despite various decisions of the Inter-American Court of Human Rights (IACtHR) that called upon the Brazilian government and judiciary to void it and conduct investigations into the crimes of the military regime.

Tensions between impunity and pro-accountability legal discourses developed in both countries, particularly after 2010. Bulgarian right-wing politicians attempted to challenge the status quo with legislative proposals that aimed to criminalize the communist regime in its entirety—a tactical decision that compromised more realistic strategies to fight impunity for major international crimes. The judicial responses to these political initiatives revealed a reluctance of the courts to employ ICL and to contain a radical anti-communist discourse. In parallel, Brazilian judges and prosecutors have become increasingly divided over the applicability of the Amnesty Law to military crimes. Attempts to prosecute gross human rights violations have been initiated across the country, but without success. The 1979 consensus over the Amnesty Law, and the 1985 negotiated transition that confirmed these arrangements, enshrined the refusal of the judiciary to alter the status quo. While pro-accountability strategies differed in Bulgaria and Brazil, the resistance to the duty to prosecute prevailed in both countries due both to a lack of political will to reverse impunity and a dominant legal education that was nearly impermeable to new ICL trends.

2. The Duty to Prosecute: An Emergent Principle of ICL

The duty to prosecute major international crimes is a relatively new ICL principle which gained momentum at the end of the 1990s, and particularly in the first decade of the twenty-first century. Even if after the Second World War this principle was inscribed in various international conventions,[3] amnesties continued to be used and promoted as appropriate solutions for reconciling post-conflict societies. In 1946, Italy pardoned crimes committed during the civil war by both fascists and partisans. In France, post-war purges of Nazi collaborators and trials of Vichy officials were followed by amnesties in 1951 and 1953. These measures were representative of a Western Europe in search for social and economic reconstruction and political reconciliation in front of a new Cold War adversary, the Soviet Union. The end of the Algerian War of Independence in 1962 produced its own series of amnesties. In the aftermath of the Bangladesh Liberation War of 1971, India and Bangladesh agreed not to pursue charges of genocide against Pakistani troops accused of killing nearly one million East Pakistanis. In 1977, the amnesty that accompanied the Spanish transition to democracy spared Francoists and—as shown in the Introduction—soon became an archetypal model for dealing with the past that ensured peaceful political change. Moreover, the 1977 Additional Protocols of the Geneva Conventions—adopted within the context of the various wars of liberation in Africa—provided for 'the broadest possible amnesty' of combatants in internal armed conflicts.[4]

In the 1980s and 1990s, when Latin American and CEE countries transitioned to democracy, the duty to prosecute remained thus a marginalized and contentious principle of international law. The attempted military coups d'état that followed Argentinian efforts to put former dictatorial officials on trial also generated fears of an authoritarian turn across Latin America and resulted in an understanding of criminal justice as detrimental to democratic consolidation. Moreover, at a European level, the fall of communist regimes in CEE triggered the prioritization of economic reform and integration over a criminalization of the past as the necessary prerequisite mechanism for entrenching liberal democracy.[5]

[3] The 1948 UN Genocide Convention; the 1968 UN Convention on the Non-Applicability of Statutory Limitation to War Crimes and Crimes against Humanity; the 1973 UN Anti-Apartheid Convention; and the UN 1984 Convention against Torture.

[4] This provision is however disputed by the Red Cross.

[5] Sophie Baby, Daniel Kressel, and James Mark, 'Decriminalisation for Transition? *Consenso* and the Global Travels of a Spanish Paradigm', paper presented at the Criminalising Violent Pasts: Multiple Roots and Forgotten Pathways (1950s–2010s) conference, London South Bank University, 15–16 November 2018.

Starting at the end of the 1980s, several global conferences discussed reckoning with the past during the 'third wave of democratization'. Their proceedings promoted the idea that national political and economic stability had to prevail over justice for mass atrocities. The protection of settlements achieved through negotiated transitions and the containment of democratic backlash became epitomes of global politics at the expense of criminal justice for gross human rights violations. In 1988, at a conference dedicated to Latin American transitions,[6] most of participants warned about the dangers of indicting former officials involved in gross human rights violations. Argentina stood as an example. According to Argentinian Jaime Malamud-Goti or Chilean José Zalaquett, applying international human rights norms in transitioning countries where the military continued to hold power could lead to military unrest and a dictatorial turn. Amnesties and pardons, together with truth-telling in the form of truth commissions, were deemed to be the best solution for addressing the legacy of dictatorship and secure democratic transitions. Only very few contributors—among them Diane Orentlicher, professor of international law at Columbia University, and Areih Neyer and Juan Méndez, from Human Rights Watch—contended that the duty to prosecute gross human rights violations existed under international law and should be respected. Allowing domestic politics to impinge upon fulfilment of international human rights norms was morally wrong and politically unproductive in the long run.[7] In 1991, Carlos Nino—the architect of Argentina's democratic Constitution and transitional justice measures—engaged in a debate with Orentlicher in the *Yale Journal of International Law*. Nino argued that the duty to prosecute was not yet a *jus cogens* principle and advised against maximalist approaches to international law that could jeopardize domestic political stability. From his perspective, an international duty to prosecute was 'too blunt an instrument to help successor governments who must struggle with the subtle complexities of re-establishing democracy'.[8] Until 2001, amnesties continued to be seen as a legitimate instrument for democratic consolidation in Latin America, despite protests from victims' associations and human rights NGOs.

Critiques of the duty to prosecute also emerged at a conference organized in Salzburg in 1992 by the Charter 77 Foundation (New York) to discuss

[6] In 1988, the Aspen Institute organized the conference 'State Crimes: Punishment or Pardon on Processes of Dealing with the Past in Latin America'.

[7] See the contributions in Neil Kritz, ed., *Transitional Justice: How Emerging Democracies Reckon with Former Regimes* (Washington, DC: United States Institute of Peace Press, 1995), Volume I.

[8] Carlos S. Nino, 'The Duty to Punish Past Abuses of Human Rights Put into Context: The Case of Argentina', *The Yale Law Journal* 100, no. 8 (1991): pp. 2619–2640.

transitional justice in post-communist CEE and lessons for this region from Latin America. Hungarian and German experts made common front with Argentinian and Chilean counterparts and raised the issue of the conflict between the obligation to prosecute and the principle of legality. In their view, in order to respect the rule of law, prosecutions should be based on national legislation in force when the crimes were committed. Even if a duty to prosecute existed under international law, removing statutory limitations for certain crimes (even if international) infringed upon the basic principle of non-retroactivity. Radical calls for trials should not sacrifice the liberal rule of law.[9] Finally, the idea that amnesties and pardons were the best solution for 'third wave' democracies was underlined by South Africa's transition from apartheid. As a post-conflict society, in which the African National Congress had also committed crimes (although with less intensity than the apartheid authorities), South Africa opted for a Truth and Reconciliation Commission (TRC) that could grant amnesty to those who confessed to political crimes committed between 1960 and 1993. Although the TRC pardoned only a handful of perpetrators, trials for gross human rights violations committed during apartheid were never initiated and offenders remained unpunished. While the TRC was considered a successful story of reconciliation by many scholars and experts, its existence was also a rejection of the idea that international crimes should necessarily be prosecuted.[10]

Only at the end of the 1990s, after the creation of various ad hoc international tribunals and of the ICC, did the duty to prosecute gain global relevance. The ICC's 1998 Rome Statute enforced this principle and prohibited amnesties and statutory limitations as a means of impeding criminal investigations. In 1998, the ICTY ruled in *Prosecutor v. Furundžija* that amnesties for torture were null and void under international law, an approach later adopted by all international tribunals for crimes such as genocide, crimes against humanity, and war crimes. Starting in 2001, with *Barrios Altos v. Peru*, the Inter-American Court of Human Rights (IACtHR) developed a doctrine that prohibited the application of amnesties and statutory limitations for grave human rights violations. Based on this jurisprudence, most Latin American countries cancelled or reinterpreted the amnesties adopted in the 1970s and 1980s and initiated

[9] Mary Albon, *The Charter Seventy-Seven Foundation: New York, Project on Justice in Times of Transition* (Report of the Project's Inaugural Meeting, Salzburg, Austria, 7–10 March 1992): pp. 5–18.

[10] For pros and cons of the TRC, see John Dugard, 'Dealing with Crimes of the Past: Is Amnesty Still an Option?', *Leiden Journal of International Law* 12, no. 4 (1999): pp. 1001–1015; Ronald Suresh Roberts, 'How "Transitional Justice" Colonized South Africa's TRC', *Modern Languages Open* 34, no. 1 (2020): pp. 1–15.

prosecutions of crimes committed under dictatorship. The European Court of Human Rights (ECtHR) also ruled in cases such as *Kolk & Kislyiy v. Estonia* (2006) and *Drėlingas v. Lithuania* (2019) that statutory limitations did not apply to communist crimes that amounted to genocide, crimes against humanity, and war crimes and could be prosecuted based on retroactive laws because they constituted major international crimes under customary international law at the moment of their commission. As shown in Chapter 2, this jurisprudence was instrumental to instigating the prosecutions of former communist officials in Romania. Finally, the African Commission on Human and People's Rights stated on several occasions that amnesties for human rights violations were inconsistent with state obligations under the African Charter.[11] Despite this new trend, the resistance to the duty to prosecute remains strong in various national jurisdictions. Bulgaria and Brazil are two such examples.

3. Legal Formalism and Socialist Continuities in Bulgaria

In November 1989, long-standing dictator Todor Zhivkov (in power from 1954 to 1989) was replaced by the reformist minister of foreign affairs Peter Mladenov in a coup d'état organized within the Politburo of the Bulgarian Communist Party (BCP). In parallel, civil society groups, such as the Independent Association for Human Rights and the Club in Support of Democracy and Perestroika, demanded a radical break with all BCP structures. Anti-communist demonstrations took place until December 1989, leading to negotiations between the BCP and opposition groups and, eventually, to the adoption of political pluralism as an organizing principle of the state. Nonetheless, the BCP (which became the Bulgarian Socialist Party, BSP, in 1990) continued to rule the country until 1997, with the exception of a brief period between November 1991 and October 1992 when the centre-right, anti-communist Union of Democratic Forces formed the government. After 1997, a series of right-wing parties held power until 2005 when the BSP won the election and became part of the government coalition until 2010. The continuity of former communist elites impeded radical state reform—including the restructuring of the judicial branch—as well as wide measures of dealing with the past.[12] As shown later in this chapter, the situation was similar in Brazil.

[11] See, for example, African Commission on Human and Peoples' Rights, Communication 245/2002, *Zimbabwe Human Rights NGO Forum v. Zimbabwe*.

[12] For transitional justice in Bulgaria, see Momchil Metodiev, 'Bulgaria', in *Transitional Justice in Eastern Europe and Former Soviet Union: Reckoning with the Communist Past*, edited by Lavinia Stan (New York: Routledge, 2009): pp. 152–157; Hristo Hristov and Alexander Kashumov, 'Justice

In January 1990, echoing public demands for systemic change, the Bulgarian judiciary began to investigate politically motivated crimes committed after 1945. The most prominent case concerned the torture and murders perpetrated in the Lovech political prison, the last Bulgarian communist labour camp, where 151 individuals died and more than 1,500 were subject to torture, starvation, and forced labour between 1959 and 1962.[13] The inquiry documented fourteen homicides and pointed to the alleged guilt of five ex-military officials, among them Mirtcho Spasov, the former deputy interior minister and one of Zhivkov's closest collaborators.[14] In March 1990, the five were placed under house arrest or imprisoned for three years, although no indictment was formulated against them until 1992. This long detention without trial reflected the continuation of former socialist legislation and legal practice, which allowed for unlimited preventive custody.

The case was investigated by military prosecutors who had built their careers under communism and had contributed to the consolidation of the BCP's rule through the indictment of political opponents.[15] While the Bulgarian judiciary underwent a certain depoliticization and reorientation towards stricter proceduralism in the 1970s, it nonetheless remained a pillar of political repression. This was evident in the 1980s, when judges and prosecutors legitimized the policy of forced assimilation of the Turkish minority through judicial verdicts. During the so-called 'Revival Process' (1984–1989), when communist authorities coerced Turks into changing their names and religion and prohibited the speaking of Turkish in public spaces, judges rejected demands for redress and endorsed the arrest of those opposing these policies.[16] As we will also see in the Brazilian case, the Bulgarian judiciary contributed to the enforcement of judicialized political repression until the demise of the regime and was

and Accountability Mechanisms in Bulgaria in the Transition Period (1989–2008)', in *After Oppression: Transitional Justice in Latin America and Eastern Europe*, edited by Vesselin Popovski and Monica Serrano (New York: United Nations University Press, 2012): pp. 273–297.

[13] Hristo Hristov, 'The Crimes during the Communist Regime and the Attempts at Their Investigation after 10 November 1989', available at www.decommunization.org/English/Articles/Hristov.htm (accessed 24 April 2023).

[14] The others were Peter Gogov and Cviatko Goranov, directors of the Lovech camp; Nikolai Gazdov, the State Security official in the camp; and Juliana Rugjeva, a jail supervisor.

[15] Raluca Grosescu and Agata Fijalkowski, 'Retrospective Justice and Legal Culture', in *Justice, Memory and Redress in Romania: New Insights*, edited by Lavinia Stan and Lucian Turcescu (Cambridge: Cambridge Scholars, 2017): pp. 100–123.

[16] Vasil Kadrinov, 'Forced Assimilation of the Turkish Minority in Bulgaria in the 1980s', paper presented at the Legal Settlement of Communist Crimes conference, European Parliament, Brussels, 5 June 2012.

not subject to radical reform or the replacement of personnel even decades after the fall of dictatorships.[17]

In 1990, when investigations into the Lovech crimes were initiated, prosecutors were forced to deal with the problem of statutory limitations. As in other countries from CEE and Latin America, the socialist Bulgarian criminal code—adopted in 1951, amended in 1968, and, in the post-communist period, in 1998 and 2017—provided for a twenty-year statute of limitations for homicide. This provision meant that after 1982, it was no longer possible to investigate homicides committed at Lovech in 1962. Moreover, the criminal code did not (and still does not in 2023) contain a provision for crimes against humanity,[18] although Bulgaria ratified the 1968 UN Convention in 1969. Within this context, Bulgarian prosecutors argued that they had no legal basis to investigate the Lovech crimes. They contended that Parliament needed to adopt a law to allow retrospective prosecutions of politically motivated crimes perpetrated before 1989.[19]

In March 1990, in the context of the negotiated transition between opposition groups and the BCP reformist wing, the last communist Parliament extended the statute of limitations for 'murder of two or more persons' from twenty to thirty-five years.[20] The declared purpose was to allow prosecutions of crimes that violated international human rights law, even if the statute of limitations had expired. Yet the legislature did not specify whether the amendment had retroactive effect into the communist period or if it referred exclusively to homicides committed after March 1990. The Prosecutors' Office addressed both Parliament and the Supreme Court of Justice to obtain clarification. Parliament did not reply, and the Supreme Court refused to issue a decision, indicating that the absence of any contradictory judicial practice did not require a response.[21] Consequently, prosecutors postponed the investigations. Victims' associations and pro-accountability NGOs—such as the Independent Association for Human Rights and the Association of Repressed People after 9 September 1944—interpreted the amendment as a strategy of the BCP

[17] Atanas Slavov, 'Constitutional Moment of Failure: Constitutional Politics in Bulgaria 2020', *ПУБЛИЧНИ ПОЛИТИКИ.bg* (Public Policies.bg) 12, no. 1 (2021): pp. 54–63.

[18] In 2023, only crimes against peace, war crimes, genocide, and apartheid were included in the criminal code and considered to be without a statute of limitations.

[19] Hristov and Kashumov, 'Justice and Accountability Mechanisms', p. 279.

[20] Art. 80, para 1, subpara 1 of the Bulgarian Criminal Code was amended to that end, *State Gazette* no. 31/1990. I would like to thank Vasil Kadrinov and Gergana Dineva for the translation of all documents in Bulgarian used in this chapter.

[21] Hristov and Kashumov, 'Justice and Accountability Mechanisms', p. 280.

reformist wing to disassociate itself from Zhivkov's administration but avoid any trials for crimes committed in the labour camps.[22]

In November 1991, the centre-right and anti-communist Union of Democratic Forces (UDF) won the election and formed the first government without representatives from the former communist, now socialist, party. The UDF favoured a rigorous decommunization programme, including the purging of former communist officials from public administration. In 1992, a lustration law (the Panev Law) prohibited former communist elites from holding positions in the executive bodies of research organizations. The law was however repealed in 1995 after the BSP returned to power. In 1998, when the UDF formed the government again, former state security officers and informers were prohibited from election to the Council for Electronic Media.[23] Socialist politicians and human rights NGOs, such as the Bulgarian Helsinki Committee, argued that these laws were discriminatory, since they excluded individuals from public office based on their political affiliations.[24] Conversely, various analysts criticized the laws for being too narrow, since they only focused on academic bodies and media outlets and failed to engage in an 'authentic lustration of public governance'.[25]

In 1992, the UDF appointed a new general prosecutor, Ivan Tatarchev. Son of a former political prisoner, Tatarchev had been banned from the law faculty in the 1950s and forced to work as a manual labourer due to his family's political background. In the 1970s, after he was finally allowed to graduate in law, he was sent to work as a lawyer in a small town near the Turkish border, where he witnessed the forced assimilation and subsequent repression of the Turkish minority. Immediately after his appointment as general prosecutor, Tatarchev drafted an indictment in the Lovech case, and the trial began at the Supreme Court of Justice in 1994. The defendants[26] were accused of murder and the mistreatment of political opponents based on the 1951 criminal code as interpreted in light of the March 1990 Amendment. Tatarchev argued that under communist rule, it was impossible to prosecute such crimes since they

[22] Hristov, 'The Crimes during the Communist Regime'; Personal interview with Vasil Kadrinov, Sofia, Bulgaria, 30 March 2017.

[23] For lustration laws in Bulgaria, see Metodiev, 'Bulgaria'; Nadège Ragaru, 'Les dossiers de la Sûreté d'État bulgare: le communisme dans les pliures du temps', *Revue des études slaves* LXXXI, nos. 2–3 (2010): pp. 203–225.

[24] Helsinki Watch, 'Decommunization in Bulgaria', *News from Helsinki Watch* 5, no. 14 (1993): pp. 1–44.

[25] Cynthia M. Horne, '"Silent Lustration" Public Disclosures as Informal Lustration Mechanisms in Bulgaria and Romania: Evaluating Measures and Their Outcome', *Problems of Post-Communism* 62, no. 3 (2015): pp. 131–144.

[26] Two of the defendants had passed away, but the most important accused, Mirtcho Spasov, was still alive.

were ordered by state officials.[27] He claimed that the law should be interpreted in its historical context, especially in cases of state criminality and political hegemony over the justice system. Given the impossibility of the judiciary to investigate political crimes during the communist dictatorship, he contended that the prescribed terms for such offences should start in 1990, once the transition to democracy was completed. He also maintained that the intention of the drafters of the March 1990 Amendment was clear in this respect: to lift the statute of limitations for political murders committed under communism.[28]

However, beyond the March 1990 Amendment, the indictment did not refer to any other national or international law that allowed for the retroactive suspension of the statute of limitations. In contrast to Romanian legislation, for instance, that conceded such a suspension if a 'legal disposition or an irremovable circumstance' hindered a trial (including the interference of the political bodies in judicial affairs), a similar provision did not exist in the Bulgarian criminal code. According to legal expert Alexander Kashumov, there was no real base in the Bulgarian legislation to lift the statutory limitation and Tatarchev's indictment was more a political and moral enterprise than a solid legal argumentation.[29] Moreover, even though the 1947 and 1971 communist Bulgarian Constitutions did not include a ban on retroactivity, Article 2 of the 1968 criminal code stated that all crimes must be judged upon the law in force at the moment of their commission.[30] Similarly, Article 5 of the democratic Constitution adopted in 1991 prohibited retroactivity.[31] Tatarchev's indictment did not touch on these sensitive aspects and relied only on a historical interpretation of the judiciary's status and the impossibility of investigating state criminality during communism. He also referred to the duty of judges to repair historical injustices and to contribute to the writing of a 'correct history' of Bulgarian communism.[32] In response, the defence argued that his approach had no legal basis, violated the 1991 Constitution and the rules of due process, and transformed justice into revenge.[33]

The trial was postponed for nine years and moved between various jurisdictions for procedural reasons. The story repeated itself with all other prosecutions of communist crimes, including attempts to try those responsible

27 Archives of the Bulgarian Supreme Court of Justice (hereafter: ABSCJ), 'Accusation Act No. 2 / 1994', pp. 1–5.

28 Ibid.

29 Personal interview with Alexander Kashumov, Sofia, Bulgaria, 18 March 2013.

30 Bulgarian Criminal Code 1968, Article 2.

31 Bulgarian Constitution 1991, Article 5(3).

32 Discourse of General Prosecutor Ivan Tatarchev before the Bulgarian Supreme Court in 1994, in Hristov and Kashumov, 'Justice and Accountability Mechanisms', p. 280.

33 Hristov, 'The Crimes during the Communist Regime'.

for the forced assimilation of Turks in the 1980s.[34] Some observers argued that this was due to an esprit de corps that was 'remarkably stubborn in [its] resistance to change'.[35] Moreover, the members of Supreme Judicial Council (SJC)—the institution that controls the appointment, promotion, and dismissal of magistrates—were first elected in 1992 and then in 1997 when the BSP was in power. Half of the Council's members are elected by the judicial body and half by Parliament, a procedure leading to its strong politicization. Until 2022, demands from the European Union to revise the structure of the SJC went unheeded.[36] The first two post-communist SJCs comprised a large majority of high-profile jurists from the communist period, including individuals who worked for the political police (such as Angel Alexandrov and Rumen Andreev), which resulted in a judicial agenda reluctant to engage in decommunization measures, including prosecutions.

In 2002, the Lovech case arrived at the Supreme Court, which acquitted all defendants. The Court acknowledged that the accused had committed the crimes in question and that from a moral point of view, they were guilty: the 'murder and mistreatment of innocent people arrested in the Lovech camp are reprehensive acts, which contradict any form of moral understanding of justice'.[37] However, the Court ruled that from a legal point of view, it was no longer possible to prosecute these crimes, since the statute of limitations had expired:

> During communism, the prosecutors were under the strict control of the Communist Party, and they could never have initiated an investigation with respect to political crimes. [. . .] But neither the 1951, nor the 1968 criminal code provided any possibility for pausing the statute of limitations. From a juridical point of view, these crimes can no longer be judged.[38]

The Court also argued that ignoring the statute of limitations violated Article 15(1) of International Covenant on Civil and Political Rights (ICCPR)—which prohibits *ex post facto* punishment. Nevertheless, the Court underlined that Article 15(2) of the ICCPR allowed Parliament to extend the statute of limitations for acts considered criminal according to the general principles of law

34 Raluca Grosescu, 'Criminal Justice and Master Historical Narratives in post-1989 Bulgaria and Germany', *European Politics and Society* 18, no. 1 (2017): pp. 66–80.

35 Bruno Schönfelder, 'Judicial Independence in Bulgaria: A Tale of Splendour and Misery', *Europe-Asia Studies* 57, no. 1 (2005): pp. 61–92, at p. 63.

36 Slavov, 'Constitutional Moment'.

37 ABSCJ, 'Decision No. 3 / 2002 of the Bulgarian Supreme Court of Justice', p. 5.

38 Ibid, p. 4.

recognized by the international community. In the absence of such a law, however, the Court had to adjourn the trial.[39]

The judge who presided over the Court and drafted the decision was Rumen Nenkov, a former secretary of the Communist Party at the Sofia regional court before 1989. He was promoted to a Supreme Court judgeship in 1992 and became a member of the Constitutional Court in 2009. In a 2014 interview, Nenkov maintained that he had no other option than to adjourn the trial, as it was not within the judiciary's purview to create laws:

> The statute of limitations for murder had expired; the 1990 March Amendment did not apply retroactively, and the category of crimes against humanity—which might have applied to the Lovech crimes—was not included in the Bulgarian criminal code. [. .] Some people say nowadays that political crimes committed under communism are international crimes, but they were not according to Bulgarian legislation [. . .] We indicated that Parliament could adopt a new law based on international human rights law, but we could not replace Parliament in creating laws.[40]

Nenkov also criticized Tatarchev's desire to 'prosecute at any price' and 'write history through judicial decisions':

> If the history of the Roman Empire is still revisited by historians today, how can judges adjudicate much more recent historical controversies? The role of the judiciary is to apply existing law, not to prosecute at any price and create new laws for the sake of engaging in historical justice.[41]

From Nenkov's perspective, the Supreme Court acknowledged the immorality of the crimes committed at Lovech, but its overarching duty was to respect the rule of law, not to engage in law- and history-making.

Bulgarian NGOs promoting justice for communist crimes—such as the Hannah Arendt Center in Sofia—criticized the ruling as overly formalistic. In their view, judges should have interpreted the Bulgarian criminal code in light of Article 15(2) of the ICCPR, Article 7(2) of the European Convention on Human Rights, and the 1968 UN Convention. Such an approach would have allowed the definition of the Lovech crimes as international crimes not subject

[39] Ibid, pp. 4–5.
[40] Personal interview with Rumen Nenkov, Sofia, Bulgaria, 30 June 2014.
[41] Ibid.

to statutory limitations. For justice activists, such as Vasil Kadrinov—founding member of the Hannah Arendt Center, militant environmentalist, and political prisoner during late socialism (1985–1986)—the Supreme Court's decision reflected the long-standing impunity for communist crimes that continued after 1990.[42]

Legal scholars also considered that in the 1990s, the Bulgarian judiciary was not equipped with the necessary legal education to try human rights violations based on international law. Socialist legal education, developed over five decades of communist rule, was highly formalistic and focused on national legislation.[43] The philosophy taught to Bulgarian law students after 1989 continued this tradition, as it continued to be influenced by legal positivism, with Hans Kelsen's *Pure Theory of Law* as a sort of 'Bible' that was never critically interrogated.[44] Also, the Bulgarian judiciary inherited from state socialism the idea that interpreting problematic laws was the task of political bodies and not of the judiciary, an aspect also illustrated by 'textbooks [that] only rephrase and summarize the codes, avoiding issues of interpretation and construction'.[45] Even in 2005, law faculties still used textbooks written under communist rule that were only superficially revised. Even derogatory references to 'bourgeois law' survived this revision.[46]

Nonetheless, one must also take into account that Bulgaria's legal system is based on civil law, where legal education and praxis emphasize the application of written law, and judges play almost no role in the production of laws (with the exception of the Constitutional Court). The absence of the category of crimes against humanity in the criminal code and the absence of a legal basis for prolonging the statutory limitations for homicide severely constricted prosecutions of communist-era crimes. As shown in Chapter 2, Estonian and Romanian judges and prosecutors did not engage in law-making either. They applied laws enforced by their parliaments but tried to find solutions to interpret them in accordance with the evolution of customary law developments since Nuremberg. In Bulgaria, political elites showed little interest in concrete strategies to fight impunity. The former communist elites that regrouped within the BSP had no desire to change the law and potentially auto-incriminate themselves, while the UDF (which governed the country from 1991 to 1992

[42] Interview with Vasil Kadrinov, Sofia, Bulgaria, 30 March 2017.

[43] Michal Bobek, 'The Fortress of Judicial Independence and the Mental Transitions of the Central European Judiciaries', *European Public Law* 14, no. 1 (2008): pp. 1–20.

[44] Personal interview with Atanas Slavov, Sofia, Bulgaria, 2 July 2014.

[45] Schönfelder, 'Judicial Independence', pp. 82 and 84.

[46] Ibid.

and from 1997 to 2001) failed to enforce progressive judicial reform.[47] In 2000, the UDF passed a law that acknowledged 'the criminal nature of the communist regime'[48] and condemned the violation of democratic values, the so-called 'moral and economic decline of the state', and the 'destruction [of] the values of European civilisation'. Yet, the law never envisaged a modification of the criminal code. It constructed state socialism as a 'monster',[49] without any legal consequences for criminal investigations.

3.1 Maximalist versus Minimalist Approaches to Communist Crimes as Crimes against Humanity

In 2009, the conservative-populist GERB party (Citizens for European Development of Bulgaria), led by Boyko Borissov, won the elections and remained in power until 2021. GERB promoted a radical anti-communist discourse that often rehabilitated former fascist officials and even war criminals as national heroes.[50] The party attempted to delegitimize the communist regime as a whole through a legislative package that banned the display of communist symbols in public spaces,[51] introduced a new history curriculum that increased the number of classes dedicated to communist political repression,[52] and lifted the statute of limitations for a long list of alleged crimes committed by former communist officials. This radical anti-communist rhetoric was aimed, among other things, at turning attention away from GERB's rampant corruption and at counter-attacking the BSP's re-emergent popularity in the 2010s.[53]

In September 2015, Parliament adopted a controversial law that modified the criminal code in two steps. First, it stipulated that 'there is no statute of limitations for major crimes against human rights when committed between 1944

[47] Hristov, 'The Crimes during the Communist Regime'.

[48] Law on Declaring the Criminal Nature of the Communist Regime in Bulgaria, promulgated in the *State Gazette*, Issue no. 37 of 5 May 2000.

[49] Ina Dimitrova, 'How We Raised a Monster: Constructing the Image of Socialism during the Post-Socialist Period in Bulgaria', *History of Communism in Europe* 1 (2010): pp. 153–165.

[50] Kristen Ghodsee, 'Tale of "Two Totalitarianisms": The Crisis of Capitalism and the Historical Memory of Communism', *History of the Present* 4, no. 2 (2014): pp. 115–142.

[51] In 2016, Parliament adopted a law that banned the public display of any communist symbol. In 2017, however, after heated debates on what 'communist symbols' meant and based on the jurisprudence of the European Court of Human Rights which had sanctioned similar laws in Hungary, the law was repealed. Personal interview with Metodi Borissov Andreev, Sofia, Bulgaria, 10 March 2017.

[52] Anemona Constantin, 'L'enseignement de l'histoire du communisme à l'Est: Bulgarie, Roumanie, République de Moldavie', *Passés Futurs* 9 (2021), available at www.politika.io/fr/article/lenseignement-lhistoire-du-communisme-a-lest (accessed 23 April 2023).

[53] Ragaru, 'Les dossiers de la Sûreté d'État bulgare'.

and 1989 under the authority of state'.[54] The law included not only illegal detention, torture, and homicide but also the violation of private property, embezzlement, the propagation of anti-democratic ideology, mismanaging hazardous waste or hiding ecological disasters that harmed the health of the population, and engaging in transactions that damaged the national economy.[55] Metodi Borissov Andreev, one of the drafters of the proposal, stated in an interview in 2017:

> Through this law we intended to criminalize the mass atrocities in labour camps, but also crimes such as not protecting the Bulgarian population from the effects of the Chernobyl disaster, the bad management of the national economy or the detrimental aid Bulgaria gave to communist parties in the Third World at the expense of the wellbeing of Bulgarian citizens.[56]

The law was thus designed to comprise gross human rights abuses, but also acts of negligence, and even economic and foreign policies engaged in by communist Bulgaria. It reflected a maximalist approach that envisioned a total delegitimization of communist rule.

The second part of the legislation introduced the category of crimes against humanity into the criminal code, as defined by the 1998 ICC Statute and 'punishable no matter when committed' according to the 1968 UN Convention. The drafters maintained that Bulgaria had ratified the 1968 UN Convention and explicitly endorsed its retrospective effect in 1969. They also quoted the 2002 Decision of the Supreme Court in the Lovech case, which stipulated that Parliament could adopt a law that retroactively criminalized gross human rights violations based on Article 15(2) of the ICCPR and Article 7(2) of the ECHR.[57] According to Andreev, this proposal was inspired by the Romanian anti-impunity tactics and the ensuing modification of the Romanian criminal code in 2014 (as seen in Chapter 2).[58] Romanian pro-accountability activists were however more cautious and less maximalist than their Bulgarian counterparts. In Romania, the goal was only to allow the prosecution of crimes against humanity, whereas in Bulgaria, GERB was concerned with criminalizing communist ideology, and its political system, in its entirety.

[54] Archives of the Hannah Arendt Center Sofia (hereafter AHACS), 'Draft Law on Amendment and Supplementation of the Criminal Code, No. 554-01-87, 08.05.2015', adopted on 26 September 2015.
[55] Ibid.
[56] Personal interview with Metodi Borissov Andreev, Sofia, Bulgaria, 10 March 2017.
[57] AHACS, 'Draft Law on Amendment and Supplementation of the Criminal Code, No. 554-01-87, 08.05.2015', adopted on 26 September 2015.
[58] Personal interview with Metodi Borissov Andreev, Sofia, Bulgaria, 10 March 2017.

In December 2015, Bulgaria's general prosecutor, backed by the SJC, contested the law at the Constitutional Court. The general prosecutor was now Sotir Tsatsarov, a jurist without ties to the former Communist Party, appointed by GERB in 2012, but with the support of other political parties. He argued that lifting the statute of limitations for ordinary criminal code violations infringed upon the Constitution in several respects. First, it went against Article 31 which stipulates that 'anyone charged with a crime shall be brought before the court within the time established by law'. Second, it violated Article 6, which prohibits discrimination based on political affiliation, because the law applied only to members of the communist apparatus. Third, it infringed upon Article 5, which prohibits retroactivity and imposes the application of the most lenient law on the defendants.[59] His arguments did not, however, refer in any way to the introduction of crimes against humanity and their prosecution no matter the time elapsed.

The Bulgarian Helsinki Committee, one of the most important human rights NGOs in the country, supported the general prosecutor's position, while the Hannah Arendt Center in Sofia backed GERB's law and particularly the codification of crimes against humanity and their punishment in line with the 1968 UN Convention.[60] Since its implementation in Bulgaria, in the early years of transition, the Helsinki Committee had advocated a future-oriented politics on human rights—such as the enforcement of the liberal rule of law and the rights of minorities—and a reconciliatory narrative about the past. In contrast, the Hannah Arendt Center gathered together former political opponents who had been jailed by communist authorities and understood reckoning with the past in the form of criminal prosecutions and lustration as major elements of democratization. The Helsinki Committee was however much more influential due to its international character and funding. In contrast, the Hannah Arendt Center was a smaller NGO with very limited financial resources and few connections to political elites.

In October 2016, in an eleven to one decision, the Constitutional Court ruled against the law that criminalized communist crimes. The Court was presided over by Boris Velchev, son of a former communist diplomat and grandson of a former member of the Politburo and close collaborator of Todor Zhivkov.

[59] Archives of the Bulgarian Constitutional Court (hereafter ABCC), 'Request from the Prosecutor General of the Republic of Bulgaria, No. 1066/15, 22.12.2015'; 'Opinion of the Supreme Judicial Council on Constitutional Case No. 13/2015, No. 514/28.04.2016'.

[60] ABCC, 'Opinion of the Bulgarian Helsinki Committee on Constitutional Case No. 13/2016, No. A-79/11.04.2016'; AHACS, 'Opinion of the Hannah Arendt Center, Sofia, on Constitutional Case No. 13/2016, 22.01.2016'.

Between 2001 and 2006, Velchev headed the legal team of socialist president Georgi Parvanov. His connections to the BSP led to his appointment as general prosecutor in 2006 and as Chairman of the Constitutional Court in 2012. With the exception of Rumen Nenkov, who had presided over the Lovech case in 2002 and had been secretary of the Communist Party at the Sofia regional court before 1989, the other judges did not have any ties to the former regime, outside of their graduation in law during the socialist period. Moreover, while most Constitutional Court members had been appointed by GERB, they often overruled GERB's legislative initiatives. In fact, since the early 1990s, the Bulgarian Constitutional Court regularly challenged politicians (both socialist and right-wing) and, in some cases, effectively disrupted their political agendas.[61]

On the one hand, the Court endorsed the general prosecutor's arguments. The law was discriminatory on political grounds, and any suspension of statutory limitations for ordinary past crimes entailed retroactivity. On the other hand, the Court rejected the possibility of prosecuting gross violations of human rights committed during the communist period as crimes against humanity. It contended that such crimes (including illegal detention, torture, and murder) could qualify as crimes against humanity under international law; but the Bulgarian socialist criminal code had never included this category. During the socialist period, only war crimes, genocide, and apartheid were considered major international crimes not subject to statutory limitations. Moreover, the judges argued that although Bulgaria had ratified the 1968 UN Convention in 1969, that instrument was not officially part of Bulgarian legislation, as, under Bulgarian law, international treaties needed not only to be ratified but also to published in the Official Gazette in order to become national law. Because the 1968 UN Convention was never published during the socialist period, it was not part of the Bulgarian body of laws.[62]

> We understand the need and will of victims to investigate and punish, but if the defendant is not provided with due process this means violation of the rule of law [. . .] If truth and judicial procedure are destroyed by propaganda, this would ruin the democratic basis of society. Prosecutions are not the final goal. The final goal is the consolidation of the rule of law.[63]

[61] Venelin Ganev, *Preying on the State: The Transformation of Bulgaria after 1989* (Ithaca, NY: Cornell University Press, 2013): pp. 136–138, 159–162.

[62] ABCC, 'Decision No. 12/13.10.2016 of the Constitutional Court, Case No. 13/2015', published in the Official Gazette no. 83 / 21 October 2016.

[63] Ibid.

The Court's understanding of the rule of law thus prioritized the right of the defendant to due process ahead of the duty to prosecute major international crimes. This view however ignored the jurisprudence of the ECtHR that, in *Papon v. France* and *Kolk and Kislyiy v. Estonia*, allowed the prosecution of crimes against humanity based on retrospective national laws because these crimes had already been sanctioned by international customary and conventional law before their inclusion in national legislations.[64] Also, in *Streletz, Kessler and Krenz v. Germany*, the ECtHR ruled that the ICCPR was part of the German Democratic Republic (GDR) legislation, even though the Covenant had never been incorporated into domestic law through a vote in Parliament, as the GDR Constitution required. The ratification of an international treaty was enough to consider it part of national legislation.[65] The interpretation of the Constitutional Court was also in contradiction with the Supreme Court's judgment in the Lovech case, which acknowledged that Parliament could adopt a retroactive law to criminalize gross human rights violations based on Article 15(2) of the ICCPR. Paradoxically, Nenkov, who had adopted this position in the Lovech case in 2002, now ruled against any retroactive criminalization of major international crimes.

Philip Dimitrov, former prime minister in the 1990s and a proponent of radical decommunization, was the only dissenting judge. He criticized the majority for being overly formalistic and overlooking principles of customary international law. In his view, crimes against humanity could be prosecuted retrospectively, because Bulgaria had adhered to the Nuremberg principles and endorsed Article 15(2) of the ICCPR and Article 7(2) of the ECHR, which imposed prosecutions of international crimes even if they were not criminalized by the national legislation at the time of commission. The 1968 UN Convention had to be interpreted in light of the entirety of ICL developed since 1945, which imposed a duty to prosecute major international crimes. Nonetheless, Dimitrov himself believed that the Bulgarian law on criminalizing communist crimes required revision since it not only concerned crimes against humanity but also felonies that were not covered by international law.[66]

In 2017, GERB introduced new legislation that ostensibly responded to the critiques of the Constitutional Court. The proposal was however almost identical to the one adopted in 2015 and did not address the Constitutional Court's

[64] ECtHR, *Papon v. France*, Decision of 15 November 2001; ECtHR, *Kolk and Kislyiy v. Estonia*, Decision of 17 January 2006.

[65] ECtHR, *Streletz, Kessler and Krenz v. Germany*, Judgment of 22 March 2001.

[66] ABCC, 'Decision No. 12/13.10.2016 of the Constitutional Court, Case No. 13/2015', 'Separate Opinion of Judge Philip Dimitrov'.

objection that the 1968 UN Convention was not part of Bulgarian law.[67] The proposal was soon abandoned, but its drafting demonstrated that GERB MPs were concerned with condemning the entirety of the communist regime as a 'radical evil' rather than developing realistic strategies to open investigations into major international crimes.

The Bulgarian approaches to judging communist crimes reflected a polarization between a maximalist view that aimed to condemn the entire former regime as criminal and a minimalist approach that maintained impunity even for crimes against humanity. On the one hand, political parties such as the UDF and GERB, and a few rare prosecutors, such as Ivan Tatarchev, attempted to end impunity, but their legal strategies were problematic and did not seriously consider the interconnections between national and international criminal law. Their approach to post-dictatorial justice was more political rhetoric than coherent legal strategy. NGOs engaged in the decommunization process, such as the Hannah Arendt Center, also lacked legal expertise as most of their members were trained in disciplines other than law.

On the other hand, the BSP and most of the judges and prosecutors implicated in debates used both national and international law whenever convenient to maintain the status quo. They were generally backed by the Bulgarian Helsinki Committee, whose activities focused on the resolution of future-oriented rights issues (particularly the rights of ethnic minorities) and opposed past-oriented policies, including lustration and retrospective justice. In the Lovech case, the Supreme Court of Justice referred to Article 7(1) of the ECHR and Article 15(1) of ICCPR to evoke the rule of non-retroactivity and deferred any interpretation of Articles 7(2) and 15(2) to Parliament. With its 2016 rejection of any application of the 1968 UN Convention, the Constitutional Court put itself at odds with ECtHR jurisprudence and ignored customary international law developed since 1945. This approach reflected a positivist and formalist legal culture, but also a selectivity toward international law that reveals the Bulgarian judiciary's 'implicit disobedience'[68] towards international norms and standards. In this respect, the Bulgarian judiciary is rhetorically European, but simultaneously refrains from advocating for the systematic judicial reform demanded by the European Commission for Democracy through Law (the Venice Commission).[69] This position was also evident in 2018, when the Constitutional Court—seating the same judges as in 2016—declared the

[67] AHACS, 'Draft Law on the Interpretation of Art. 79, para. 2, item 1 of the Criminal Code, No. 754-01-7', introduced on 18 January 2017.

[68] Slavov, 'Constitutional Momentum'.

[69] Ibid.

ratification of the 2011 Istanbul Convention (on preventing domestic violence and violence against women) unconstitutional. The Court argued that the instrument propagated 'gender ideology' and went against the Bulgarian Constitution, which was 'based on the understanding of the binary existence of human species'. Moreover, in a twisted interpretation of a constitutional article on the right to maternity leave, the Court concluded that 'the female biological sex was related to social roles such as "mother", "giving birth", and "home care"'.[70] While judging communist crimes and preventing domestic violence are separate issues, they both reflect how reluctantly Bulgarian judges approached international law in general and thereby prevented any adjustments to the national status quo.

4. Judicial Divisions over the Amnesty Law in Brazil

As in Bulgaria, the Brazilian military dictatorship (1964–1985) was characterized by an 'authoritarian legality' that provided legalistic justifications for acts of political repression and relied on the judiciary to enforce them.[71] In comparison to Argentina, Uruguay, and Chile, the number of enforced disappearances was much lower in Brazil (although torture was widespread), and most political opponents were imprisoned based on trials held in mixed military-civilian courts. Verdicts could be appealed but were generally upheld by the higher courts. The number of deaths and disappearances for political reasons is estimated at 434 people (although at least 8,350 people from Indigenous communities were also killed during military rule), but more than 7,000 were tried and imprisoned.[72] The judicial structures of the Brazilian military regime resembled those of CEE communist dictatorships, where judicial decisions were instrumental in legitimizing repression and enforcing state ideology through criminal law. Similarly, as in CEE countries, repression decreased significantly after the regime's consolidation and the overall number of victims was relatively small in comparison to the size of the population. In 1974, military President Ernesto Geisel initiated a gradual liberalization, and lethal violence declined to nearly zero in the final years of dictatorship.

[70] Radosveta Vassileva, 'Bulgaria's Constitutional Troubles with the Istanbul Convention', *Verfassungsblog*, 2 August 2018, available at https://verfassungsblog.de/bulgarias-constitutional-troubles-with-the-istanbul-convention/ (accessed 25 April 2023).

[71] For the role of the judiciary and repression, see Anthony W. Pereira, *Political (In) Justice: Authoritarianism and the Rule of Law in Brazil, Chile, and Argentina* (Pittsburgh, PA: University of Pittsburgh Press, 2005).

[72] National Truth Commission, *Final Report* (Brasilia, 2014), vol. I, p. 963, and vol. II, pp. 197–255.

Starting in 1974 opposition groups found more space for political protest. They created the Brazilian Committee for Amnesty (Comitê Brasileiro pela Anistia, CBA), which gained momentum and international support from 1978 onwards. Comprising various social and political groups,[73] the CBA advocated for the amnesty of the political opponents of the military regime, the rehabilitation of those purged from public offices, and the return of those exiled. The movement was, however, divided in its approach to the scope of the amnesty—a division that continued in the decades after the 1985 democratic transition.[74] Some organizations claimed amnesty for political opponents and punishment for gross human rights violations committed by the military; others favoured an amnesty without prosecutions, but with clarifications about forced disappearances and the dismantling of repressive institutions; a third group promoted reconciliation through forgiveness and forgetting of all crimes—including military violence—'an amnesty which [would] reconcile the Brazilian family'.[75]

Finally, in 1979, after negotiations between the only legal opposition party, the Brazilian Democratic Movement, the government, and military hardliners, the Brazilian Congress adopted an amnesty law that de facto protected both the regime's officials and its opponents from charges for politically motivated crimes. Nonetheless, the majority of the pardons were to the benefit of the military. First, the law provided a wide definition of political crimes which included torture and murder committed by state officials.[76] Second, amnesty excluded 'terrorism' and so-called 'blood crimes'—namely attacks on the life of other persons. This provision targeted only leftist militants involved in the armed struggle against the regime. Third, army officials forced to retire for political reasons were not rehabilitated, and purged academics and civil servants were only allowed to reoccupy their posts after they had been 'cleared' by a special investigation committee. Most political prisoners were however released, exiled persons could return to Brazil, and politicians who had lost their

[73] For an analysis of this heterogenous movement, see Cecília MacDowell Santos, Édson Teles, and Janaína Teles, *Desarquivando a ditadura: memoria e justiça no Brasil* (São Paulo: Aderaldo & Rothschild, 2009); Nina Schneider, 'Waiting for a Meaningful State Apology: Has Brazil Apologized for Authoritarian Repression?', *Journal of Human Rights* 13, no. 1 (2014): pp. 69–84, at pp. 72–74.

[74] Nina Schneider, 'Impunity in Post-authoritarian Brazil: The Supreme Court's Recent Verdict on the Amnesty Law', *European Review of Latin American and Caribbean Studies* 90 (2011): pp. 39–54, at p. 47.

[75] Carlos Fico, 'A negociação parlamentar da anistia de 1979 e o chamado "perdão aos torturadores"', 2009, available at www.corteidh.or.cr/tablas/r30005.pdf (accessed 25 April 2023); Aarão D. Reis, 'Ditadura e sociedade: as reconstruções da memoria', in *O golpe e a ditadura militar: 40 anos depois (1964–2004)*, edited by Aarão D. Reis, Marcelo Ridenti, and Rodrigo Sá Motta (Bauru: EDUSC, 2004): pp. 29–52.

[76] Ann M. Schneider, 'Legislative Efforts against Impunity in the 1979 Amnesty Debate in Brazil', *Bulletin of Latin American Research* 37, no. 1 (2018): pp. 18–32.

political rights could resume their careers. The CBA understood this approach as a suitable strategy for that specific historical moment, even if the law granted impunity to military officials.[77]

The elite-driven transition that took place from 1974 to 1985 resulted in a notable continuity in dictatorial power structures. After 1985, military elites retained considerable influence and corporate cohesion. They succeeded in shaping the narrative of 'a transition in which a feigned amnesia— combined with overt pride in the authoritarian past—was the order of the day'.[78] There were no important reforms of the judicial and military structures after 1985. The relatively small scale of lethal violence in the last ten years of dictatorship helped apologists of the military regime to propagate a 'fairy tale about the benevolence and fairness of Brazil's military courts during the dictatorship'.[79] Moreover, the military successfully enforced the image of a humane regime that had formally maintained the country's democratic structures and had achieved economic growth (the so-called 'economic miracle') during the 1970s.[80]

In 1988, Article 8 of the Transitory Constitutional Disposition Act reaffirmed the validity of the Amnesty Law. It established categories of victims and survivors and recognized the rights of resistance and reparation. The *Act* was however silent about the amnesty granted to the military, leading various analysts to posit that it rejected the bilateral amnesty.[81] They also emphasized that Article 5 of the 1988 Constitution prohibited 'bail, clemency or amnesty' for 'torture, illicit trafficking in narcotics, terrorism, and heinous crimes'.[82] Nevertheless, the Constitution also forbade retroactivity unless it benefited the defendant.[83] This provision allowed the proponents of the bilateral amnesty to make their case: because military officials had benefited from the Amnesty Law until 1988, curtailing this advantage was retroactive and hindered their right to be judged under the most lenient law. Over the years, the bilateral amnesty was endorsed by the judiciary and by political elites who underlined that the democratic transition depended on pardoning the regime's crimes.

[77] Fico, 'A negociação', pp. 1 and 13.
[78] Pereira, *Political (In)Justice*, pp. 159, 162.
[79] Ibid, p. 165.
[80] Schneider, 'Impunity in Post-authoritarian Brazil', p. 41.
[81] Paulo Abrão and Marcelo D. Torelly, 'Resistance to Change: Brazil's Persistent Amnesty and Its Alternatives for Truth and Justice' in *Amnesty in the Age of Human Rights Accountability: Comparative and International Perspectives*, edited by Francesca Lessa and Leigh Payne (Cambridge: Cambridge University Press, 2012): pp. 152–181, at p. 156.
[82] Brazilian Constitution 1988, Article 5 (XLIII).
[83] Brazilian Constitution 1988, Article 5 (XL).

The criminal code also imposed legal constraints on prosecutions, similar to the Bulgarian case. First, Brazil never incorporated the category of crimes against humanity into its criminal code, even after the country ratified the Rome Statute in 2002. Second, the statute of limitations for murder was twenty years, meaning that homicides committed in the late 1960 and the 1970s could no longer be prosecuted in the 1990s. Third, torture was criminalized only in 1997, even if a similar category (lesão corporal) existed in the criminal code during the dictatorship but submitted to a statute of limitation of twelve years. The Amnesty Law and these provisions of the criminal code rendered prosecutions impossible. As in Bulgaria, impunity was also enforced by a monist doctrine of international law and a legal culture reluctant to engage the direct application of international law in domestic jurisprudence.[84]

4.1 Reparations for Victims, Impunity for Perpetrators

In the first ten years after the 1985 return to democracy, there was silence with regard to truth and justice for dictatorial crimes, except for private investigative reports on the torture and enforced disappearances committed during the regime, such as *Brazil: Never Again* (1985) and *Report of the Families of Dead and Disappeared Persons* (1996). NGOs and victims' associations—including Torture Never More or the Commission of the Families of the Killed and Disappeared—pressured the state to reckon with its military legacy. However, as in Bulgaria, these organizations represented only a small segment of Brazilian civil society, the majority of whom turned to present and future-oriented causes after 1985, such as land reform, anti-racism, and the environment.[85] Moreover, the first two civilian presidents, José Sarney (1985–1990) and Fernando Color de Mello (1990–1992), were former allies of the military. The following president, Iamar Franco (1992–1994), ruled during a period of severe economic crisis which forced attention away from confronting the past to present-day economic reforms. It is only in 1995, under the mandate of Fernando Cardoso (1995–2003), that the Brazilian state started to enforce reparatory measures for the victims of the dictatorship, but without any initiatives centred on retributive justice.[86] A former exile himself, Cardoso was

[84] Fauzi Hassan Choukr, 'Droit Brasilien', in *Juridictions Nationales et Crimes Internationaux*, edited by Antonio Cassese and Mireille Delmas-Marty (Paris: PUF, 2002): pp. 333–344.

[85] Abrão and Torelly, 'Resistance to Change', p. 174.

[86] For transitional justice in Brazil, see Abrão and Torelly, 'Resistance to Change'; Glenda Mezarobba, 'Brazil: The Tortuous Path to Truth and Justice', in *Transitional Justice in Latin America: The Uneven*

among the first theorists of peaceful transitions to democracy through pacts between oppositional groups and reformist segments of the bureaucratic authoritarian elite. He was also an advocate of the bilateral amnesty. Moreover, his state secretary for human rights, Paulo Sérgio Pinhero, was part of a network of Latin American scholars and politicians who, in the late 1980s, saw trials as a potential source of military unrest, based on the Argentinian experience.[87]

In 1995, during Cardoso's government, the Congress adopted a 'Law of the Disappeared' which acknowledged state responsibility for past violence, made provisions for reparations, and established a Special Commission to investigate Political Deaths and Disappearances. Until 2006, the Special Commission granted financial reparations to the families of around 300 victims killed by the military regime.[88] However, the Commission itself recognized the limits of its activity: many investigations were sabotaged by state authorities, and many victims were not aware of the Commission's existence, as the government did not conduct information campaigns about the right to reparations.[89] In 2002, in response to pressure from labour unions, the government established an Amnesty Commission, with the aim of granting reparations to victims of political purges, torture, arbitrary arrest, and forced exile.[90] By 2011, around 35,000 citizens were granted political amnesty but less than a half received financial compensation.[91] Both the Commission for Deaths and Disappearances and the Amnesty Commission rehabilitated numerous victims and created a critical memory of the former regime. Neither questioned, however, the amnesty granted to the military, an aspect that would emerge on the state's agenda only in 2008.

Another important element of the recognition of state responsibility in acts of repression were civil legal actions brought by victims against the state and particular military officers. While criminal trials were blocked by the Amnesty Law, Brazilian legislation allowed for civil litigation claiming moral and material compensation for harm inflicted by state authorities. Such civil legal

Road from Impunity towards Accountability, edited by Elin Skaar, Jemima Garcia-Godos, and Cath Collins (New York: Routledge, 2016): pp. 103–125.

[87] Paige Arthur, 'How "Transitions" Reshaped Human Rights: A Conceptual History of Transitional Justice', *Human Rights Quarterly* 31, no. 2 (2009): pp. 321–367.

[88] Glenda Mezarobba, 'Between Reparations, Half Truths and Impunity: The Difficult Break with the Legacy of the Dictatorship in Brazil', *International Journal on Human Rights* 7, no. 13 (2010): pp. 7–27, at p. 14.

[89] MacDowell Santos, Teles, and Teles, *Desarquivando*, pp. 473–391; Mezarobba, 'Between Reparations', p. 13.

[90] Abrão and Torelly, 'Resistance to Change', pp. 154–155.

[91] Mezarobba, 'Between Reparations', pp. 14–15.

actions had been initiated as early as the 1970s, but the final verdicts were handed down only after the end of the dictatorship. Such cases included the torture and killing of journalist Vladimir Herzog (1975, with a final decision in 1994), the Araguaia Guerrilla case (2003, with a final decision in 2007), and the Teles Family case against notorious torturer Carlos Alberto Brilhante Ustra (2008, with a final decision in 2014).[92] These civil trials represented a form of moral reparations and truth-telling without any criminal consequence. They created a historical record that clearly condemned dictatorial crimes, but never questioned the bilateral amnesty and the political discourse concerning its importance for Brazil's democratization.

Starting in 2005, and particularly after 2009, the left-wing governments of Luiz Inácio Lula da Silva (2003–2011) and Dilma Rousseff (2011–2016) promoted a new memory narrative that valued the struggle for social justice of left-wing groups in the 1970s and condemned their repression by the military. Both presidents had played key roles in contesting the former regime: Lula as a union leader and Dilma as a member of Marxist urban guerrilla that fought against the dictatorship. Both recruited former guerrilla fighters, political exiles, and student leaders who opposed the regime to join their political staff. Nearly half of the ministers in Lula's two governments, for instance, had been part of the clandestine opposition to the dictatorship.[93] The rise to power of former leftist opponents was a turning point in the writing of a new history of the military regime, one that denounced its violent character and questioned its conservative politics and neoliberal economic foundations.

International pressure was also instrumental for this shift in memory politics. In 2005, the Italian judiciary issued eleven international arrest warrants against Brazilian military officials accused of killing Italian citizens during the Condor Operation in the 1970s.[94] In 2008, the Inter-American Commission on Human Rights called on the Brazilian government to end impunity and investigate the enforced disappearance of around seventy members of the Araguaia Guerrilla—an armed offshoot of the Communist Party of Brazil, formed to resist the military regime—between 1973 and 1974. The Inter-American Commission found that the Amnesty Law violated the rights to

[92] Cecília MacDowell Santos, 'Transitional Justice from the Margins: Legal Mobilizations and Memory Politics in Brazil', in *Legacies of Violence and Transitional Justice in Latin America: A Janus-Faced Paradigm?*, edited by Nina Schneider and Marcia Esparza (London: Lexington Books, 2015): pp. 37–72, at pp. 52–65.

[93] Maria Celina D'Araujo, 'Os ministros da Nova República: Notas para entender a democratização do Poder Executivo', paper presented at II Consad, Brasilia, 6–8 May 2009, available at https://1library.org/document/9yn9ejlq-ministros-nova-republica-notas-entender-democratizacao-poder-executivo.html (accessed 30 April 2023).

[94] Procura della Repubblica. Presi Il Tribunale di Roma, 'Procedimento Penale n. 31079/2005'.

life, justice, and truth as protected by the American Convention on Human Rights (ACHR). In 2009, the Commission referred the case to the IACtHR (see *infra*). In 2009, the UN High Commissioner for Human Rights also requested the Brazilian government to establish a programme to combat impunity, arguing that the lack of justice for past acts of violence was likely to strengthen current practices of torture and police violence.[95] International pressure was thus a driving force behind the state's public engagement with the military past during Lula da Silva and Rousseff's mandates, as Brazil was keen to comply with UN human rights standards in its aspiration to attain a permanent seat at the UN Security Council.[96]

It is in this new national and international political context that the Brazilian state began to challenge the impunity status quo. Several public officers played a key role in contesting the application of amnesty to military crimes: Paulo Vennuchi, Minister of Human Rights between 2006 and 2010, a political prisoner between 1971 and 1976 and co-author of the 1985 report *Brazil: Never Again*; Claudio Fonteles, Brazil's general prosecutor from 2003 to 2010 and a former member of an opposition student organization in the 1960s; Marlon Weichert, deputy in chief of Brazil's Ombudsman between 1999 and 2002 and collaborator of the Auschwitz Institute for Peace and Reconciliation; and Maria do Rosario, Minister of Human Rights between 2011 and 2014. The efforts of these individuals resulted in museums, memory campaigns and educational programmes about past human rights abuses, and the establishment of a truth commission in 2011.[97] Attempts to open criminal trials and void the bilateral amnesty were also initiated, but without success.

4.2 Failed Attempts to Revoke the Bilateral Amnesty

Encouraged by Lula da Silva's new memory regime and in response to pressure from the Inter-American Commission on Human Rights and the Italian judiciary, various prosecutors and legal experts began to question the scope of the Amnesty Law. In 2008, both the Amnesty Commission and the Congress'

[95] Nina Schneider, 'Breaking the "Silence" of the Military Regime: New Politics of Memory in Brazil', *Bulletin of Latin American Research* 30, no. 2 (2011): pp. 198–212, at p. 208.

[96] Nina Schneider, '"Too Little Too Late or 'Premature"? The Brazilian Truth Commission and the Question of "Best Timing"', *Journal of Iberian and Latin American Research* 19, no. 1 (2013): pp. 149–162, at p. 157.

[97] Schneider, 'Waiting for a Meaningful State Apology', p. 74.

Commission on Human Rights organized public hearings to discuss this issue. Three different opinions emerged during these debates.

The first one was formulated by prosecutors such as Eugênia Fávero and Marlon Weichert, who argued that amnesties and statutory limitations did not apply to major international crimes according to customary international law, the 1968 UN Convention, and IACtHR jurisprudence. They asked for the annulment of the Amnesty Law in cases of major international crimes and the opening of trials based on the Argentinian model.[98] Since the end of the 1990s, both Weichert and Fávero had led forensic investigations to excavate mass graves (including the Araguaia Guerrilla case in 2001) and had collaborated to this end with the Argentine Forensic Anthropology Team. According to Weichert, their legal reasoning on the illegality of the Brazilian Amnesty Law was inspired by Argentinian anti-impunity strategies and by the IACtHR jurisprudence in cases such as *Barrio Alto v. Peru* (2001) and *Almonacid Arellano v. Chile* (2006)—which had established that amnesties and statutory limitations did not apply to international crimes.[99]

The second opinion came from the Amnesty Commission, the Brazilian Lawyers' Organization (Ordem dos Advogados, OAB), and the Ministry of Justice. It was more modest in so far as it only questioned the applicability of amnesty to cases of torture and did not make reference to international law. From this perspective, acts of torture did not constitute a political crime, but an atrocious private crime that was not within the scope of the Amnesty Law. Moreover, the OAB argued that exonerating perpetrators of torture contradicted Article 5 the 1988 Brazilian Constitution which stipulated that no 'bail, clemency or amnesty' should apply to torture and 'crimes defined as heinous'.[100] The OAB also highlighted that the Amnesty Law explicitly excluded acts of 'terrorism'. This exception, the OAB claimed, should not only be applied to the militant opposition but also to officials involved in 'state terrorism', understood as 'the systematic and organized practice [. . .] of homicide, torture, and rape against political opponents'.[101] This view was however problematic because the concept of 'state terrorism' had no legal basis in national legislation or international law. According to Weichert, this legal reasoning was chosen to circumvent debates on how customary international law could be applied in a civil law country with a positivistic legal tradition. He warned its

[98] Comissão de Direitos Humanos, Seminário no. 1357/08 from 16/10/2008.

[99] Personal interview with Marlon Weichert, online, 1 December 2021.

[100] 'ADPF: Petição OAB', available at www.ajd.org.br/documentos/769-93adpf-peticao-oab (accessed 25 April 2023).

[101] Ibid.

limits: it could trigger debates on retroactivity, as the Amnesty Law had been adopted prior to the 1988 Constitution; it did not solve the issue of the expired statute of limitations for crimes committed in the 1970s—an 'absolute dogma' of Brazilian legal education.[102]

Such arguments were indeed formulated in a third opinion advanced by the Ministry of Defence and various legal experts such as Carlos Velloso (president of the Brazilian Supreme Court of Justice between 1994 and 1996) or law professors such as Thiago Bottino do Amaral and Dimitri Dimoulis. In their view, revisiting the Amnesty Law was unconstitutional because it represented a retroactive measure. It was also a useless initiative because the statute of limitations for the crimes under consideration had expired. Brazil had never codified crimes against humanity in its criminal legislation nor ratified the 1968 UN Convention ruling that crimes against humanity do not elapse. Furthermore, the bilateral amnesty had been the political foundation of the Brazilian transition to democracy.[103] Dimoulis, who would later testify on behalf of the Brazilian government at the IACtHR in the *Herzog* case (see *infra*), explained in a 2021 interview:

> Revoking the bilateral amnesty was unconstitutional because it infringed on the right of the defendant to the most lenient punishment. Also, Brazil is a monist legal system in which the Constitution is above international law. Moreover, one must understand that most Brazilians see the Amnesty Law as a fundamental pillar of the peaceful transition.[104]

Born in Greece during the military junta, Dimoulis considered the retributive justice measures engaged in by the Greek government after the fall of the military dictatorship as excessive and vindictive. In his view, 'trials are confrontational and antagonistic and can do little for reconciliation and democracy'.[105] In contrast, the Brazilian approach was 'reconciliatory' since it was based on amnesty—'a legitimate instrument of any sovereign state'—but also on reparations and truth-telling. Dimoulis's view was representative of most Brazilian legal positivists, who consider that

[102] Personal interview with Marlon Weichert, online, 1 December 2021.
[103] 'ADPF: Petição OAB', available at www.ajd.org.br/documentos/769-93adpf-peticao-oab (accessed 25 April 2023).
[104] Personal interview with Dimitri Dimoulis, online, 14 December 2021.
[105] Ibid.

> ignoring the statute of limitations, the non-retroactivity of criminal law, and the imperative *non bis in idem* violates the 1988 Constitution and, in part, the ACHR [. . .]. Due to its constitutive, hence, creative nature, accountability is a mechanism for reconstructing the past, and it is always *retroactive*. Accountability elaborates a narrative about the past that allows the subsumption of a behaviour to current norms.[106]

The proponents of this viewpoint thus also doubted that criminal justice could contribute to clarifying the past. Like the Bulgarian judges, they consider the 'truth' to be difficult to establish given the continuous reinterpretation of historical events during specific periods of time and according to prevailing ideologies. Moreover, in their view, the 'right to truth' and the duty of the state to establish a historical narrative about the past stand in contradiction to democratic principles such as freedom of expression and political pluralism.[107]

Following these debates, the OAB addressed the Brazilian Supreme Court of Justice (Supremo Tribunal Federal, STF) to formulate an opinion on the constitutionality of the bilateral amnesty. In April 2010, the STF rejected, by a vote of seven to two, the initiative to revoke the bilateral amnesty.[108] From a legal point of view, the majority of the judges argued that Article 1 of the Amnesty Law clearly encompassed any crime committed on political grounds, including murder and torture. They emphasized that the Amnesty Law should be interpreted in the historical and legal context in which it had been adopted, not in the sense of any new arrangements that might follow: The 1979 amnesty predated the 1988 Constitution, the 1984 UN Convention against Torture, and Brazil's ratification of the ACHR in 1992. Some judges also argued that IACtHR jurisprudence concerning the illegality of amnesties for gross human rights violations (such as *Barrios Altos v. Peru*) could not be applied to any period prior to Brazil's recognition of the IACtHR's jurisdiction in 1998. Such an application would have amounted to retroactivity.[109] Moreover, some judges, such as Celso de Melo and Cezar Peluso, emphasized that even without the

[106] Dimitri Dimoulis, 'Justiça de transição e função anistiante no Brasil: Hipostasiações indevidas e caminhos de responsabilização', in *Justiça de transição no Brasil. Direito, responsabilização e verdade*, edited by Dimitri Dimoulis, Antonio Martins, Lauro Joppert, and Swensson Junior (São Paulo: Saraiva, 2010): pp. 91–127.

[107] Ibid.

[108] Supremo Tribunal Federal (hereafter: STF), 'Arguição de Descumprimento de Preceito Fundamental-ADPF no. 153, 29 April 2010'. For a summary of each judge's vote, see Carlos Artur Gallo, *Um Acerto de Contas com o Passado: Crimines da ditadura, 'Leis de Impunidade' e decisões das Supremas Cortes no Brasil e na Argentina* (Brazil: Appris Editora, 2018): pp. 68–91.

[109] Paulo Sotero, 'El desafío brasileño: cómo gestionar las relaciones regionales asimétricas más allá de la OEA', *Revista CIDOB d'Afers Internacionais* 97–98 (2012): pp. 101–116, at p. 107.

Amnesty Law, it was no longer possible to prosecute crimes committed during the Brazilian dictatorship because any statutory limitations had expired. Since Brazil never incorporated the category of crimes against humanity into its criminal code, any use of this category was retroactive.[110]

From a political point of view, the majority labelled the Amnesty Law a 'landmark of democratization' that had underpinned the 1985–1988 transition.[111] They emphasized that most segments of Brazilian society, including the Brazilian Committee for Amnesty and the OAB itself, had supported it because it formed the political basis of the peaceful transition from authoritarianism. Moreover, the 1988 Constitution reaffirmed the validity of the Amnesty Law. Revising this consensus twenty-five years after the Brazilian transition to democracy amounted to retroactivity. It was also, the majority claimed, an attempt to 'rewrite' and 'reconstruct' history and annul a political agreement that had significantly contributed to the pacification of Brazilian society.[112] Within this logic, certain judges, such as Gilmar Mendes, emphasized a 'two demons' theory. While the military had imposed a regime of terror, left-wing armed groups had also been violent in their attempt to impose a 'totalitarian regime with a Stalinist, Castroists or Maoist foundation'.[113] Amnesty should thus be bilateral. Moreover, as in Bulgaria, the judges argued that only Congress could revoke the law because the STF was not a legislative body. They rejected the idea that judges possessed any creative power and referred any possible legal transformations to political authorities. The majority's ruling endorsed the long-standing historical and legal interpretation of the broad, bilateral amnesty, which had been backed by military elites, but also by some victims. In fact, the reporting judge, Eros Grau, had himself been a victim of torture. He voted in favour of the bilateral amnesty, emphasizing that processes of truth-telling should continue, but changing the 1979 arrangements would amount to political and historical revisionism.[114]

Two judges, Carlos Ayres Britto and Ricardo Lewandowski, challenged the interpretation of the amnesty as general and unrestricted. Britto asserted that torture was not a political crime, because the 'torturer is not an ideologist. [. . .] He is a monster, inhuman, a perverse maniac'.[115] In Britto's view, the 1988

[110] As summarized by Gallo, *Um Acerto*, pp. 77–79.

[111] Jorge Barrientos-Parra and Jorge Luís Mialhe, 'Lei de Anistia Comentários à sentença do Supremo Tribunal Federal no caso da ADPF 153', *Revista de Informação Legislativa*, no. 194 / 2012, pp. 23–40.

[112] STF, 'Arguição de Descumprimento de Preceito Fundamental: ADPF no. 153'. 29 April 2010.

[113] Alessandro Cristo, 'Lea a Voto de Gilmar Mendes sobre la Lei de Anistia', available at www.conjur.com.br/2010-ago-08/leia-voto-ministro-gilmar-mendes-lei-anistia (accessed 23 April 2023).

[114] Abrão and Torelly, 'Resistance to Change', p. 177.

[115] Quoted by Gallo, *Um Acerto*, p. 90.

Brazilian Constitution prevailed over the 1979 Amnesty Law. Maintaining legal impunity for torture was unconstitutional. Britto did not refer to international law, nor to IACtHR jurisprudence.[116] His dissenting opinion dissociated torture from state politics and situated such practices in the sphere of individual abuses. In contrast, Lewandowski argued that political crimes committed during the dictatorship had been crimes against humanity. Quoting IACtHR jurisprudence, as well as Chilean jurisprudence, which affirmed that amnesties could not apply to major international crimes, he contended that the amnesty for military crimes was illegal under both conventional and customary international law.[117] Lewandowski also referred to a 2009 STF decision to extradite a Uruguayan citizen to Argentina to be put on trial for murder, torture, and enforced disappearances committed within Operation Condor. In that case, the STF acknowledged that crimes against humanity should be prosecuted no matter the lapse of time.[118] Lewandowski was in fact the only STF judge to favour the application of ICL as far as Brazilian dictatorial crimes were concerned. Britto and Lewandowski also engaged in historical debates, criticizing the 'hypocrisy' of hiding military atrocities behind the supposed virtue of a non-violent transition. The military regime had been criminal and had transformed its officials into monsters.

The different perspectives of the STF judges mirrored wider conflicts within the Brazilian legal community between those embracing a 'monist and positivist legal approach' that refers only to national laws and the Constitution, and those with an 'internationalist, dialogical' approach that interrogates the Amnesty Law from the point of view of its validity under international law.[119] This second approach however relied mainly on IACtHR jurisprudence and the ACHR, which Brazil only ratified in 1992. These temporal limitations remained an important critique of those who opposed the revision of the 1979 Amnesty Law.

The majority ruling was acclaimed by the armed forces and by certain politicians and legal experts who systematically rejected the revision of the Amnesty Law. In contrast, the decision was criticized by the OAB, the Ministry of Human Rights, the Ministry of Justice, and various national and international human

[116] Ibid, p. 140.

[117] Barrientos-Parra and Mialhe, 'Lei de Anistia'.

[118] Mariane Morato Stival, 'Direitos humanos: análise dos votos no julgamento da ADPF 153 pelo Supremo Tribunal Federal', June 2015, available at https://jus.com.br/artigos/40881/direitos-humanos-analise-dos-votos-no-julgamento-da-adpf-153-pelo-supremo-tribunal-federal (accessed 23 April 2023).

[119] Anderson Luiz Brasil Silva, 'ADPF 153, Direito penal e justiça transicional a luz dos princípios de Chicago', in *Justiça de Transição no Brasil*, edited by Eneá de Stutz e Almeida (Brasil: Editora CRV, 2017): pp. 51–68, at pp. 61–62.

rights organizations including Torture Never More, Amnesty International, and the UN Committee against Torture. According to the latter, the judgment was an offence to victims' families, a legitimization of human rights abuses with implications for violations in present-day Brazil, and a sign of an unfinished transition towards full democracy. The STF was accused of 'juridical provincialism', since 'self-pardoning' was no longer acceptable in the twenty-first century and the duty to prosecute gross human rights violations had firmly established itself as a fundamental principle of international law.[120]

Indeed, the STF verdict resulted both from the judges' desire to maintain the political status quo and from a dualist vision of international law, which had dominated Brazilian legal culture for decades. According to the 1988 Constitution, international agreements ratified by Brazil are part of national legislation, but they have infra-constitutional status (i.e., at a lower hierarchy than the Constitution itself). Treaties that specifically concern the protection of human rights only achieve full constitutional authority upon congressional approval. The direct application of *jus cogens* and customary international law is thus often seen as an infringement of the principle of legality, unless these norms are incorporated into domestic positive law.[121] The ACHR has not yet acquired constitutional status and its application prior to 1992 continued to be interpreted by most Brazilian judges as a violation of the principle of non-retroactivity. However, by maintaining the application of the Amnesty Law to acts of torture, the STF judgment engaged in a choice between two constitutional provisions: one that prohibits clemency and amnesty for torture and one that affirms the right of the defendant to the most lenient punishment. As in Bulgaria, the Court prioritized the right of the defendant to due process over the duty to prosecute major international crimes and provided a conservative approach to international law, which was overridden by domestic legal provisions.

4.3 The Inter-American Court of Human Rights and the Duty to Prosecute

In November 2010, several months after the STF verdict, the IACtHR ruled in the Araguaia Guerrilla case and found that the Amnesty Law was inconsistent

[120] Schneider, 'Impunity in Post-authoritarian Brazil', p. 50; Gallo, *Um Acerto*, p. 138.

[121] Yi Shin Tang, 'International Justice through Domestic Courts: Challenges in Brazil's Judicial Review of the Amnesty Law', *International Journal of Transitional Justice* 9, no. 2 (2015): pp. 259–277, at p. 266.

with the ACHR, at least in cases of enforced disappearances. First, the Court affirmed that the enforced disappearances of the Araguaia Guerrilla members violated the right to life, the right to juridical personality, and the right to personal integrity and personal liberty, protected by Articles 3, 4, 5, and 7 of the ACHR. Since enforced disappearances were continuous crimes[122]—a doctrine that IACtHR adopted in 1999—the Court possessed the jurisdiction to ask the Brazilian state to open criminal inquires. Second, the lack of investigations violated the right to a fair trial and judicial protection and the right to truth inscribed in Articles 8, 25 and 5 of the ACHR.[123]

Nevertheless, the IACtHR acknowledged that its temporal jurisdiction prevented the examination of events that occurred prior to Brazil's recognition of its jurisdiction in 1998. The Court expressly stated that the Amnesty Law lacked effect only for the crime of enforced disappearances, given that they are continuous crimes and, consequently, were still formally committed since Brazil's ratification of the ACHR. In contrast, the Court refrained from expanding its argument to extrajudicial killings, torture, and illegal detentions committed during the dictatorship or to discuss them as international crimes.[124]

This limitation was underlined by the concurring opinion of Brazilian (ad hoc) judge, Roberto de Figueiredo Caldas, who argued that the IACtHR should have highlighted that torture and extrajudicial executions perpetrated by the Brazilian dictatorship were crimes against humanity—not subject to amnesties and statutory limitations. In his view, the Court took a conservative approach that departed from its previous, more progressive, jurisprudence such as *Goiburú v. Paraguay* and *Almonacid Arellano v. Chile*. In these cases, the IACtHR had engaged with the nature of the crimes under international law and the duty to prosecute them. Moreover, underlined the judge, even if Brazil had not signed the relevant international treaties, the duty to prosecute crimes against humanity derived from international custom.[125] Caldas also emphasized the STF's obligation to conform with the IACtHR's decision: while domestic supreme or constitutional courts engage in constitutional control, the IACtHR has control over the application of the American Convention on Human Rights and thus has the last word on human rights issues. Consequently, the Brazilian legislature should annul the bilateral amnesty since its duty is to adapt national legislation to the ACHR and IACtHR

[122] International law concerning enforced disappearances stipulates that until a body is recovered, a person cannot be declared dead, and the crime thus does not lapse.

[123] IACtHR, *Gomes Lund et al. v. Brazil*, Judgment of 24 November 2010.

[124] Ibid.

[125] IACtHR, *Gomes Lund et al. v. Brazil*, 'Concurring Opinion of Judge Roberto de Figueiredo Caldas'.

jurisprudence, 'not vice versa'. Caldas called for the invalidation of 'a law that generates impunity, lack of trust regarding protection from the state, and an eternally opened social wound, needing to be healed by [. . .] more incisive application of law and justice'.[126]

The difference between the majority's vote and Caldas's concurring opinion reflected the differing approaches taken by IACtHR judges towards the question of its jurisdiction to interpret the nature of the crimes in question. As in the Guatemalan genocide case (see Chapter 3), most of the judges believed that it was not in their purview to elaborate on their categorization or on whether the crimes committed were major international crimes. In *Plan de Sánchez v. Guatemala*, another Brazilian judge, A.A. Cançado Trinidade, stressed in a separate opinion that the IACtHR should have recognized, or at least engaged with, the nature of the crimes under international law. In fact, in the 1980s, Caldas had studied law at the University of Brasilia, where Cançado Trinidade was professor of international law.

Even if the Araguaia Guerrilla case acknowledged only the inapplicability of amnesty to enforced disappearances, the case gave Brazilian prosecutors a strong legal basis to initiate new investigations. Between 2011 and 2016—when Dilma Rousseff was impeached—the Federal Prosecutor's Office (Ministerio Publico Federal—MPF) lodged thirty-six criminal complaints against public agents for crimes against humanity committed during the dictatorship. On the one hand, the MPF argued that the Brazilian judiciary had to conform with the IACtHR decision and investigate enforced disappearances. On the other hand, the MPF relied on Judge Caldas's arguments to maintain that extrajudicial killings and torture were crimes against humanity, not subject to amnesties or statutes of limitations.[127] Yet, the MPF's approach was widely rejected by Brazilian judges: only seven indictments were accepted by the courts, but the trials were later stopped based on the argument that Brazilian courts were bound by the 2010 STF decision and not by the IACtHR judgment.[128]

Judge Paulo Fontes, from the Appellate Court of São Paulo, was among those who tried to begin criminal proceedings against Carlos Alberto Brilhante Ustra, former head of the army's intelligence service and a notorious torturer,

[126] Ibid.

[127] Ministerio Público Federal, *Crimes da Ditadura Militar: Relatório sobre as atividades de persecução penal desenvolvidas pelo MPF em matéria de graves violações a DH cometidas por agentes do Estado durante o regime de exceção* (Brasilia: MPF, 2017).

[128] Emilio Peluso Neder Meyer and Fabrício Bertini Pasquot Polido, 'Brazil in the Dock: The Inter-American Court of Human Rights Rulings Concerning the Dictatorship of 1964–1985', *Verfassungsblog*, 3 December 2018, available at https://verfassungsblog.de/brazil-in-the-dock-the-inter-american-court-of-human-rights-rulings-concerning-the-dictatorship-of-1964-1985/ (accessed 23 April 2023).

accused of the extrajudicial killing of a leftist militant in 1972. Born in 1970, Fontes had been close to Lula da Silva's Labour Party in his student days and had worked within the MPF for more than ten years before being appointed to the Appellate Court of São Paulo. Fontes had completed a master's degree and postdoctoral studies in France, where he had worked on the legal philosophy of Robert Alexy—a German legal scholar who engaged with conflicts between natural law and legal positivism and defended the Radbruch theory that unjust or evil laws lose their validity when they deliberately disavow justice. Fontes emphasized in a 2021 interview:

> Any judge has his own political visions and values. Even if my father was in the military, I always stood against the values and practices of the military dictatorship. I had left-wing political views. [. . .] I also engaged with the law in a comprehensive way that included both national and international law, as well as moral principles.[129]

In 2013, Fontes was the reporting judge in the Ustra case, in which the Appellate Court of São Paulo decided two to one that the MPF could open a criminal trial based on IACtHR jurisprudence; moreover, dictatorial crimes constituted crimes against humanity—not subject to amnesties and statutory limitations. Yet, the decision was soon reversed by a superior chamber of the same Court, which invoked the 2010 STF decision.[130] In Fontes's view, this divergence within the Brazilian judiciary had both political and juridical motives. On the one hand, there was a consensus among most Brazilian judges—including many with leftist political views—that the Amnesty Law was essential for enforcing democratic stability. Only very few considered that impunity pacts were detrimental to the Brazilian society and justice system. On the other hand, Brazilian legal culture and education had been dominated for decades by monist theories of international law. Most legal practitioners were thus reluctant to apply ICL without its clear codification in the national legislation.[131]

Indeed, the deployment of Inter-American case law and ICL within the Brazilian constitutional order was very limited. Brazil only recognized the IACtHR's jurisdiction in 1998, and the first IACtHR ruling against Brazil was issued as late as 2002. The STF, which has a 'totemic status' in the 'judicial

[129] Personal interview with Paulo Fontes, online, 14 December 2021.

[130] São Paulo Appellate Court, 'Recurso em Sentido Estrito Nr. 0004823-25.2013.4.03.6181/SP'; 'Embargos Infringentes e de Nulidade Nr. 0004823- 25.2013.4.03.6181/SP'.

[131] Personal interview with Paulo Fontes, online, 14 December 2021.

architecture of the state', developed after the 1985 transition without any link to the IACtHR. Even after 1998, it continued to maintain its resistance to international law and to emphasize the infra-Constitutional status of international treaties.[132]

Disputes on the scope of the amnesty also took place within the Comissão Nacional da Verdade (CNV, National Truth Commission), established in 2011.[133] While the Commission only had a historical research function, without judicial investigative power, it gathered numerous legal experts who engaged with the legality of the bilateral amnesty. Two competing narratives emerged:[134] on the one hand, a 'status quo-driven conciliatory narrative' was endorsed by commissioners José Paulo Cavalcanti, a former legal adviser to President Sarney, José Carlos Dias, President Cardoso's former minister of justice, and Gilson Dipp, a judge appointed by Cardoso at the second highest Brazilian court, the Superior Court of Justice. On the other hand, an anti-impunity narrative was advocated by Claudio Fonteles, former general prosecutor under Lula da Silva, and Rosa Cardoso, a human rights lawyer who defended political prisoners during the dictatorship. Cardoso's former secretary for human rights, Paulo Sérgio Pinheiro, also overruled the impunity provisions for human rights violations. Since the mid-1990s, Pinheiro had been a UN Special Rapporteur on human rights for countries such as Togo, Burundi, and Myanmar; between 2003 and 2007, he was a member of the Inter-American Commission on Human Rights. Within an international context that had begun to emphasize 'the duty to prosecute', Pinheiro became a vocal opponent of the Brazilian Amnesty Law, which he had previously endorsed in the 1990s. Conflicts between these two groups within the CNV replicated the divisions within the Brazilian judiciary and political class.

Nevertheless, the CNV report delivered in 2014 was progressive in nature. It emphasized the systemic political crimes of the dictatorship and labelled them crimes against humanity—a narrative that went further than the IACtHR decision in the *Araguaia* case. It also stipulated Brazil's duty to conform with international accountability standards and suspend the blanket amnesty for crimes against humanity.[135] With Dilma Rousseff's impeachment in 2016 and

[132] Tom Gerald Day, 'Brazilian 'Supremocracy' and the Inter-American Court of Human Rights: Unpicking an Unclear Relationship', in *Law and Policy in Latin America: Transforming Courts, Institutions, and Rights*, edited by Pedro Fortes, Larissa Boratti, Andrés Palacios Lleras, and Tom Gerald Daly (London: Palgrave Macmillan, 2017): pp. 3–20.

[133] For an analysis of the Brazilian Truth Commission, see Schneider, 'Too Little Too Late'; Marcelo Torelly, 'Assessing a Late Truth Commission: Challenges and Achievements of the Brazilian National Truth Commission', *International Journal of Transitional Justice* 12, no. 2 (2018): pp. 194–215.

[134] For these divisions, see Torelly, 'Assessing a Late Truth Commission', p. 194 and pp. 204–206.

[135] Torelly, 'Assessing a Late Truth Commission'.

Jair Bolsonaro's rise to power, however, the CNV's recommendations to prosecute former military officials, prohibit any apology of the dictatorship, and reform of the army and military education had no practical effect.

4.4 Bolsonaro's Revisionism and the Continued Divisions within the Judiciary

Jair Bolsonaro—a former army officer himself—had a long history of celebrating the military dictatorships of the Southern Cone and praising notorious perpetrators of human rights violations. On several occasions, he declared himself in favour of torture and even stated in 2016 that 'the dictatorship's mistake was to torture but not kill'.[136] During his mandate, the role of the army in Brazilian politics expanded, with approximately 6,100 military appointed to political positions between 2018 and 2021.[137] In 2020, more than a third of Bolsonaro's government, including the president and the vice-president, were former or active military personnel.[138] In terms of memory politics, Bolsonaro appointed new commissioners to head the Amnesty Commission, including Henrique de Freitas, a lawyer who had previously attempted to block reparation payments to victims. In 2019, Bolsonaro's minister of education, Ricardo Vélez, announced a revision of history textbooks to provide 'a broader version of history', one that would describe the dictatorship as 'a democratic regime by force'.[139] That same year, the president issued a decree to celebrate the fifty-fifth anniversary of the 1964 military coup, which he defined as a 'democratic revolution'.[140]

Bolsonaro's memory agenda generated protests from various segments of Brazilian society and the international community. Moreover, it split, once again, the judiciary over the legal and historical narratives about the dictatorship. In 2019, the MPF attacked Bolsonaro's decree celebrating the military coup in court, arguing that it offended the victims and contradicted previous

[136] For Bolsonaro's memory politics, see Nina Schneider, 'Bolsonaro in Power: Failed Memory Politics in Post-Authoritarian Brazil?' *Modern Languages Open* 1 (2020), available at https://modernlanguagesopen.org/articles/10.3828/mlo.v0i0.324 (accessed 26 April 2023).

[137] Emilio Peluso Neder Meyer and Ulisses Levy Silvério dos Reis, 'Brazilian Democracy under Military Tutelage', *Verfassungsblog*, 19 February 2018, available at https://verfassungsblog.de/brazilian-democracy-under-military-tutelage/ (accessed 25 April 2023).

[138] Schneider, 'Bolsonaro in Power'.

[139] Ibid.

[140] Emilio Peluso Neder Meyer and Juliano Zaiden Benvindo, 'Bolsonaro's Unconstitutional Support for the Brazilian Civil-Military Dictatorship of 1964–1985', *International Journal of Constitutional Law Blog*, 12 April 2019.

reparation laws and the CNV report. A judge initially ruled to bar the celebration, contending that it was incompatible with 'the process of democratic reconstruction' and required the approval of Congress. His decision, however, was quickly overturned by an appeals judge, Maria do Carmo Cardoso, a close friend of the Bolsonaro family. She argued that Brazil's democracy was sufficiently robust for a 'pluralism of ideas'. Freedom of expression was a constitutional right, and 'similar demonstrations took place in the barracks in preceding years, with no negative consequences'. While it is true that revisionist military clubs had commemorated the 1964 coup in the past, they had done so privately and not by presidential order. Victims' associations appealed to the STF, arguing that Bolsonaro's decree violated the Constitution, because it incited propaganda for non-democratic regimes and infringed on the international right of victims to truth and memory. STF judge Gilmar Mendes—a staunch defender of the bilateral amnesty—rejected the petition. Paradoxically, he argued that the presidential order represented only 'an act of (personal) opinion', expressed through a presidential decree that was not legally binding.[141] Both judges ignored the IACtHR decision in *Araguaia Guerrilla v. Brazil* and the second IACtHR verdict handed down against Brazil in 2018, *Herzog v. Brazil*.

In 2018, in *Herzog v. Brazil*, the IACtHR condemned Brazil for not prosecuting the public agents responsible for the torture and murder of journalist Vladimir Herzog in 1975.[142] The Court ruled that extrajudicial killings and torture committed on political grounds by the Brazilian military regime constituted crimes against humanity. It also stated that the 1968 UN Convention codified pre-existing customary law and *jus cogens* norms. Brazil was bound by such norms, even if it did not ratify the Convention. The IACtHR concluded that *jus cogens* imposes the duty to prosecute major international crimes and states cannot impose statutes of limitations, amnesties, or any other legal provisions that prevent criminal liability.

Nevertheless, as in the *Araguaia Guerrilla* case, *Herzog v. Brazil* had little impact on revisiting the bilateral amnesty. The STF remained indifferent to the various petitions asking for a revision of its 2010 decision in response to IACtHR jurisprudence. In 2019, the Superior Tribunal of Justice (Superior Tribunal de Justiça, STJ), the second highest court in Brazil, ruled, in a five to two decision, that the category of crimes against humanity could not be used in trials related to dictatorial crimes. The category had never been incorporated in

[141] Varla Osmo and Danilo Tavares. 'A chancela do Judiciário à comer'. *Carta Capital*, 2 April 2019, available at www.cartacapital.com.br/ (accessed 9 July 2021).

[142] IACtHR, *Herzog et. al. v. Brazil*, Judgment of 12 March 2018.

the Brazilian criminal code, and the statute of limitations for ordinary crimes, such as homicide, had expired. Any prosecution would thus infringe upon the principle of legality and would be politically untenable since it would cast doubt on the 1979 consensus. Two dissenting judges referred to Brazil's obligation to enforce the IACtHR's decision in *Herzog v. Brazil*, but the majority argued that such a position was in contradiction with the principle of legality.[143] The two highest courts in Brazil, the STF and the STJ, therefore ignored IACtHR jurisprudence, an approach subsequently followed by most lower courts.

In June 2021 however, a São Paulo lower court accepted an MPF criminal complaint and convicted a former military officer, Carlos Alberto Augusto, of the kidnapping and enforced disappearance of a dissident ex-marine in 1971. The judge, Silvio César Arouck Gemaque, used the Argentinian double classification of deeds under both national and international law. He condemned Alberto Augusto for kidnapping based on the national law, while classifying his deeds as crimes against humanity under international law (and thus not subject to amnesty and statutory limitations). Arouck Gemaque made extensive use of ICL conventions and customary law and relied on the IACtHR decisions in *Araguaia* and *Herzog* cases to emphasize Brazil's duty to prosecute.[144] In a 2022 interview, the judge acknowledged that his decision was driven by the desire to comply with international standards and align Brazil with the progressive jurisprudence coming out of countries such as Argentina and Chile:

> I studied international law during my doctoral studies, between 2007 and 2010. I also studied the Argentinian and the Chilean case law, which reversed impunity in both countries. My verdict was not a matter of politics or ideology—my politics changed several times over the years, and my grandfather was himself a member of the military. I wanted to create a precedent that complies with international standards, one that even if rejected by the superior courts could be used by other judges in future and align Brazil to the new international and regional trends.[145]

Like Weichert and Fontes, Arouck Gemaque emphasized the international duty to prosecute—at least in cases of enforced disappearances—over the dominant national jurisprudence. While his verdict was praised by pro-accountability actors as historical and courageous, it was contested by the defendant at the

[143] Superior Tribunal de Justiça, 'Recurso Especial 1798903/RJ, 25/09/2019'.
[144] 'Sentença de Arouck Gemaque é aula de História e de Direito', available at https://monitormercantil.com.br/sentenca-de-arouck-gemaque-e-aula-de-historia-e-de-direito/ (accessed 23 April 2023).
[145] Personal interview with Silvio César Arouck Gemaque, online, 21 January 2022.

Appellate Court of São Paulo, and it can still be appealed a second time at the STJ. Without a reformulation of the 2010 STF decision on the validity of the bilateral amnesty, it seems improbable that impunity in Brazil will come to an end.

Despite their different historical and regional contexts, Bulgaria and Brazil present important similarities in terms of the resistance to the duty to prosecute. Both countries were characterized by long-standing experiences of dictatorship, judicialized repression, and negotiated transitions. The continuity of former political and military elites and the lack of judicial reform after the transition to democracy led to weak policies for dealing with the past, despite the fact that Brazil established robust reparation programmes and a truth commission. In both Bulgaria and Brazil, pro-accountability coalitions were quite weak: after the fall of their respective dictatorships, most civil society groups were more interested in the future than in reckoning with past human rights violations. In Brazil, this situation was accentuated by the consensus surrounding the Amnesty Law at the moment of its adoption, while in Bulgaria it was triggered more broadly by a weak civil society. Both countries had a legal culture characterized by legal positivism, a monist approach to international law, and a deference to political authorities as far as major legal transformations and interpretations were concerned. The Bulgarian and Brazilian judiciaries prioritized legal arguments based on national law and maintained legal practices marked by reluctance towards new developments in ICL. The highest courts saw non-retroactivity and written laws as the driving principle guiding their jurisprudence and ignored customary law. They prioritized the right of the defendant based on a minimalist use of international law over a victim's right to justice and over the international duty to prosecute. Moreover, both judiciaries refused to engage in what they perceived as revisionist history-writing and were keen to maintain the political arrangements agreed upon at a parliamentary level during the dictatorship and in the early years of the transition to democracy. Amnesties and statutory limitations thus became a magna carta for rejecting attempts to end impunity and open investigations into dictatorial crimes.

One important difference between the two countries must however be underlined: in Bulgaria, the legislative initiatives to change the status quo were more political rhetoric—designed to condemn communism in its entirety—than a realistic strategy for indicting major international crimes perpetrated during state socialism. Also, given the weak mobilizations of NGOs and victims' associations, there were no attempts to challenge impunity at the European level. As such, no ECtHR jurisprudence emerged on the duty to prosecute crimes against humanity in Bulgaria. In contrast, Brazilian pro-accountability actors, especially prosecutors and judges who attempted to initiate prosecutions, relied on strong legal arguments previously used in other Latin American countries such as Argentina and Chile. They also invoked broader IACtHR jurisprudence on the duty to prosecute, including two decisions handed down against Brazil. Given the anti-impunity activism of various Brazilian legal experts and members of the judiciary, the annulment of the bilateral amnesty in the future is not an impossibility. In contrast, the Bulgarian judiciary remains unified in its rigid interpretation of the principle of legality as a fundamental pillar of the rule of law and its weak political interest in dealing with the past. This context renders future prosecutions of communist crimes unlikely.

Epilogue

1. Introduction

By bringing together histories of Latin American and Central Eastern European (CEE) engagements with international criminal law (ICL), this book aimed to offer both a fresh perspective on the fragmentation of this body of law and a new method to study it. It placed two semi-peripheries of the global system in the centre of the analysis in order to clarify how and why their national courts, judicial officials, and human rights activists attempted—and often succeeded—in altering long-standing, hegemonic visions of ICL. The book also proposed a sociological alternative to the prevailing scholarship that explains the fragmentation of ICL exclusively through institutional and structural legal factors. It focused instead on the actors who apply ICL and the way their legal educations, their understandings of national and international politics in terms of dealing with violent pasts, and their subjective attitudes towards the historical episodes they address through ICL impacted interpretations and revisions of this body of law. I believe that such an approach is vital to overcoming the shortcomings of both alarmist and often Eurocentric accounts that warn against the alleged danger of deviating from international standards and normative, textual legal analyses that overlook the social life of the law.

2. Transforming ICL to End Impunity

The case studies analysed in this book reveal that pro-accountability actors from the two regions turned to ICL as a powerful tool with the potential to unblock criminal trials at home and render justice for egregious human rights violations. Faced, however, with the limits of ICL codification at both the national and international levels, they began to adapt prevailing definitions and principles in order to render them applicable to the crimes of the previous military and communist dictatorships in their home countries. Justice activists very frequently had to choose between opening prosecutions based on

Justice and Memory after Dictatorship. Raluca Grosescu, Oxford University Press. © Raluca Grosescu 2024.
DOI: 10.1093/oso/9780192870346.003.0006

unconventional interpretations of ICL or applying dominant readings and thereby renouncing their chance at criminal justice.

In both regions, anti-impunity lawyers and judicial officials endorsed a more flexible vision of the principle of non-retroactivity to overcome the legal constraints—in particular the obstacles of amnesties and statutory limitations—that obstructed criminal investigations. They used unsettled principles of customary international law to legitimize retrospective prosecutions; they coined new forms of criminalization, such as the 'double classification of deeds' under national and international law (in Latin America); and they revived and employed the 1968 UN Convention on the Non-Applicability of Statutory Limitations to War Crimes and Crimes against Humanity—a marginalized ICL instrument, dismissed by Western governments, that allows retroactive prosecutions of international crimes. These tactics were alternative solutions to positivist visions of the law that demanded a strict interpretation of *nullum crimen sine lege*, but which inevitably impeded criminal investigations into dictatorial crimes. Such legal manoeuvres were determined by the absence—throughout the twentieth century—of a generally recognized international instrument that defined and sanctioned crimes against humanity committed in times of peace; the non-codification of this international category in the national legislations in force during the military and the communist regimes; and the lack of an international jurisdiction that CEE and Latin American justice activists could have addressed in order to redress impunity at home.

The use of the concept of 'ideological auto-genocide' by the Spanish Audiencia Nacional can also be explained by the absence of crimes against humanity in the Spanish Criminal Code at the time of the proceedings and in the Ley Orgánica del Poder Judicial, which enabled extraterritorial prosecutions based on universal jurisdiction. As soon as this category was introduced in Spanish legislation, it became the prevailing charge retained by Spanish courts.[1] In Lithuania, the notion of *ethno-national-political genocide* was employed to sanction the extrajudicial killings of anti-Soviet partisans. Justice for such crimes would have been impossible based on other categories inscribed in Lithuanian law at the time of their commission. The inclusion of 'cultural genocide' in Ríos Montt's trial in Guatemala aimed to prevent a narrow criminalization of the destruction of Indigenous

[1] Cristina Fernández-Pacheco Estrada, 'Domestic Prosecution of Genocide: Fragmentation or Natural Diversity?', in *The Diversification and Fragmentation of International Criminal Law*, edited by Larissa van den Herik and Carsten Stahn (Leiden: Martinus Nijhoff, 2012): pp. 429–459, at p. 449.

groups and encompass not only acts of physical destruction but also the systematic obliteration of Indigenous social cohesion and ways of life due to structural racism and the alleged cultural superiority of Westernized Guatemalan elites.

Finally, CEE and Latin American activists also resorted to strategies of transnationalizing justice to overcome the lack of legal responses by national governments and UN offices to the crimes of the communist and military dictatorships. CEE anti-communist memory entrepreneurs picked an inefficient battle, namely the creation of a European tribunal for communist crimes. Their cross-border mobilizations had little effect on the development of ICL due to pan-European divisions across the left–right political spectrum and due to East–West polarizations centred around the uniqueness of the Holocaust. The connection between radical conservative politics and claims of criminalizing communism also impeded any consensus over prosecutions of communist crimes at both the national and European levels. In contrast, the transregional cooperation between Latin American and Western European lawyers and investigative judges was particularly important for enforcing universal jurisdiction as a principle of ICL. Nonetheless, this principle remains politically contentious, and its legitimacy continued to be contested by many legal scholars and politicians.

In both regions, legal interventions into ICL stemmed in fact from the reality of an international regime that left numerous gross human rights violations committed during the twentieth century without response—including crimes perpetrated on political grounds, policies of ethnic assimilation and racial discrimination and exploitation, or the widespread destruction of Indigenous groups in the name of Western economic modernization projects and 'civilizational emancipation'. From this point of view, critical interrogations of the politics of ICL-making and subsequent reformulations of this body of law are likely to emerge, more widely from the semi-peripheries and peripheries of the global system, and more specifically from subaltern groups that have been silenced in the international negotiation of ICL principles. This was the case with various CEE, Latin American, and Spanish legal actors who took a bold stand against the limits of the 1948 UN Genocide Convention, condemned the formalist interpretations of the principle of non-retroactivity, and criticized legal discourses that privileged the right of the accused to due process over a victim's rights to justice. Such approaches were built upon and further expanded previously formulated arguments that had (exceptionally) been endorsed in the jurisprudence since 1945, but which remained at the margins of the dominant doctrine and practice of international justice.

Rather than a harmful and pathological phenomenon, such ICL reinterpretations can be analysed as transformative visions that contribute to the gradual development of a more inclusive ICL. Looking back into the history of ICL jurisprudence since the Nuremberg trial, deviations from standard principles and norms have in fact been quite frequent. Both the Nuremberg and the Tokyo international tribunals relied in part on *ex-post facto* laws. So did many domestic trials organized after 1945 against Nazi officials and their collaborators in both Western and Eastern Europe. In the 1960s, statutory limitations were lifted across Europe for certain categories of international crimes to enable the prosecutions of Nazi crimes—a measure amounting to retroactivity if understood in the strictest sense. The convictions for crimes against humanity upheld by the Extraordinary Chambers in the Courts of Cambodia and endorsed by the UN can also be interpreted as retroactive, since they refer to gross human rights violations committed by the Khmer Rouge between 1975 and 1979, during a period when—according to many legal scholars—crimes against humanity perpetrated in times of peace were not recognized under customary law and were certainly not codified in Cambodian legislation. Further examples include the Eichmann trial—conducted based on an Israeli law adopted in 1950—or the proceedings of the International Crimes Tribunal of Bangladesh, established in 2010 to adjudicate crimes against humanity committed in 1971 during the Bangladesh liberation war.[2] Similarly, the category of political genocide was employed by the Ethiopian courts in 2007 in a trial against former communist leaders in power between 1977 and 1991. Although the convictions relied on the 1957 Ethiopian criminal code, which included political groups in the social categories protected against genocide, the trial was criticized by both certain judges and international legal experts for deviating from the UN definition of genocide.[3] In 2007, a German court in Düsseldorf ruled in a case concerning the Yugoslav war that genocide should be understood not only as the intent to destroy an ethnic group physically or biologically but also as the intent to extinguish the group in its social existence and self-perception as a group.[4]

These examples, together with those examined in this book, show that trials for gross human rights violations in post-dictatorial and post-conflict societies

[2] Nicholas N. Kittrie, 'A Post Mortem of the Eichmann Case: The Lessons for International Law', *Journal of Criminal Law and Criminology* 55, no. 1 (1964): pp. 16–28; Maruf Billah, 'Non-retroactivity in Prosecuting Crimes against Humanity and International Crimes Tribunal Bangladesh', *Journal of Politics and Law* 13, no. 3 (2020): pp. 180–195.

[3] Firew Kebede Tiba, 'The *Mengistu* Genocide Trial in Ethiopia', *Journal of International Criminal Justice* 5, no. 2 (2007): pp. 513–528.

[4] Fernández-Pacheco Estrada, 'Domestic Prosecution', pp. 449–450.

are often possible only if judges abandon strict legal formalism. Courts in such societies frequently reshape and vernacularize international norms and practices to fit local contexts and specific historical episodes. A cultural–historical approach to the application of ICL would thus be more lenient to institutional innovations and variations of norms and judicial practices. It would also acknowledge the limits of ICL, stemming from its origins within inherently political negotiations at specific moments in history; and it would properly explain the selective adaptations of ICL to local perceptions and understandings and the subsequent modification of rules, principles, and practices in light of domestic contexts.[5]

3. Actors, Legal Education, and Mnemonic Visions about Dictatorial Pasts

Another methodological point emphasized in this book is the importance of studying the legal actors who apply ICL, with their legal educations and theoretical perspectives on the law, as well as their historical understanding of the dictatorial regimes and the subsequent 'best' solutions for reckoning with their egregious crimes. The focus on actors—and their interactions with national and international institutional and opportunity structures—allows a greater appreciation of how and to what end norms are enacted and why conflicts over specific interpretations of the law coexist within national judiciaries. At the risk of overgeneralizing, I want to summarize a few trends that emerged from the case studies analysed in this book. Legal actors who opposed prosecutions have usually embraced legal positivism: they accepted criminal trials only if they were based on the written national law in force at the moment when the crimes were committed; they resisted the direct application of international law, disregarded rules of customary international law, and even refused to interpret the national legislation in connection to ICL and human rights treaties ratified by their countries. They also deferred any decision regarding legal transformations to the political authorities in power, believing that it was not in the purview of the judiciary to create law. This approach was supported by

[5] Randall Peerenboom, 'What Have We Learned about Law and Development? Describing, Predicting, and Assessing Legal Reforms in China', *Michigan Journal of International Law* 27, no. 3 (2006): pp. 823–871, at p. 867; Edda Kristjánsdóttir, André Nollkaemper, and Cedric Ryngaert, 'Concluding Observations', in *International Law in Domestic Courts: Rule of Law Reform in Post-Conflict States*, edited by Edda Kristjánsdóttir, André Nollkaemper, and Cedric Ryngaert (Cambridge: Intersentia, 2012): pp. 311–335, at p. 325.

international experts who considered that domestic judges should not engage in altering and changing international law, and should apply the law 'conscientiously and objectively', giving up their 'subjective preference' towards the historical episodes they address in their jurisprudence.[6]

Such an approach stemmed from a legal education dominant across CEE and Latin America that—until very recently—endorsed legal formalism, paid little attention to ICL and human rights law, defended a strict dualist approach to international law, and overlooked the evolution of customary international law. This legal education tended to have permeated further in countries that experienced longer periods of dictatorship, such as Paraguay, Brazil, and the socialist regimes of Eastern Europe. In such settings, judicial independence was restricted for longer, leading to extended periods wherein the law was used as an instrument of control rather than emancipation. Reforms of the judicial system were instigated only many years after the transition to democracy, leading to a more conformist attitude towards the national political body and its politics of dealing with the past.

While justified by their proponents in the name of the predictability and foreseeability of the law, such approaches also arose from the visions of the dictatorial past and the subsequent political transition ingrained in the legal actors in question. As shown in the case of Brazil, the reluctance to engage in the duty to prosecute was connected to the conviction held by the judges involved that the bilateral amnesty had been a key element of the peaceful transition to democracy. Consequently, they could not imagine its annulment, even if it did not comply with current ICL standards and the decision of the IACtHR. However, certain proponents of the bilateral amnesty endorsed the 'two demons' theory, which morally equated leftist political insurgency and military state repression and even justified past military violence in the name of fighting communism. In Bulgaria, judges actively circumvented any critical interrogation of the former regime: they operationalized and carefully selected ICL principles to justify the termination of criminal procedures and argued against any involvement of the courts in law-making and historical justice. During the 1990s and the first decade of the 2000s, Romanian military prosecutors adopted the same legal strategy towards communist crimes and validated an anti-impunity political narrative formulated by communist elites who continued to hold power after the end of the dictatorship. This is not to say that all these legal actors extolled former dictatorships. They did nevertheless avoid a critical engagement

[6] These approaches are largely accounted in Sharon Weill, *The Role of National Courts in Applying International Humanitarian Law* (Oxford: Oxford University Press, 2014).

with its history and legality and endorsed positivist legal criteria, historically protective of conservative interests.

In contrast, justice activists and judicial officials inclined to open prosecutions had visions of ICL that more closely aligned to natural law philosophy, inclusive positivism, and critical criminology. They also saw judicial activism as essential to correcting political arrangements that had closed down justice for dictatorial crimes. This attitude led them to a more solid inquiry into human rights law, ICL, legal doctrines, and judicial precedents that favoured prosecutions in other national and international settings. Some of these pro-accountability actors, particularly in Latin America and Spain, had also been part of transnational networks of judicial officials that had investigated transnational criminality, a dynamic that facilitated a broader understanding of ICL in a period when ICL education was underdeveloped in national curricula. Such a legal education was a crucial factor in shifting judicial imagination away from legal formalism and a narrow focus on domestic law and constituted an essential condition for the explosion of trials in the 2000s. The Romanian convictions of political crimes perpetrated in the 1950s were adjudicated by judicial officials belonging to a young generation of lawyers, trained in human rights law and European jurisprudence. They extensively used both the existing ECtHR case law that endorsed retrospective justice for gross human rights violations and interpretations of recent laws linked to the development of international customary law since 1945 to justify their own legal decisions. Similarly, the judges who unblocked prosecutions in Argentina had extensive training in ICL, IACtHR judgments, and jurisprudence concerning Nazi crimes. They also built upon previous investigations and trials held in Western Europe against Latin American military officials. They creatively combined national constitutional law and customary international law to annul the impunity laws that had governed Argentina from 1986 to 2001. In Brazil, the prosecutors and judges who opened criminal trials despite the persistence of the amnesty law also had training in ICL and human rights jurisprudence and were inclined to support principles of natural law philosophy developed by scholars such as Lon Fuller, Gustav Radbruch, and Robert Alexy.

However, these struggles over legal interpretation also encompassed political, ideological, and mnemonic issues. Using and adapting ICL was primarily an anti-impunity solution, but also a method for overcoming a perceived peripheralization of the history of military and communist repression in the memory politics of the global twentieth century. Across CEE, justice activism was informed by a quest to equate Nazi and communist crimes and overcome a Western historical narrative based on the uniqueness of the Holocaust. This mnemonic militantism accelerated after 2004, as Eastern European countries began to integrate into the structures of the European Union. In countries such as Bulgaria, Czechia, Romania, and Slovakia, it stemmed mainly from frustrations with incremental impunity both at home and at the European level. For the Baltic states, it was also a matter of condemning the double Nazi and Soviet occupation and counter-attacking the Russian Federation's revisionist mnemonic agenda regarding this historical episode. Drawing parallels between the Holocaust and the 'communist genocide' was however often accompanied by a downplaying of the role of CEE governments and segments of the civilian population in the extermination of European Jews during the Second World War. Moreover, condemning communist crimes often descended into attempts to delegitimize any leftist thinking and into radical conservative politics, characterized by Eurosceptic and nationalist discourses, Islamophobia, racism, and attacks against gender equality. Far from being embraced by all CEE justice activists and judicial officials involved in trials for communist crimes, these discourses produced political discomfort at both the national and European levels.

In contrast, the transnational mobilizations of Latin American activists contributed to the consolidation of a liberal vocabulary of human rights, based on the universal defence of civil and political rights and the duty to punish major international crimes based on universal jurisdiction. After the reopening of trials across the continent, leftist aspirations for social justice were included in the Madrid–Buenos Aires principles. This new doctrine of universal jurisdiction, which intended to reflect the voices of the semi-peripheries and subaltern groups such Indigenous populations and to include economic and environmental crimes, gained little momentum in a global context dominated by neoliberal policies. The Western-designed Princeton Principles, which focus only on the legitimacy of universal jurisdiction for the Nuremberg categories of crimes, remain the most quoted and resonant doctrine in the legal scholarship.

That being said, the use of the category of genocide in Argentina was not a necessary tactic to end impunity, since many courts had already convicted former military officials for crimes against humanity, but a political strategy employed by certain judges who believed that labelling the military repression as the 'crime of crimes' was more persuasive to the wider public in their attempts to foster solidarity with the victims and achieve a social consensus about the criminality of the former dictatorship. These judicial officials, together with victims' associations and various social scientists, also sought to assign the same position in international mnemopolitics to the Argentinian military repression as that already acquired by the Holocaust, the genocides in Yugoslavia and Rwanda, or the Armenian genocide. Such activism was problematic, since ICL was not adapted to render prosecutions of egregious crimes possible but to enforce a particular strand of political rhetoric. The criminal investigations opened in Argentina based on universal jurisdiction also mirrored how 'universality' was selectively used by right-wing lawyers to condemn Chinese crimes against the Falun Gong and the rise of the Kirchner administration's memory politics; and by left-wing lawyers to create transnational solidarities against crimes perpetrated under right-wing military dictatorships, such as Spain under Franco and Paraguay under Stroessner. In Guatemala, the incorporation of the destruction of Indigenous culture and social cohesion in the genocide charges against Ríos-Montt were interconnected with the will of certain judges and Mayan activists to emphasize the enduring racism and neocolonial oppression against Indigenous populations not only during the civil war, but throughout Guatemala's entire modern history.

Studying the legal actors who apply ICL, their legal educations, political inclinations, and visions of the past reveals that legal norms are the product of the specific historical and social experiences of those who create and implement them. Individual actors and the advocacy networks they create or integrate endorse or rise against existing political and legal structures, dominant ideas, and hegemonic historical and legal narratives. Despite the impartiality and universality to which some ICL practitioners aspire, the development of law (be it national or intranational) is always contingent on the subjective attitudes of legal actors towards the social world. Indeed, those working in CEE and Latin America did not conceive ICL as an objective, neutral body of jurisprudence, but sought—through the medium of ICL—to reinforce specific political positions and historical narratives, and, in some instances, to interrogate an international order that peripheralized the political violence that had unfolded in their home countries under dictatorship.

This epilogue thus calls for more ethnographic, sociological, and cultural research alongside the analysis of the jurisprudence in order to fully understand how judicial officials and justice activists employ and understand international law across the globe. As the CEE and Latin American cases reveal, although justice activists from both regions pursued the same goal—prosecuting egregious crimes—their political preferences were different and reflected different historical and ideological contexts. Such diversity can also be seen at the global level and within struggles to advance specific human rights and ICL regimes at national, regional, and international levels. Furthermore, a Bourdieusian approach to ICL making—similar to the studies of international commercial arbitration conducted by Yves Dezalay and Bryant Garth[7]—would complement and widen the scope of this book, by emphasizing how the emergence and reformulation of international norms are marked by 'turf battles' between competing networks and professionals as they endeavour to amend international regulations, while also trying to consolidate their professional positions and control over the financial and symbolic resources intrinsic to these regulatory processes. Such a methodological perspective would also highlight how ICL is shaped by a variety of social groups, driven by both principled advocacy and instrumentally motivated goals, who are often in competition with one another and thereby create a fragmented field of knowledge and practice. Finally, analysing the perceptions and deployment of ICL by subaltern groups, local communities, and grass-roots movement, alongside decolonial appraisals of this body of law, would contribute to a more inclusive and critical perspective on both the history of ICL and its limited applicability in the contemporary world. Ultimately, the final thoughts presented here are not simply a contemplation about how best to write an ever-more comprehensive history of the evolution of both current and future ICL jurisprudence for a select audience of insiders. It is also a call to take seriously the lived experiences of those who both write the law and live with its consequences, in order to better understand the coexistence of diverse visions of human rights, democracy, and economic systems across the world.

[7] Yves Dezalay and Bryant Garth, *Dealing in Virtue: International Commercial Arbitration and the Construction of a Transnational Legal Order* (Chicago: University of Chicago Press, 1996); see also Yves Dezalay and Bryant Garth, eds., *Lawyers and the Construction of Transnational Justice* (New York: Routledge, 2012).

List of Interviews

Argentina

Marienala Ahumada, Buenos Aires, 5 December 2014
Octavio Araoz de Lamadrid, online, 12 April 2022
León Carlos Arsalian, Buenos Aires, 27 November 2014
Julio Leonardo Bavio, Tucuman, 22 June 2016
Martin Bohmer, Buenos Aires, 18 December 2014
Adolfo Casabal Elia, Buenos Aires, 27 May 2022
Gabriel Cavallo, Buenos Aires, 4 December 2014 and 14 June 2016
Alejandro Cowes, online, 13 April 2022
Hernan Folgueiro, Buenos Aires, 6 July 2016
Pablo Llonto, Buenos Aires, 9 December 2014
Jaime Malamud-Goti, Buenos Aires, 14 November 2014
Luis Moreno Ocampo, Buenos Aires, 13 November 2014
Pablo Ouviña, Buenos Aires, 14 November 2014
Luz Palmas, Buenos Aires, 14 June 2016
Pablo Parenti, online, 14 February 2018
Tomas Quintana, online, 12 May 2022
Daniel Rafecas, Buenos Aires, 2 March 2015
Carlos Rico, Buenos Aires, 3 December 2014
Carlos Rozanski, La Plata, 16 June 2016
Leopoldo Schiffrin, La Plata, 1 July 2016
Carolina Varsky, Buenos Aires, 3 December 2014

Brazil

Silvio César Arouck Gemaque, online, 21 January 2022
Dimitri Dimoulis, online, 14 December 2021
Paulo Fontes, online, 14 December 2021
Marlon Weichert, online, 1 December 2021

Bulgaria

Metodi Borissov Andreev, Sofia, 10 March 2017
Daniela Dokovska, Sofia, 3 July 2014
Vasil Kadrinov, Sofia, 30 March 2017
Alexander Kashumov, Sofia, 18 March 2013
Ina Lulcheva, Sofia, 3 July 2014
Rumen Nenkov, Sofia, 30 June 2014
Blagovest Punev, Sofia, 1 July 2014
Atanas Slavov, Sofia, 2 July 2014 and 14 March 2017

Czechia

Neela Winkelmann-Heyrovská, online, 27 January 2022

Estonia

Illimar Lepik von Wirén, online, 2 March 2022

Germany

Ana Kaminski, Berlin, 11 March 2014
Hubertus Knabe, Berlin, 5 March 2014
Annelen Micus, Berlin, 25 April 2014
Christian Tomuschat, Berlin, 3 July 2019

Guatemala

Edwin Canil, Guatemala City, 21 August 2019
Esteban Cesar, Guatemala City, 14 August 2019
Aura Cumes, Guatemala City, 19 August 2019
Angel Valdez, Guatemala City, 21 August 2019

Lithuania

Egidijus Kūris, Strasbourg, France, 27 February 2019
Rimvydas Valentukevičius, Vilnius, 16 October 2018
Dainius Žalimas, Vilnius, 17 October 2018
Justinas Žilinskas, Vilnius, 17 October 2018
Anonymous, Vilnius, 16 October 2018

Paraguay

Martin Almada, Asunción, 31 January 2015
Rodolfo Manuel Aseretto, Asunción, 4 February 2015
Clemente Barrios Monges, Asunción, 20 July 2016
Santiago Bibolini, Asunción, 11 February 2015
Alfredo Boccia Paz, Asunción, 18 February 2015
Pelao Carvallo, Asunción, 7 February 2015
Arnaldo Fleitas Ortiz, Asunción, 18 February 2015
Rogelio Goiburú, Asunción, 21 July 2016
Lurdi Guibi, Asunción, 20 February 2015
Guillermina Karnikov, Asunción, 20 July 2016
Luis Lezcano Claude, Asunción, 18 July 2016
Aitor Martínez Jiménez, Asunción, 4 February 2015
Philippe Edeb Piragi, Asunción, 8 February 2015
Carlos Portillo, Asunción, 13 February 2015
Yudith Rolón, Asunción, 4 February 2015 and 18 July 2016
Delio Antonio Vera Navarro, Asunción, 17 February 2015

Romania

Cosmin Budeanca, Bucharest, 16 June 2018
Gheorghe Ciubotaru, Bucharest, 23 July 2014
Denisa Cristodor, Bucharest, 15 September 2014
Luciana Jinga, online, 8 February 2022
Marius Oprea, Bucharest, 1 March 2008
Mihai Popov, Bucharest, 22 February 2007
Antonie Popescu, Bucharest, 16 September 2015
Oana Soare, Bucharest, 12 June 2014

Adriana Stamatescu, Bucharest, 8 April 2013
Valerian Stan, email correspondence, 27 August 2007
Dan Voinea, Bucharest, 18 June 2014

Slovenia

Jernej Letnar Černič, online, 3 February 2022

Spain

Dolores Delgado, Madrid, 18 November 2015
José Ricardo de Prada, Madrid, 20 November 2015
Baltasar Garzón, Madrid, 18 November 2015
Joaquín Giménez García, Madrid, 28 May 2016
Manuel Ollé Sésé, Madrid, 19 November 2015
Ana Messuti, online, 28 April 2022
Luciano Varela, Madrid, 28 May 2016
Manuel Vergara, Madrid, 17 November 2015

List of Archives Consulted

Archives Juicios de Lesa Humanidad (Argentina, online)
Archives of La Dirección General de Verdad, Justicia y Reparación (Director General for Truth, Justice and Reparation, Paraguay)
Archives of the Argentinian Parliament
Archives of the Bulgarian Constitutional Court (ABCC)
Archives of the Bulgarian Supreme Court of Justice (ABSCJ)
Archives of the Equipo Nizkor (online)
Archives of the Hannah Arendt Center Sofia (AHACS)
Archives of the Institute for the Investigation of Communist Crimes in Romania
Archives of the Romanian Parliament
Archives of the Romanian Supreme Court of Justice
Archives of the Bucharest Appellate Military Court

Bibliography

Abente Brun, Diego. 'Estatalidad y calidad de la democracia en Paraguay', *América Latina Hoy* 60 (2012): pp. 43–66.

Abrão, Paulo and Marcelo D. Torelly. 'Resistance to Change. Brazil's Persistent Amnesty and Its Alternatives for Truth and Justice', in *Amnesty in the Age of Human Rights Accountability: Comparative and International Perspectives*, edited by Francesca Lessa and Leigh Payne (Cambridge: Cambridge University Press, 2012): pp. 152–181.

Acuña, Carlos H. and Catalina Smulovitz. 'Guarding the Guardians in Argentina: Some Lessons about the Risks and Benefits of Empowering the Courts', in *Transitional Justice and the Rule of Law in New Democracies*, edited by James McAdams (Notre Dame: University of Notre Dame Press, 1997): pp. 93–122.

Albon, Mary. '"Justice in Times of Transition": Report of the Project's Inaugural Meeting', in *Transitional Justice: How Emerging Democracies Reckon with Former Regimes*, edited by Neil J. Kritz (Washington, DC: U.S. Institute of Peace Press, 1995): pp. 42–54.

Alexy, Robert. 'A Defence of Radbruch's Formula', in *Recrafting the Rule of Law: The Limits of Legal Order*, edited by David Dyzenhaus (Oxford: Hart, 1999): pp. 15–39.

Alfonso, Cesar. 'Paraguay', in *Jurisprudencia latinoamericana sobre derecho penal internacional: Con un informe adicional sobre la jurisprudencia italiana*, edited by Kai Ambos, Ezequil Malarino, and Gisela Elsner (Montevideo: Konrad Adenauer Stiftung, 2008): pp. 261–270.

Alvarez, Alejandro E., Eduardo A. Bertoni, and Mihuel Boo. 'Droit Argentin', in *Juridictions Nationales et Crimes Internationaux*, edited by Antonio Cassese and Mireille Delmas-Marty (Paris: Presses Universitaires de France, 2002): pp. 299–331.

Ambos, Kai. 'The Crime of Genocide and the Principle of Legality under Article 7 of the European Court of Human Rights', *Human Rights Law Review* 17 (2017): pp. 175–186.

Ambos, Kai and Ezequiel Malarino, eds., *Persecución penal nacional de crímenes internacionales en América Latina y España* (Montevideo: Konrad Adenauer Stiftung, 2003).

Ambos, Kai, Cesar Alfonso, and Roberto Ubeda. 'Paraguay', in *Encyclopaedia of Transitional Justice*, edited by Lavinia Stan and Nadya Nedelsky (Cambridge: Cambridge University Press, 2013): pp. 364–370.

Anayiotos, Daphne. 'The Cultural Genocide Debate: Should the UN Genocide Convention Include a Provision on Cultural Genocide, or Should the Phenomenon Be Encompassed in a Separate International Treaty?', *New York International Law Review* 99, no. 2 (2009): pp. 99–129.

Ankumah, Evelyn A. 'The Cairo-Arusha Principles on Universal Jurisdiction in Respect of Gross Human Rights Offenses: An African Perspective', *Proceedings of the ASIL (American Society of International Law) Annual Meeting*, 98 (2004): pp. 238–240.

Arias, Arturo. 'The Maya Movement, Postcolonialism and Cultural Agency', *Journal of Latin American Cultural Studies* 15, no. 2 (2006): pp. 251–262.

Armenian, Andre Vartan. 'Selectivity in International Criminal Law: An Assessment of the "Progress Narrative"', *International Criminal Law Review* 16, no. 4 (2016): pp. 642–672.

Arthur, Paige. 'How "Transitions" Reshaped Human Rights: A Conceptual History of Transitional Justice', *Human Rights Quarterly* 31, no. 2 (2009): pp. 321–367.

Aseretto, Rodolfo Manuel, ed., *Compañero Julián Cubas* (Asunción: CIPAE, 2003).

Aseretto, Rodolfo Manuel, ed., *Fallos judiciales sobre casos de violaciones a los DD.HH* (Asunción: CIPAE, 2011).

Aveces, William J. *The Anatomy of Torture: A Documentary History of Filártiga v. Peña-Irala* (Leiden: Martinus Nijhoff, 2007).

Balaban, Oded and Amos Megged, eds., *Impunidad y Derechos Humanos en America Latina: Perspectivas Teóricas* (La Plata: Ediciones al Margen, 2003).

Baniker, Onur. 'Between Politics and History: The Baltic Truth Commissions in Global Perspective', in *Transitional Justice and the Former Soviet Union: Reviewing the Past, Looking toward the Future*, edited by Lavinia Stan and Nadya Nedelsky (Cambridge: Cambridge University Press, 2018): pp. 155–176.

Barkan, Elazar. 'Genocide of Indigenous People', in *The Spectre of Genocide: Mass Murder in Historical Perspective*, edited by Robert Gellately and Ben Kiernan (Cambridge: Cambridge University Press, 2003): pp. 117–140.

Basch, Fernando Felipe. 'The Doctrine of the Inter-American Court of Human Rights Regarding States' Duty to Punish Human Rights Violations and Its Dangers', *American University International Law Review* 23, no. 1 (2007): pp. 195–229.

Bass, Gary J. 'The Adolf Eichmann Case: Universal and National Jurisdiction', in *Universal Jurisdiction: National Courts and the Prosecution of Serious Crimes under International Law*, edited by Stephen Macedo (Philadelphia: Pennsylvania University Press, 2004): pp. 75–90.

Bassiouni, M. Cherif. *Crimes against Humanity: Historical Evolution and Contemporary Application* (New York: Cambridge University Press, 2011).

Bassiouni, M. Cherif. 'The History of Universal Jurisdiction and Its Place in International Law', in *Universal Jurisdiction: National Courts and the Prosecution of Serious Crimes under International Law*, edited by Stephen Macedo (Philadelphia: Pennsylvania University Press, 2004): pp. 39–63.

Bassiouni, M. Cherif. 'Chronology of Efforts to Establish an International Criminal Court', *Revue Internationale de Droit Penal* 86, nos. 3–4 (2015): pp. 1163–1194.

Becker Lorca, Arnulf. 'International Law in Latin America or Latin American International Law? Rise, Fall, and Retrieval of a Tradition of Legal Thinking and Political Imagination', *Harvard International Law Journal* 47, no. 1 (2006): pp. 283–305.

Behr, Valentin Muriel Blaive, Anenoma Constantin, Laure Neumayer, and Máté Zombory. 'An Anti-Communist Consensus: The Black Book of Communism in Pan-European Perspective', *Revue d'Études Comparative Est-Ouest*, nos. 2–3 (2020): pp. 55–88.

Belavusau, Uladzislau and Anna Wójcik. 'La criminalisation de l'expression historique en Pologne: la loi mémorielle de 2018', *Archives de Politique Criminelle* 40 (2018): pp. 175–188.

Billah, Maruf. 'Non-retroactivity in Prosecuting Crimes against Humanity and International Crimes Tribunal Bangladesh', *Journal of Politics and Law* 13, no. 3 (2020): pp. 180–195.

Bilsky, Leora. 'The Eichmann Trial and the Legacy of Jurisdiction', in *Politics in Dark Times: Encounters with Hannah Arendt*, edited by Seyla Benhabib (Cambridge: Cambridge University Press, 2010): pp. 198–218.

Bilsky, Leora and Rachel Klagsbrun. 'The Return of Cultural Genocide?', *European Journal of International Law* 29, no. 2 (2018): pp. 373–396.

Binder, Christina. 'The Prohibition of Amnesties by the Inter-American Court of Human Rights', *German Law Journal* 12, no. 5 (2011): pp. 1203–1230.

Bobek, Michal. 'The Fortress of Judicial Independence and the Mental Transitions of the Central European Judiciaries', *European Public Law* 14, no. 1 (2008): pp. 1–20.

Boot, Machteld. *Genocide, Crimes against Humanity and War Crimes: Nullum Crimen Sine Lege and the Subject Matter Jurisdiction of the International Criminal Court* (Cambridge: Intersentia, 2002).

Bosdriesz, Hanna and Sander Wirken. 'An Imperfect Success: The Guatemalan Genocide Trial and the Struggle against Impunity for International Crimes', *International Criminal Law Review* 14, no. 6 (2014): pp. 1067–1094.

Bourdieu, Pierre. 'Le force du droit: Eléments pour une sociologie du champs juridique', *Actes de la recherche en sciences sociales* 64 (1986): pp. 3–19.

Brasil Silva and Anderson Luiz. 'ADPF 153, Direito penal e justiça transicional a luz dos princípios de Chicago', in *Justiça de Transição no Brasil*, edited by Eneá de Stutz e Almeida (Brasil: Editora CRV, 2017): pp. 51–68.

Brems, Eve. 'Transitional Justice in the Case Law of the European Court of Human Rights', *The International Journal of Transitional Justice* 5, no. 2 (2011): pp. 282–303.

Brysk, Alison. *The Politics of Human Rights in Argentina: Protest*, Change and Democratization (Stanford: Stanford University Press, 1994).

Budytre, Dovile. *Taming Nationalism? Political Community Building in the Post-Soviet* Baltic States (Aldershot: Ashgate, 2013).

Budrytė, Dovilė. 'We Call It Genocide: Soviet Deportations in the Memory of the Lithuanians', in *The Genocidal Temptation. Auschwitz, Hiroshima, Rwanda, and Beyond*, edited by Robert S. Frey (Lanham, MD: University Press of America, 2004): pp. 79–95.

Bultz, Ariel. 'Redefining Apartheid in International Criminal Law', *Criminal Law Forum* 24 (2013): pp. 205–233.

Burauskaite, Birutė, ed., *Genocide of Lithuanian People*, Volume II (1944–1947) (Vilnius: Institute of Philosophy, Sociology and Law, Research Center of Repressions in Lithuania, 1998).

Burt, Jo-Marie. 'From Heaven to Hell in Ten Days: The Genocide Trial in Guatemala', *Journal of Genocide Research* 18, nos. 2–3 (2016): pp. 143–169.

Capdepón, Ulrike. 'The Selectivity of Universal Jurisdiction: The History of Transnational Human Rights Prosecutions in Latin America and Spain', in *The Routledge History of Human Rights*, edited by Jean H. Quataert and Lora Wildenthal (London: Routledge, 2019): pp. 507–522.

Carcano, Andrea. 'Of Fragmentation and Precedents in International Criminal Law: Possible Lessons from Recent Jurisprudence on Aiding and Abetting Liability', *Journal of International Criminal Justice* 14, no. 4 (2016): pp. 771–792.

Cassese, Antonio. 'Balancing the Prosecution of Crimes against Humanity and Non-Retroactivity of Criminal Law. The *Kolk and Kislyiy v. Estonia Case* before the ECHR', *Journal of International Criminal Justice* 4, no. 2 (2006): pp. 410–418.

Cassese, Antonio and Mireille Delmas-Marty. *Juridictions Nationales et Crimes Internationaux* (Paris: PUF, 2002).

Cassese, Antonio and Paula Gaeta. *Cassese's International Criminal Law*, third edition (Oxford: Oxford University Press, 2013).

CEH, *Guatemala: Memoria del Silencio*, vol. 1 (Guatemala: UNOPS, 1999).

Centeno Martin, Héctor. 'Comisión del Esclarecimiento Histórico: Guatemala, entre la memoria del silencio y el silencio de la memoria', *Informe de CMI* 13 (2018): pp. 1–74.

Chalk, Frank and Kurt Jonassohn. 'The Conceptual Framework', in *The History and Sociology of Genocide*, edited by Frank Chalk and Kurt Jonassohn (New Haven: Yale University Press, 1991): pp. 17–26.

Charney, Israel W. 'Toward a Generic Definition of Genocide', in *Genocide, Conceptual and Historical Dimensions*, edited by George J. Andreopoulos (Philadelphia: University of Pennsylvania Press, 1994): pp. 64–94.

Choukr, Fauzi Hassan. 'Droit Brasilien', in *Juridictions Nationales et Crimes Internationaux*, edited by Antonio Cassese and Mireille Delmas-Marty (Paris: PUF, 2002): pp. 333–344.

Clark, Anne Marie. *Diplomacy of Conscience: Amnesty International and Changing Human Rights Norms* (Princeton: Princeton University Press, 2011).

Collins, Cath. 'Paraguay. Accountability in the Shadow of Stroessner', in *Transitional Justice in Latin America: The Uneven Road from Impunity towards Accountability*, edited by Elin Skaar, Jemima Garcia-Godos, and Cath Collins (London: Routledge, 2016): pp. 151–177.

Constantin, Anemona. 'L'enseignement de l'histoire du communisme à l'Est: Bulgarie, Roumanie, République de Moldavie', *Passés Futurs* 9 (2021).

Crenzel, Emilio. 'The Crimes of the Last Dictatorship in Argentina and Its Qualification as Genocide: A Historicization', *Global Society* 33, no. 3 (2019): pp. 365–381.

Crutchley, Julie. 'How Can a Decolonial Critique Rearticulate Concepts of Peace and Victims in International Criminal Law?' Research Paper No. 2017/05 (London, UK: The City Law School, 2017).

Cryer, Robert. *Prosecuting International Crimes: Selectivity and the International Criminal Law Regime* (New York: Cambridge University Press, 2005).

Currie, Robert J. and Hugh M. Kindred. 'Flux and Fragmentation in International Law of State Jurisdiction: The Synecdochal Example of Canada's Domestic Court Conflicts over Accountability for International Human Rights Violations', in *The Practice of International and National Courts and the (De-)Fragmentation of International Law*, edited by Ole Kristian Fauchald and André Nollkaemper (London: Hart Publishing, 2012): pp. 217–243.

Davis, Madeleine. *The Pinochet Case: Origins, Progress, and Implications* (London: ILAS, University of London, 2003).

Day, Tom Gerald. 'Brazilian 'Supremocracy' and the Inter-American Court of Human Rights: Unpicking an Unclear Relationship', in *Law and Policy in Latin America: Transforming Courts, Institutions and Rights*, edited by Pedro Fortes, Larissa Boratti, Andrés Palacios Lleras, and Tom Gerald Daly (London: Palgrave Macmillan, 2017): pp. 3–20.

Deak, Istvan, Jan T. Gross, and Tony Judt, eds., *The Politics of Retribution in Europe* (Princeton: Princeton University Press, 2000).

De la Rasilla del Moral, Ignacio. 'The Swan Song of Universal Jurisdiction in Spain', *International Criminal Law Review* 9 (2009): pp. 777–808.

de la Rasilla del Moral, Ignacio. *International Law and History:* Modern Interfaces (Cambridge: Cambridge University Press, 2021).

De Nike, Howard J., John Quigley, and Kenneth J. Robinson. *Genocide in Cambodia: Documents of the Trial of Pol Pot and Ieng Sary* (Pennsylvania, PA: University of Pennsylvania Press, 2000).

del Valle Escalante, Emilio. *Maya Nationalisms and Postcolonial Challenges in Guatemala: Coloniality, Modernity, and Identity Politics* (Santa Fe, NM: School for Advanced Research, 2009).

Dezalay, Yves and Bryant Garth. *Dealing in Virtue: International Commercial Arbitration and the Construction of a Transnational Legal Order* (Chicago: University of Chicago Press, 1996).

Dezalay, Yves and Bryant Garth, eds., *Lawyers and the Construction of Transnational Justice* (New York: Routledge, 2012).

Dimitrova, Ina. 'How We Raised a Monster: Constructing the Image of Socialism during the Post-Socialist Period in Bulgaria', *History of Communism in Europe* 1 (2010): pp. 153–165.

Dimoulis, Dimitri. 'Justiça de transição e função anistiante no Brasil: Hipostasiações indevidas e caminhos de responsabilização', in *Justiça de transição no Brasil. Direito, responsabilização e verdade*, edited by Dimitri Dimoulis, Antonio Martins, and Lauro Joppert Swensson Junior (São Paulo: Saraiva, 2010): pp. 91–127.

Druliolle, Vincent. 'The Struggle for Recognition of the Stolen Children and the Politics of Victimhood in Spain', in *The Politics of Victimhood in Post-conflict Societies*, edited by Vincent Druliolle and Roddy Brett (Cham: Springer International, 2018): pp. 77–99.

Dugard, John. 'Dealing with Crimes of the Past. Is Amnesty Still an Option?', *Leiden Journal of International Law* 12, no. 4 (1999): pp. 1001–1015.

Dujisin, Zoltan. 'A History of Post-communist Remembrance: From Memory Politics to the Emergence of a Field of Anticommunism', *Theory and Society* 50, no. 1 (2021): pp. 65–96.

Eckel, Jan. *The Ambivalence of Good: Human Rights in International Politics since the 1940s* (Oxford: Oxford University Press, 2019).

Eckel, Jan and Samuel Moyn, eds., *The Breakthrough: Human Rights in the 1970s* (Philadelphia: University of Pennsylvania Press, 2014).

Esteve Moltó, José Elías. 'Requiem for Universal Jurisdiction in Spain', *Quebec Journal of International Law* 33, no. 1 (2020): pp. 55–84.

Fauchald, Ole Kristian and André Nollkaemper, eds., *The Practice of International and National Courts and the (De-)Fragmentation of International Law* (London: Hart, 2012).

Feierstein, Daniel. *Cinco Estudios Sobre Genocidio* (Buenos Aires: Acervo Cultural, 1997).

Feierstein, Daniel. *El genocidio como **práctica social**. Entre el nazismo y la experiencia argentina* (*Buenos Aires*: Fondo de Cultura, 2007).

Feierstein, Liliana. '"A Quilt of Memory": The Shoah as a Prism in the Testimonies of Survivors of the Dictatorship in Argentina', *European Review* 22 (2014): pp. 585–593.

Fein, Helen. 'Scenarios of Genocide: Models of Genocide and Critical Responses', in *Towards the Understanding and Prevention of Genocide*, edited by Israel W. Charny (Boulder, CO: Westview Press, 1984): pp. 3–31.

Ferdinandusse, N. Ward. *Direct Application of International Criminal Law in National Courts* (Hague: T.M.C. Asser, 2006).

Fernández-Pacheco Estrada, Cristina. 'Domestic Prosecution of Genocide: Fragmentation or Natural Diversity?' in *The Diversification and Fragmentation of International Criminal Law*, edited by Larissa van den Herik and Carsten Stahn (Leiden: Martinus Nijhoff, 2012): pp. 429–459.

Fijalkowski, Agata. 'Historical Politics and Court Redress in the Baltic States', in *Transitional Justice and the Former Soviet Union: Reviewing the Past, Looking toward the Future*, edited by Lavinia Stan and Nadya Nedelsky (Cambridge: Cambridge University Press, 2018): pp. 216–240.

Fournier, Dominique and Sean W. Burges. 'Form before Function: Democratization in Paraguay', *Canadian Journal of Latin American and Caribbean Studies* 25, no. 49 (2000): pp. 5–32.

Friedman, Lawrence. 'Some Thoughts on Comparative Legal Culture', in *Comparative and Private International Law: Essays in Honor of John Henry Merryman on His Seventieth Birthday*, edited by David S. Clark (Berlin: Duncker and Humblot, 1990): pp. 49–57.

Fuller, Lon L. 'Positivism and Fidelity to Law: A Reply to Professor Hart', *Harvard Law Review* 71, no. 4 (1958): pp. 630–672.

Gallant, Kenneth S. *The Principle of Legality in International and Comparative Law* (Cambridge: Cambridge University Press, 2008).

Gallo, Carlos Artur. *Um Acerto de Contas com o Passado: Crimines da ditadura, "Leis de Impunidade" e decisões das Supremas Cortes no Brasil e na Argentina* (Brazil: Appris Editora, 2018).

Ganev, Venelin. *Preying on the State: The Transformation of Bulgaria after 1989* (Ithaca, NY: Cornell University Press, 2013).

Garcia, Nicolás and Máximo Sozzo. 'For a "Marginal Criminological Realism": Zaffaroni and the Birth of a Critical Perspective on the Criminal Question from the Global South', *Justice, Power and Resistance* XX, no. XX (2023): pp. 1–19.

Garzón, Baltasar. 'Justicia de Otro Lado del Charco: Los 10 Años de la Querella Argentina contra el Franquismo', *La Jurisdicción Universal en el Juicio al Franquismo: La Querella Argentina contra el Genocidio en España*, edited by Eugenio Raul Zaffaroni (Buenos Aires: Ediciones Olejnik, 2021): pp. 35–36.

Gatti, Gabriel. '"Lo nuestro, como en Argentina": Humanitarian Reason and the Latin Americanization of Victimhood in Spain', *Journal of Latin American Cultural Studies* 25, no. 1 (2022): pp. 147–165.

Ghodsee, Kristen. 'Tale of "Two Totalitarianisms": The Crisis of Capitalism and the Historical Memory of Communism', *History of the Present* 4, no. 2 (2014): pp. 115–142.

Gil Gil, Alicia. 'La sentencia de la Audiencia Nacional en el caso Scilingo', *Revista Electrónica de Ciencia Penal y Criminología* 7 (2005): pp. 1–18.

Gil Gil, Alicia. 'The Flows of the Scilingo Judgement', *Journal of International Criminal Justice* 3, no. 5 (2005): pp. 1082–1091.

Gil Lavedra, Ricardo. 'The Possibility of Criminal Justice: The Argentinean Experience', *The Role of Courts in Transitional Justice: Voices from Latin America and Spain*, edited by Jessica Almqvist and Carlos Espósito (New York: Routledge, 2012): pp. 56–80.

Glaser, Stefan. *Droit International Pénal Conventionnel* (Brussels: Bruylant, 1970).

González-Ocantos, Ezequiel A. *Shifting Legal Visions: Judicial Change and Human Rights Trials in Latin America* (Cambridge: Cambridge University Press, 2016).

Grandin, Greg. 'The Instruction of Great Catastrophe: Truth Commissions, National History, and State Formation in Argentina, Chile, and Guatemala', *The American Historical Review* 110, no. 1 (2005): pp. 46–67.

Graven, Jean. 'Projet de convention sur les crimes de guerre, les crimes contre la paix et les crimes contre l'humanité Introduction et Questionnaire', *Revue Internationale de Droit Pénal* 3–4 (1966): pp. 393–449.

Grosescu, Raluca. 'Criminal Justice and Master Historical Narratives in post-1989 Bulgaria and Germany', *European Politics and Society* 18, no. 1 (2017): pp. 66–80.

Grosescu, Raluca. 'Judging Communist Crimes in Romania: Transnational and Global Influences', *International Journal of Transitional Justice* 11, no. 3 (2017): pp. 505–524.

Grosescu, Raluca. 'State Socialist Endeavours for the Non-Applicability to Statutory Limitations to International Crimes: Historical Roots and Present Implications', *Journal of the History of International Law* 21, no. 2 (2019): pp. 239–269.

Grosescu, Raluca and Agata Fijalkowski. 'Retrospective Justice and Legal Culture', in *Justice, Memory and Redress in Romania: New Insights*, edited by Lavinia Stan and Lucian Turcescu (Cambridge: Cambridge Scholars, 2017): pp. 100–123.

Grosescu, Raluca and Raluca Ursachi. *Justiţia penală de tranziţie de la Nürnberg la postcomunismul românesc* (Iaşi: Polirom, 2009).

Grover, Sonja. *The European Court of Human Rights as a Pathway to Impunity for International Crimes* (Berlin: Springer, 2010).

Gutman, Tara H. 'Cambodia, 1979: Trying Khmer Rouge Leaders for Genocide', in *Trials for International Crimes in Asia*, edited by Kirsten Sellars (Cambridge: Cambridge University Press, 2016): pp. 167–190.

Hart, Herbert L.A. 'Positivism and the Separation of Law and Morals', *Harvard Law Review* 71, no. 4 (1958): pp. 593–629.

Haldemann, Frank. 'Gustav Radbruch v. Hans Kelsen: A Debate on Nazi Evil', *Ratio Juris* 18, no. 2 (2005): pp. 162–178.

Hannum, Hurst. 'International Law and Cambodian Genocide: The Sounds of Silence', *Human Rights Quarterly* 11, no. 1 (1989): pp. 82–138.

Herzog, Jacques-Bernard. 'Étude des lois concernant la prescription des crimes contre l'humanité', *Revue de Science criminelle et de Droit pénal comparé* 1 (1965): pp. 337–371.

Hevey, Kirstyn. 'Estonian Transitional Justice: Predicated on a Collective Memory', PhD Dissertation (Budapest: Central European University, 2014).

Hoffmann, Tamás. 'Trying Communism through International Criminal Law?: The Experiences of the Hungarian Historical Justice Trials', in *Hidden Histories of War Crimes Trials*, edited by Kevin Jon Heller and Gerry Simpson (Oxford: Oxford University Press, 2013): pp. 229–247.

Hon, Kristina. 'Bringing Cultural Genocide in by the Backdoor: Victim Participation at the ICC', *Seton Hall Law Review* 43, no. 1 (2013): pp. 359–407.

Horne, Cynthia M. '"Silent Lustration" Public Disclosures as Informal Lustration Mechanisms in Bulgaria and Romania: Evaluating Measures and Their Outcome', *Problems of Post-Communism* 62, no. 3 (2015): pp. 131–144.

Hristov, Hristo and Alexander Kashumov. 'Justice and Accountability Mechanisms in Bulgaria in the Transition Period (1989–2008)', in *After Oppression: Transitional Justice in Latin America and Eastern Europe*, edited by Vesselin Popovski and Monica Serrano (New York: United Nations University Press, 2012): pp. 273–297.

Hudson, Andrew and Alexandra W. Taylor. 'The International Commission against Impunity in Guatemala: A New Model for International Criminal Justice Mechanisms', *Journal of International Criminal Justice* 8, no. 1 (2010): pp. 53–74.

Huneeus, Alexandra. 'International Criminal Law by Other Means: The Quasi-Criminal Jurisdiction of Human Rights Courts', *American Journal of International Law* 107, no. 1 (2013): pp. 1–44.

Iňigo, María. 'Conversation with Aura Cumes on Maya Epistemology, Postcolonial Theory and the Struggle for Identity', *Re-visiones* 7 (2017).

Jaulin, Robert. *La Paix Blanche : Introduction à l'Éthnocide* (Paris: Seuil, 1970).

Jones, Harry W. 'The Rule of Law and the Welfare State', *Columbia Law Review* 58, no. 2 (1958): pp. 143–156.

Kahan, Emmanuel and Daniel Lvovich. 'Los usos del Holocausto en Argentina: Apuntes sobre las apropiaciones y resignificaciones de la memoria del genocidio nazi', *Revista Mexicana de Ciencias Políticas y Sociales* LXI, no. 228 (2016): pp. 1–26.

Kalfayan, Philippe. *La France et l'imprescriptibilité des crimes internationaux* (Paris: Éditions Pedone, 2015).

Karstedt, Susanne, ed., *Legal Institutions and Collective Memory* (Oxford: Hart, 2009).

Kattago, Siobhan. 'Agreeing to Disagree on the Legacies of Recent History: Memory, Pluralism and Europe after 1989', *European Journal of Social Theory* 12, no. 3 (2009): pp. 1–21.

Keck, Margaret E. and Kathryn Sikkink. *Activist beyond Borders:* Advocacy Networks in International Politics (Ithaca: Cornell University Press, 2014).

Kemp, Susan. 'Guatemala Prosecutes Former President Rios Montt', *Journal of International Criminal Justice* 12 (2014): pp. 133–156.

Keys, Barbara. 'Anti-Torture Politics: Amnesty International, the Greek Junta, and the Origins of the Human Rights "Boom" in the United States', in *The Human Rights Revolution: An International History*, edited by Akira Iriye, Petra Goedde, and William I. Hitchcock (New York: Oxford University Press, 2012): pp. 201–222.

Kingston, Lindsey. 'The Destruction of Identity: Cultural Genocide and Indigenous People', *Journal of Human Rights* 14 (2015): pp. 63–83.

Kittichaisaree, Kriangsak. *The Rohingya, Justice and International Law* (New York: Routledge, 2022).

Kittrie, Nicholas N. 'A Post Mortem of the Eichmann Case: The Lessons for International Law', *Journal of Criminal Law and Criminology* 55, no. 1 (1964): pp. 16–28.

Koskiennemi, Martti and Päivi Leino. 'Hague International Tribunals : Fragmentation of International Law? Postmodern Anxieties', *Leiden Journal of International Law* 15, no. 3 (2002): pp. 553–579.

Kressel, Daniel Gunnar. '"Getting of the Tiger": The Spanish Transitional Model and Its Influence on the Democratic Transitions in Argentina and Chile 1977–1990', *Global Society* 33, no. 3 (2019): pp. 316–331.

Kristjánsdóttir, Edda, André Nollkaemper, and Cedric Ryngaert, eds., *International Law in Domestic Courts: Rule of Law Reform in Post-Conflict States* (Cambridge: Intersentia, 2012).

Kritz, Neil, ed., *Transitional Justice: How Emerging Democracies Reckon with Former Regimes* (Washington, DC: United States Institute of Peace Press, 1995).

Lamb, Susan. 'Nullum Crimen, Nulla Poena Sine Lege in International Criminal Law', in *The Rome Statute of the International Criminal Court: A Commentary*, vol. 1, edited by Antonio Cassese, Paola Gaeta, and John R.W.D. Jones (Oxford: Oxford University Press, 2002): pp. 735–742.

Lambert, Peter and Andrew Nickson, eds., *The Transition to Democracy in Paraguay* (London: MacMillan, 1997).

Langer, Máximo. 'Universal Jurisdiction Is Not Disappearing: The Shift from 'Global Enforcer' to 'No Safe Haven' Universal Jurisdiction', *Journal of International Criminal Justice* 13 (2015): pp. 245–256.

Langer, Máximo and Mackenzie Eason. 'The Quiet Expansion of Universal Jurisdiction', *The European Journal of International Law* 30, no. 3 (2019): pp. 779–817.

Lattanzi, Flavia. 'Introduction', in *The Diversification and Fragmentation of International Criminal Law*, edited by Larissa van den Herik and Carsten Stahn (Leiden: Martinus Nijhoff, 2012): pp. 1–20.

Lessa, Francesca. *Memory and Transitional Justice in Argentina and Uruguay: Against Impunity* (New York: Palgrave Macmillan, 2013).

Lessa, Francesca. 'Operation Condor on Trial: Justice for Transnational Human Rights Crimes in South America', *Journal of Latin American Studies* 51 (2019): pp. 409–439.

Lessa, Francesca. *The Condor Trials: Transnational Repression and Human Rights in the South America* (Yale: Yale University Press, 2022).

Lessa, Francesca and Leigh Payne, eds., *Amnesty in the Age of Human Rights Accountability: Comparative and International Perspectives* (Cambridge: Cambridge University Press, 2012).

Levy, Daniel and Natan Sznaider. *Human Rights and Memory* (University Park, PA: Pennsylvania State University Press, 2010).

Lippman, Matthew. 'The Drafting of the 1948 Convention on the Prevention and Punishment of the Crime of Genocide', *Boston University International Law Journal* 3 (1985): pp. 1–65.

Lippman, Matthew. 'The Trial of Adolf Eichmann and the Protection of Universal Human Rights under International Law', *Huston Journal of International Law* 5 no. 1 (1982): pp. 1–34.

Lippman, Matthew. 'The 1948 UN Convention on the Prevention and Punishment of the Crime of Genocide: Forty Years Later', *Temple International & Comparative Law Journal* 8, no. 1 (1994): pp. 1–84.

Łoś, Maria. *Communist Ideology, Law and Crime: A Comparative View of the USSR and Poland* (New York: St. Martin's Press, 1988).

Łoś, Maria and Andrzej Zybertowicz. *Privatizing the Police-State: The Case of Poland* (New York: St. Martin's Press, 2000).

Lyman Bruun, Lory. 'Beyond the 1948 Convention: Emerging Principles of Genocide in Customary International Law', *Maryland Journal of International Law and Trade* 17, no. 2 (1993): pp. 193–226.

Malarino, Ezequil. 'Argentina', in *Persecución penal nacional de crímenes internacionales en América Latina y España*, edited by Kai Ambos and Ezequil Malarino (Montevideo: Konrad Adenauer Stiftung, 2003): pp. 35–81.

Mälksoo, Lauri. 'Soviet Genocide? Communist Mass Deportations in the Baltic States and International Law', *Leiden Journal of International Law* 14 (2001): pp. 757–787.

Mälksoo, Maria. 'A Baltic Struggle for a "European Memory": The Militant Mnemopolitics of *The Soviet Story*', *Journal of Genocide Research* 20, no. 8 (2018): pp. 530–544.

Mälksoo, Maria. 'The Memory Politics of Becoming European: The East European Subalterns and the Collective Memory of Europe', *European Journal of International Relations* 15, no. 4 (2009): pp. 653–680.

Mälksoo, Maria. *The Politics of Becoming European: A Study of Polish and Baltic Post-Cold War Security Imaginaries* (London: Routledge, 2010).

Manili, Pablo Luis. 'Sobre la Constitucionalidad de la ley 25779, Nos guste o no nos guste', *Antecedentes Parlamentarios* 1 (2003): pp. 1749–1752.

Mark, James. *The Unfinished Revolution: Making Sense of the Communist Past in Central-Eastern* (New Haven: Yale University Press, 2014).

Mark, James and Paul Betts, eds., *Socialism Goes Global: The Soviet Union and Eastern Europe in the Age of Decolonization* (Oxford: Oxford University Press, 2022).

Mark, James, Bogdan C. Iacob, Tobias Rupprecht, and Ljubica Spaskovska. *1989: A Global History of Eastern Europe* (Cambridge: Cambridge University Press, 2019).

Markarian, Vania. *Left in Transformation: Uruguayan Exiles and the Latin American Human Rights Networks, 1967–1984* (New York: Routledge, 2005).

Martens, Pierre. *L'imprescriptibilité des crimes de guerre et contre l'humanité. Étude de droit international et de droit pénal comparé* (Brussels: Éditions de l'Université de Bruxelles, 1974).

Matus Acuña, Jean Pierre. 'Informe sobre la ejecución de la sentencia en el caso Almonacid presentado a la Cámara de Diputados', *Revista Ius et Praxis* 12, no. 2 (2006): pp. 385–396.

May, Larry. *Genocide: A Normative Account* (Cambridge: Cambridge University Press, 2010).

Meron, Theodor. 'Public International Law Problems and the Jurisdiction of the State of Israel', *Journal du Droit International* 88, no. 2 (1961): pp. 1054–1056.

Mersky, Marcie and Naomi Roht-Arriaza. 'Guatemala', in *Victims Unsilenced: The Inter-American System and Transitional Justice in Latin America* (Washington DC: Due Process of Law Foundation, 2007): pp. 7–32.

Metodiev, Momchil. 'Bulgaria', in *Transitional Justice in Eastern Europe and Former Soviet Union: Reckoning with the Communist Past*, edited by Lavinia Stan (New York: Routledge, 2009): pp. 152–157.

Mezarobba, Glenda. 'Between Reparations, Half Truths and Impunity: The Difficult Break with the Legacy of the Dictatorship in Brazil', *International Journal on Human Rights* 7, no. 13 (2010): pp. 7–27.

Mezarobba, Glenda. 'Brazil: The Tortuous Path to Truth and Justice', in *Transitional Justice in Latin America: The Uneven Road from Impunity towards Accountability*, edited by Elin Skaar, Jemima Garcia-Godos, and Cath Collins (New York: Routledge, 2016): pp. 103–125.

Miller, Robert H. 'The Convention on the Non-Applicability of Statutory Limitations to War Crimes and Crimes against Humanity', *The American Journal of International Law* 65, no. 3 (1971): pp. 476–501.

Moses, A. Dirk. *The Problems of Genocide: Permanent Security and the Language of Transgression* (Cambridge: Cambridge University Press, 2021).

Moses, A. Dirk. 'Empire, Colony, Genocide: Keywords and the Philosophy of History', in *Empire, Colony, Genocide: Conquest, Occupation, and Subaltern Resistance in World History*, edited by Dirk Moses (New York: Berghahn, 2010): pp. 3–54.

Mouralis, Guillaume. *Une épuration allemande: La RDA en procès 1949–2004* (Paris: Fayard, 2008).

Moyn, Samuel. *The Last Utopia: Human Rights in History* (Cambridge, MA: Harvard University Press, 2012).

Nash Rojas, Claudio. *El Sistema Interamericano de Derechos Humanos en Acción. Aciertos y Desafíos* (México: Porrua, 2010).

Neumann, Gerald. 'Import, Export and Regional Consent in the Inter-American Court of Human Rights', *The European Journal of International Law* 19, no. 1 (2008): pp. 101–123.

Neumayer, Laure. *Criminalising Communism in the European Political Space after the Cold War* (London: Routledge, 2018).

Neumayer, Laure. 'Integrating the Central European Past into a Common Narrative: The Mobilizations around the "Crimes of Communism" in the European Parliament', *Journal of Contemporary European Studies* 23, no. 3 (2015): pp. 344–363.

Nino, Carlos S. 'The Duty to Punish Past Abuses of Human Rights Put into Context: The Case of Argentina', *The Yale Law Journal* 100, no. 8 (1991): pp. 2619–2640.

Novic, Elisa. *The Concept of Cultural Genocide: An International Law Perspective* (Oxford: Oxford University Press, 2016).

Ollé Sesé, Manuel. 'Tribuna Abierta: Contribución de la Justicia Universal a Latinoamérica', *Revista Electrónica Iberoamericana* 4, no. 2 (2010): pp. 5–7.

Olsen, Tricia D., Leigh A. Payne, and Andrew G. Reiter. 'Transitional Justice in the World, 1970–2007: Insights from a New Dataset', *Journal of Peace Research* 47, no. 6 (2010): pp. 803–809.

Osiel, Marc. *Mass Atrocity, Collective Memory, and the Law* (New Brunswick, NJ: Transaction, 1997).

Pakier, Małgorzata and Bo Straåth, eds., *A European Memory? Contested Histories and Politics of Remembrance* (New York: Berghahn, 2010).

Parenti, Pablo. 'Argentina', in *Jurisprudencia Latinoamericana sobre Derecho Penal International: Con Informes Adicionales de España e Italia*, edited by Kai Ambos and Ezequiel Malarino (Montevideo: Konrad Adenauer Stiftung, 2008): pp. 21–66.

Parenti, Pablo. 'The Prosecution of International Crimes in Argentina', *International Criminal Law Review* 10 (2010): pp. 491–507.

Peerenboom, Randall. 'What Have We Learned about Law and Development?: Describing, Predicting, and Assessing Legal Reforms in China', *Michigan Journal of International Law* 27, no. 3 (2006): pp. 823–871.

Pendas, Devin O. 'Retroactive Law and Proactive Justice: Debating Crimes against Humanity in Germany, 1945–1950', *Central European History* 43, no. 3 (2010): pp. 428–463.

Pereira, Anthony W. *Political (In)Justice: Authoritarianism and the Rule of Law in Brazil, Chile, and Argentina* (Pittsburgh, PA: University of Pittsburgh Press, 2005).

Perlin, Jan. 'The Guatemalan Historical Clarification Commissions Finds Genocide', *ILSA Journal of International & Comparative Law* 6, no. 2 (2000): pp. 289–413.

Peto, Andrea. 'The Illiberal Memory Politics in Hungary', *Journal of Genocide Research* 24, no. 2 (2022): pp. 241–249.

Pettai, Eva-Clarita. 'Negotiating History for Reconciliation: A Comparative Evaluation of the Baltic Presidential Commissions', *Europe-Asia Studies* 67, no. 7 (2015): pp. 1079–1101.

Pettai, Eva-Clarita and Vello Pettai, *Transitional and Retrospective Justice in the Baltic States* (Cambridge: Cambridge University Press, 2014).

Popovsky, Vesselin and Monica Serrano, eds. *After Oppression: Transnational Justice in Latin America and Eastern Europe* (New York: United Nations University, 2012).

Prakash Sinha, Surya. *Legal Polycentricity and International Law* (Durham, NC: Carolina Academic Press, 1996).

Prusin, Alexander. 'Poland's Nuremberg: The Seven Court Cases at the Supreme National Tribunal 1946–1948', *Holocaust and Genocide Studies* 24, no. 1 (2010): pp. 1–25.

Radbruch, Gustav. 'Injustice légale et droit supralégal', *Archives de l'Association française de Philosophie du Droit* 1(1994): pp. 309–320.

Rafecas, Daniel. 'La reapertura de los procesos judiciales por crímenes contra la humanidad en la Argentina', in *Juicios por crímenes de Lesa Humanidad en Argentina*, edited by Gabriele Andreozzi (Buenos Aires: Cara o ceca, 2011): pp. 155–176.

Raffin, Marcelo. *La experiencia del horror* (Buenos Aires: Ed. Del Puerto, 2006).

Ragaru, Nadège. 'Les dossiers de la Sûreté d'État bulgare: le communisme dans les pliures du temps', *Revue des études slaves* LXXXI, nos. 2–3 (2010): pp. 203–225.

Ramcharan, Bertrand. *The Advent of Universal Protection of Human Rights: Theo van Boven and the Transformation of the UN Role* (Cham, Switzerland: Springer, 2018).

Ratner, Michael and Reed Broody, eds., *The Pinochet Papers: The Case of Augusto Pinochet in Spain and Britain* (The Hague: Kluwer International Law, 2000).

Ratner, Steven R. 'Belgium's War Crimes Statute: A Postmortem', *American Journal of International Law* 97, no. 4 (2003): pp. 888–897.

Reis, Aarão D. 'Ditadura e sociedade: as reconstruções da memoria', in *O golpe e a ditadura militar: 40 anos depois (1964–2004)*, edited by Aarão D. Reis, Marcelo Ridenti, and Rodrigo Sá Motta (Bauru: EDUSC: 2004): pp. 29–52.

Rezses, Eduardo. 'La Figura de Genocidio y el Caso Argentino: La Posibilidad de Adecuar Jurídicamente una Figura Penal a Una Realidad Política', in *Aportes Jurídicos para el análisis y juzgamiento del genocidio en Argentina*, edited by Eduardo Rezses (Buenos Aires: Secretaria de Derechos Humanos, 2007): pp. 61–63.

Richardson-Little, Ned, Hella Dietz, and James Mark, eds., 'New Perspectives on Socialism and Human Rights in East Central Europe after 1945', special issue of *East Central Europe* 46, nos. 2–3 (2019): pp. 169–187.

Rivers, Julian. 'The Interpretation and Invalidity of Unjust Laws', in *Recrafting the Rule of Law: The Limits of Legal Order*, edited by David Dyzenhaus (Oxford: Hart, 1999): pp. 40–65.

Roht-Arriaza, Naomi. 'Guatemala Genocide Case', *The American Journal of International Law* 100 (2008): pp. 207–231.

Roht-Arriaza, Naomi. 'Making the State Do Justice: Transnational Prosecutions and International Support for Criminal Investigations in Post-Armed Conflict Guatemala', *Chicago Journal of International Law* 9, no. 1 (2008): pp. 79–104.

Roht-Arriaza, Naomi. *The Pinochet Effect: Transitional Justice in the Age of Human Rights* (Philadelphia, PA: University of Pennsylvania Press, 2005).

Roht-Arriaza, Naomi and Javier Mariezcurrena, eds., *Transitional Justice in the Twenty-First Century: Beyond Truth versus Justice* (Cambridge: Cambridge University Press, 2006).

Rozanski, Carlos. 'Delitos de lesa humanidad y genocidio, origen y sentido de las prohibiciones', in *Juicios por crímenes de lesa humanidad en Argentina*, edited by Gabriele Andreozzi (Buenos Aires: Editorial Atuel, 2011): pp. 177–198.

Rummel, Rudolf Joseph. *Lethal Politics: Soviet Genocide and Mass Murder since 1917* (New Brunswick, NJ: Transaction, 1990).

Sadat, Leila Nadya. 'Codifying the "Laws of Humanity" and the "Dictates of the Public Conscience": Towards a New Global Treaty on Crimes against Humanity', in *On the Proposed Crimes against Humanity Convention*, edited by Morten Bergsmo and Tianying Song (Brussels: Torkel Opsahl, 2014): pp. 17–46.

Santos, Cecília MacDowell. 'Transitional Justice from the Margins: Legal Mobilizations and Memory Politics in Brazil', in *Legacies of Violence and Transitional Justice in Latin America: A Janus-Faced Paradigm?*, edited by Nina Schneider and Marcia Esparza (London: Lexington Books, 2015): pp. 37–72.

Santos, Cecília MacDowell, Édson Teles, and Janaína Teles. *Desarquivando a ditadura: memoria e justiça no Brasil* (São Paulo: Aderaldo & Rothschild, 2009).

Satkauskas, Rytis. 'Soviet Genocide Trials in the Baltic States: The Relevance of International Law', *Yearbook of International Humanitarian Law* 7 (2004): pp. 388–409.

Schabas, William A. *Genocide in International Law: The Crimes of Crimes* (Cambridge: Cambridge University Press, 2009).

Schabas, William. 'The Contribution of the Eichmann Trial to International Criminal Law', *Leiden Journal of International Law* 26 (2013): pp. 667–699.

Schabas, William A. *The UN International Criminal Tribunals: The Former Yugoslavia, Rwanda and Sierra Leone* (Cambridge: Cambridge University Press, 2006).

Schiffrin, Leopoldo. 'La primacía del derecho internacional sobre el derecho argentino', in *La aplicación de los tratados sobre derechos humanos por los tribunales locales*, edited by Martin Abregú and Christian Courtis (Buenos Aires: Del Puerto, 1997): pp. 115–125.

Schneider, Ann M. 'Legislative Efforts against Impunity in the 1979 Amnesty Debate in Brazil', *Bulletin of Latin American Research* 37, no. 1 (2018): pp. 18–32.

Schneider, Howard. 'Political Genocide in Latin America: The Need of Reconsidering the Current Internationally Accepted Definition of Genocide in the Light of Spanish and Latin America Jurisprudence', *American University Law Review* 25, no. 2 (2010): pp. 313–355.

Schneider, Nina. 'Breaking the "Silence" of the Military Regime: New Politics of Memory in Brazil', *Bulletin of Latin American Research* 30, no. 2 (2011): pp. 198–212.

Schneider, Nina. '"Too Little Too Late or Premature"? The Brazilian Truth Commission and the Question of "Best Timing"', *Journal of Iberian and Latin American Research* 19, no.1 (2013): pp. 149–162.

Schneider, Nina. 'Impunity in Post-authoritarian Brazil: The Supreme Court's Recent Verdict on the Amnesty Law', *European Review of Latin American and Caribbean Studies* 90 (2011): pp. 39–54.

Schneider, Nina. 'Waiting for a Meaningful State Apology: Has Brazil Apologized for Authoritarian Repression?', *Journal of Human Rights* 13, no. 1 (2014): pp. 69–84.

Schönfelder, Bruno. 'Judicial Independence in Bulgaria: A Tale of Splendour and Misery', *Europe-Asia Studies* 57, no. 1 (2005): pp. 61–92.

Schoultz, Lars. *Human Rights and United States Policy toward Latin America* (Princeton: Princeton University Press, 1981).

Sellars, Kirsten, ed., *Trials for International Crimes in Asia* (Cambridge: Cambridge University Press, 2016).

Seroussi, Julian. 'The Cause of Universal Jurisdiction: The Rise and Fall of an International Mobilisation', in *Lawyers and the Construction of Transnational Justice*, edited by Yves Dezalay and Bryant G. Garth (New York: Routledge, 2012): pp. 48–59.

Shafir, Michael. *Between Denial and 'Comparative Trivialization': Holocaust Negationism in Post-Communist East Central Europe*. Jerusalem: Vidal Sassoon International Center for the Study of Antisemitism, ACTA, No. 19, 2002.

Shany, Yuval. *The Competing Jurisdictions of International Courts and Tribunals* (New York: Oxford University Press, 2003).

Sikkink, Kathryn. 'From Pariah State to Global Protagonist: Argentina and the Struggle for International Human Rights', *Latin American Politics and Society* 50, no. 1 (2008): pp. 1–29.

Slavov, Atanas. 'Constitutional Moment of Failure: Constitutional Politics in Bulgaria 2020', *ПУБЛИЧНИ ПОЛИТИКИ.bg* (Public Policies.bg) 12, no. 1 (2021): pp. 54–63.

Sotero, Paulo. 'El desafío brasileño: cómo gestionar las relaciones regionales asimétricas más allá de la OEA', *Revista CIDOB d'Afers Internacionais* 97–98 (2012): pp. 101–116.

Stabili, Maria Rosaria. 'OPAREI. La Justicia de Transición en Paraguay', *America Latina Hoy: Revista de Ciencias Sociales* 61 (2012): pp. 137–162.

Stan, Lavinia. 'Reckoning with the Communist Past in Romania: A Scorecard', *Europe-Asia Studies* 65, no. 1 (2013): pp. 127–146.

Stan, Lavinia, ed., *Transitional Justice in Eastern Europe and Former Soviet Union: Reckoning with the Communist Past* (New York: Routledge, 2009).

Stan, Lavinia. *Transitional Justice in Post-Communist Romania: The Politics of Memory* (Cambridge: Cambridge University Press, 2013).

Stanton, Gregory H. 'The Cambodian Genocide and International Law', in *Genocide and Democracy in Cambodia: The Khmer Rouge, the United Nations and the International Community*, edited by Ben Kiernan (New Haven, CT: Yale University Southeast Asia Studies, 1993): pp. 141–161.

Su, Anna. 'The Rise and Fall of Universal Jurisdiction', *Human Rights Quarterly* 41, no. 4 (2019): pp. 849–872.

Suresh Roberts, Ronald. 'How "Transitional Justice" Colonized South Africa's TRC', *Modern Languages Open* 34, no. 1 (2020): pp. 1–15.

Sweeney, James A. *The European Court of Human Rights in the Post-Cold War Era: Universality in Transition* (London: Routledge, 2013).

Tang, Yi Shin. 'International Justice through Domestic Courts: Challenges in Brazil's Judicial Review of the Amnesty Law', *International Journal of Transitional Justice* 9, no. 2 (2015): pp. 259–277.

Tarica, Estelle. 'The Holocaust Again? Dispatches from the Jewish 'Internal Front' in Dictatorship Argentina', *Journal of Jewish Identities* 5, no. 1 (2012): pp. 89–110.

Tiba, Firew Kebede. 'The *Mengistu* Genocide Trial in Ethiopia', *Journal of International Criminal Justice* 5, no. 2 (2007): pp. 513–528.

Tismaneanu, Vladimir and Bogdan C. Iacob, eds., *Ideological Storms: Intellectuals, Dictators, and the Totalitarian Temperton* (Budapest: CEU Press, 2019).

Tittemore, Brian D. 'Ending Impunity in the Americas: The Role of the Inter-American Human Rights System in Advancing Accountability for Serious Crimes under International Law', *Southwestern Journal of Law and Trade in the Americas* 12, no. 2 (2006): pp. 429–476.

Tomuschat, Christian. 'Issue of Universal Jurisdiction in the Scilingo Case', *Journal of International Criminal Justice* 3, no. 5 (2005): pp. 1074–1081.

Torelly, Marcelo. 'Assessing a Late Truth Commission: Challenges and Achievements of the Brazilian National Truth Commission', *International Journal of Transitional Justice* 12, no. 2 (2018): pp. 194–215.

Tuori, Kaius. *Empire of Law: Nazi Germany, Exile Scholars and the Battle for the Future of Europe* (Cambridge: Cambridge University Press, 2020).

van den Herik, Larissa and Carsten Stahn, eds., *The Diversification and Fragmentation of International Criminal Law* (Leiden: Martinus Nijhoff, 2012).

van Schaack, Beth. 'Crimen Sine Lege: Judicial Lawmaking at the Intersection of Law and Morals', *Georgetown Law Journal* 97, no. 119 (2008): pp. 119–192.

van Schaack, Beth. 'The Crime of Political Genocide: Repairing the Genocide Convention's Blind Sport', *Yale Law Journal* 106 (1997): 2259–2291.

Vezetti, Hugo. *Pasado y Presente: Guerra, Dictadura y Sociedad en Argentina* (Buenos Aires: Siglo Veintiuno, 2002).

Weill, Sharon. *The Role of National Courts in Applying International Humanitarian Law* (Oxford: Oxford University Press, 2014).

Weiss-Wendt, Anton. *The Soviet Union and the Gutting of the UN Genocide Convention* (Madison, WI: University of Wisconsin Press, 2017).

Weiss-Wendt, Anton. *A Rhetorical Crime: Genocide in the Geopolitical Discourse of the Cold War* (New Brunswick, NJ: Rutgers University Press, 2018).

Wilson, Ashby Richard. *Writing History in International Criminal Trials* (Cambridge: Cambridge University Press, 2011).

Wilson, Richard J. 'Prosecuting Pinochet: International Crimes in Spanish Domestic Law', *Human Rights Quarterly* 21, no. 4 (1999): pp. 927–979.

Wouters, Nico, ed., *Transitional Justice and Memory in Europe (1945–2013)* (Cambridge: Intersentia, 2017).

Zaffaroni, Eugenio Raúl, ed., *La Jurisdicción Universal en el Juicio al Franquismo: La Querella Argentina contra el Genocidio en España* (Buenos Aires: Ediciones Olejnik, 2021).

Zake, Ieva, ed., *Anti-Communist Minorities in the US: Political Activism of Ethnic Refugees* (New York: Palgrave Macmillan, 2009).

Žalimas, Dainius. 'Crimes Committed by the Communist Regimes from the Standpoint of International Legislation: Lithuanian Case Study', in *Crimes of the Communist Regimes: An Assessment by Historian and Legal Experts. Proceedings of an International Conference* (Prague: Institute of the Study of Totalitarian Regimes, 2011): pp. 43–81.

Žalimas, Dainius. 'Legal Issues on the Continuity of the Republic of Lithuania', *Baltic Yearbook of International Law* 1 (2001): pp. 1–22.

Žilinskas, Justinas. 'Broadening the Concept of Genocide in Lithuania's Criminal Law and the Principle of Nullum Crimen Sine Lege', *Jurisprudencija/Jurisprudence* 4, no. 118 (2009): pp. 333–348.

Žilinskas, Justinas. 'Status of Members of Ani-Soviet Armed Resistance (Partisans' War) of 1944–1953 in Lithuania under International Law', *Baltic Yearbook of International Law* 11 (2011): pp. 31–65.

Žilinskas, Justinas. 'Vasiliauskas vs. Lithuania: Battle Lost in the War to Come?', *International Comparative Jurisprudence* 2 (2016): pp. 67–71.

Index

For the benefit of digital users, indexed terms that span two pages (e.g., 52–53) may, on occasion, appear on only one of those pages.
Boxes are indicated by *b* following the page number